Waiting for Spring 13

Anashin

Waiting
for Spring
vol.13
Presented by
Anashin

CONTENTS

WAITING FOR SPRING
Harumatsu Bokura

Character & Story

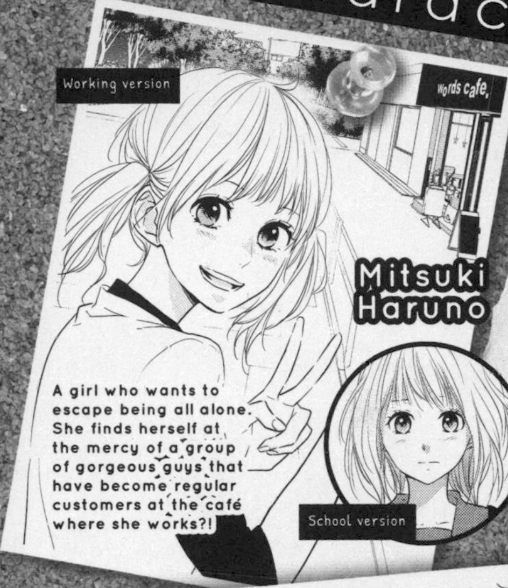

Working version
words cafe
School version

Mitsuki Haruno

A girl who wants to escape being all alone. She finds herself at the mercy of a group of gorgeous guys that have become regular customers at the café where she works?!

Mitsuki is a loner, but she's determined to make lasting friendships in high school. One day, the school celebrities—the Elite Four Hotties of the basketball team—appear at the café where she works! Mitsuki gets caught up in their silly hijinks, and gradually falls for her classmate Towa. But after reuniting with her best friend Aya-chan, she learns Aya-chan has a crush on her! Though Towa also tells Mitsuki he likes her, they have to press pause since his team's not allowed to date. The coach promises to change this rule if they can win the New Team Tournament, but they are narrowly defeated by Aya-chan and Team Hōjō. Luckily, a new coach steps in and abolishes the rule! Mitsuki and Towa are officially a couple now! ♡ Aya-chan goes to America, and everyone moves forward, including Ryūji, who confesses his love to Nana-san! How will she respond...?

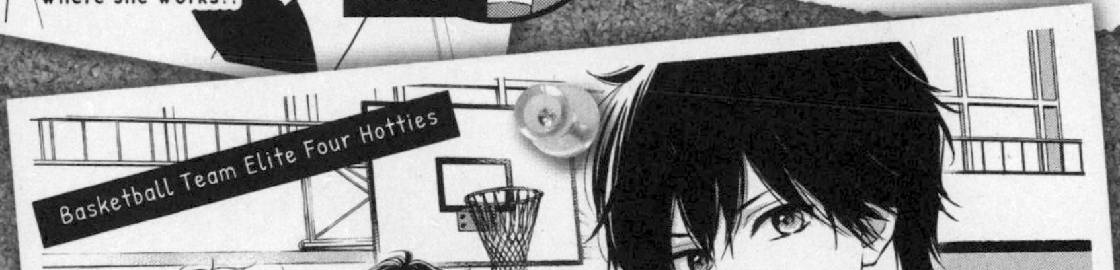

Basketball Team Elite Four Hotties

Towa Asakura

Mitsuki's classmate. He's quiet and a bit spacey, but he's always there to help her.

Rui Miyamoto

A first-year in high school. His innocent smile is adorable, but it hides a wicked heart?!

Kyōsuke Wakamiya

A second-year in high school. Mysterious and always cool-headed, he's like a big brother to everyone.

Ryūji Tada

A second-year. Comes off as a bad boy but is rather naïve. He's crushing on the Boss's daughter, Nanase-san.

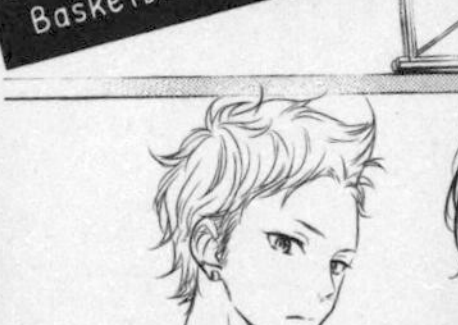

Aya-chan

Mitsuki's best friend from elementary school. When they finally meet again, she discovers he was a boy!

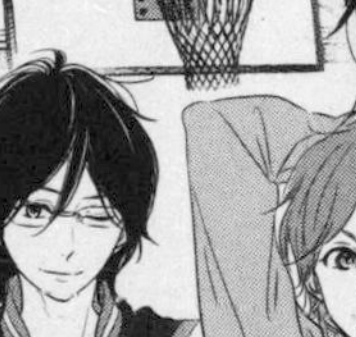

Reina Yamada

Mitsuki's first friend from her class. She has somewhat eccentric tastes?!

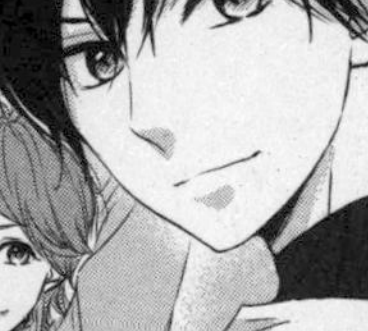

Maki-chan

A first-year on the girls' basketball team who gets along with Mitsuki. Apparently she has a crush on Towa?!

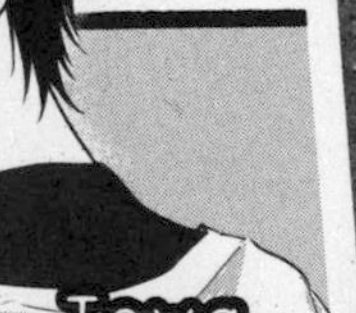

Nana-san

The Boss's daughter. Straightforward and resolute, she is a reliable, big sister type.

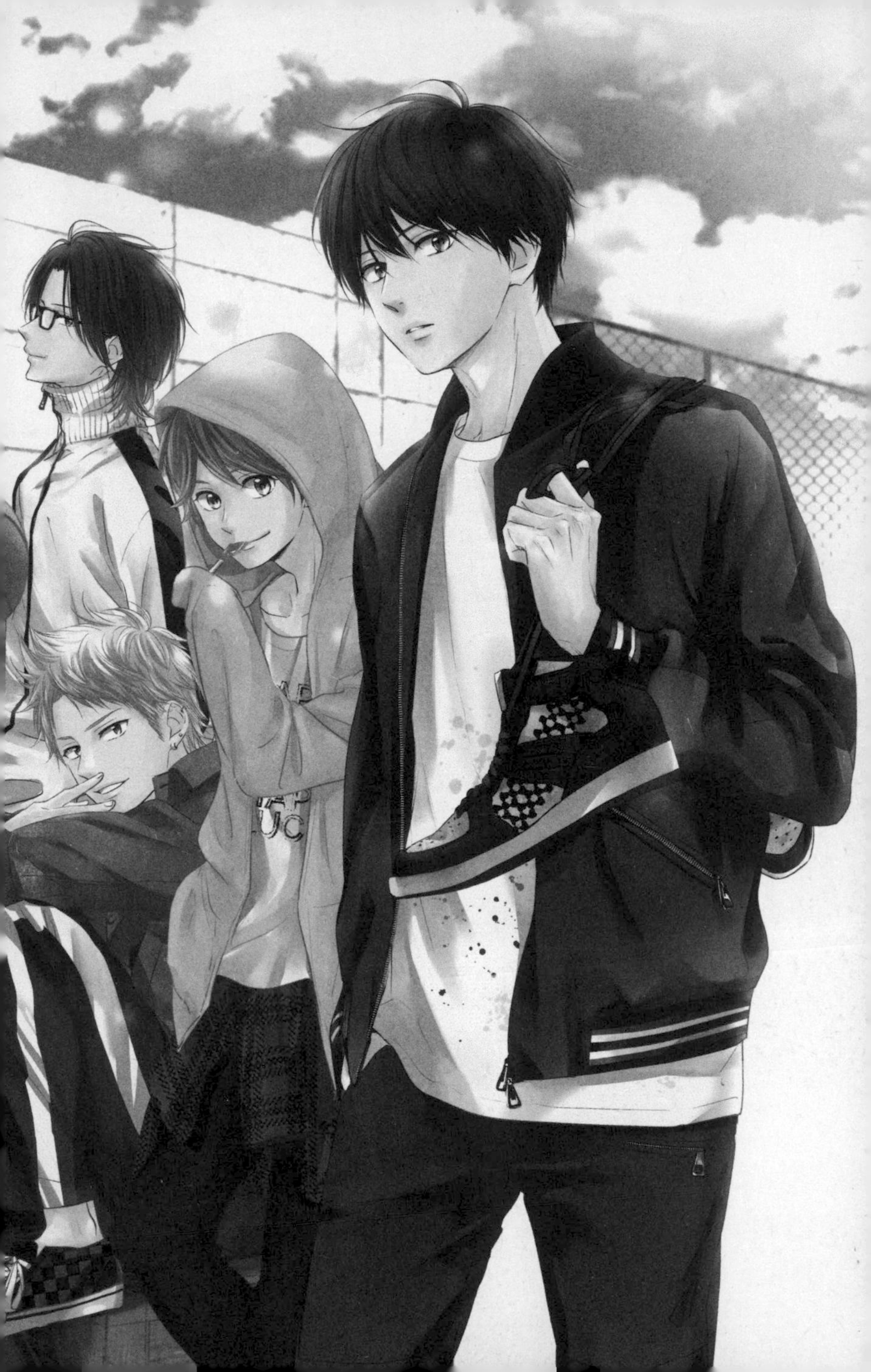

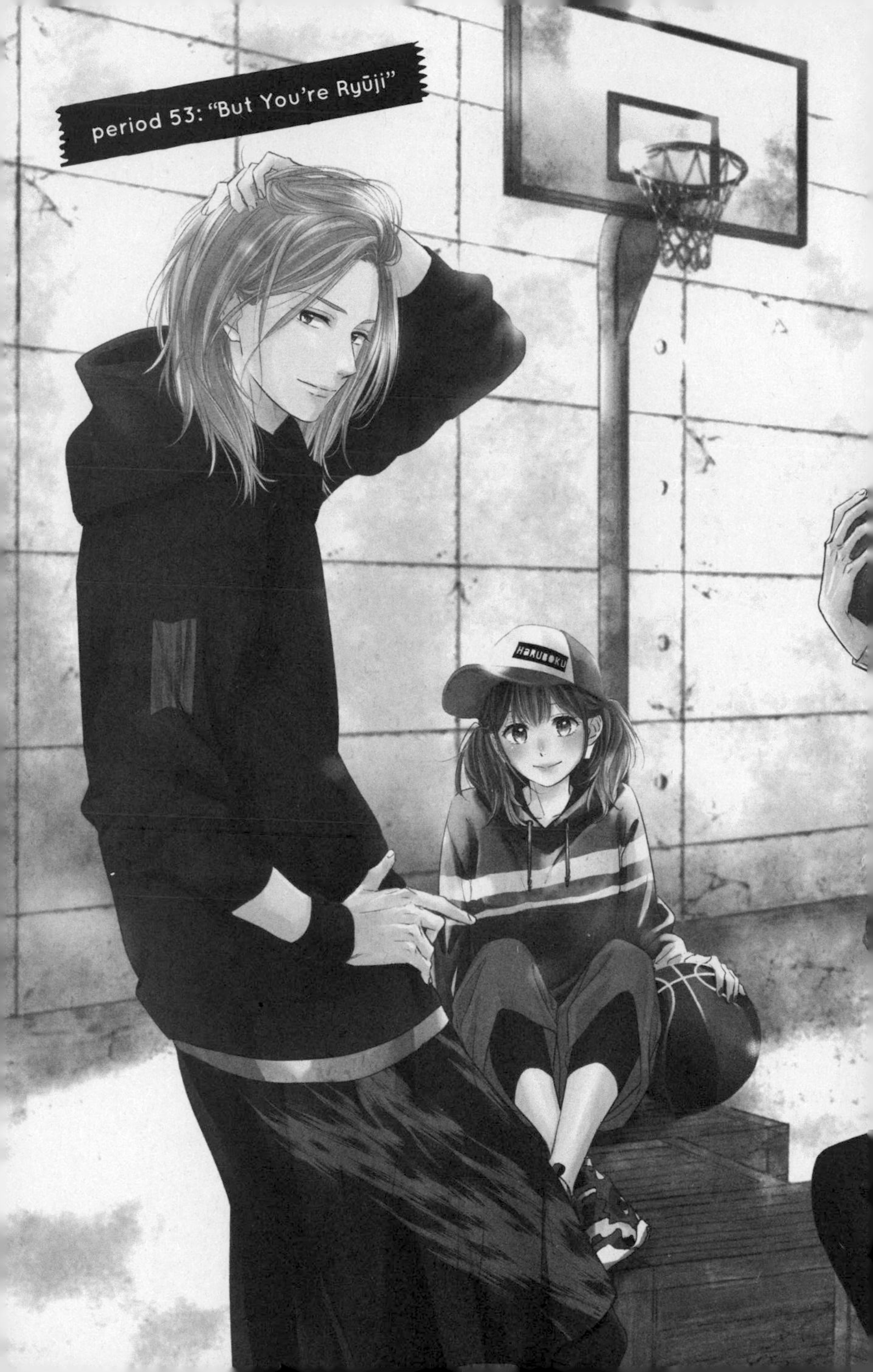
period 53: “But You’re Ryūji”

Hello! Anashin here.

Thank you so much for
picking up this volume!!

We finally made it to volume 13! I did it—I drew everyone on the cover!! And I'm sorry. In the last volume, I wrote that I would draw all five of them. ⸚
But there are six of them. Six...!

I started this series in 2014, and it's been more than five and a half years. I have nothing but gratitude for all of you who read and supported the series. I had plenty of painstakingly frustrating moments due to my relative inexperience, but I got to draw this series with everything I had right down to the last chapter, and for that I feel blessed.

Now that I've finished the main story, I'm drawing some bonus chapters, and I'm taking my time with them and having a lot of fun. I know that it's everything we've built up to this point that makes this possible, and I face my desk every day with renewed gratitude for all of you. Really, thank you very (x100) much for everything.

...That being said, the series may be over, but the characters' stories will surely go on, and I hope you will watch over them always.

I hope you enjoy volume 13!!

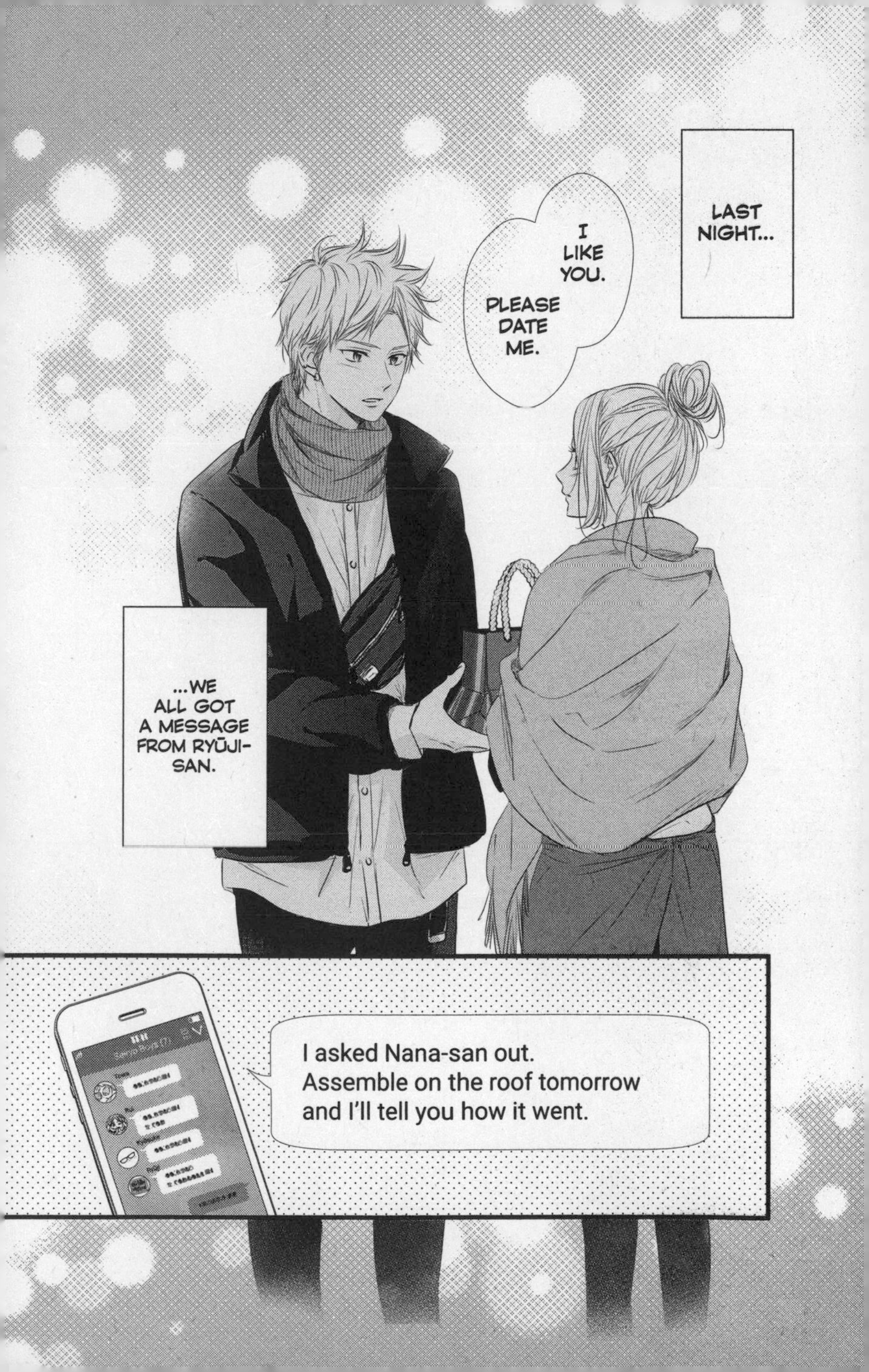
LAST NIGHT...
I LIKE YOU. PLEASE DATE ME.
...WE ALL GOT A MESSAGE FROM RYŪJI-SAN.
I asked Nana-san out. Assemble on the roof tomorrow and I'll tell you how it went.

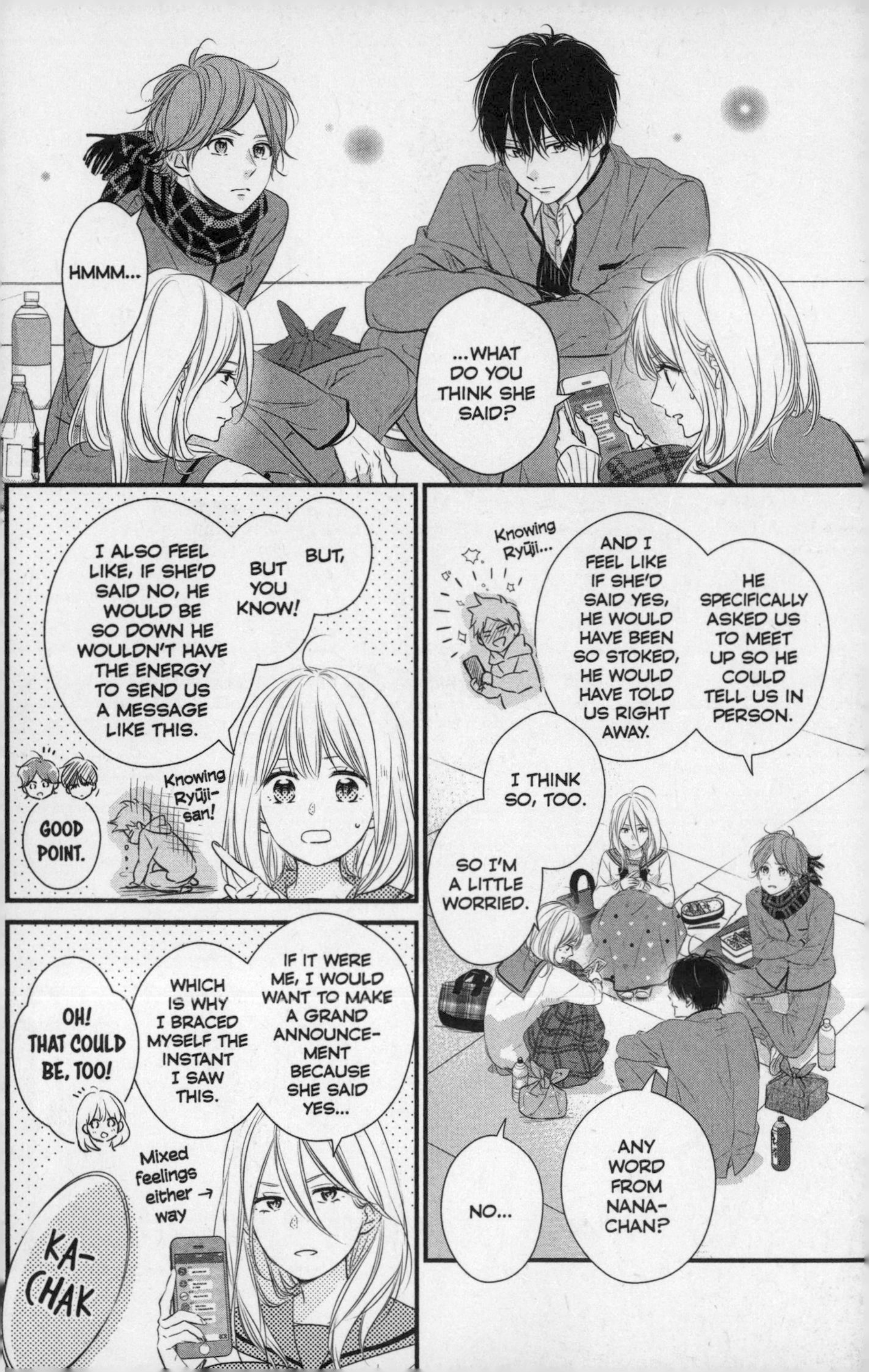
...WHAT DO YOU THINK SHE SAID?
HMMM...
HE SPECIFICALLY ASKED US TO MEET UP SO HE COULD TELL US IN PERSON.
AND I FEEL LIKE IF SHE'D SAID YES, HE WOULD HAVE BEEN SO STOKED, HE WOULD HAVE TOLD US RIGHT AWAY.
Knowing Ryūji...
I THINK SO, TOO.
SO I'M A LITTLE WORRIED.
ANY WORD FROM NANA-CHAN?
NO...
BUT,
BUT YOU KNOW!
I ALSO FEEL LIKE, IF SHE'D SAID NO, HE WOULD BE SO DOWN HE WOULDN'T HAVE THE ENERGY TO SEND US A MESSAGE LIKE THIS.
Knowing Ryūji-san!
GOOD POINT.
IF IT WERE ME, I WOULD WANT TO MAKE A GRAND ANNOUNCE-MENT BECAUSE SHE SAID YES...
WHICH IS WHY I BRACED MYSELF THE INSTANT I SAW THIS.
OH! THAT COULD BE, TOO!
Mixed feelings either → way
KA-CHAK

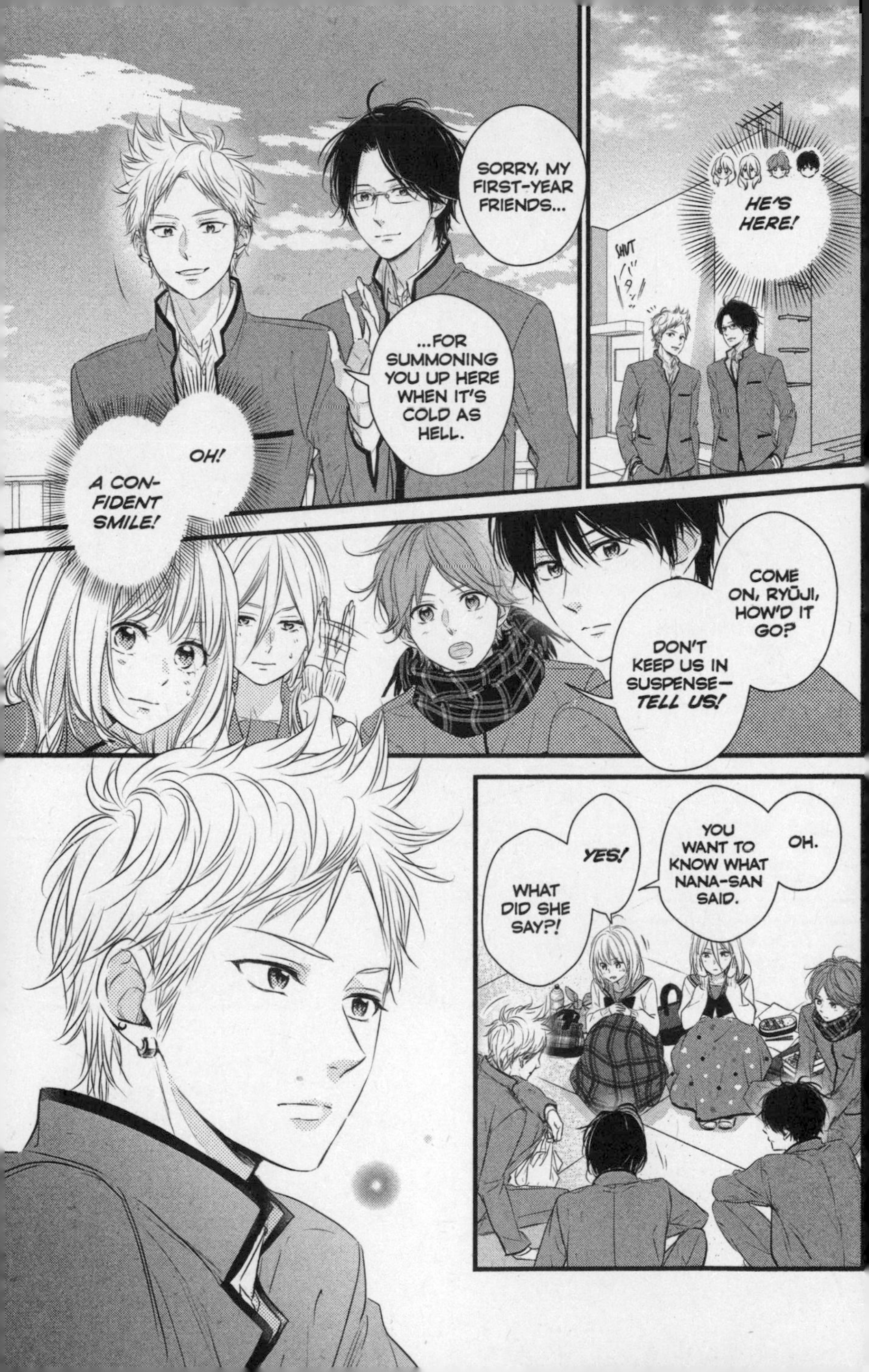
SHUT
HE'S HERE!
SORRY, MY FIRST-YEAR FRIENDS...
...FOR SUMMONING YOU UP HERE WHEN IT'S COLD AS HELL.
OH! A CON-FIDENT SMILE!
COME ON, RYŪJI, HOW'D IT GO?
DON'T KEEP US IN SUSPENSE—TELL US!
OH.
YOU WANT TO KNOW WHAT NANA-SAN SAID.
YES!
WHAT DID SHE SAY?!

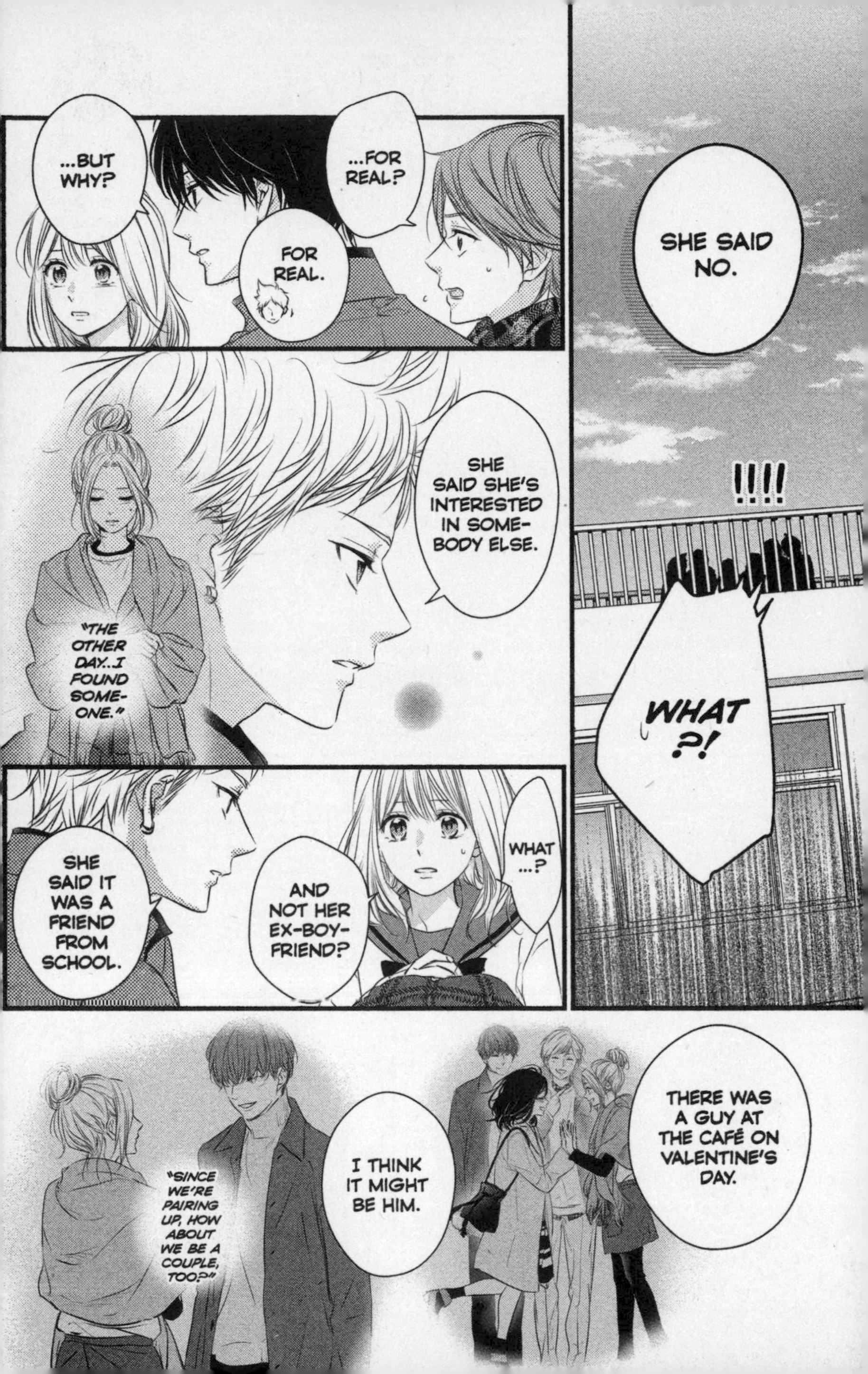
SHE SAID NO.
!!!!
WHAT ?!
...FOR REAL?
FOR REAL.
...BUT WHY?
SHE SAID SHE'S INTERESTED IN SOMEBODY ELSE.
"THE OTHER DAY..I FOUND SOMEONE."
WHAT ...?
AND NOT HER EX-BOYFRIEND?
SHE SAID IT WAS A FRIEND FROM SCHOOL.
THERE WAS A GUY AT THE CAFÉ ON VALENTINE'S DAY.
I THINK IT MIGHT BE HIM.
"SINCE WE'RE PAIRING UP, HOW ABOUT WE BE A COUPLE, TOO?"

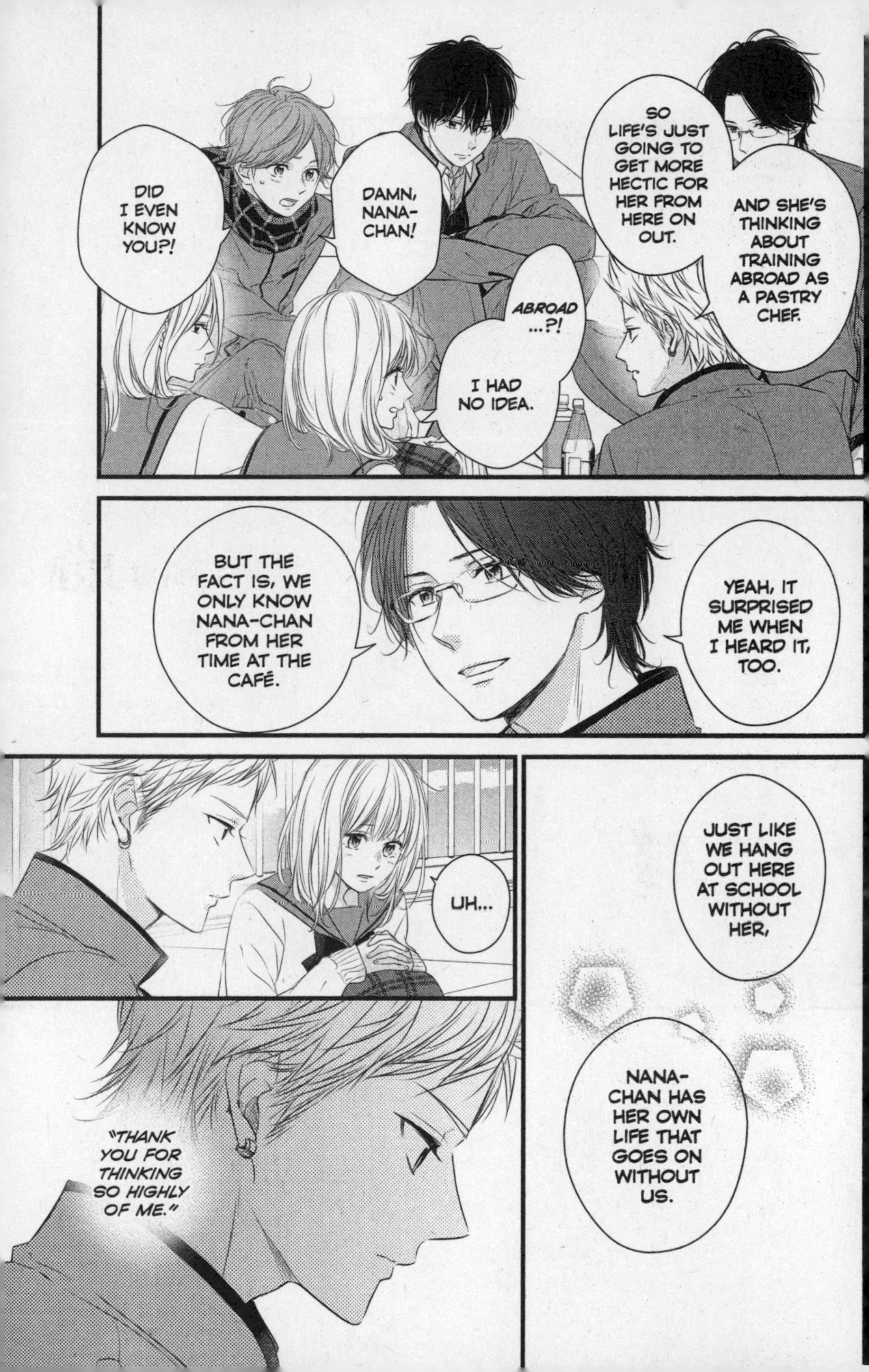
SO LIFE'S JUST GOING TO GET MORE HECTIC FOR HER FROM HERE ON OUT.
AND SHE'S THINKING ABOUT TRAINING ABROAD AS A PASTRY CHEF.
ABROAD ...?!
I HAD NO IDEA.
DAMN, NANA-CHAN!
DID I EVEN KNOW YOU?!
YEAH, IT SURPRISED ME WHEN I HEARD IT, TOO.
BUT THE FACT IS, WE ONLY KNOW NANA-CHAN FROM HER TIME AT THE CAFÉ.
JUST LIKE WE HANG OUT HERE AT SCHOOL WITHOUT HER,
NANA-CHAN HAS HER OWN LIFE THAT GOES ON WITHOUT US.
UH...
"THANK YOU FOR THINKING SO HIGHLY OF ME."

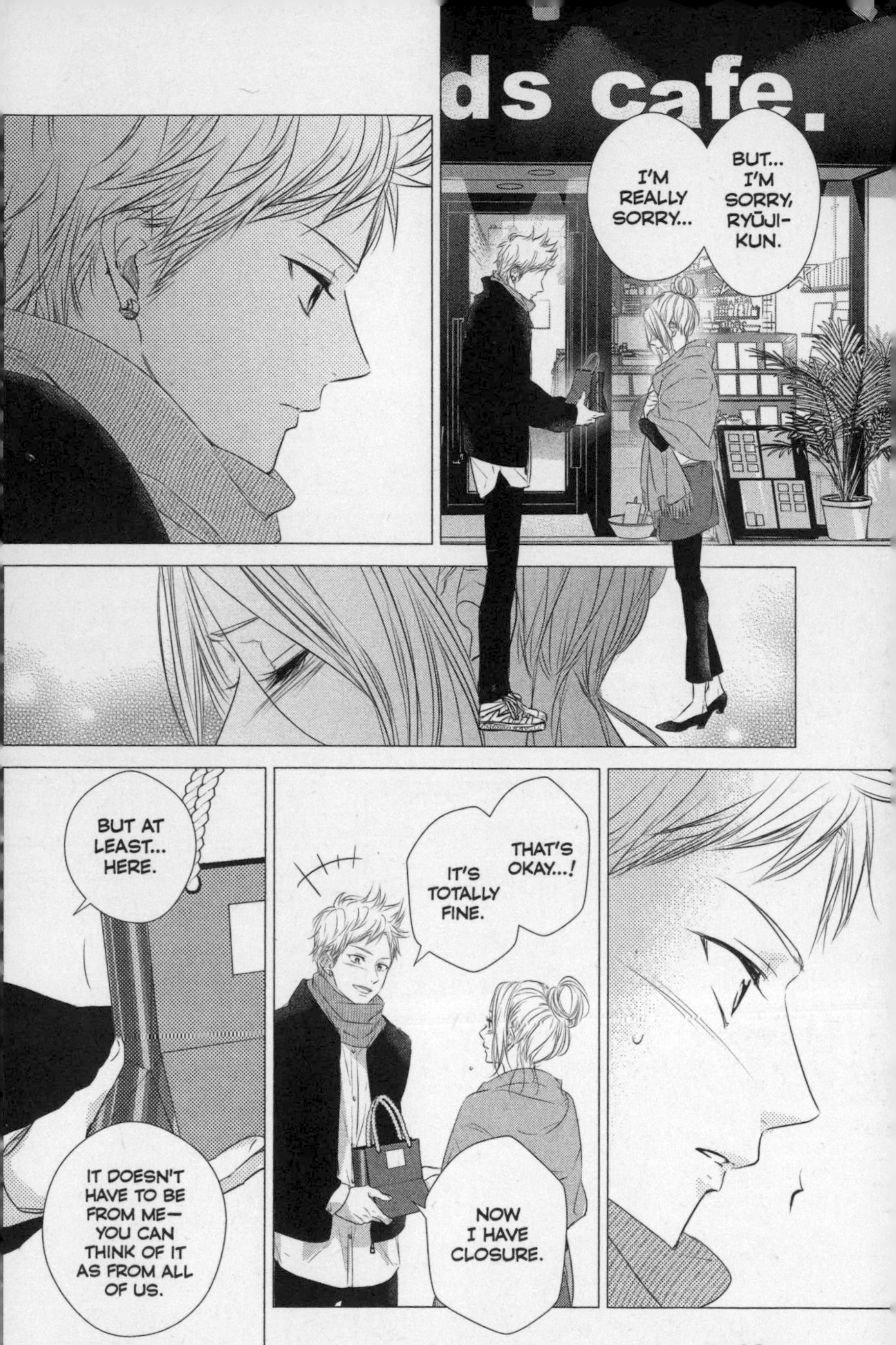
ds cafe.
BUT... I'M SORRY, RYŪJI-KUN.
I'M REALLY SORRY...
THAT'S OKAY...!
IT'S TOTALLY FINE.
NOW I HAVE CLOSURE.
BUT AT LEAST... HERE.
IT DOESN'T HAVE TO BE FROM ME— YOU CAN THINK OF IT AS FROM ALL OF US.

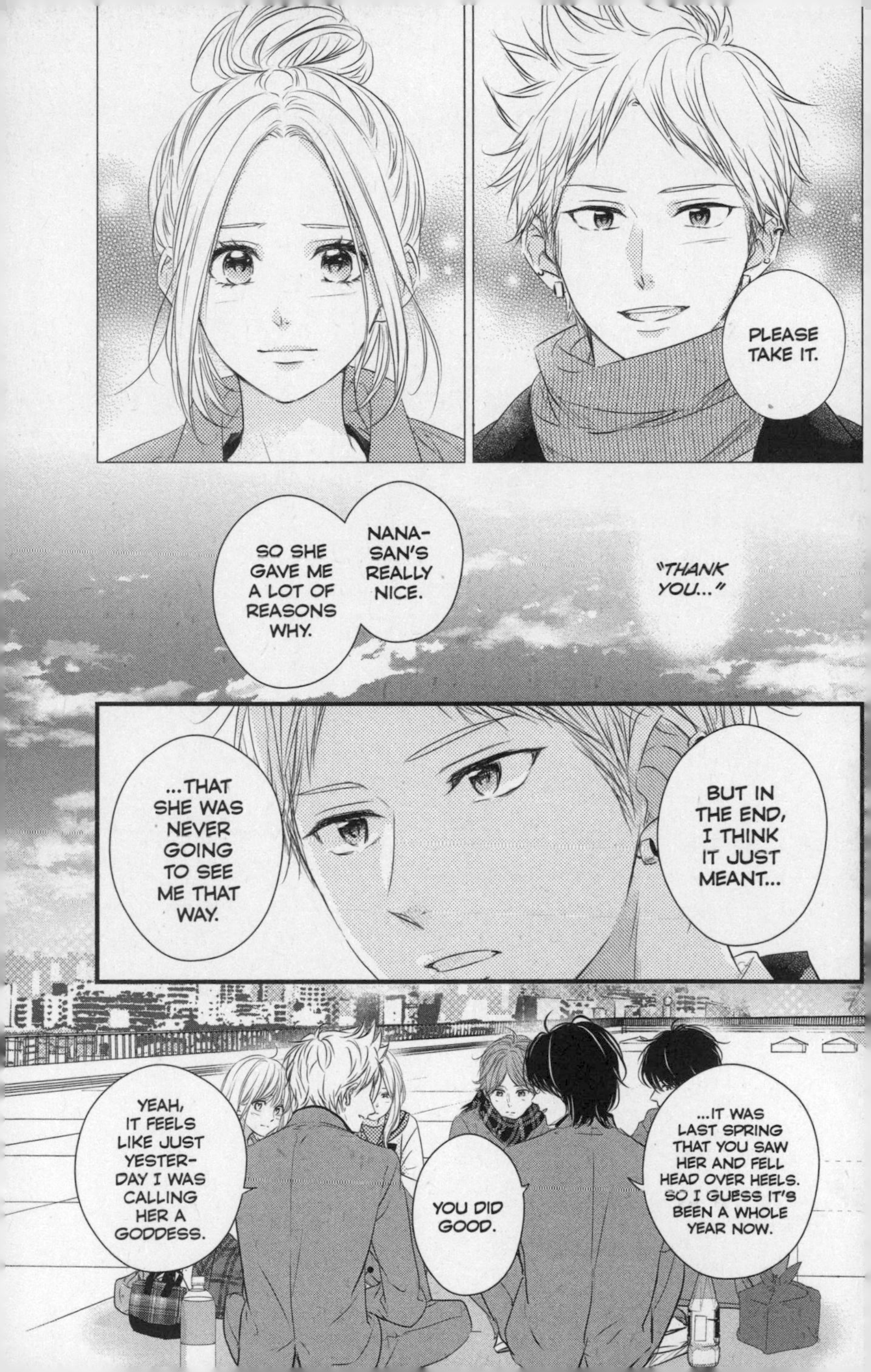
PLEASE TAKE IT.
"THANK YOU..."
NANA-SAN'S REALLY NICE.
SO SHE GAVE ME A LOT OF REASONS WHY.
BUT IN THE END, I THINK IT JUST MEANT...
...THAT SHE WAS NEVER GOING TO SEE ME THAT WAY.
...IT WAS LAST SPRING THAT YOU SAW HER AND FELL HEAD OVER HEELS. SO I GUESS IT'S BEEN A WHOLE YEAR NOW.
YOU DID GOOD.
YEAH, IT FEELS LIKE JUST YESTER-DAY I WAS CALLING HER A GODDESS.

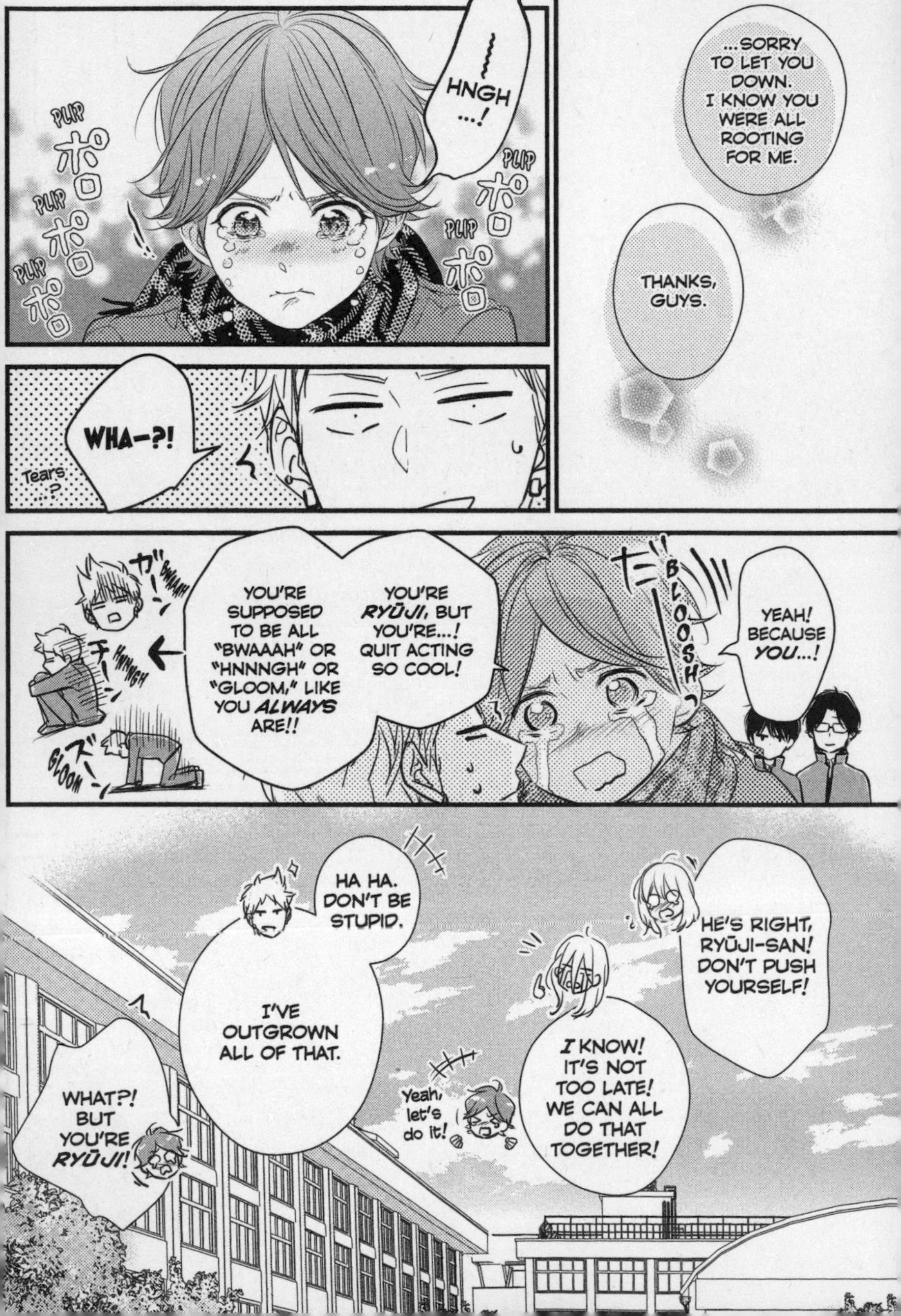
...SORRY TO LET YOU DOWN. I KNOW YOU WERE ALL ROOTING FOR ME.
THANKS, GUYS.
~~~ HNGH ...!
PLIP
PLIP
PLIP
PLIP
PLIP
WHA-?!
Tears ...?
YEAH! BECAUSE YOU...!
BLOOSH
YOU'RE RYŪJI, BUT YOU'RE...! QUIT ACTING SO COOL!
YOU'RE SUPPOSED TO BE ALL "BWAAAH" OR "HNNNGH" OR "GLOOM," LIKE YOU ALWAYS ARE!!
BWAAAH
HNNNGH
GLOOM
HE'S RIGHT, RYŪJI-SAN! DON'T PUSH YOURSELF!
I KNOW! IT'S NOT TOO LATE! WE CAN ALL DO THAT TOGETHER!
Yeah, let's do it!
HA HA. DON'T BE STUPID.
I'VE OUTGROWN ALL OF THAT.
WHAT?! BUT YOU'RE RYŪJI!
~~~

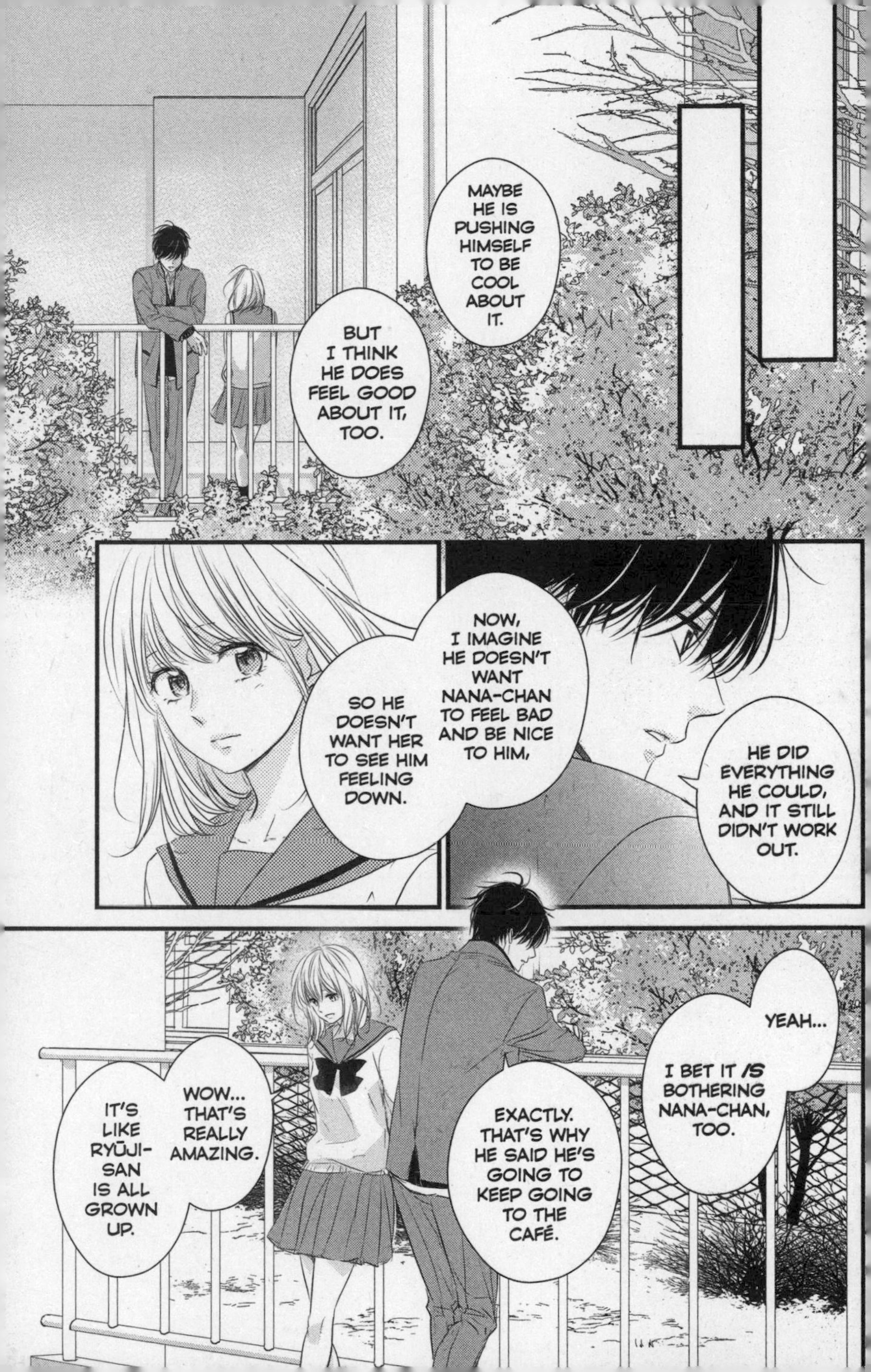
MAYBE HE IS PUSHING HIMSELF TO BE COOL ABOUT IT.
BUT I THINK HE DOES FEEL GOOD ABOUT IT, TOO.
HE DID EVERYTHING HE COULD, AND IT STILL DIDN'T WORK OUT.
NOW, I IMAGINE HE DOESN'T WANT NANA-CHAN TO FEEL BAD AND BE NICE TO HIM,
SO HE DOESN'T WANT HER TO SEE HIM FEELING DOWN.
YEAH...
I BET IT *IS* BOTHERING NANA-CHAN, TOO.
EXACTLY. THAT'S WHY HE SAID HE'S GOING TO KEEP GOING TO THE CAFÉ.
WOW... THAT'S REALLY AMAZING.
IT'S LIKE RYŪJI-SAN IS ALL GROWN UP.

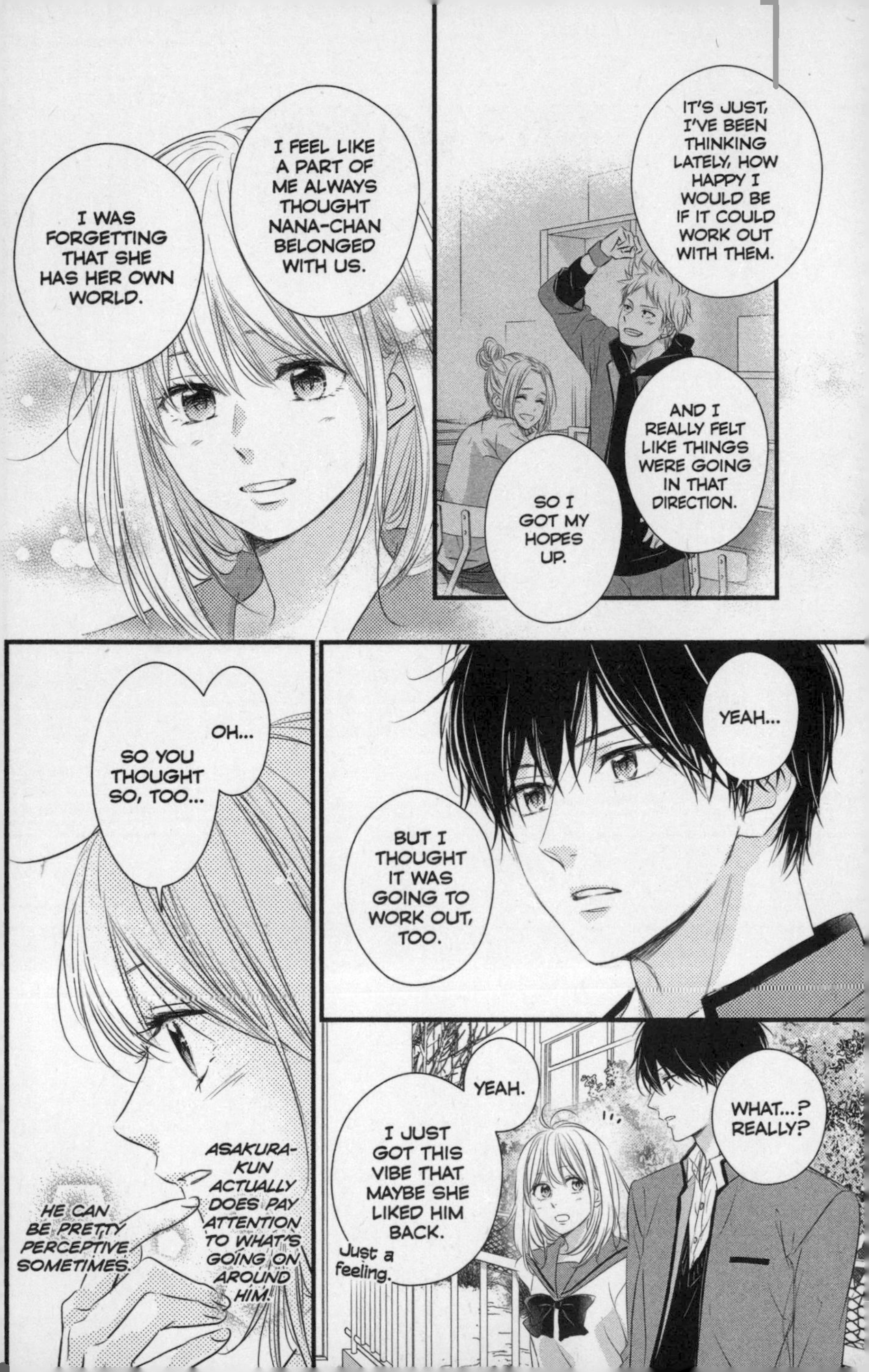
IT'S JUST, I'VE BEEN THINKING LATELY, HOW HAPPY I WOULD BE IF IT COULD WORK OUT WITH THEM.
AND I REALLY FELT LIKE THINGS WERE GOING IN THAT DIRECTION.
SO I GOT MY HOPES UP.
I FEEL LIKE A PART OF ME ALWAYS THOUGHT NANA-CHAN BELONGED WITH US.
I WAS FORGETTING THAT SHE HAS HER OWN WORLD.
YEAH...
BUT I THOUGHT IT WAS GOING TO WORK OUT, TOO.
WHAT...? REALLY?
YEAH.
I JUST GOT THIS VIBE THAT MAYBE SHE LIKED HIM BACK.
Just a feeling.
OH... SO YOU THOUGHT SO, TOO...
ASAKURA-KUN ACTUALLY DOES PAY ATTENTION TO WHAT'S GOING ON AROUND HIM.
HE CAN BE PRETTY PERCEPTIVE SOMETIMES.

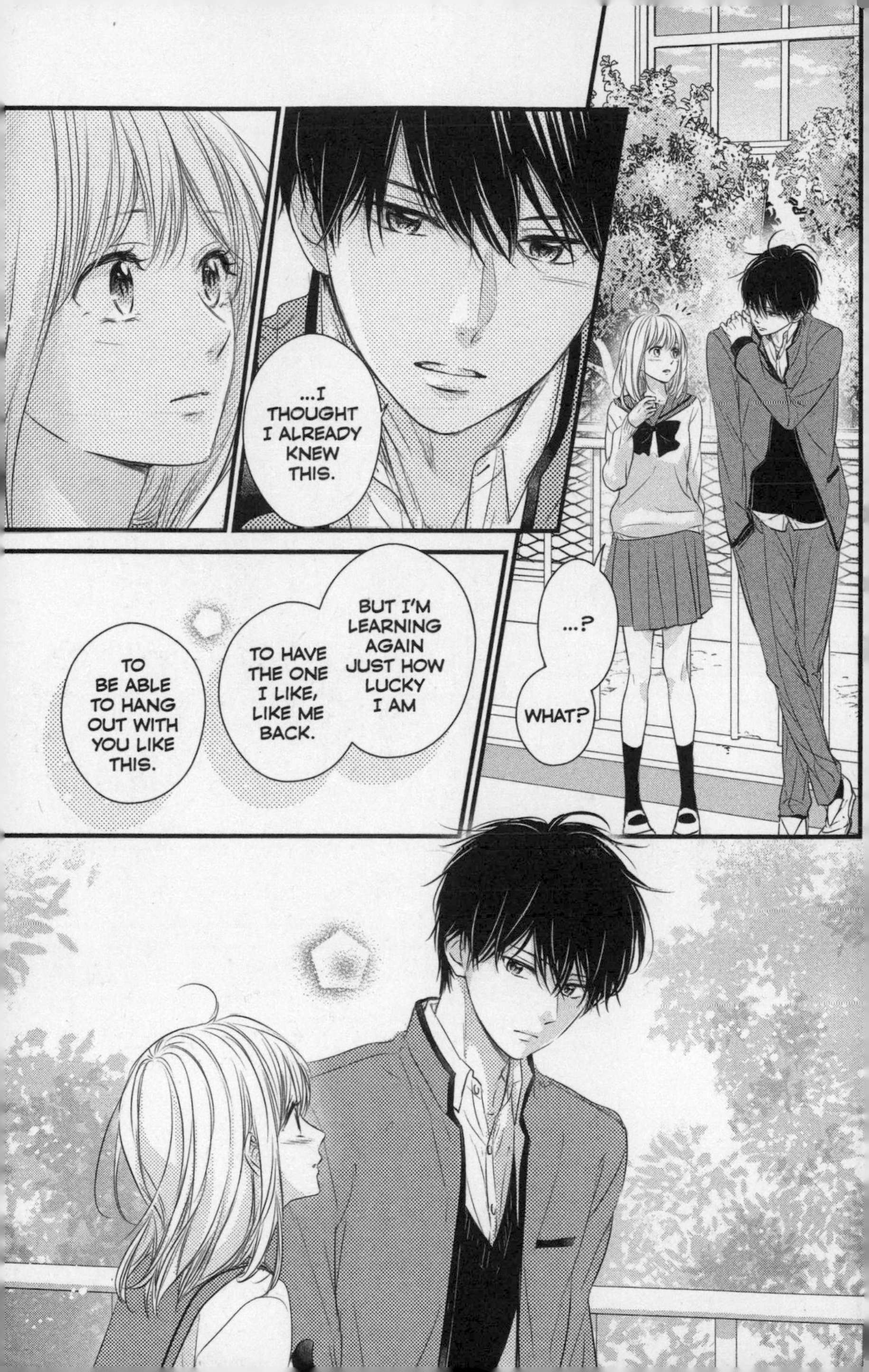
...?
WHAT?
...I THOUGHT I ALREADY KNEW THIS.
BUT I'M LEARNING AGAIN JUST HOW LUCKY I AM
TO HAVE THE ONE I LIKE, LIKE ME BACK.
TO BE ABLE TO HANG OUT WITH YOU LIKE THIS.

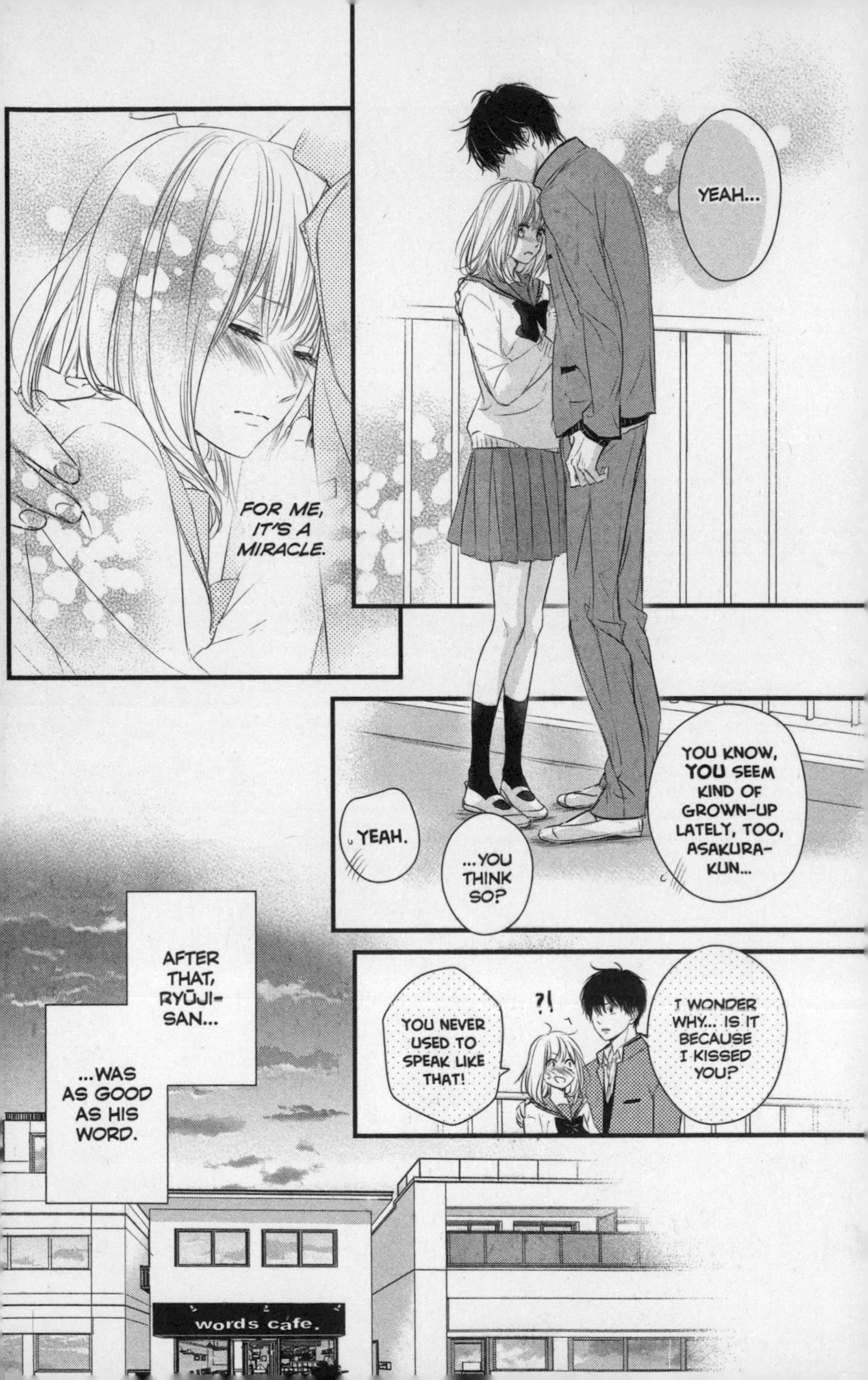
YEAH...
FOR ME, IT'S A MIRACLE.
YOU KNOW, YOU SEEM KIND OF GROWN-UP LATELY, TOO, ASAKURA-KUN...
...YOU THINK SO?
YEAH.
I WONDER WHY... IS IT BECAUSE I KISSED YOU?
?!
YOU NEVER USED TO SPEAK LIKE THAT!
AFTER THAT, RYŪJI-SAN...
...WAS AS GOOD AS HIS WORD.
words café.

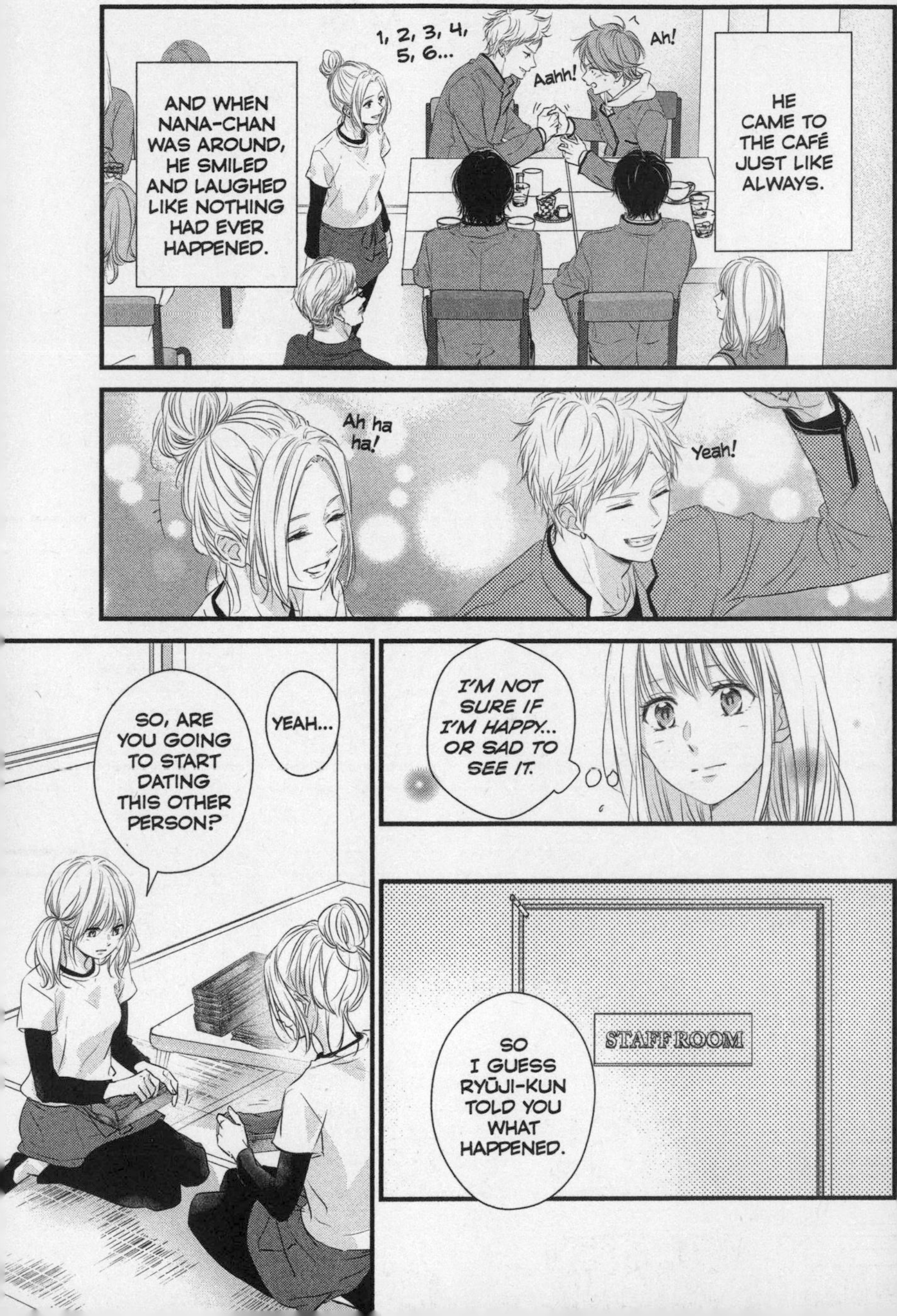
HE CAME TO THE CAFÉ JUST LIKE ALWAYS.
Ah!
Aahh!
1, 2, 3, 4, 5, 6...
AND WHEN NANA-CHAN WAS AROUND, HE SMILED AND LAUGHED LIKE NOTHING HAD EVER HAPPENED.
Yeah!
Ah ha ha!
I'M NOT SURE IF I'M HAPPY... OR SAD TO SEE IT.
STAFF ROOM
SO I GUESS RYŪJI-KUN TOLD YOU WHAT HAPPENED.
YEAH...
SO, ARE YOU GOING TO START DATING THIS OTHER PERSON?

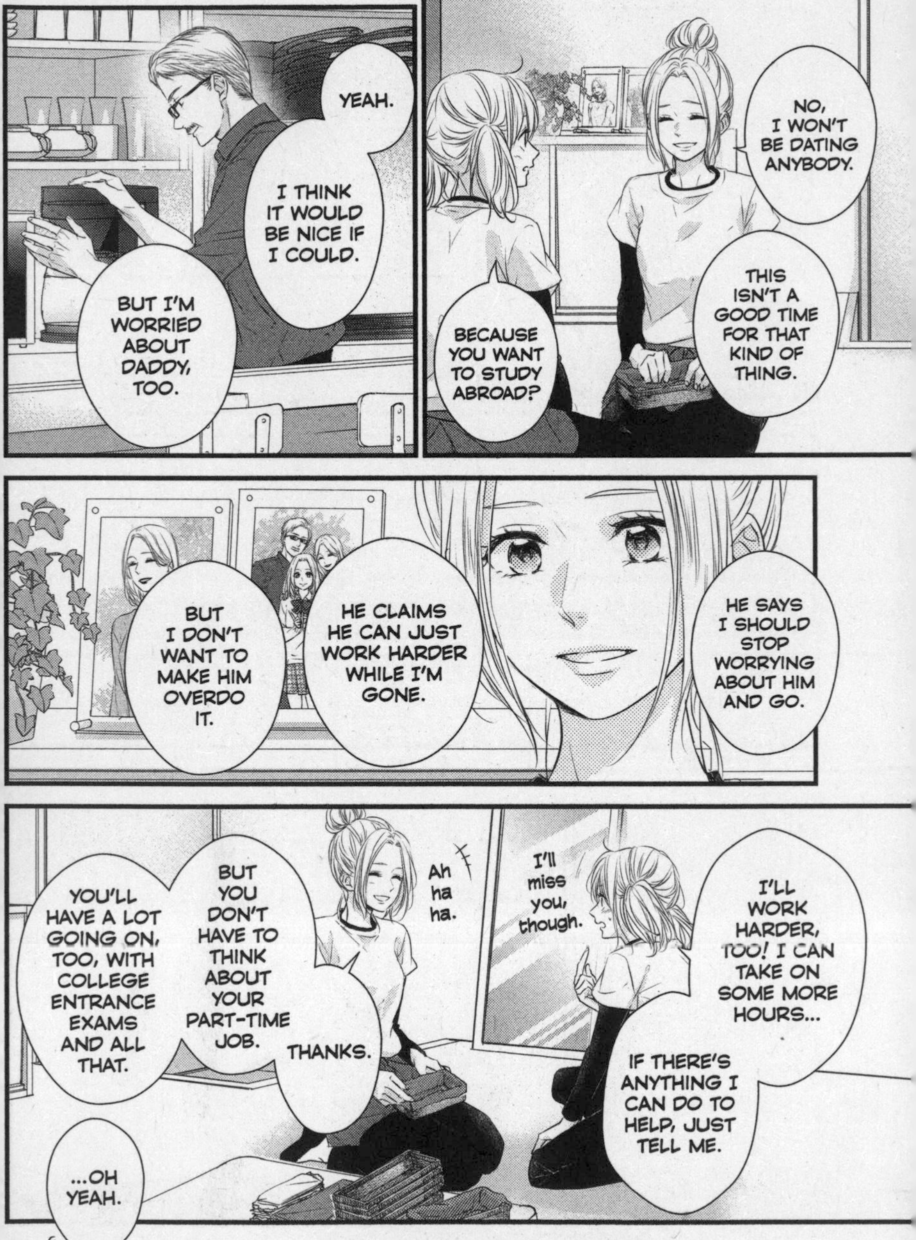
NO, I WON'T BE DATING ANYBODY.
THIS ISN'T A GOOD TIME FOR THAT KIND OF THING.
BECAUSE YOU WANT TO STUDY ABROAD?
YEAH.
I THINK IT WOULD BE NICE IF I COULD.
BUT I'M WORRIED ABOUT DADDY, TOO.
HE SAYS I SHOULD STOP WORRYING ABOUT HIM AND GO.
HE CLAIMS HE CAN JUST WORK HARDER WHILE I'M GONE.
BUT I DON'T WANT TO MAKE HIM OVERDO IT.
I'LL WORK HARDER, TOO! I CAN TAKE ON SOME MORE HOURS...
IF THERE'S ANYTHING I CAN DO TO HELP, JUST TELL ME.
I'll miss you, though.
Ah ha ha.
THANKS.
BUT YOU DON'T HAVE TO THINK ABOUT YOUR PART-TIME JOB.
YOU'LL HAVE A LOT GOING ON, TOO, WITH COLLEGE ENTRANCE EXAMS AND ALL THAT.
...OH YEAH.

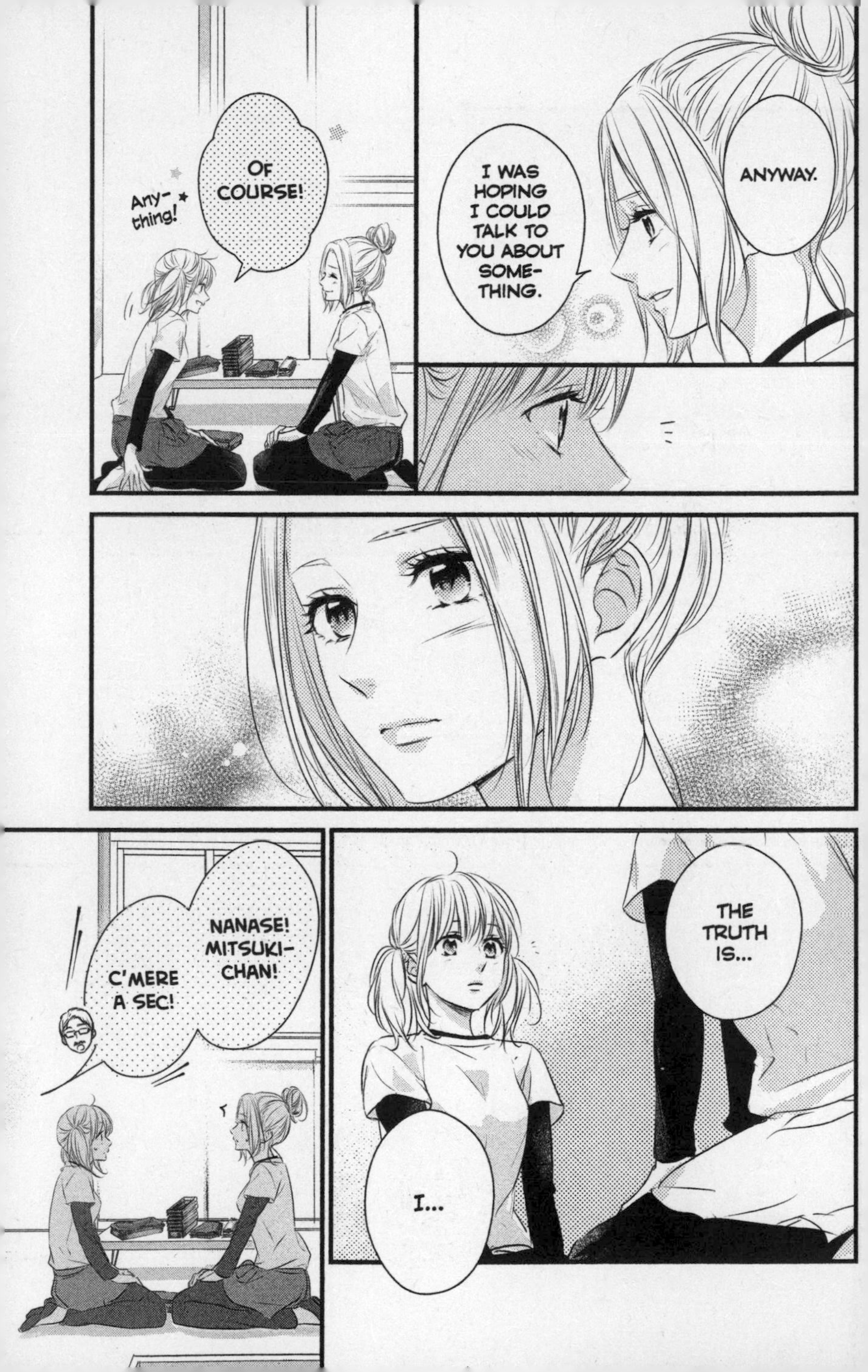
ANYWAY.
I WAS HOPING I COULD TALK TO YOU ABOUT SOME-THING.
OF COURSE!
Any-thing!
THE TRUTH IS...
I...
NANASE! MITSUKI-CHAN!
C'MERE A SEC!

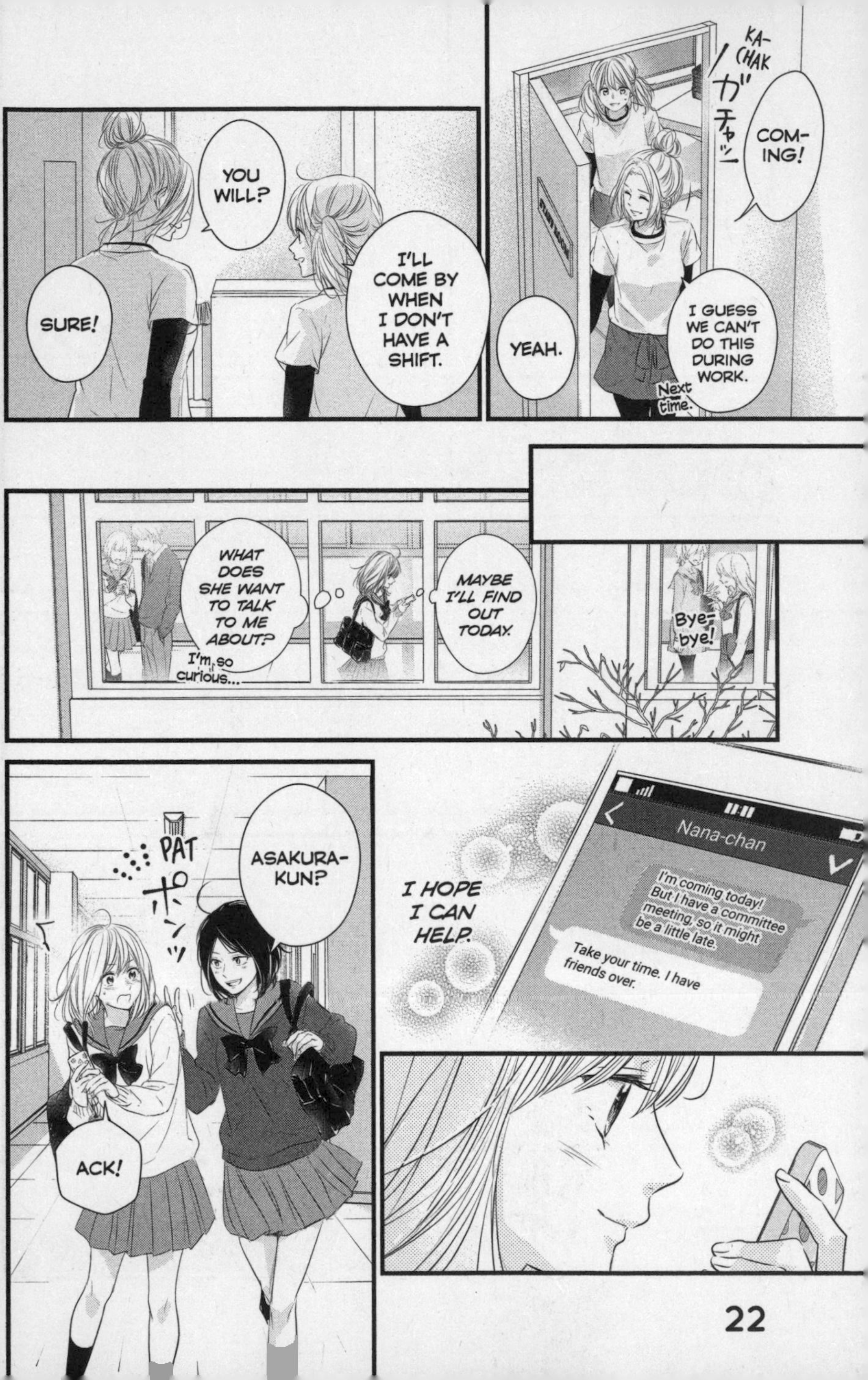
KA-CHAK
COM-ING!
I GUESS WE CAN'T DO THIS DURING WORK.
Next time.
YEAH.
I'LL COME BY WHEN I DON'T HAVE A SHIFT.
YOU WILL?
SURE!
Bye-bye!
MAYBE I'LL FIND OUT TODAY.
WHAT DOES SHE WANT TO TALK TO ME ABOUT?
I'm so curious...
Nana-chan
I'm coming today! But I have a committee meeting, so it might be a little late.
Take your time. I have friends over.
I HOPE I CAN HELP.
PAT
ASAKURA-KUN?
ACK!

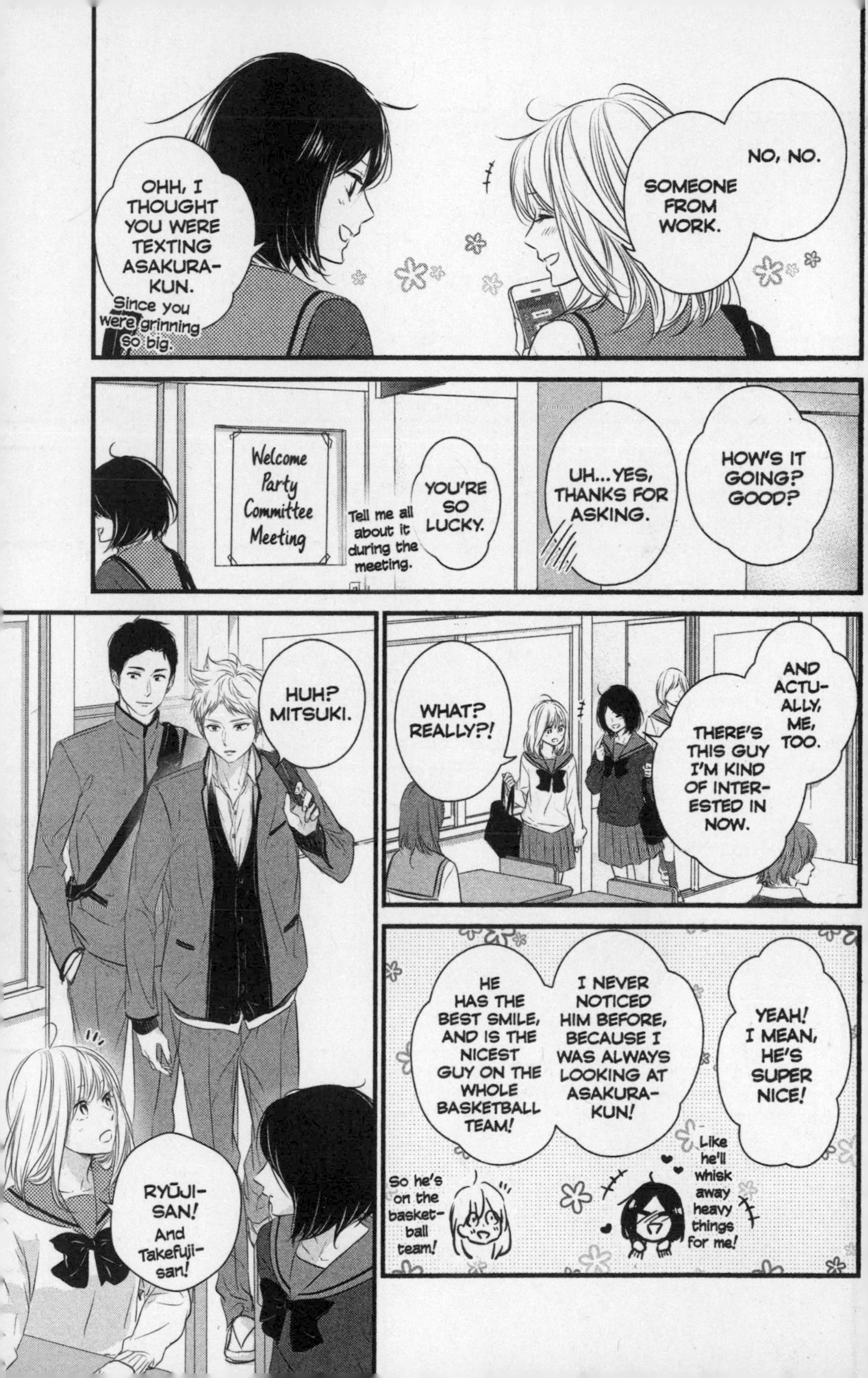
NO, NO. SOMEONE FROM WORK.
OHH, I THOUGHT YOU WERE TEXTING ASAKURA-KUN.
Since you were grinning so big.
HOW'S IT GOING? GOOD?
UH...YES, THANKS FOR ASKING.
YOU'RE SO LUCKY.
Tell me all about it during the meeting.
Welcome Party Committee Meeting
AND ACTUALLY, ME, TOO.
THERE'S THIS GUY I'M KIND OF INTERESTED IN NOW.
WHAT? REALLY?!
YEAH! I MEAN, HE'S SUPER NICE!
I NEVER NOTICED HIM BEFORE, BECAUSE I WAS ALWAYS LOOKING AT ASAKURA-KUN!
HE HAS THE BEST SMILE, AND IS THE NICEST GUY ON THE WHOLE BASKETBALL TEAM!
Like he'll whisk away heavy things for me!
So he's on the basketball team!
HUH? MITSUKI.
RYŪJI-SAN! And Takefuji-san!

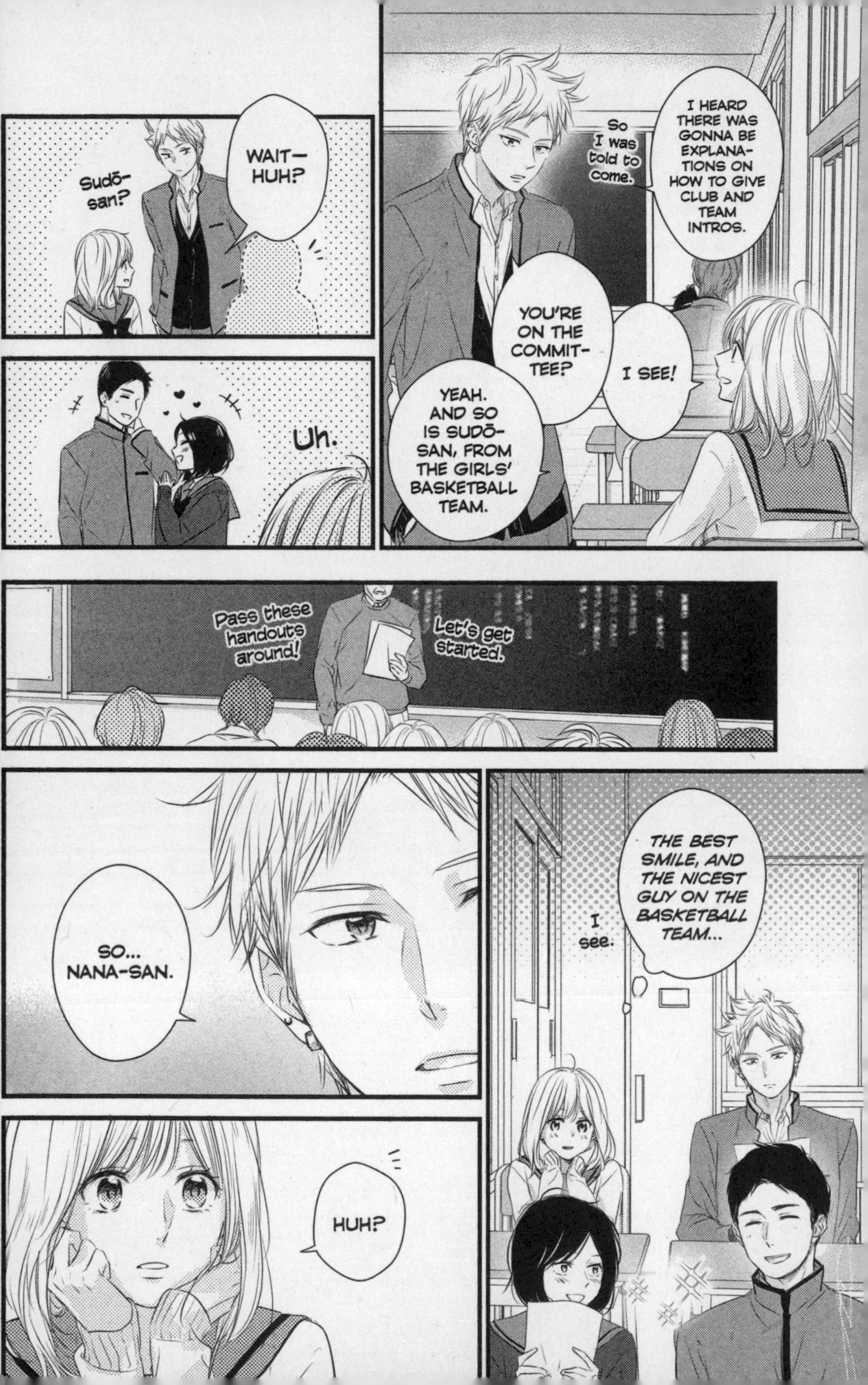
I HEARD THERE WAS GONNA BE EXPLANATIONS ON HOW TO GIVE CLUB AND TEAM INTROS.
So I was told to come.
I SEE!
YOU'RE ON THE COMMITTEE?
YEAH. AND SO IS SUDŌ-SAN, FROM THE GIRLS' BASKETBALL TEAM.
WAIT—HUH?
Sudō-san?
Uh.
Let's get started.
Pass these handouts around!
THE BEST SMILE, AND THE NICEST GUY ON THE BASKETBALL TEAM...
I see.
SO... NANA-SAN.
HUH?

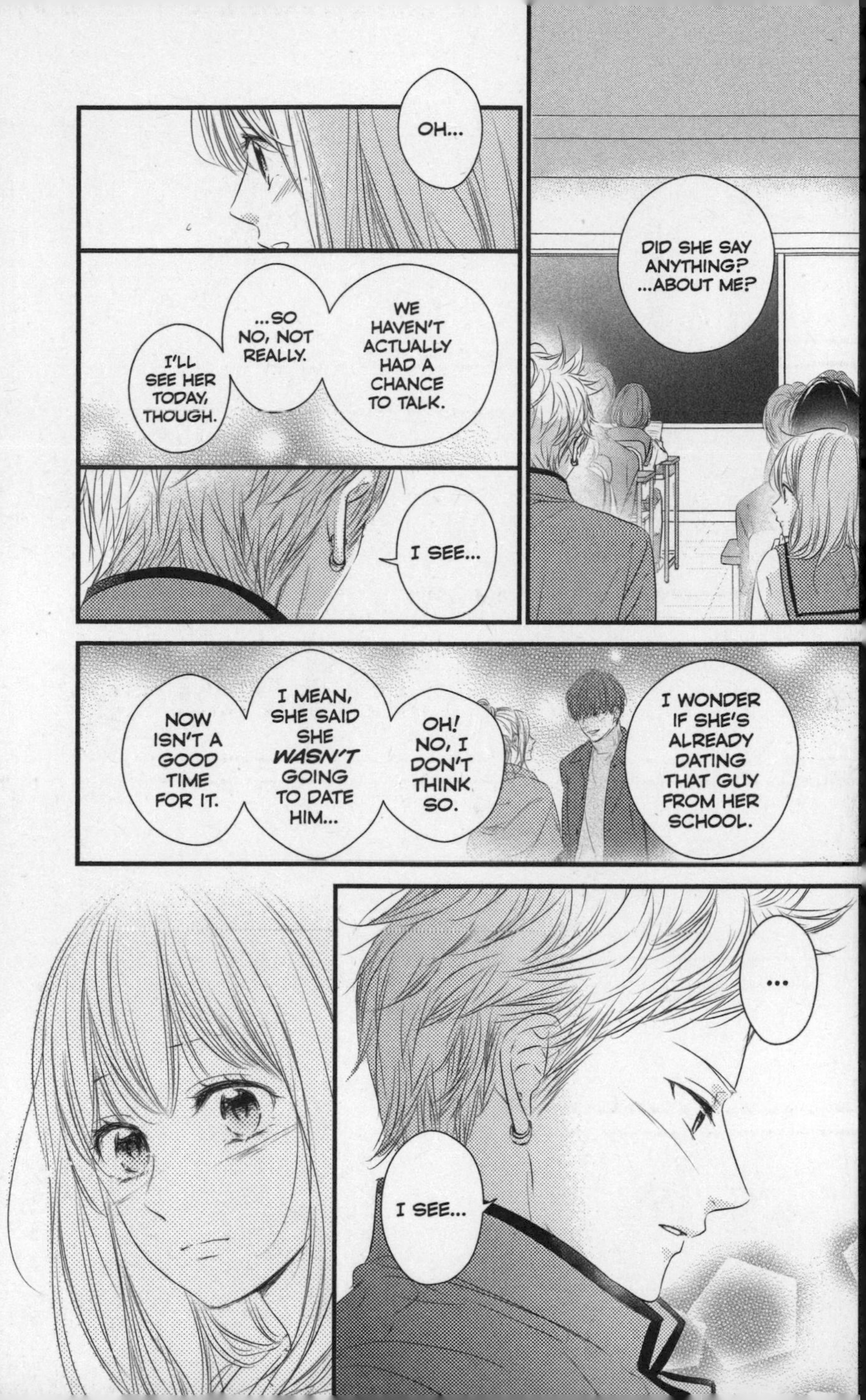
DID SHE SAY ANYTHING? ...ABOUT ME?
OH...
WE HAVEN'T ACTUALLY HAD A CHANCE TO TALK.
...SO NO, NOT REALLY.
I'LL SEE HER TODAY, THOUGH.
I SEE...
I WONDER IF SHE'S ALREADY DATING THAT GUY FROM HER SCHOOL.
OH! NO, I DON'T THINK SO.
I MEAN, SHE SAID SHE *WASN'T* GOING TO DATE HIM...
NOW ISN'T A GOOD TIME FOR IT.
...
I SEE...

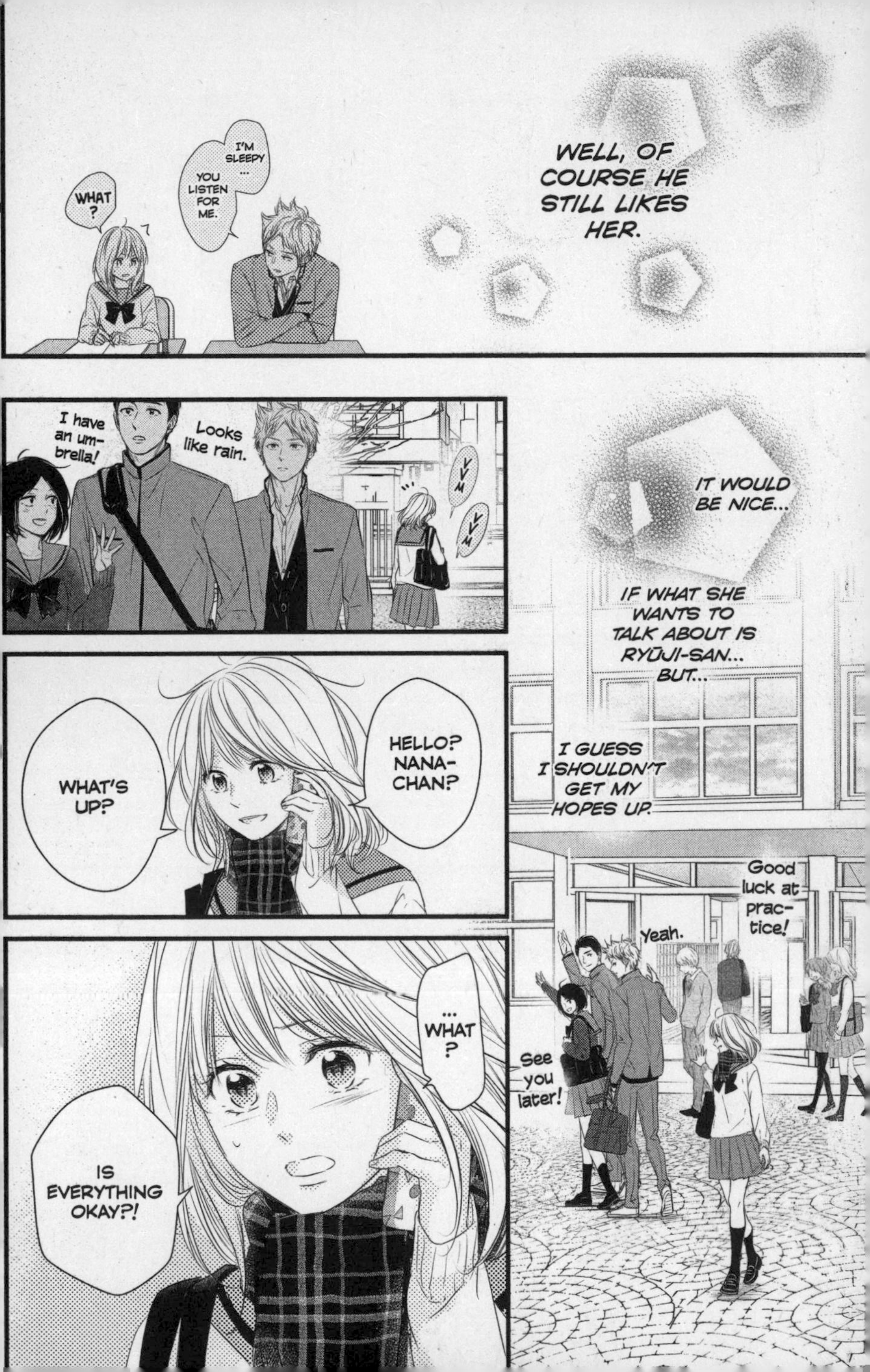
WELL, OF COURSE HE STILL LIKES HER.
I'M SLEEPY ...
YOU LISTEN FOR ME.
WHAT ?
IT WOULD BE NICE...
IF WHAT SHE WANTS TO TALK ABOUT IS RYŪJI-SAN... BUT...
I GUESS I SHOULDN'T GET MY HOPES UP.
Good luck at prac-tice!
Yeah.
See you later!
Looks like rain.
I have an um-brella!
VVM
VVM
HELLO? NANA-CHAN?
WHAT'S UP?
... WHAT ?
IS EVERYTHING OKAY?!

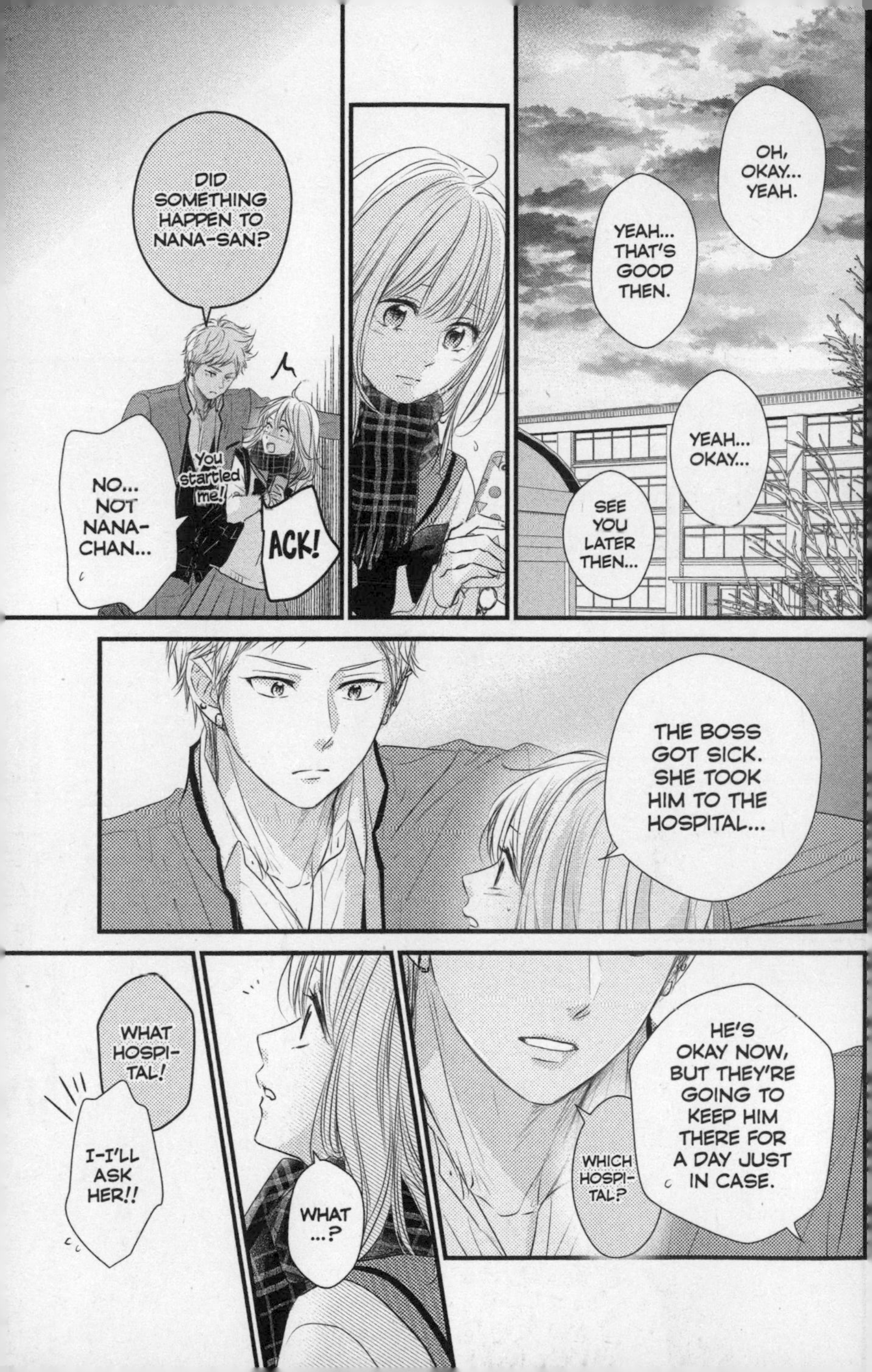
OH, OKAY... YEAH.
YEAH... THAT'S GOOD THEN.
YEAH... OKAY...
SEE YOU LATER THEN...
DID SOMETHING HAPPEN TO NANA-SAN?
ACK!
You startled me!
NO... NOT NANA-CHAN...
THE BOSS GOT SICK. SHE TOOK HIM TO THE HOSPITAL...
HE'S OKAY NOW, BUT THEY'RE GOING TO KEEP HIM THERE FOR A DAY JUST IN CASE.
WHICH HOSPI-TAL?
WHAT ...?
WHAT HOSPI-TAL!
I-I'LL ASK HER!!

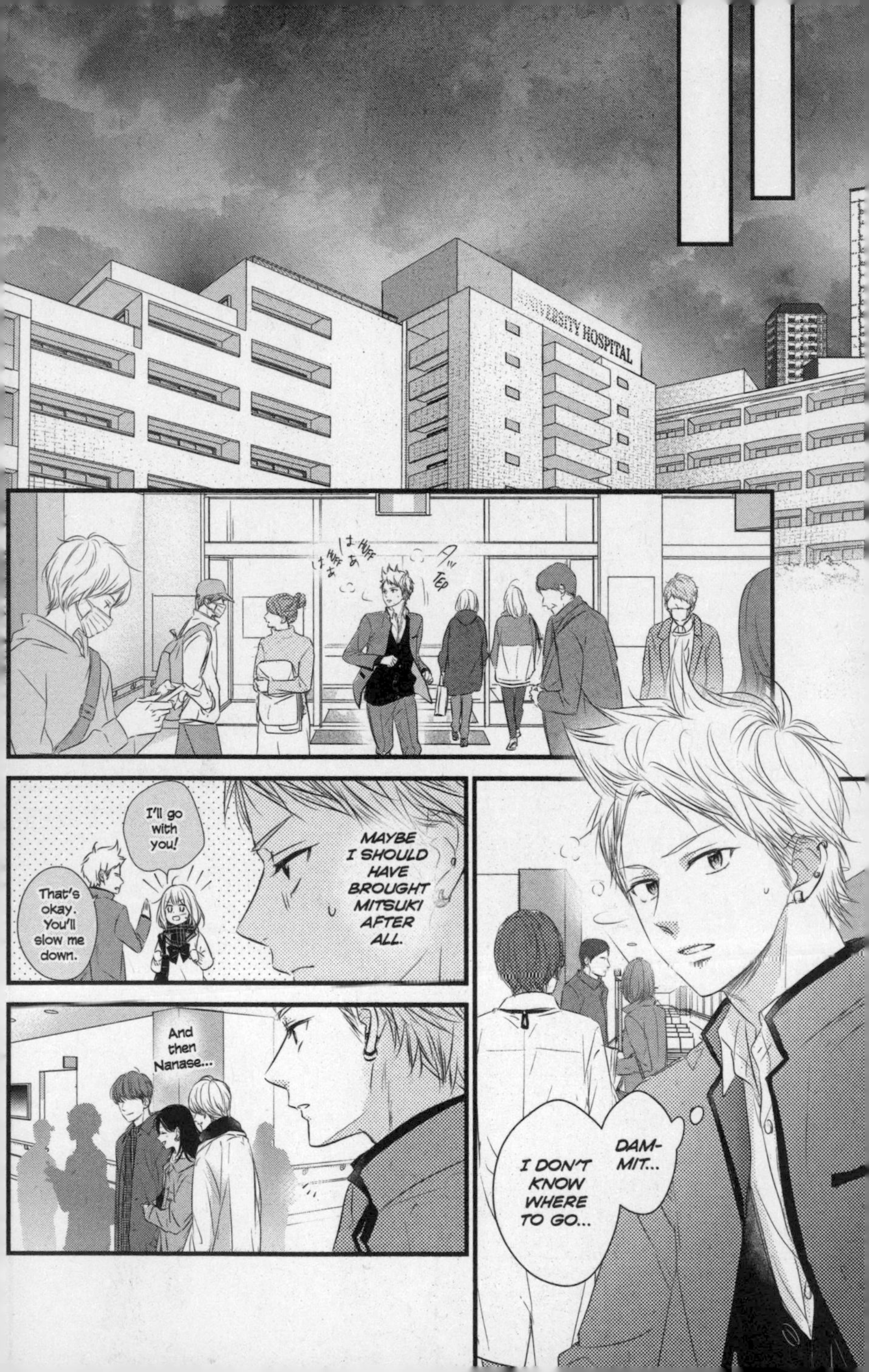
HOSPITAL
はぁ HUFF
はぁ HUFF
タッ TAP
DAM-MIT...
I DON'T KNOW WHERE TO GO...
MAYBE I SHOULD HAVE BROUGHT MITSUKI AFTER ALL.
I'll go with you!
That's okay. You'll slow me down.
And then Nanase...

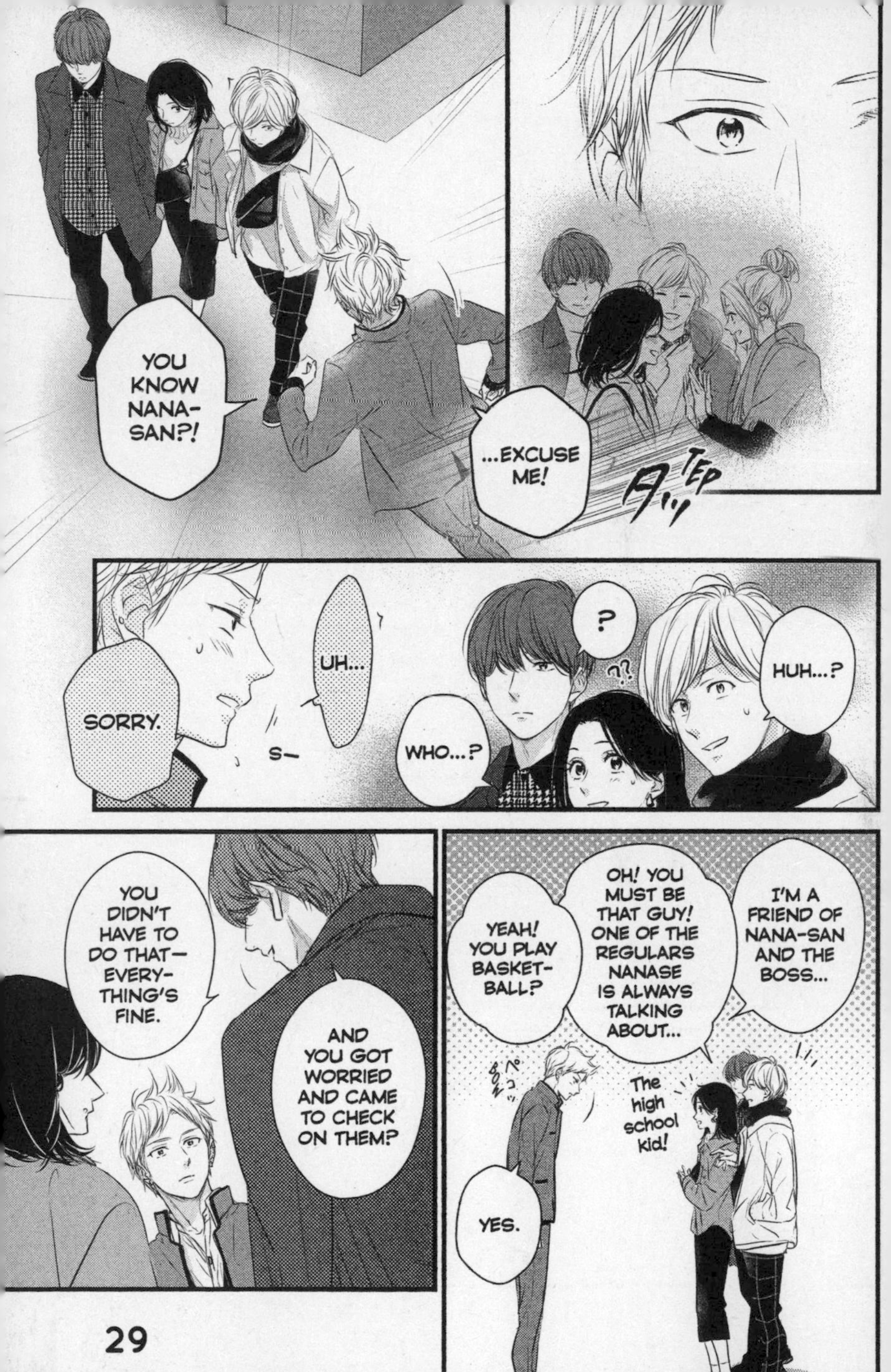

TEP
...EXCUSE ME!
YOU KNOW NANA-SAN?!
HUH...?
?
??
WHO...?
UH...
S–
SORRY.
I'M A FRIEND OF NANA-SAN AND THE BOSS...
OH! YOU MUST BE THAT GUY! ONE OF THE REGULARS NANASE IS ALWAYS TALKING ABOUT...
YEAH! YOU PLAY BASKET-BALL?
The high school kid!
YES.
YOU DIDN'T HAVE TO DO THAT—EVERY-THING'S FINE.
AND YOU GOT WORRIED AND CAME TO CHECK ON THEM?

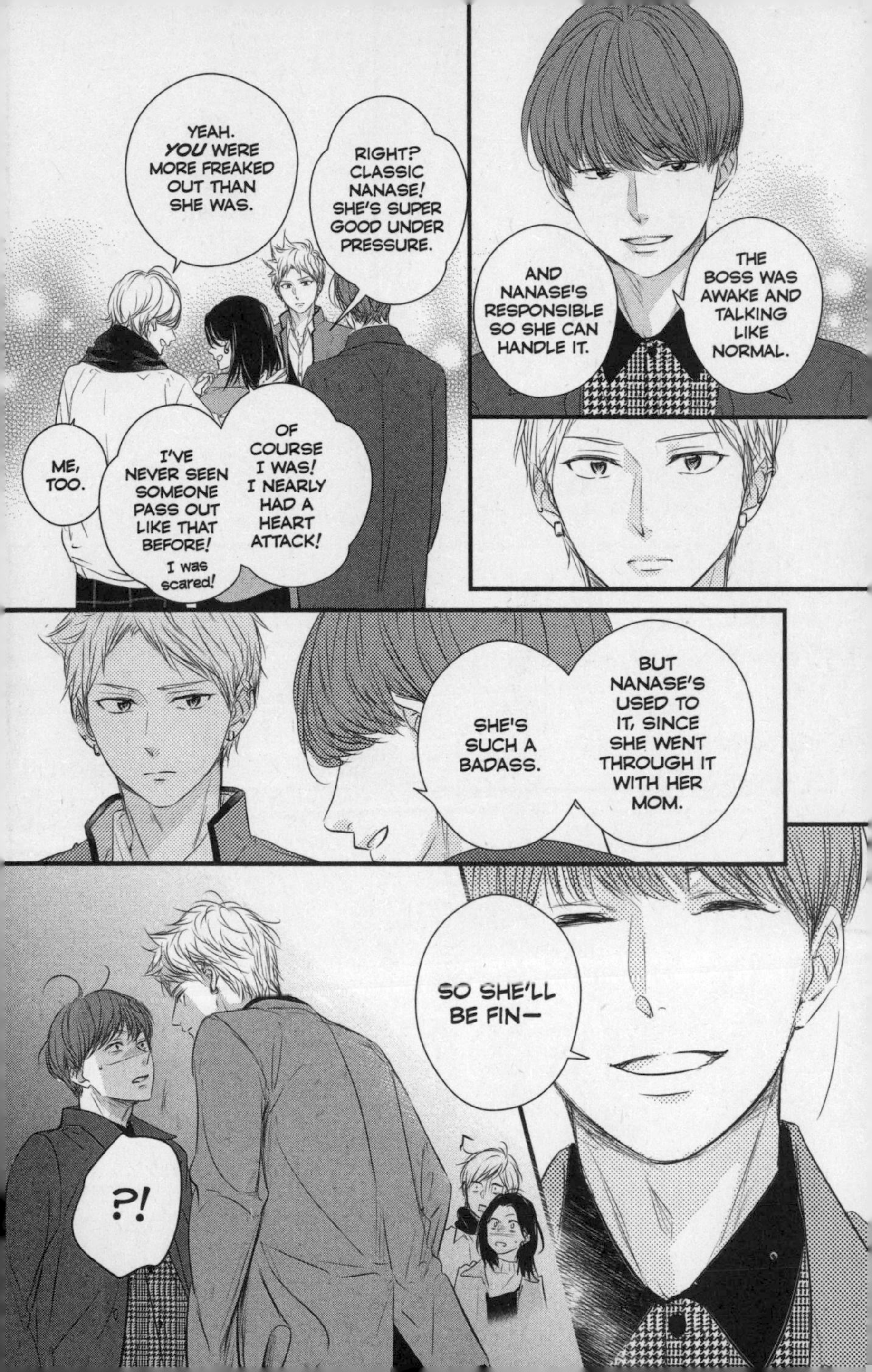
THE BOSS WAS AWAKE AND TALKING LIKE NORMAL.
AND NANASE'S RESPONSIBLE SO SHE CAN HANDLE IT.
RIGHT? CLASSIC NANASE! SHE'S SUPER GOOD UNDER PRESSURE.
YEAH. *YOU* WERE MORE FREAKED OUT THAN SHE WAS.
OF COURSE I WAS! I NEARLY HAD A HEART ATTACK!
I'VE NEVER SEEN SOMEONE PASS OUT LIKE THAT BEFORE!
I was scared!
ME, TOO.
BUT NANASE'S USED TO IT, SINCE SHE WENT THROUGH IT WITH HER MOM.
SHE'S SUCH A BADASS.
SO SHE'LL BE FIN—
?!

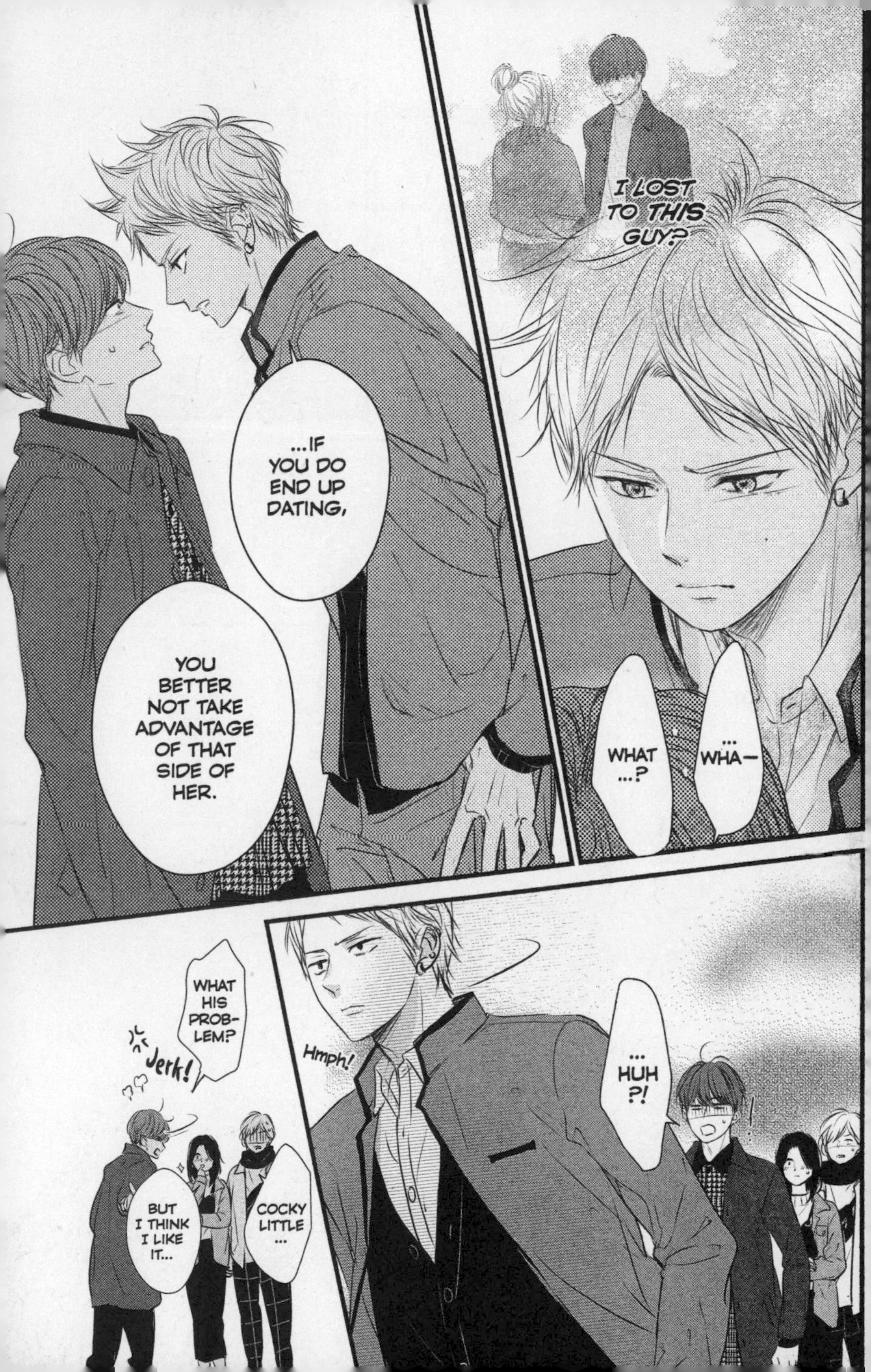

I LOST TO THIS GUY?
... WHA—
WHAT ...?
...IF YOU DO END UP DATING,
YOU BETTER NOT TAKE ADVANTAGE OF THAT SIDE OF HER.
... HUH ?!
Hmph!
WHAT HIS PROB-LEM?
Jerk!
COCKY LITTLE ...
BUT I THINK I LIKE IT...

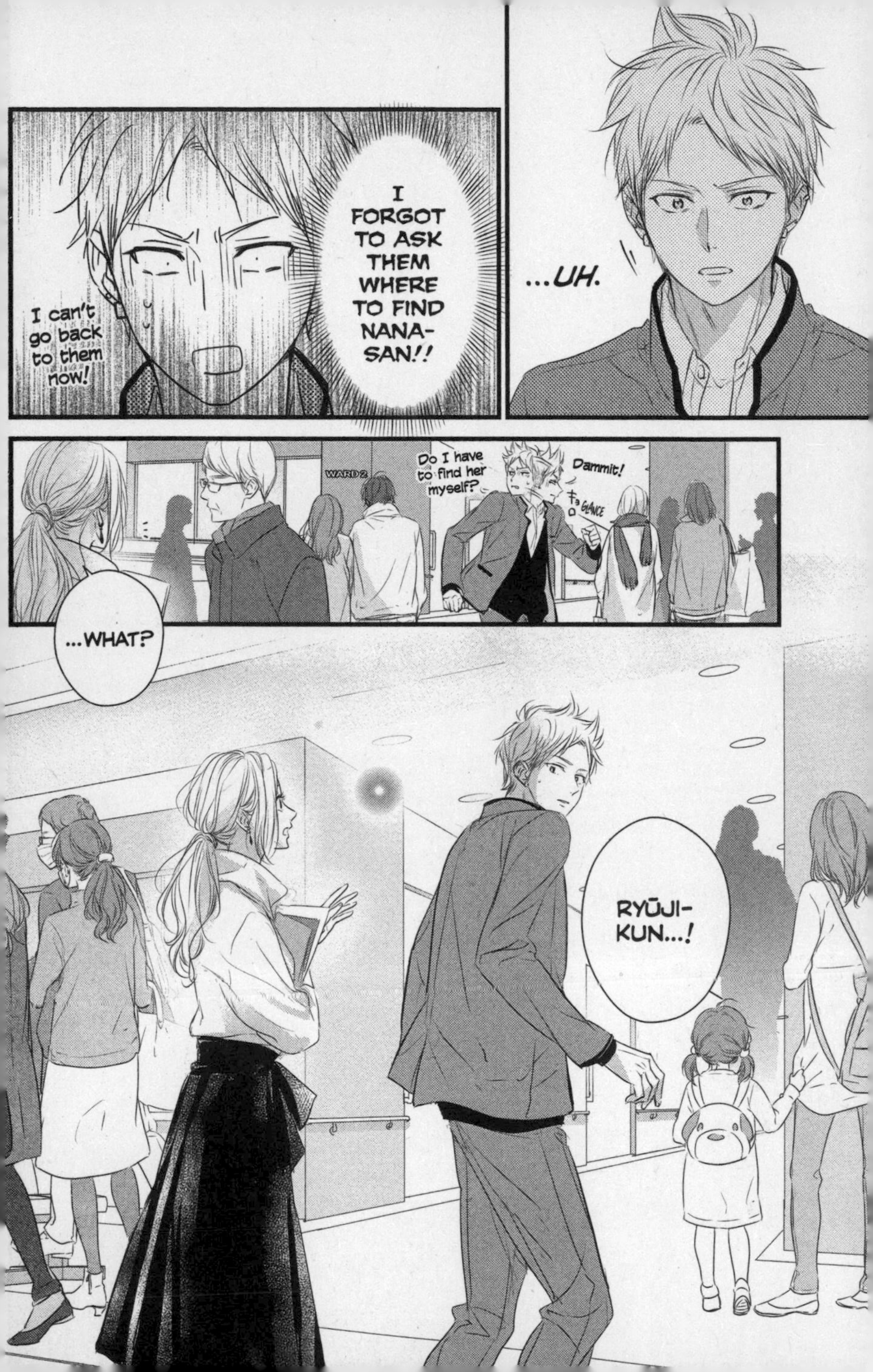
...UH.
I FORGOT TO ASK THEM WHERE TO FIND NANA-SAN!!
I can't go back to them now!
Dammit!
GLANCE
Do I have to find her myself?
WARD 2
...WHAT?
RYŪJI-KUN...!

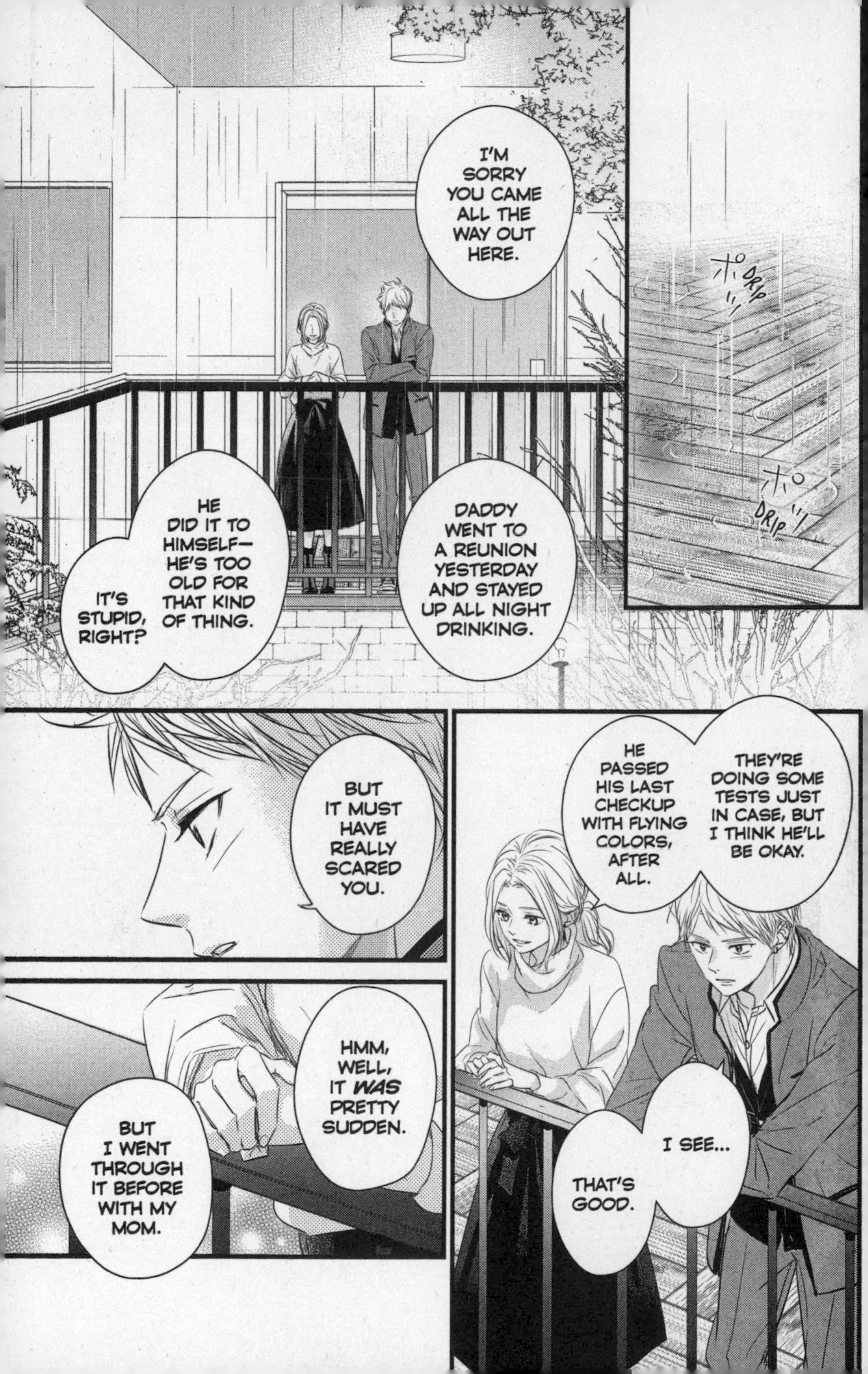
ポツ DRIP
ポツ DRIP
I'M SORRY YOU CAME ALL THE WAY OUT HERE.
DADDY WENT TO A REUNION YESTERDAY AND STAYED UP ALL NIGHT DRINKING.
HE DID IT TO HIMSELF— HE'S TOO OLD FOR THAT KIND OF THING.
IT'S STUPID, RIGHT?
THEY'RE DOING SOME TESTS JUST IN CASE, BUT I THINK HE'LL BE OKAY.
HE PASSED HIS LAST CHECKUP WITH FLYING COLORS, AFTER ALL.
I SEE...
THAT'S GOOD.
BUT IT MUST HAVE REALLY SCARED YOU.
HMM, WELL, IT *WAS* PRETTY SUDDEN.
BUT I WENT THROUGH IT BEFORE WITH MY MOM.

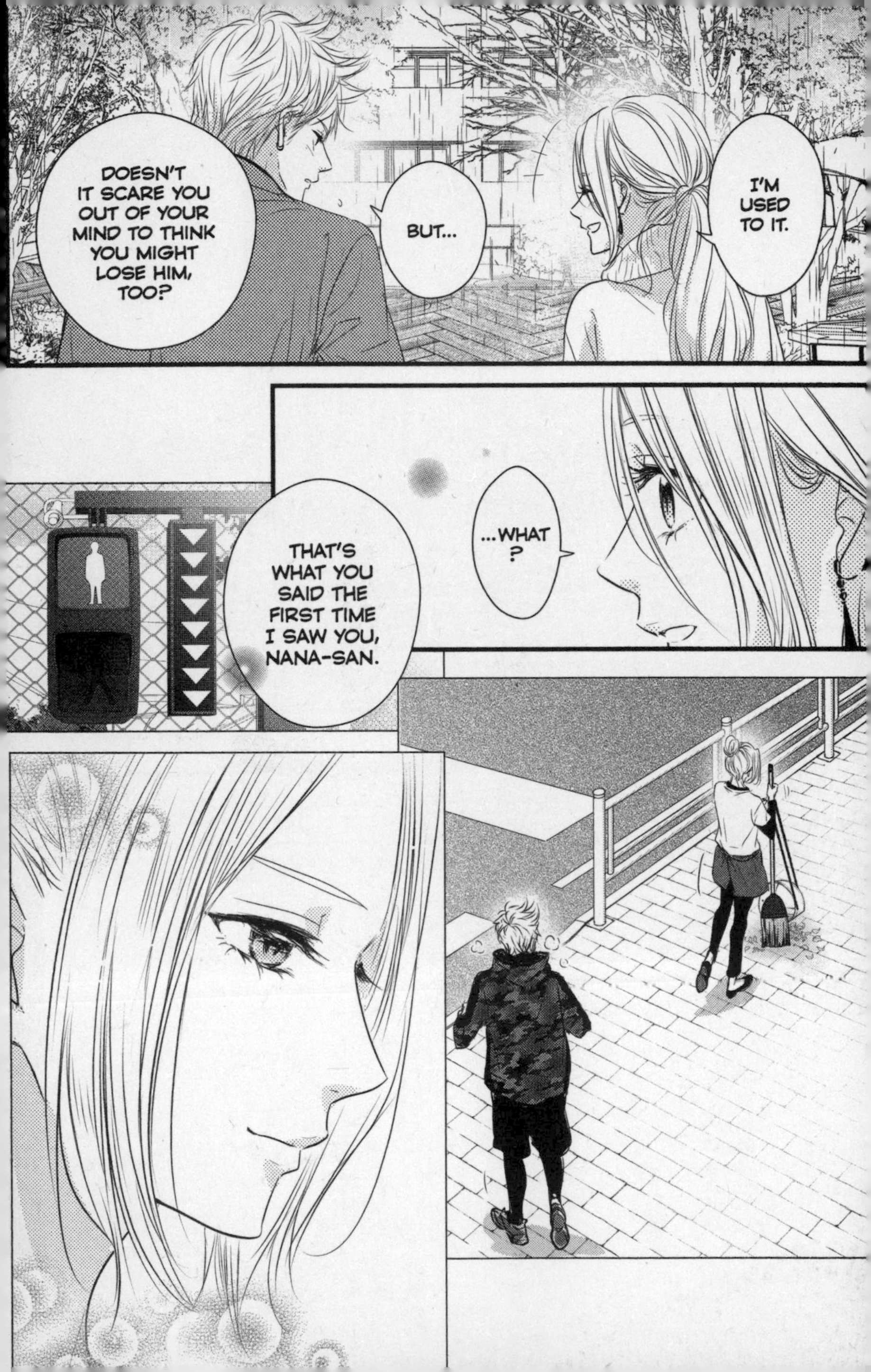
I'M USED TO IT.
BUT...
DOESN'T IT SCARE YOU OUT OF YOUR MIND TO THINK YOU MIGHT LOSE HIM, TOO?
...WHAT?
THAT'S WHAT YOU SAID THE FIRST TIME I SAW YOU, NANA-SAN.

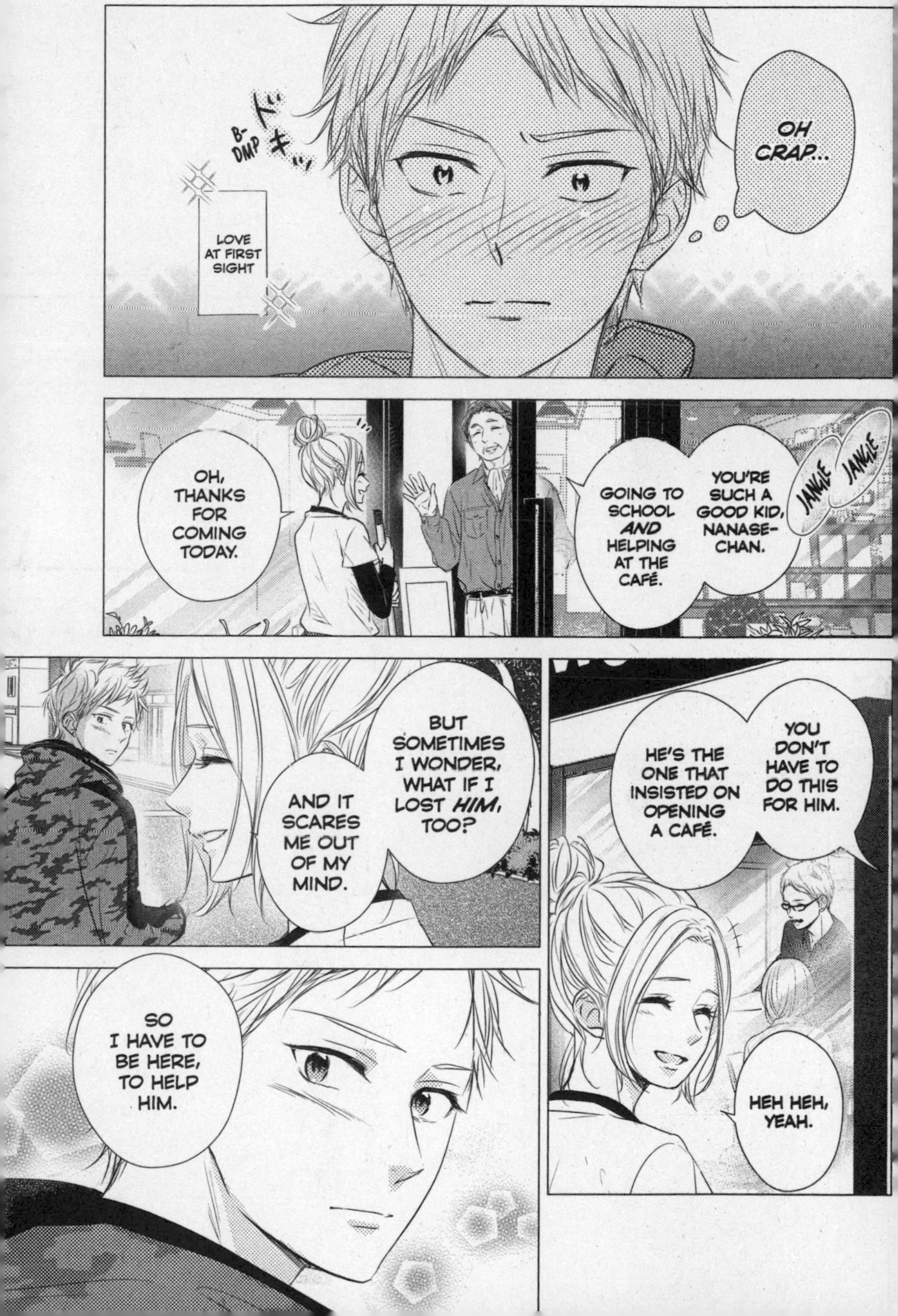
OH CRAP...
B-DMP ドキッ
LOVE AT FIRST SIGHT
JANGLE JANGLE
YOU'RE SUCH A GOOD KID, NANASE-CHAN.
GOING TO SCHOOL *AND* HELPING AT THE CAFÉ.
OH, THANKS FOR COMING TODAY.
YOU DON'T HAVE TO DO THIS FOR HIM.
HE'S THE ONE THAT INSISTED ON OPENING A CAFÉ.
HEH HEH, YEAH.
BUT SOMETIMES I WONDER, WHAT IF I LOST *HIM*, TOO?
AND IT SCARES ME OUT OF MY MIND.
SO I HAVE TO BE HERE, TO HELP HIM.

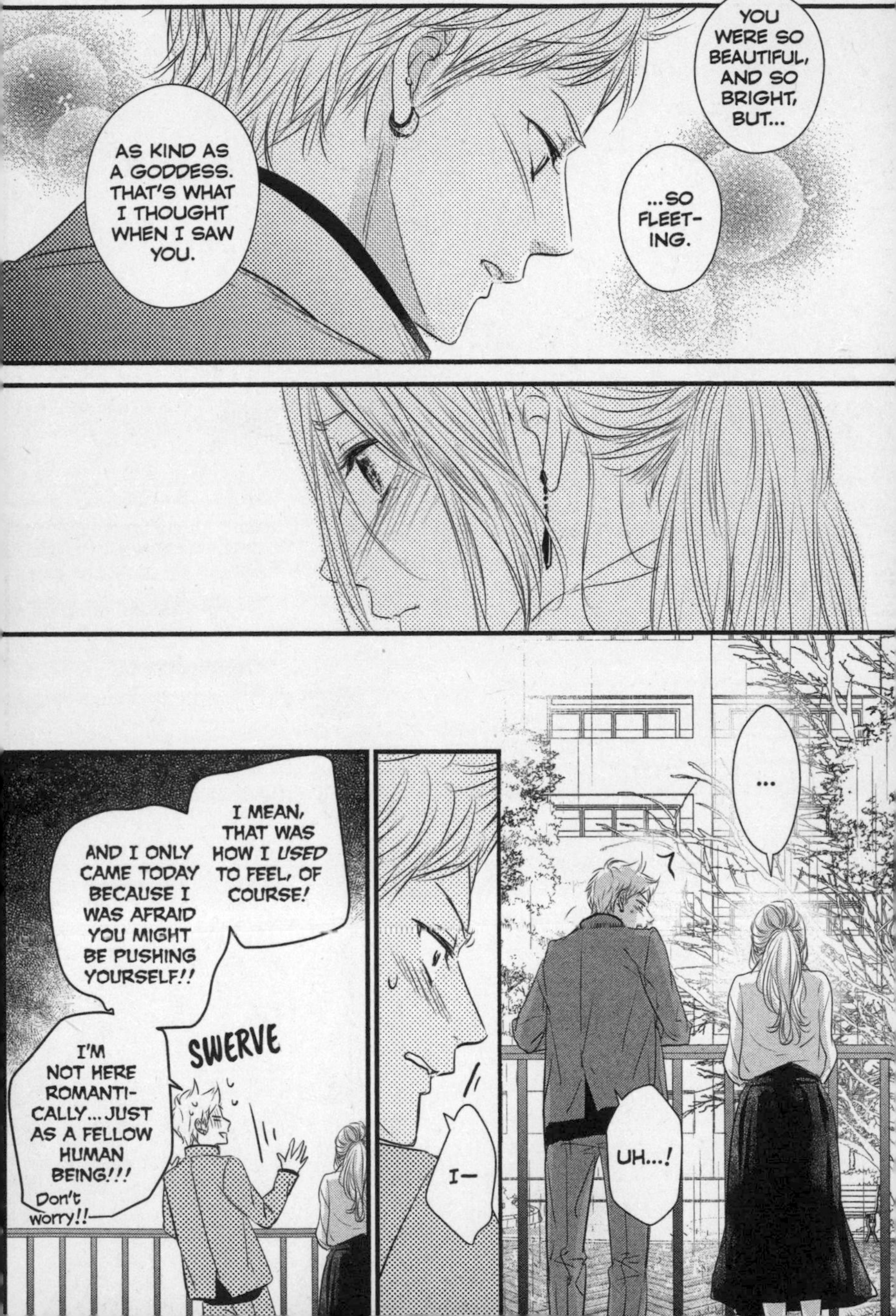
YOU WERE SO BEAUTIFUL, AND SO BRIGHT, BUT...
...SO FLEET-ING.
AS KIND AS A GODDESS. THAT'S WHAT I THOUGHT WHEN I SAW YOU.
...
UH...!
I—
I MEAN, THAT WAS HOW I *USED* TO FEEL, OF COURSE!
AND I ONLY CAME TODAY BECAUSE I WAS AFRAID YOU MIGHT BE PUSHING YOURSELF!!
SWERVE
I'M NOT HERE ROMANTI-CALLY... JUST AS A FELLOW HUMAN BEING!!!
Don't worry!!

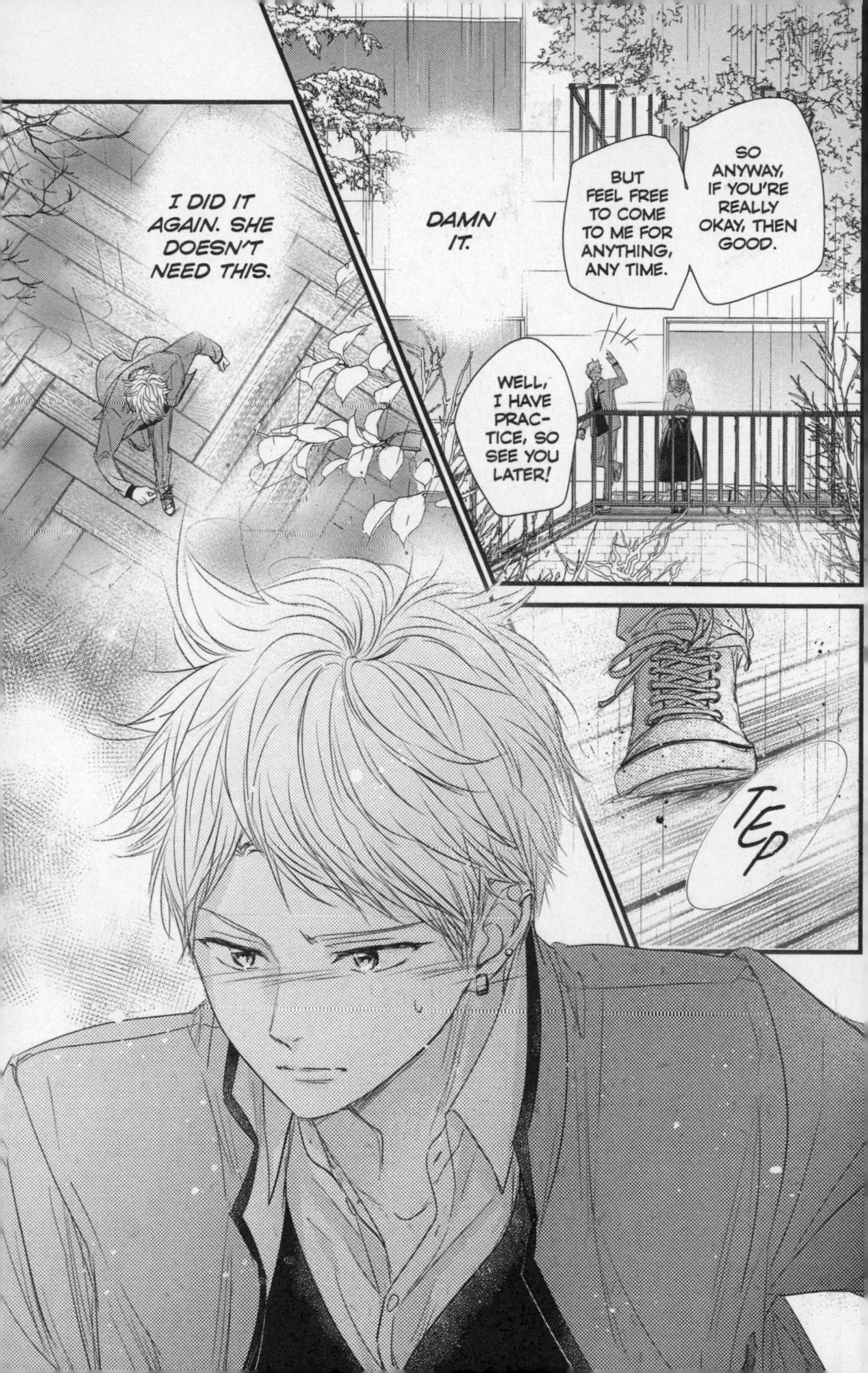
SO ANYWAY, IF YOU'RE REALLY OKAY, THEN GOOD.
BUT FEEL FREE TO COME TO ME FOR ANYTHING, ANY TIME.
WELL, I HAVE PRAC-TICE, SO SEE YOU LATER!
DAMN IT.
I DID IT AGAIN. SHE DOESN'T NEED THIS.
TEP

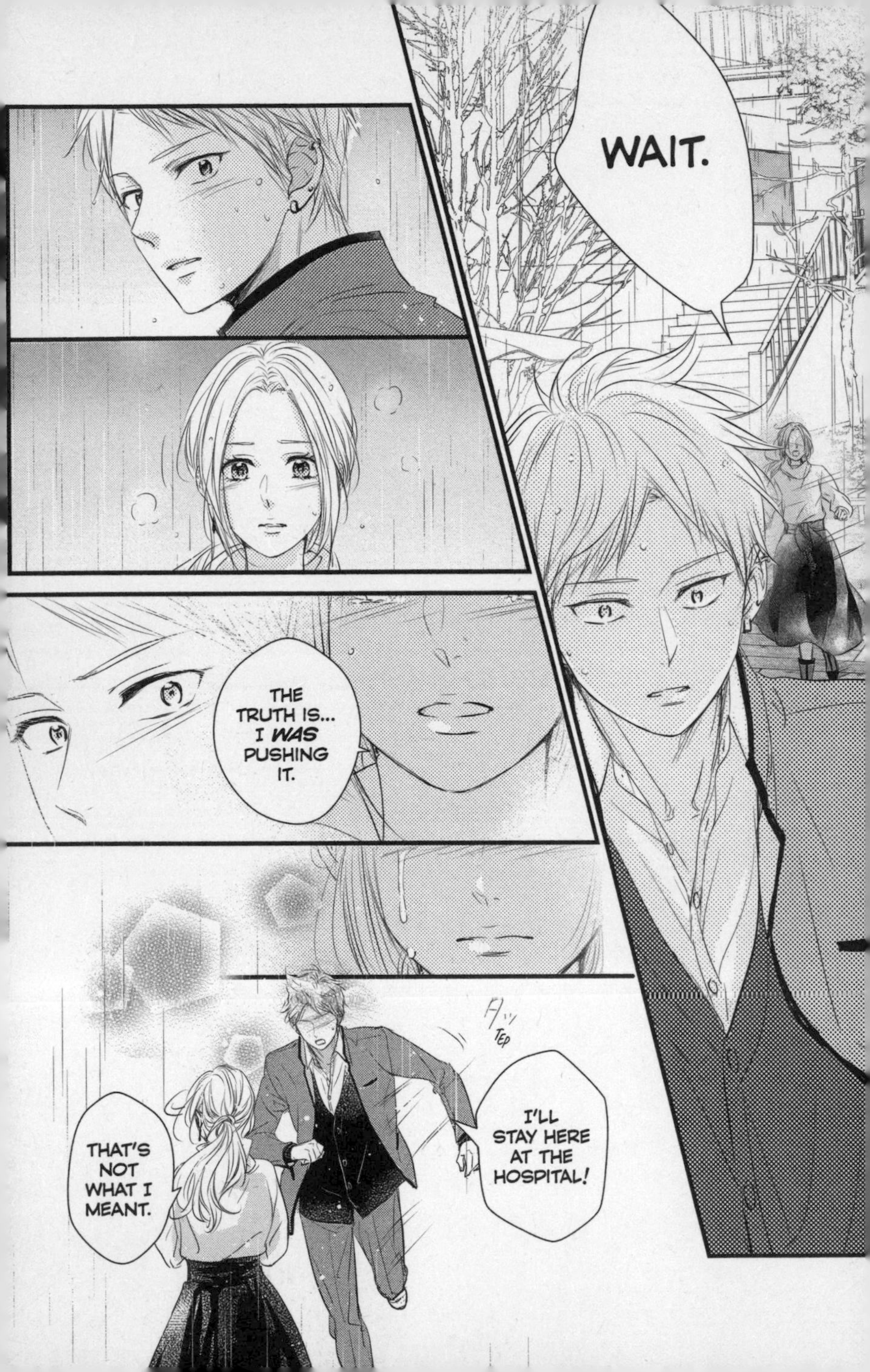
WAIT.
THE TRUTH IS... I *WAS* PUSHING IT.
TEP
I'LL STAY HERE AT THE HOSPITAL!
THAT'S NOT WHAT I MEANT.

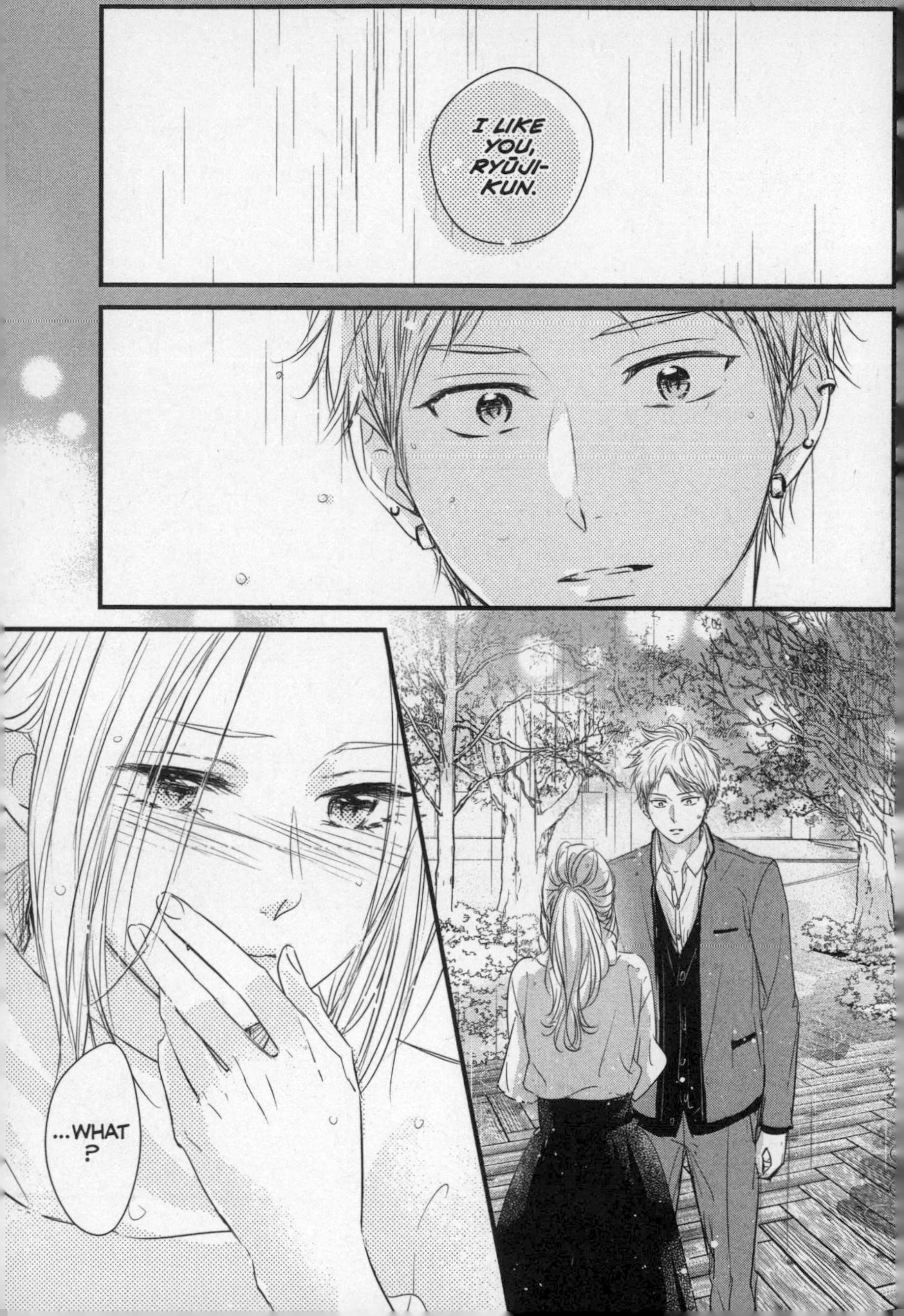
I LIKE YOU, RYŪJI-KUN.
...WHAT ?

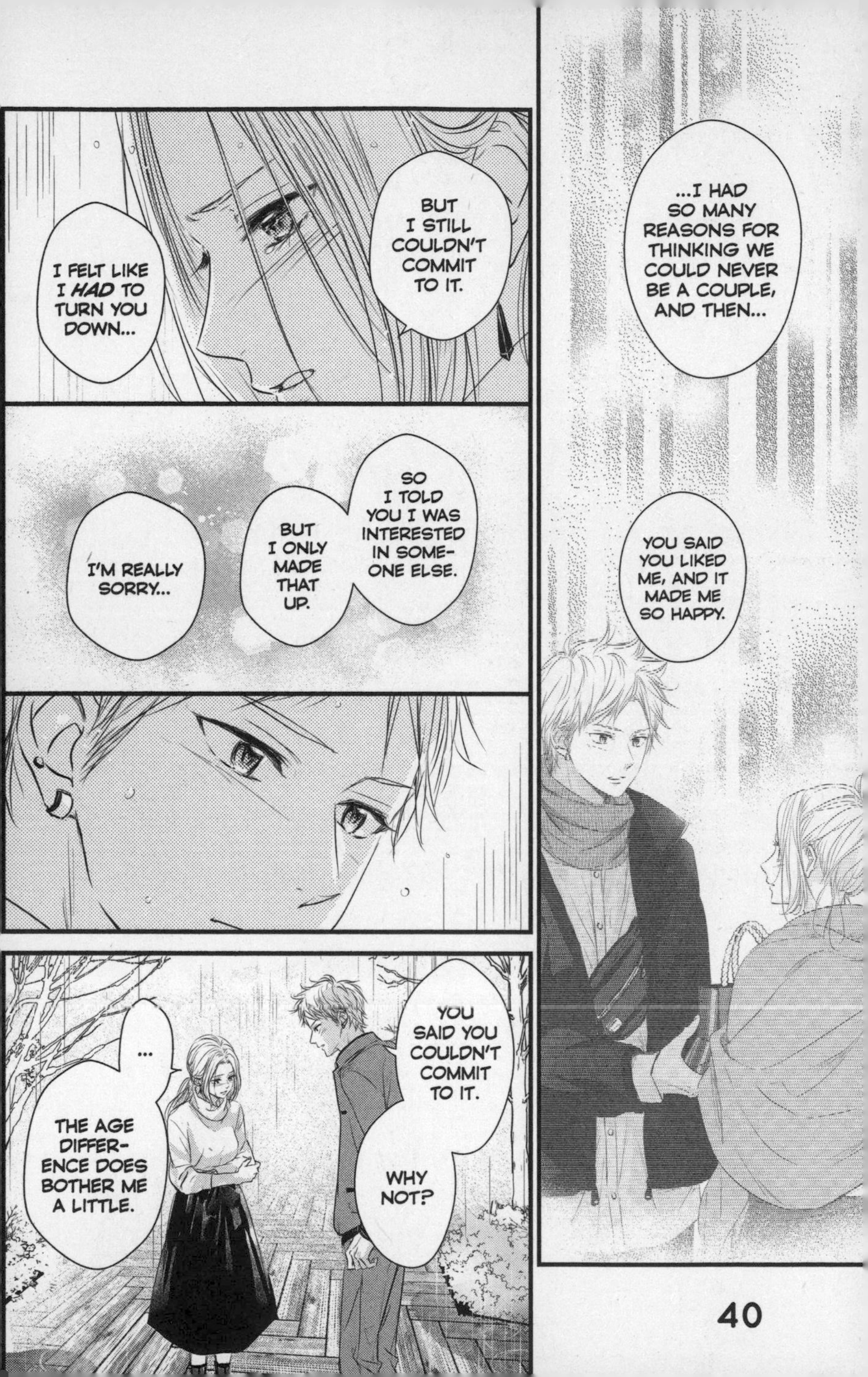
...I HAD SO MANY REASONS FOR THINKING WE COULD NEVER BE A COUPLE, AND THEN...
YOU SAID YOU LIKED ME, AND IT MADE ME SO HAPPY.
BUT I STILL COULDN'T COMMIT TO IT.
I FELT LIKE I *HAD* TO TURN YOU DOWN...
SO I TOLD YOU I WAS INTERESTED IN SOME-ONE ELSE.
BUT I ONLY MADE THAT UP.
I'M REALLY SORRY...
YOU SAID YOU COULDN'T COMMIT TO IT.
WHY NOT?
...
THE AGE DIFFER-ENCE DOES BOTHER ME A LITTLE.

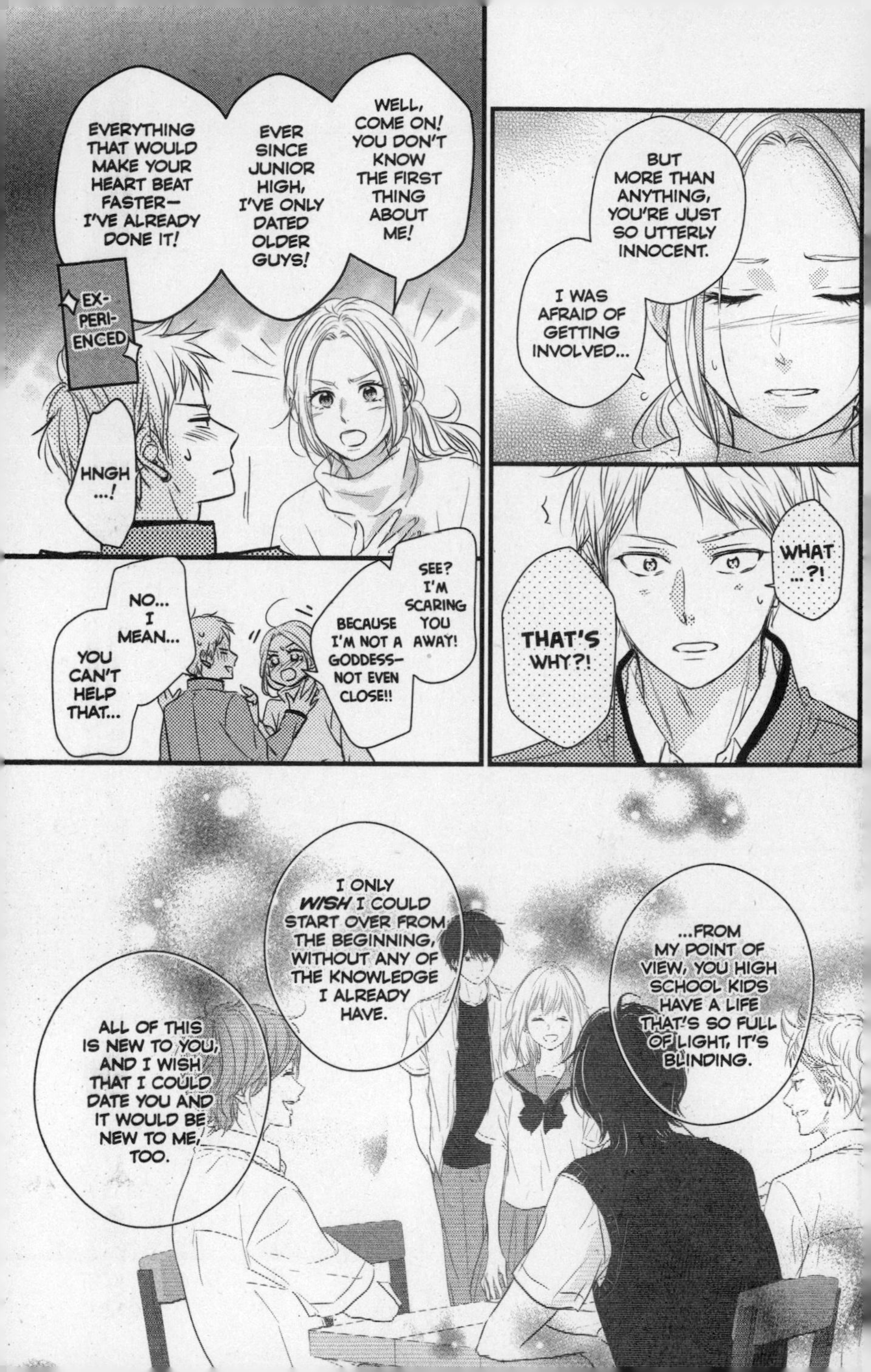

WELL, COME ON! YOU DON'T KNOW THE FIRST THING ABOUT ME!
EVER SINCE JUNIOR HIGH, I'VE ONLY DATED OLDER GUYS!
EVERYTHING THAT WOULD MAKE YOUR HEART BEAT FASTER— I'VE ALREADY DONE IT!
EX-PERI-ENCED
HNGH ...!
SEE? I'M SCARING YOU AWAY!
BECAUSE I'M NOT A GODDESS— NOT EVEN CLOSE!!
NO... I MEAN...
YOU CAN'T HELP THAT...
BUT MORE THAN ANYTHING, YOU'RE JUST SO UTTERLY INNOCENT.
I WAS AFRAID OF GETTING INVOLVED...
WHAT ...?!
THAT'S WHY?!
...FROM MY POINT OF VIEW, YOU HIGH SCHOOL KIDS HAVE A LIFE THAT'S SO FULL OF LIGHT, IT'S BLINDING.
I ONLY WISH I COULD START OVER FROM THE BEGINNING, WITHOUT ANY OF THE KNOWLEDGE I ALREADY HAVE.
ALL OF THIS IS NEW TO YOU, AND I WISH THAT I COULD DATE YOU AND IT WOULD BE NEW TO ME, TOO.

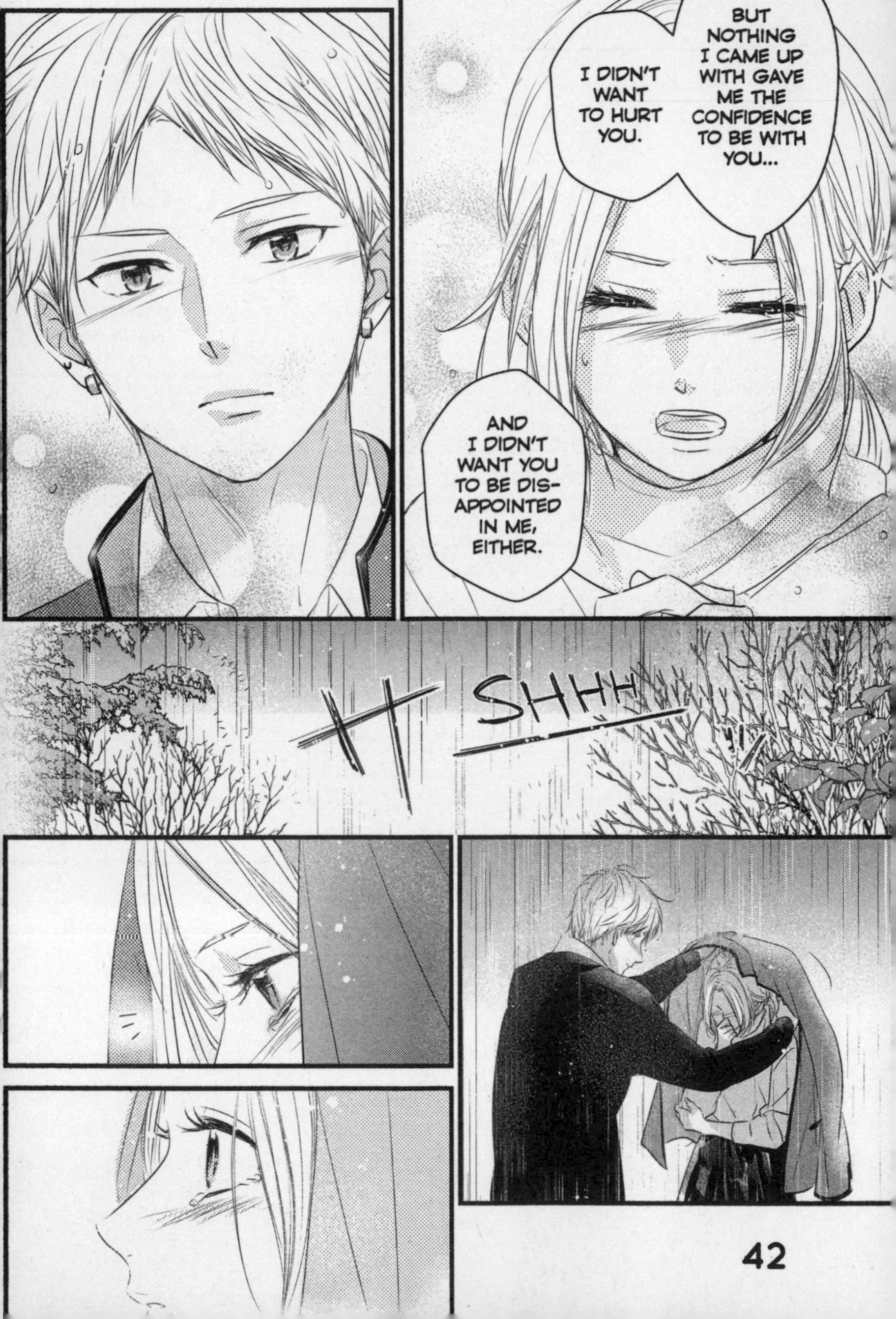
BUT NOTHING I CAME UP WITH GAVE ME THE CONFIDENCE TO BE WITH YOU...
I DIDN'T WANT TO HURT YOU.
AND I DIDN'T WANT YOU TO BE DIS-APPOINTED IN ME, EITHER.
SHHH

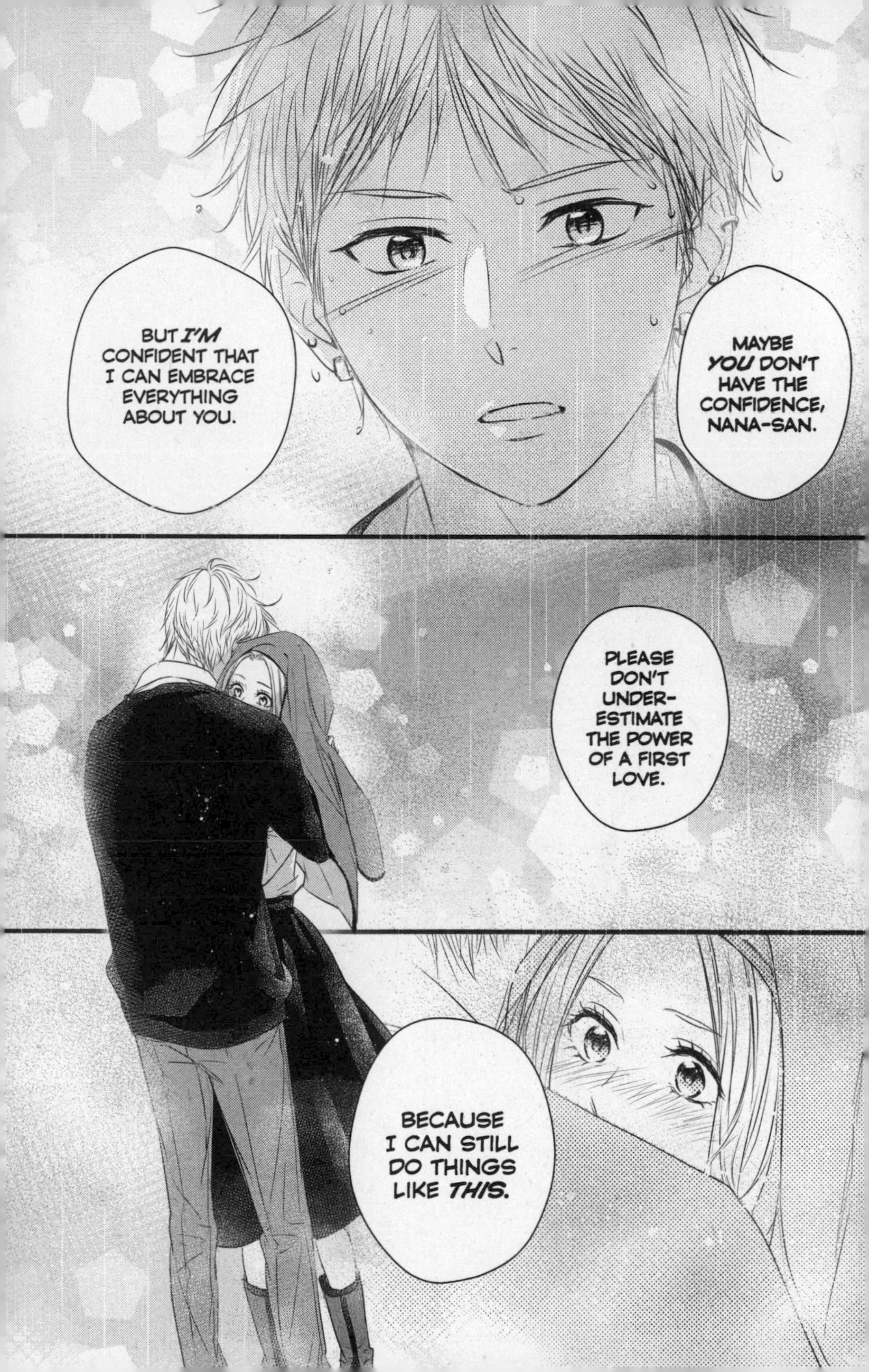
MAYBE *YOU* DON'T HAVE THE CONFIDENCE, NANA-SAN.
BUT *I'M* CONFIDENT THAT I CAN EMBRACE EVERYTHING ABOUT YOU.
PLEASE DON'T UNDER-ESTIMATE THE POWER OF A FIRST LOVE.
BECAUSE I CAN STILL DO THINGS LIKE *THIS*.

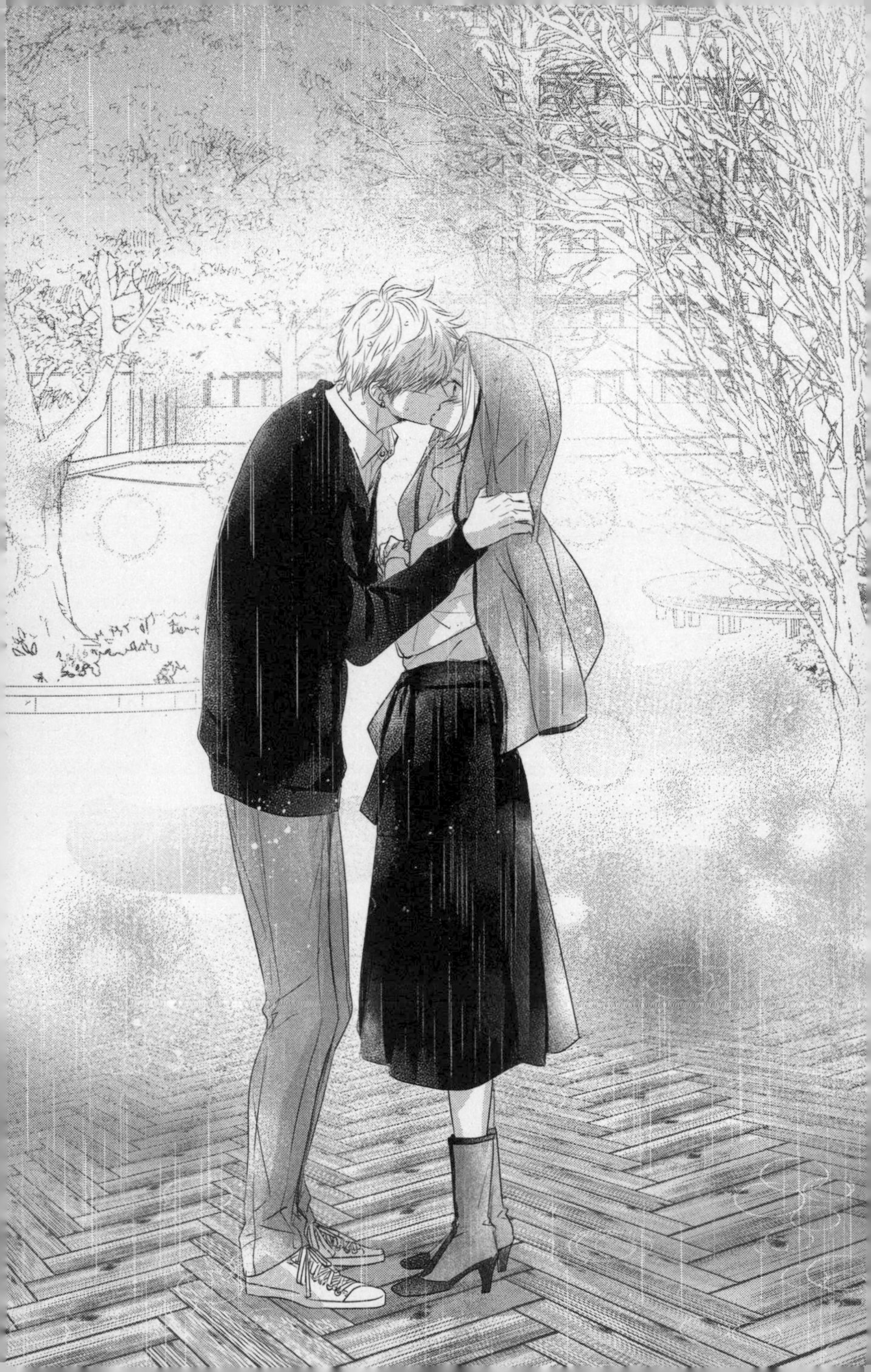

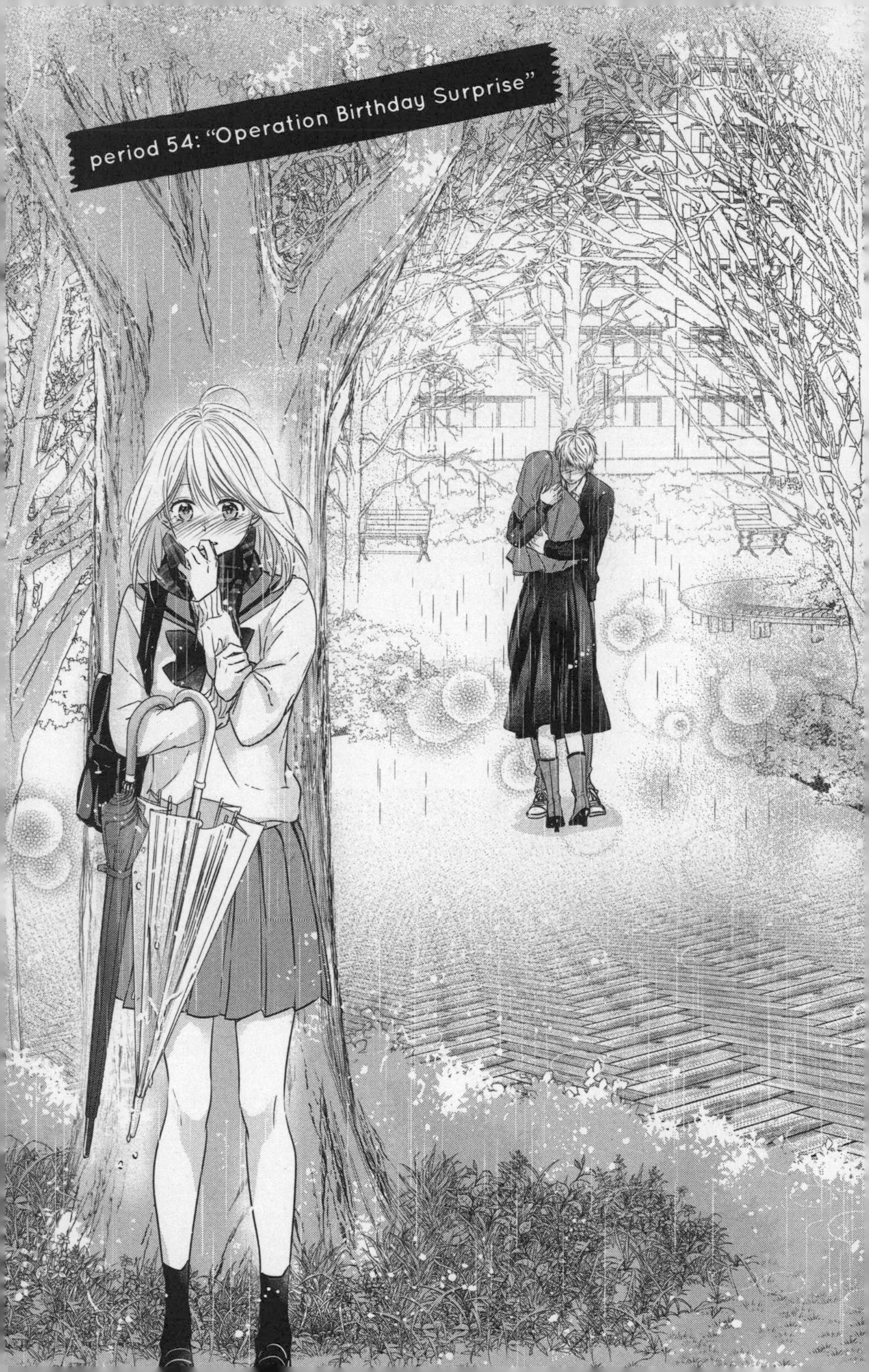
period 54: "Operation Birthday Surprise"

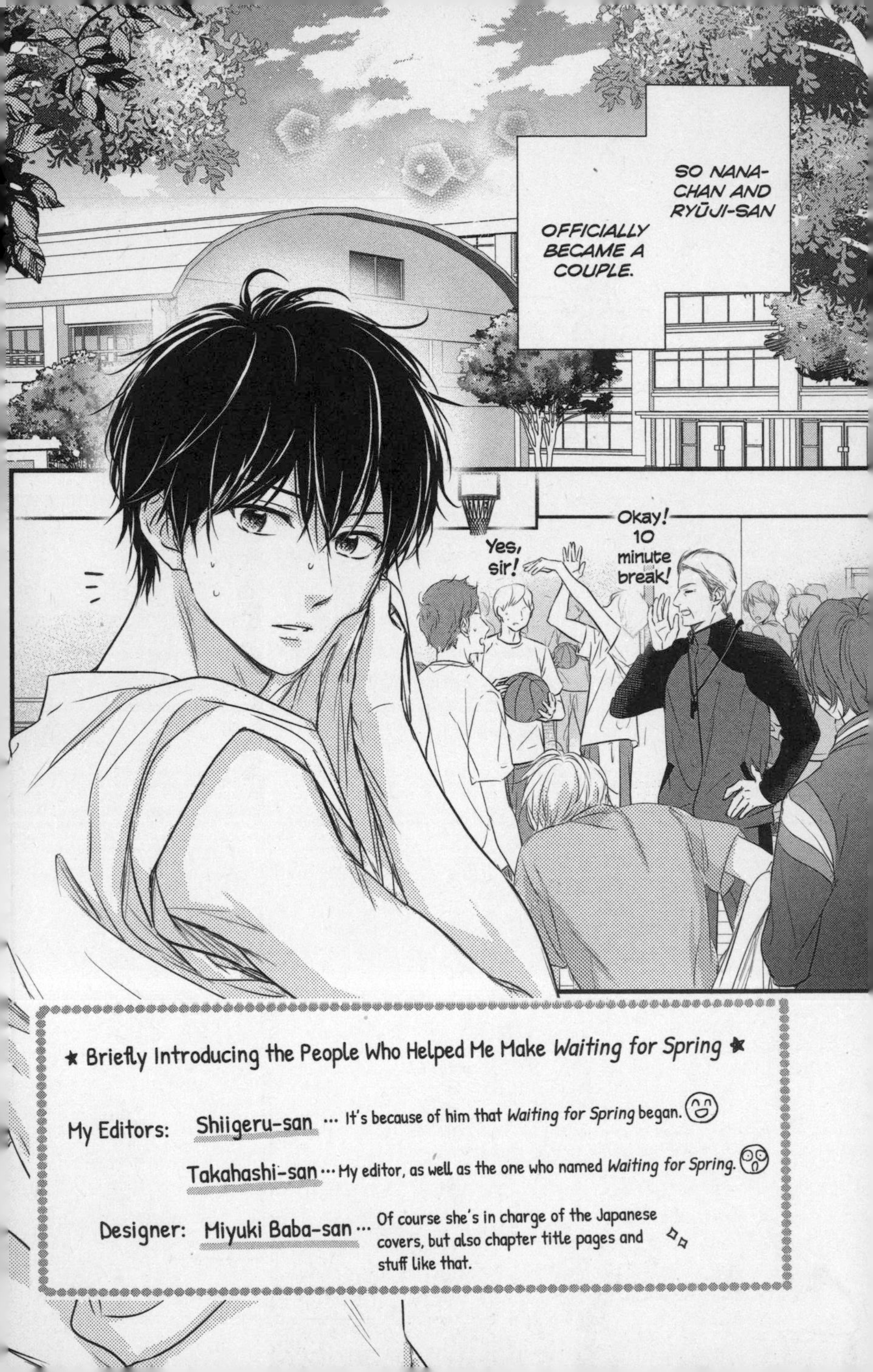
SO NANA-CHAN AND RYŪJI-SAN
OFFICIALLY BECAME A COUPLE.
Okay! 10 minute break!
Yes, sir!

★ Briefly Introducing the People Who Helped Me Make *Waiting for Spring* ★

My Editors: Shiigeru-san … It's because of him that *Waiting for Spring* began.

Takahashi-san … My editor, as well as the one who named *Waiting for Spring*.

Designer: Miyuki Baba-san … Of course she's in charge of the Japanese covers, but also chapter title pages and stuff like that.

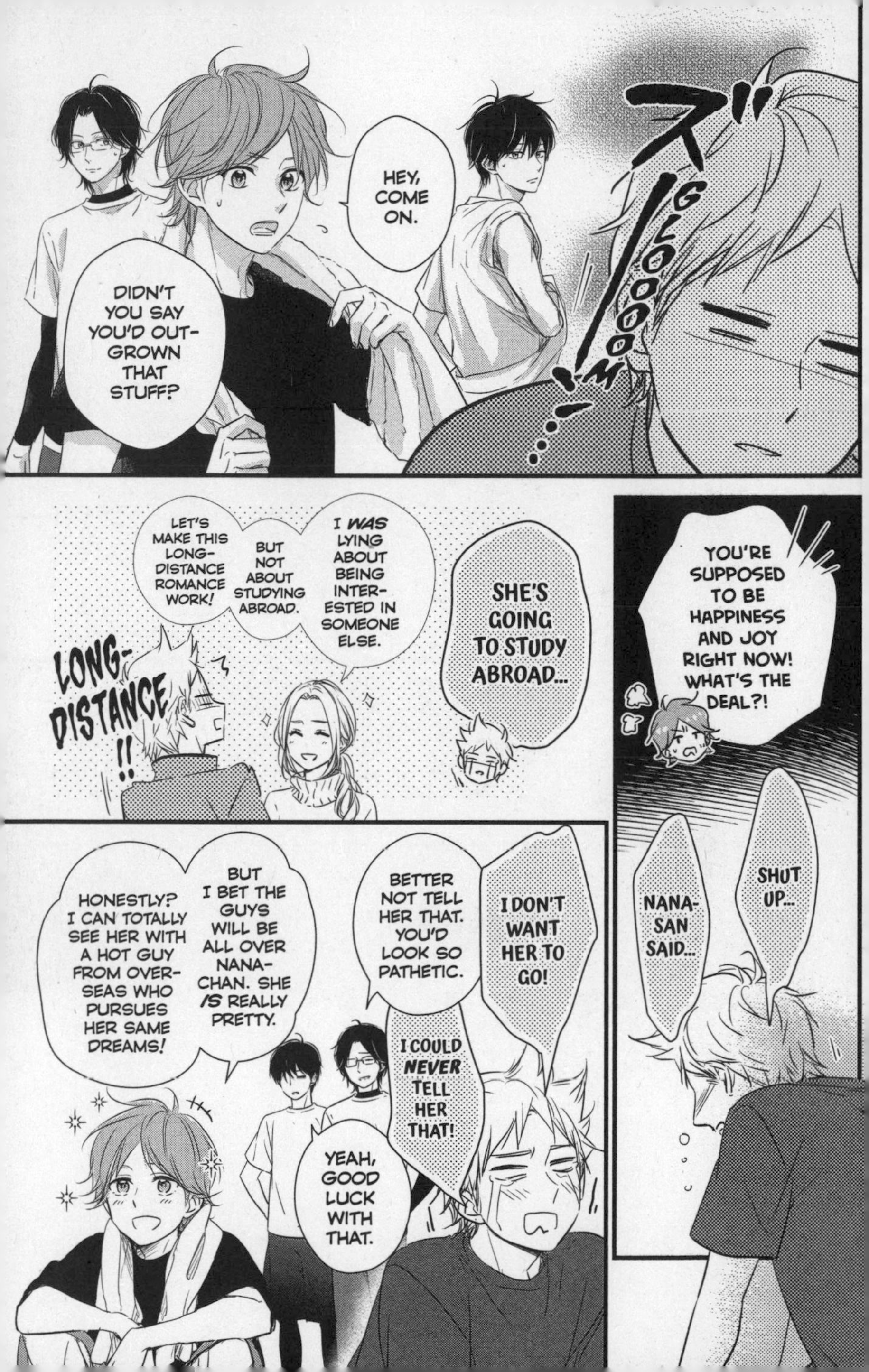
GLOOOOOOM
HEY, COME ON.
DIDN'T YOU SAY YOU'D OUT-GROWN THAT STUFF?
YOU'RE SUPPOSED TO BE HAPPINESS AND JOY RIGHT NOW! WHAT'S THE DEAL?!
SHUT UP...
NANA-SAN SAID...
SHE'S GOING TO STUDY ABROAD...
I *WAS* LYING ABOUT BEING INTER-ESTED IN SOMEONE ELSE.
BUT NOT ABOUT STUDYING ABROAD.
LET'S MAKE THIS LONG-DISTANCE ROMANCE WORK!
LONG-DISTANCE!!
I DON'T WANT HER TO GO!
BETTER NOT TELL HER THAT. YOU'D LOOK SO PATHETIC.
BUT I BET THE GUYS WILL BE ALL OVER NANA-CHAN. SHE *IS* REALLY PRETTY.
HONESTLY? I CAN TOTALLY SEE HER WITH A HOT GUY FROM OVER-SEAS WHO PURSUES HER SAME DREAMS!
I COULD *NEVER* TELL HER THAT!
YEAH, GOOD LUCK WITH THAT.

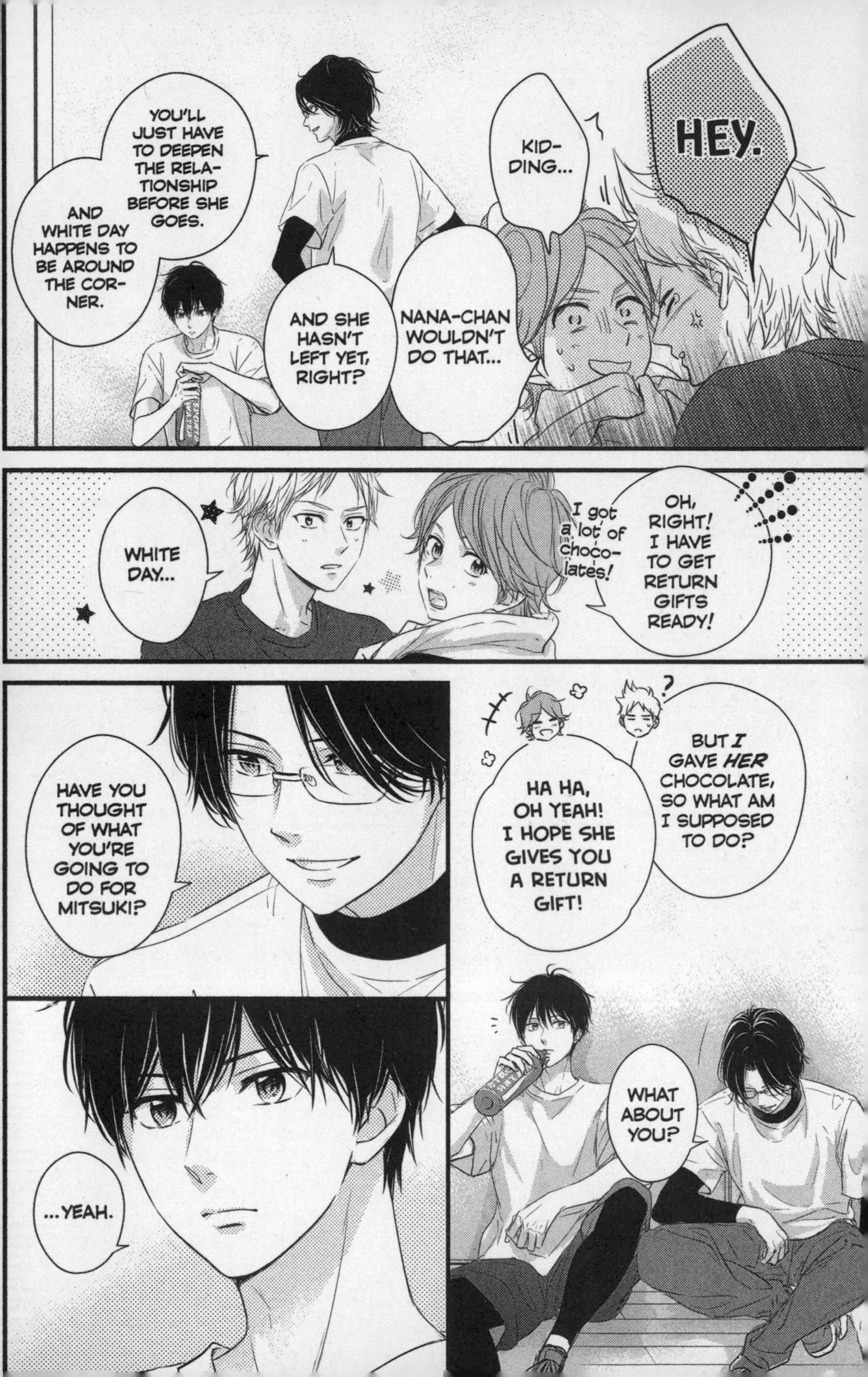
HEY.
KID-DING...
NANA-CHAN WOULDN'T DO THAT...
AND SHE HASN'T LEFT YET, RIGHT?
YOU'LL JUST HAVE TO DEEPEN THE RELA-TIONSHIP BEFORE SHE GOES.
AND WHITE DAY HAPPENS TO BE AROUND THE COR-NER.
OH, RIGHT! I HAVE TO GET RETURN GIFTS READY!
I got a lot of choco-lates!
WHITE DAY...
BUT I GAVE HER CHOCOLATE, SO WHAT AM I SUPPOSED TO DO?
HA HA, OH YEAH! I HOPE SHE GIVES YOU A RETURN GIFT!
HAVE YOU THOUGHT OF WHAT YOU'RE GOING TO DO FOR MITSUKI?
...YEAH.
WHAT ABOUT YOU?

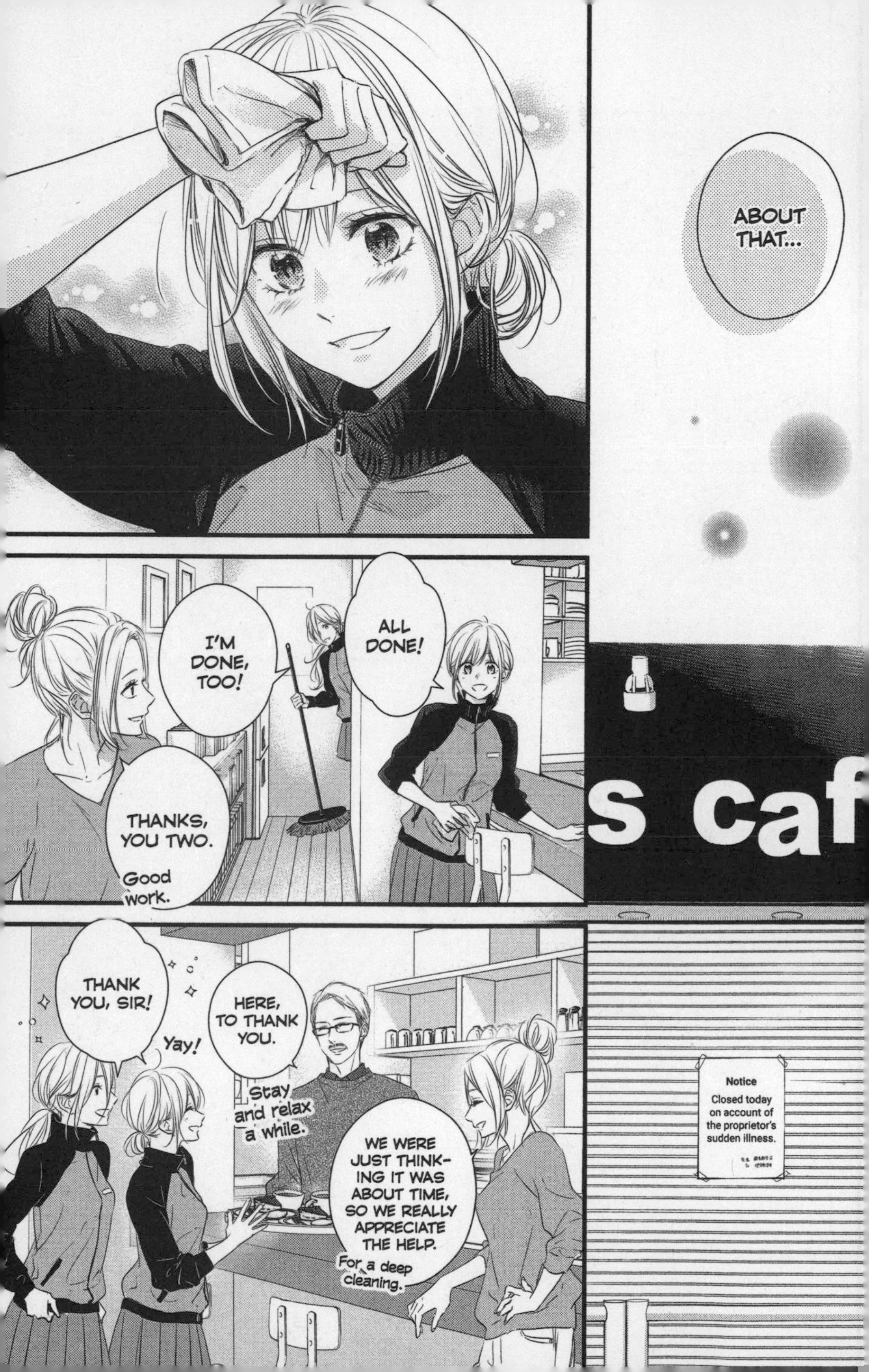
ABOUT THAT...
s caf
ALL DONE!
I'M DONE, TOO!
THANKS, YOU TWO.
Good work.
Notice
Closed today on account of the proprietor's sudden illness.
HERE, TO THANK YOU.
Stay and relax a while.
THANK YOU, SIR!
Yay!
WE WERE JUST THINKING IT WAS ABOUT TIME, SO WE REALLY APPRECIATE THE HELP.
For a deep cleaning.

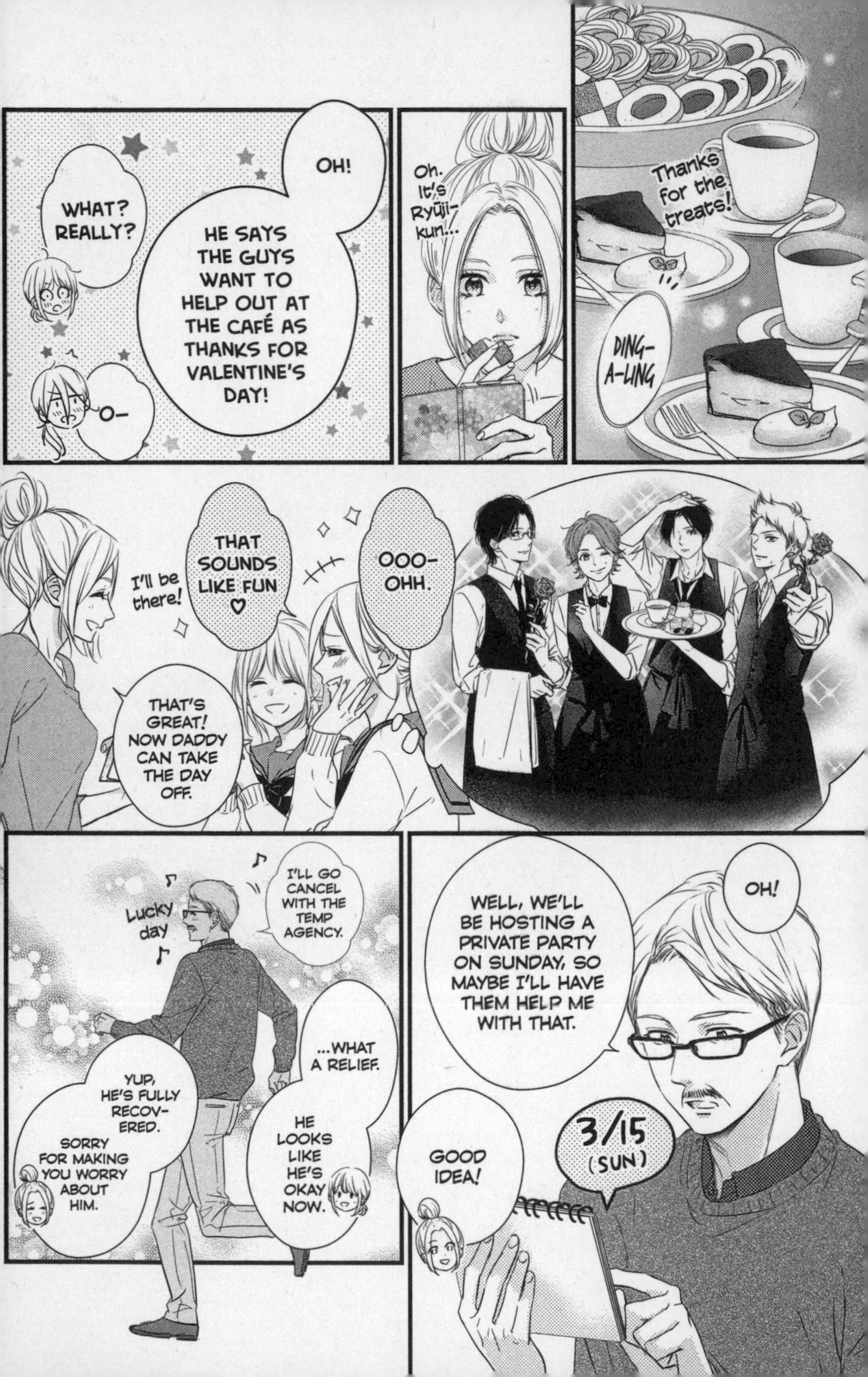
Thanks for the treats!
DING-A-LING
Oh. It's Ryūji-kun...
OH!
HE SAYS THE GUYS WANT TO HELP OUT AT THE CAFÉ AS THANKS FOR VALENTINE'S DAY!
WHAT? REALLY?
O–
OOO-OHH.
THAT SOUNDS LIKE FUN ♡
I'll be there!
THAT'S GREAT! NOW DADDY CAN TAKE THE DAY OFF.
OH!
WELL, WE'LL BE HOSTING A PRIVATE PARTY ON SUNDAY, SO MAYBE I'LL HAVE THEM HELP ME WITH THAT.
3/15 (SUN)
GOOD IDEA!
I'LL GO CANCEL WITH THE TEMP AGENCY.
Lucky day
...WHAT A RELIEF.
HE LOOKS LIKE HE'S OKAY NOW.
YUP, HE'S FULLY RECOV-ERED.
SORRY FOR MAKING YOU WORRY ABOUT HIM.

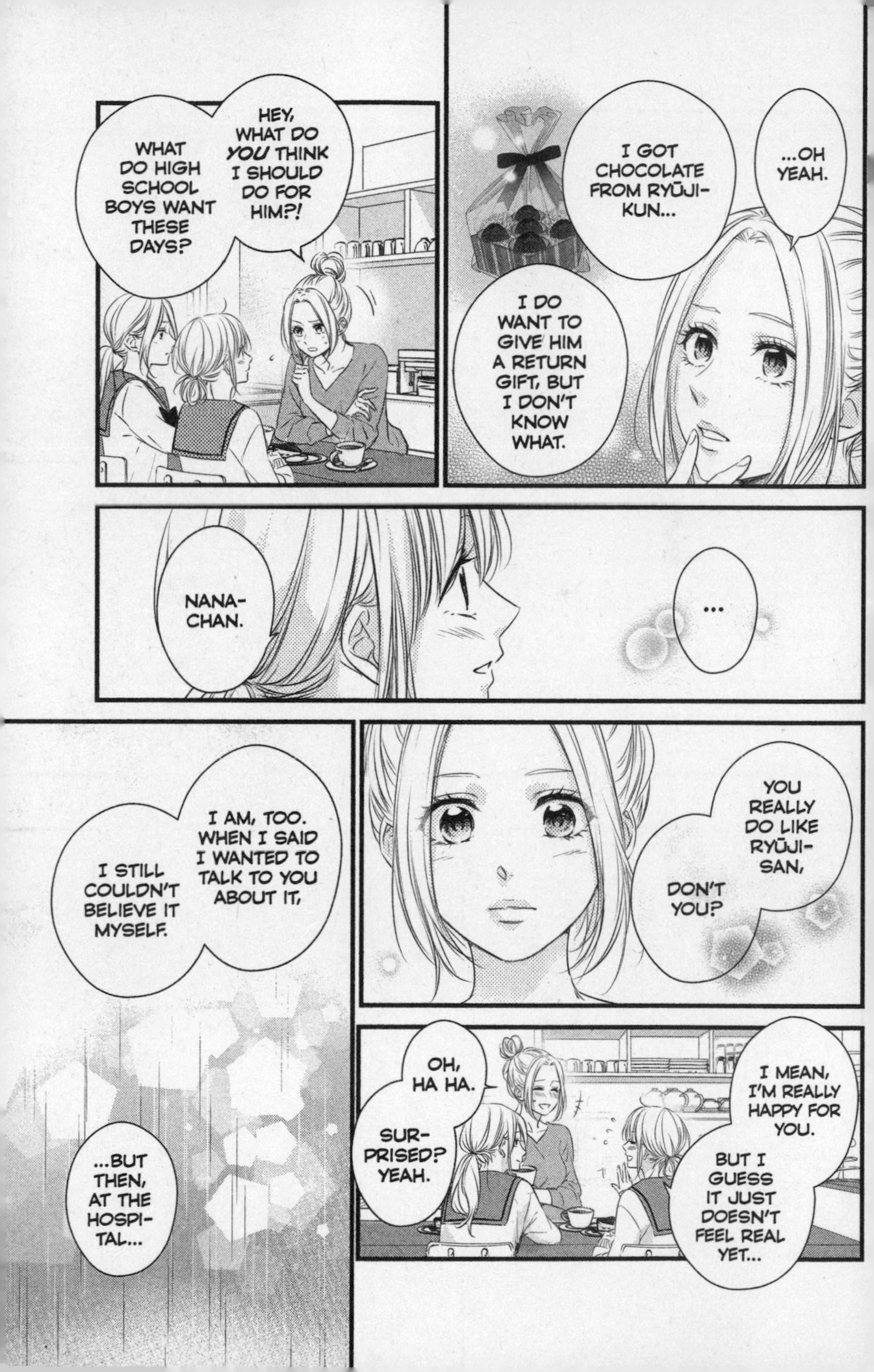
...OH YEAH.
I GOT CHOCOLATE FROM RYŪJI-KUN...
I DO WANT TO GIVE HIM A RETURN GIFT, BUT I DON'T KNOW WHAT.
HEY, WHAT DO *YOU* THINK I SHOULD DO FOR HIM?!
WHAT DO HIGH SCHOOL BOYS WANT THESE DAYS?
...
NANA-CHAN.
YOU REALLY DO LIKE RYŪJI-SAN,
DON'T YOU?
I MEAN, I'M REALLY HAPPY FOR YOU.
BUT I GUESS IT JUST DOESN'T FEEL REAL YET...
OH, HA HA.
SUR-PRISED? YEAH.
I AM, TOO. WHEN I SAID I WANTED TO TALK TO YOU ABOUT IT,
I STILL COULDN'T BELIEVE IT MYSELF.
...BUT THEN, AT THE HOSPI-TAL...

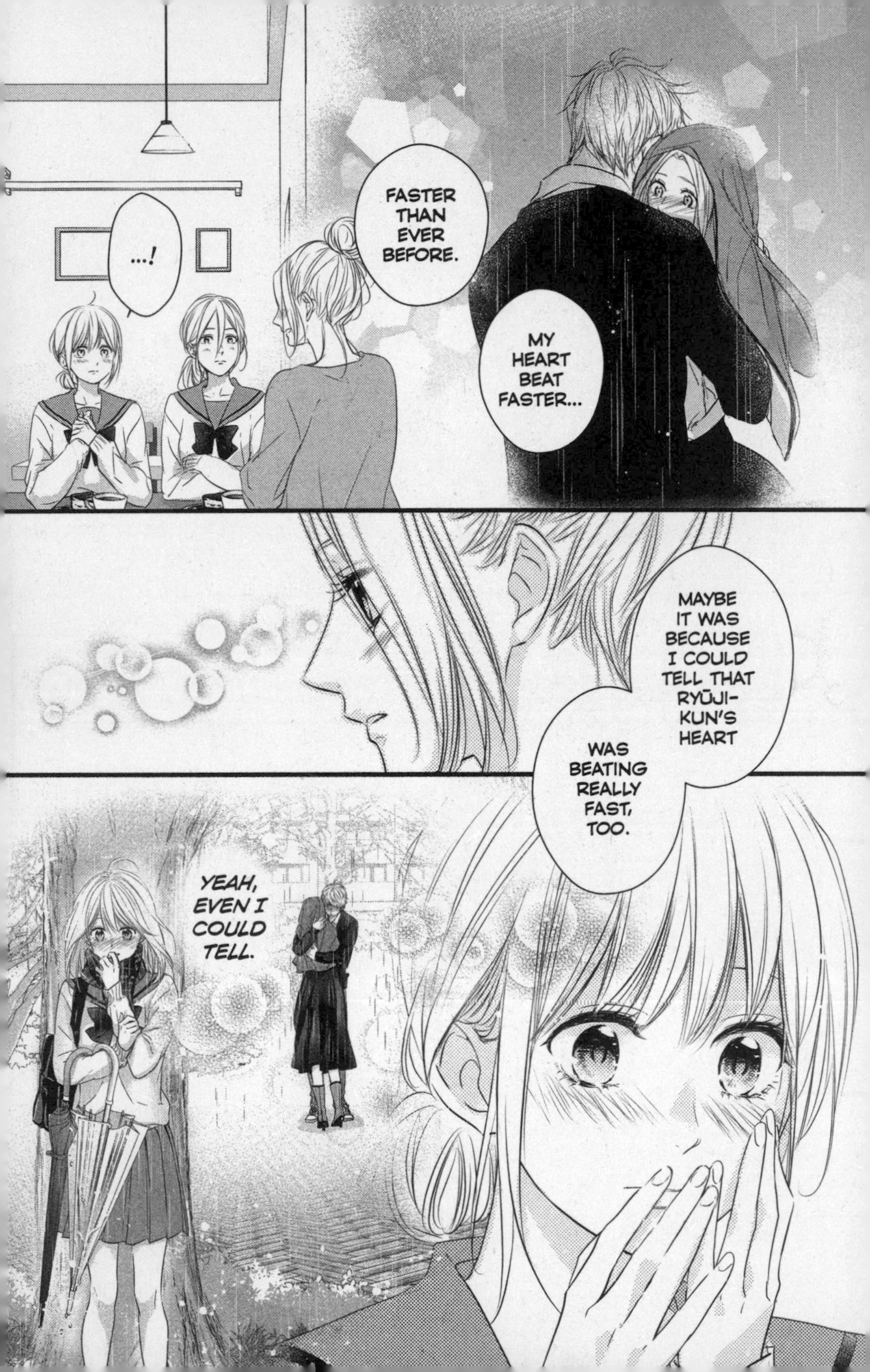
MY HEART BEAT FASTER...
FASTER THAN EVER BEFORE.
...!
MAYBE IT WAS BECAUSE I COULD TELL THAT RYŪJI-KUN'S HEART
WAS BEATING REALLY FAST, TOO.
YEAH, EVEN I COULD TELL.

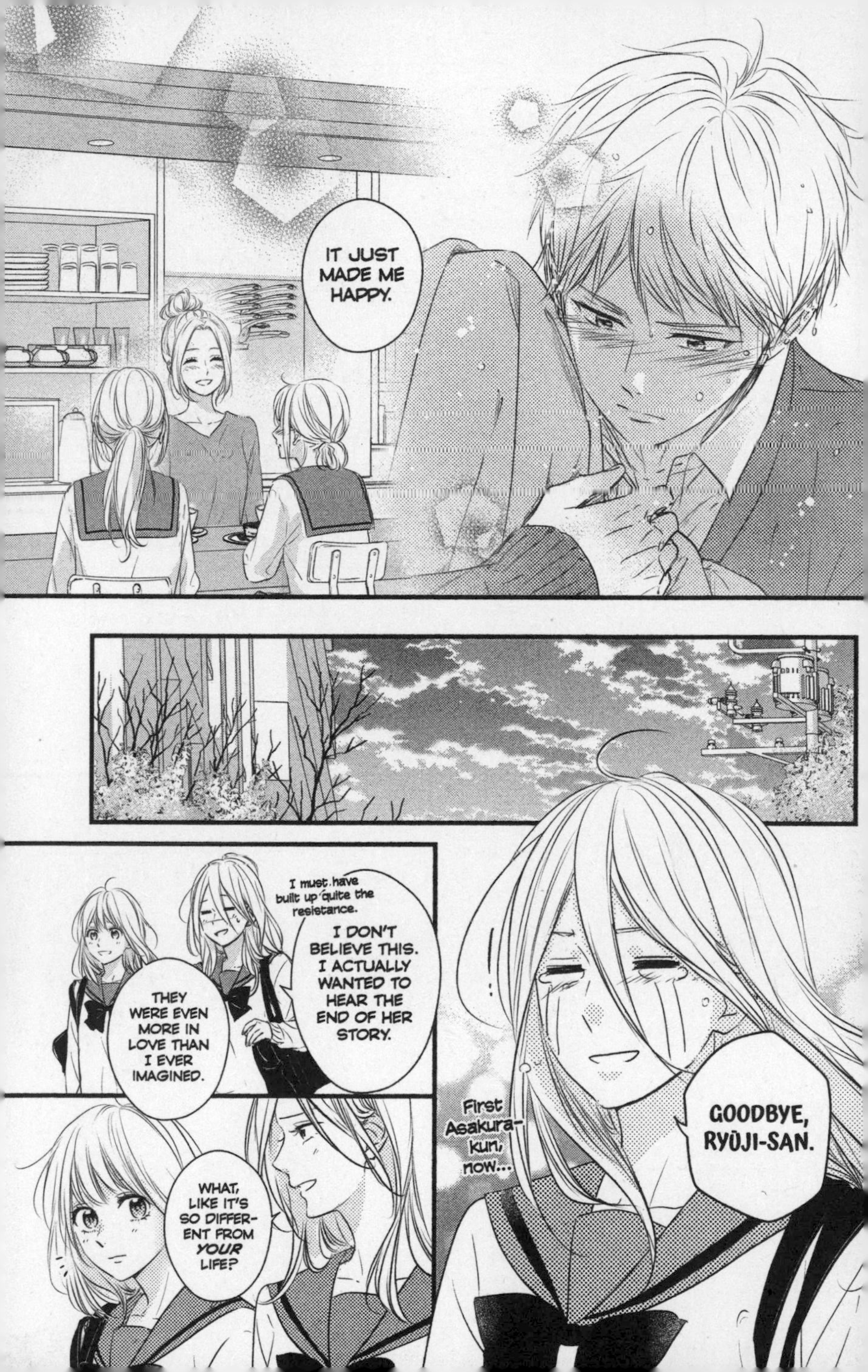
IT JUST MADE ME HAPPY.
GOODBYE, RYŪJI-SAN.
First Asakura-kun, now...
I DON'T BELIEVE THIS. I ACTUALLY WANTED TO HEAR THE END OF HER STORY.
I must have built up quite the resistance.
THEY WERE EVEN MORE IN LOVE THAN I EVER IMAGINED.
WHAT, LIKE IT'S SO DIFFER-ENT FROM *YOUR* LIFE?

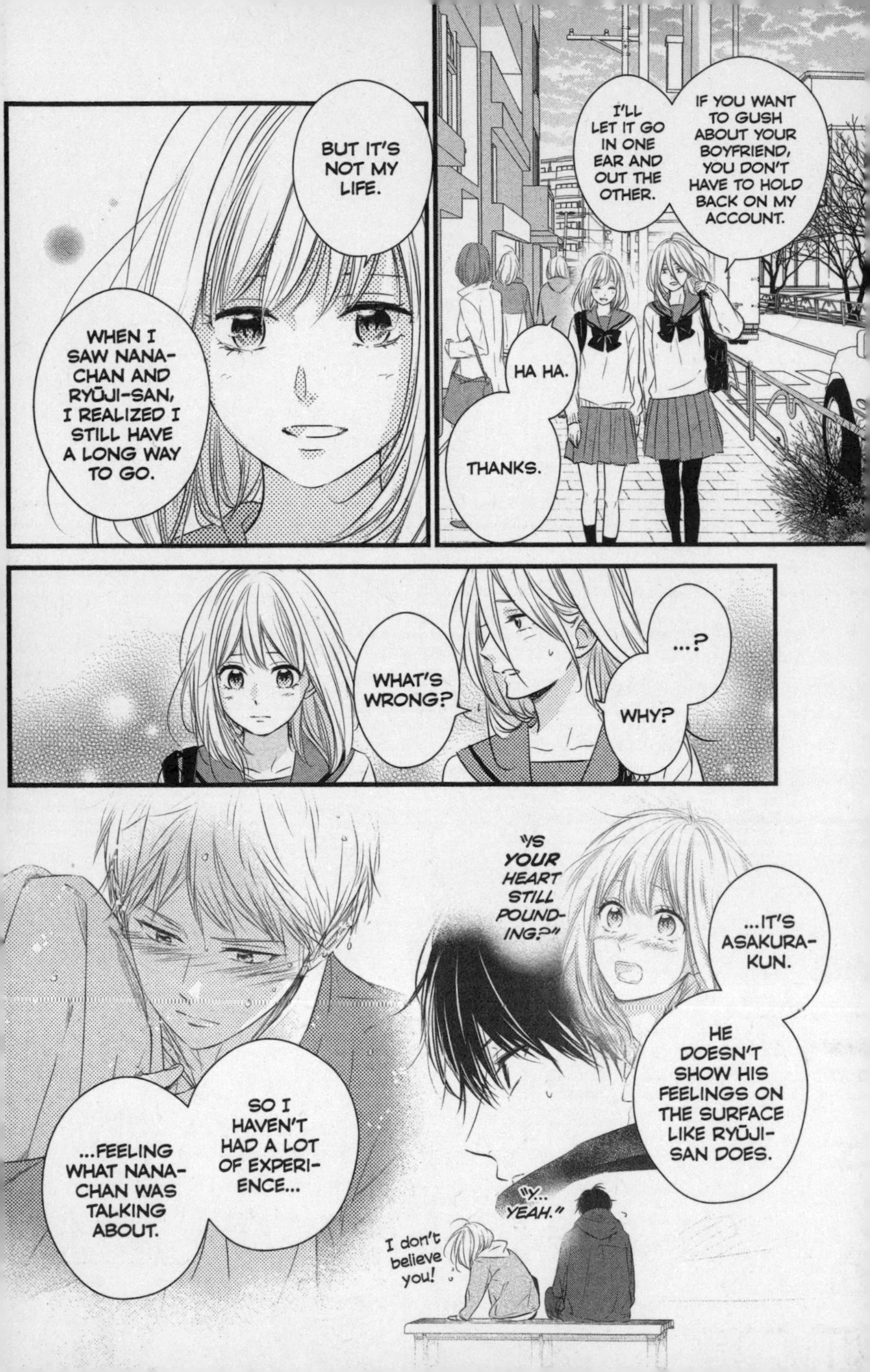
IF YOU WANT TO GUSH ABOUT YOUR BOYFRIEND, YOU DON'T HAVE TO HOLD BACK ON MY ACCOUNT.
I'LL LET IT GO IN ONE EAR AND OUT THE OTHER.
HA HA.
THANKS.
BUT IT'S NOT MY LIFE.
WHEN I SAW NANA-CHAN AND RYŪJI-SAN, I REALIZED I STILL HAVE A LONG WAY TO GO.
...?
WHY?
WHAT'S WRONG?
...IT'S ASAKURA-KUN.
HE DOESN'T SHOW HIS FEELINGS ON THE SURFACE LIKE RYŪJI-SAN DOES.
"IS *YOUR* HEART STILL POUNDING?"
"Y... YEAH."
I don't believe you!
SO I HAVEN'T HAD A LOT OF EXPERIENCE...
...FEELING WHAT NANA-CHAN WAS TALKING ABOUT.

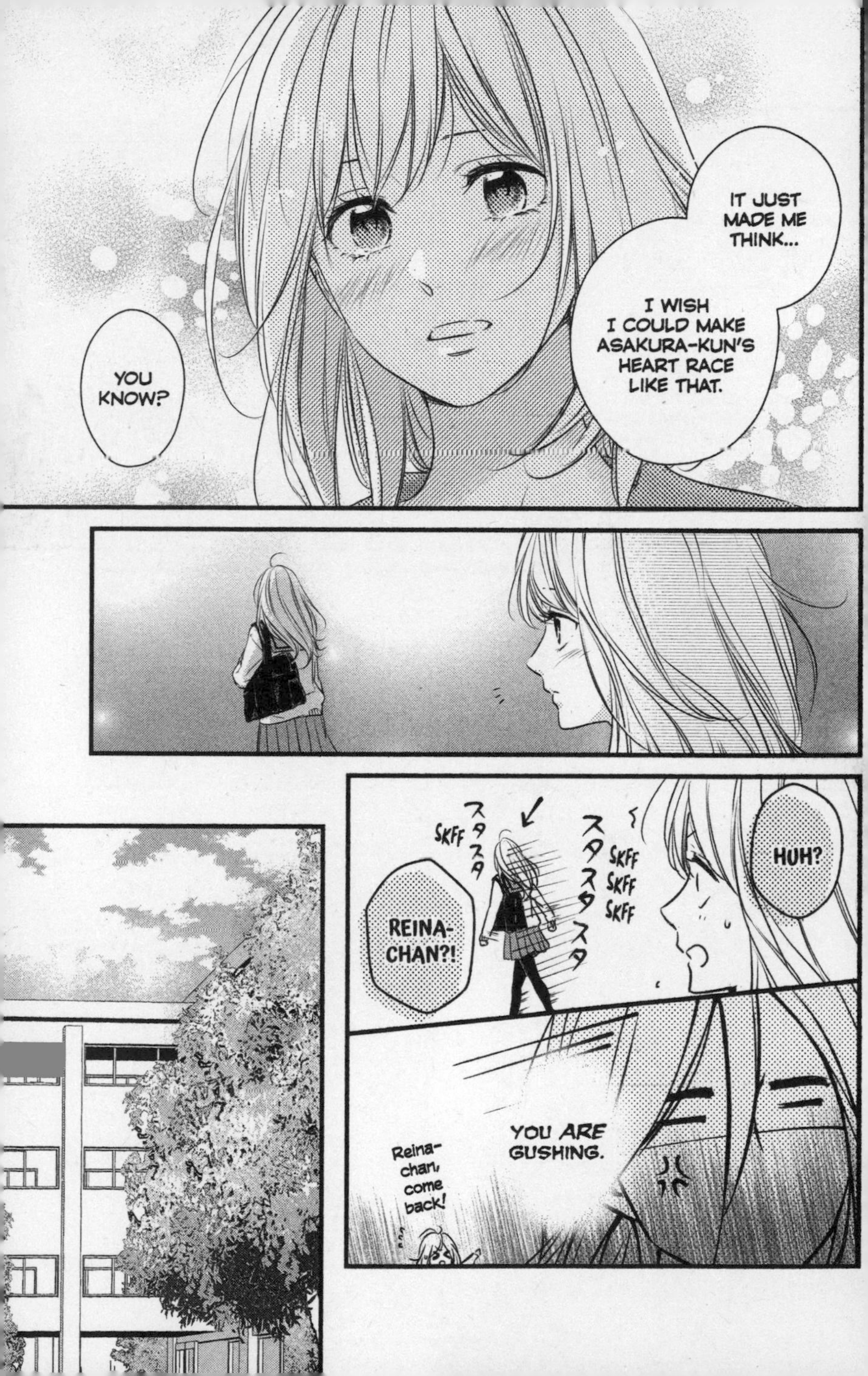
IT JUST MADE ME THINK...
I WISH I COULD MAKE ASAKURA-KUN'S HEART RACE LIKE THAT.
YOU KNOW?
HUH?
スタスタスタ
SKFF SKFF SKFF
REINA-CHAN?!
スタスタ
SKFF
YOU ARE GUSHING.
Reina-chan, come back!

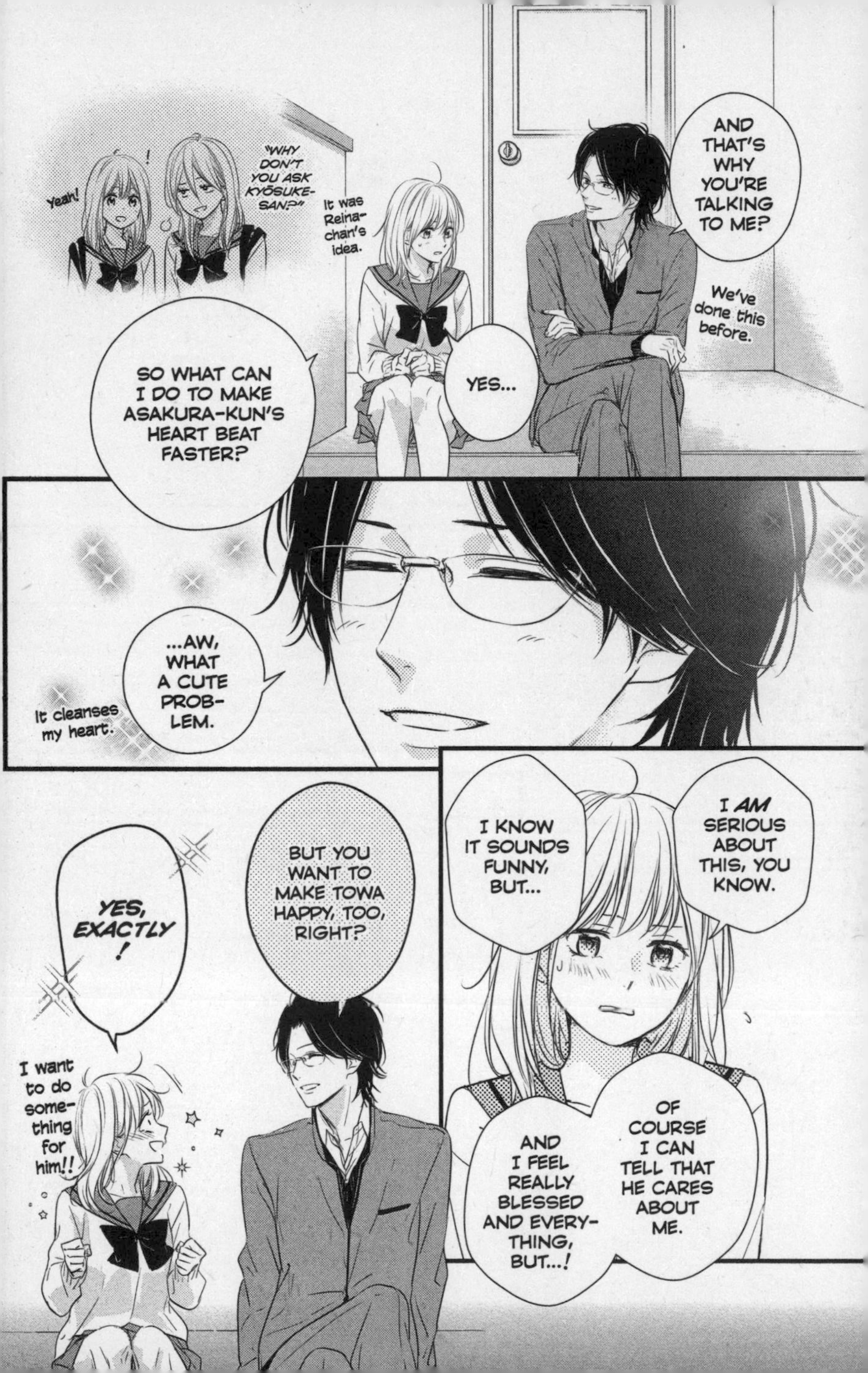
AND THAT'S WHY YOU'RE TALKING TO ME?
We've done this before.
It was Reina-chan's idea.
"WHY DON'T YOU ASK KYŌSUKE-SAN?"
Yeah!
YES...
SO WHAT CAN I DO TO MAKE ASAKURA-KUN'S HEART BEAT FASTER?
...AW, WHAT A CUTE PROB-LEM.
It cleanses my heart.
I *AM* SERIOUS ABOUT THIS, YOU KNOW.
I KNOW IT SOUNDS FUNNY, BUT...
OF COURSE I CAN TELL THAT HE CARES ABOUT ME.
AND I FEEL REALLY BLESSED AND EVERY-THING, BUT...!
BUT YOU WANT TO MAKE TOWA HAPPY, TOO, RIGHT?
YES, EXACTLY!
I want to do some-thing for him!!

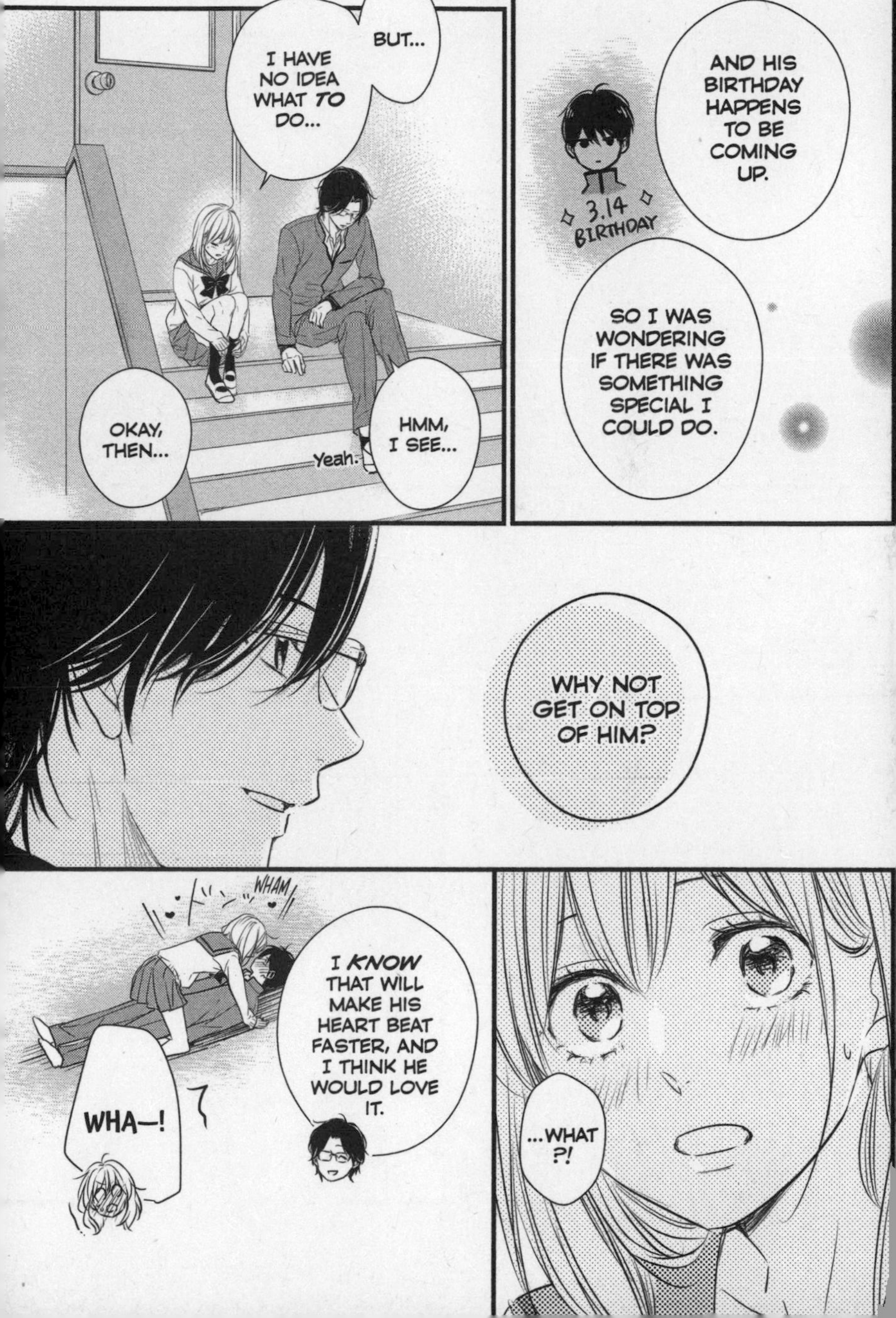
AND HIS BIRTHDAY HAPPENS TO BE COMING UP.
3.14 BIRTHDAY
SO I WAS WONDERING IF THERE WAS SOMETHING SPECIAL I COULD DO.
BUT...
I HAVE NO IDEA WHAT *TO* DO...
HMM, I SEE...
Yeah.
OKAY, THEN...
WHY NOT GET ON TOP OF HIM?
...WHAT ?!
WHAM
I *KNOW* THAT WILL MAKE HIS HEART BEAT FASTER, AND I THINK HE WOULD LOVE IT.
WHA—!

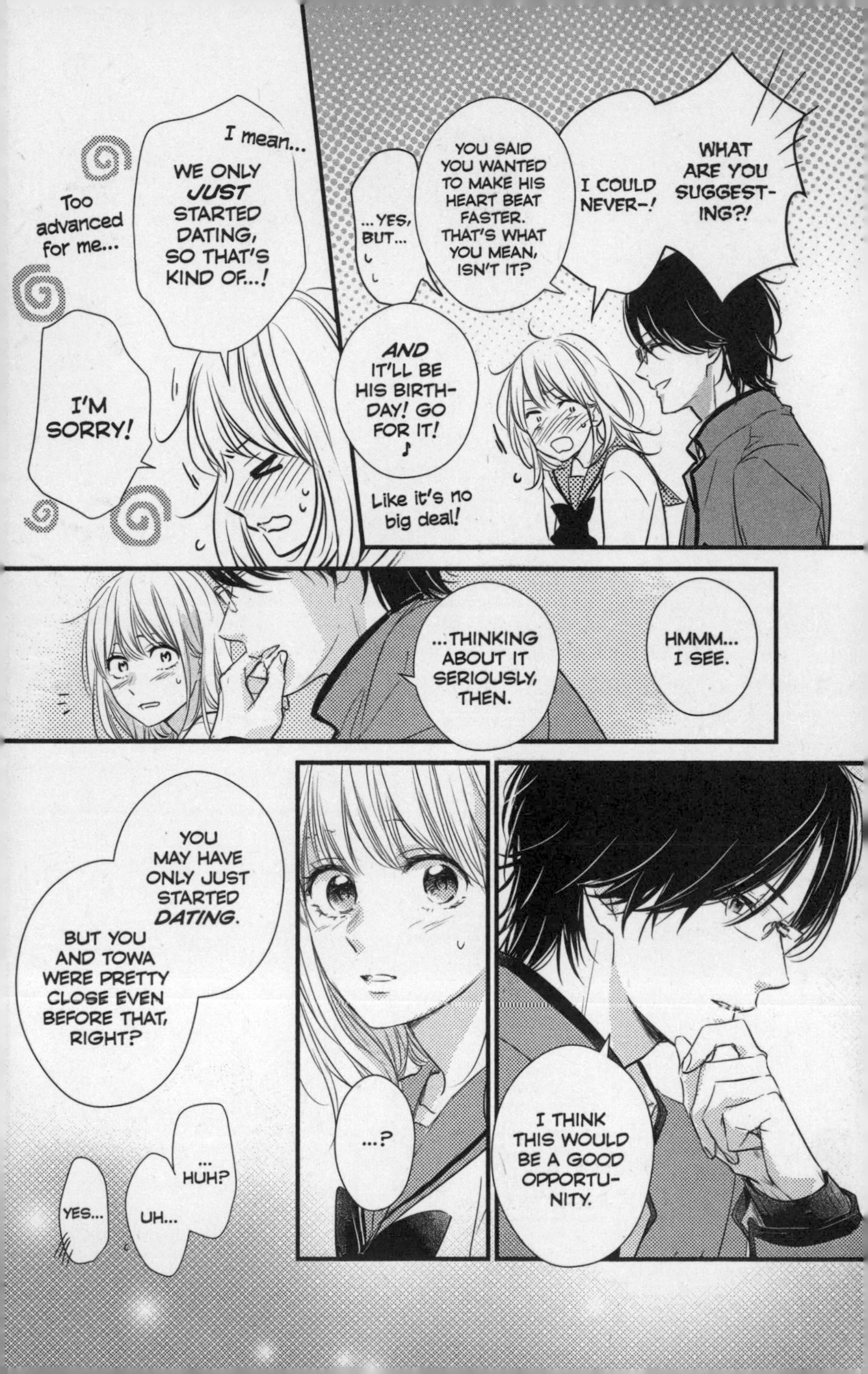
WHAT ARE YOU SUGGEST-ING?!
I COULD NEVER–!
YOU SAID YOU WANTED TO MAKE HIS HEART BEAT FASTER. THAT'S WHAT YOU MEAN, ISN'T IT?
...YES, BUT...
AND IT'LL BE HIS BIRTH-DAY! GO FOR IT! ♪
Like it's no big deal!
I mean...
WE ONLY *JUST* STARTED DATING, SO THAT'S KIND OF...!
Too advanced for me...
I'M SORRY!
HMMM... I SEE.
...THINKING ABOUT IT SERIOUSLY, THEN.
I THINK THIS WOULD BE A GOOD OPPORTU-NITY.
...?
YOU MAY HAVE ONLY JUST STARTED *DATING*.
BUT YOU AND TOWA WERE PRETTY CLOSE EVEN BEFORE THAT, RIGHT?
... HUH?
UH...
YES...

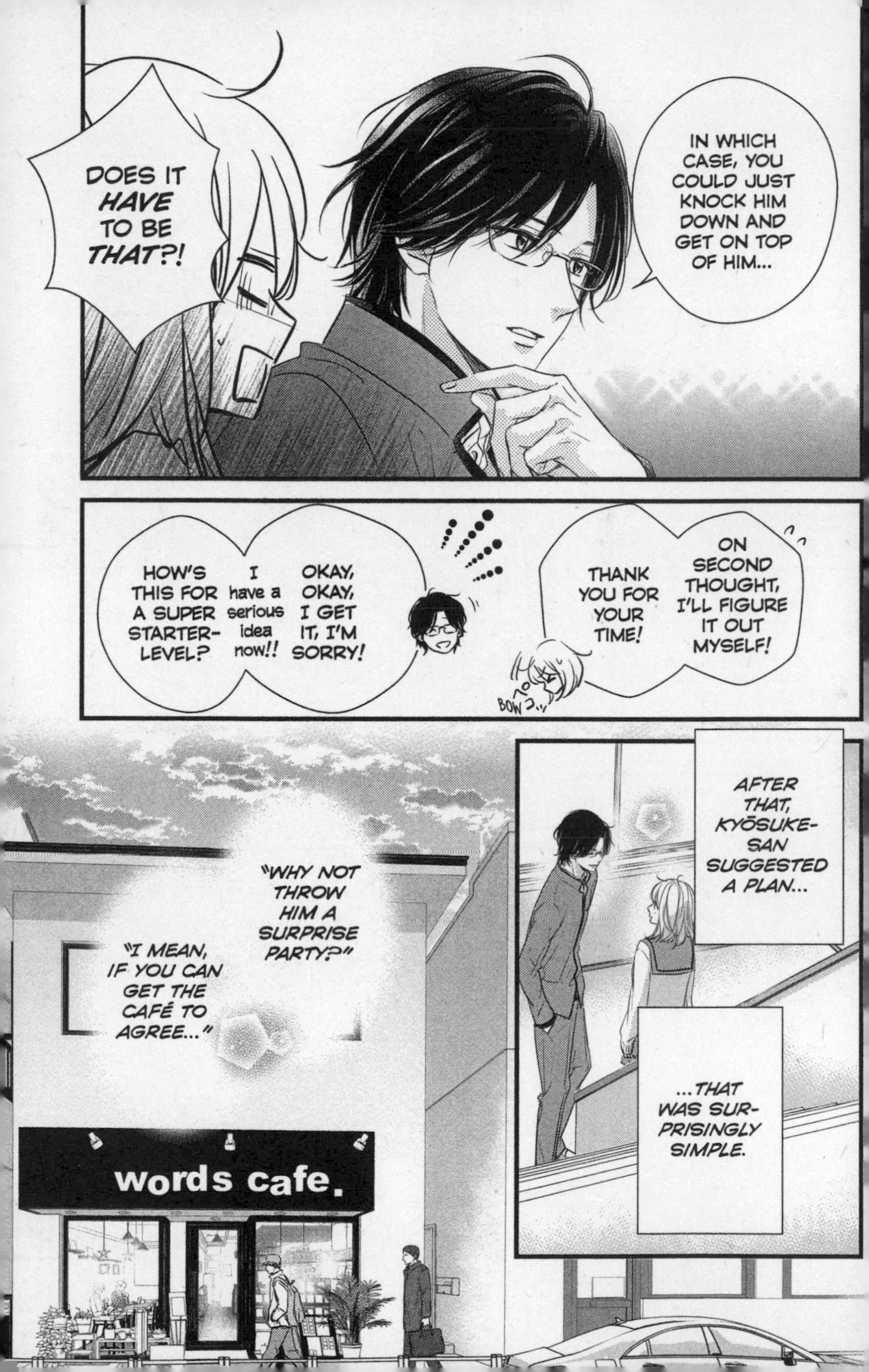
IN WHICH CASE, YOU COULD JUST KNOCK HIM DOWN AND GET ON TOP OF HIM...
DOES IT *HAVE* TO BE *THAT*?!
ON SECOND THOUGHT, I'LL FIGURE IT OUT MYSELF!
THANK YOU FOR YOUR TIME!
BOW
OKAY, OKAY, I GET IT, I'M SORRY!
I have a serious idea now!!
HOW'S THIS FOR A SUPER STARTER-LEVEL?
AFTER THAT, KYŌSUKE-SAN SUGGESTED A PLAN...
...THAT WAS SURPRISINGLY SIMPLE.
"WHY NOT THROW HIM A SURPRISE PARTY?"
"I MEAN, IF YOU CAN GET THE CAFÉ TO AGREE..."
words cafe.

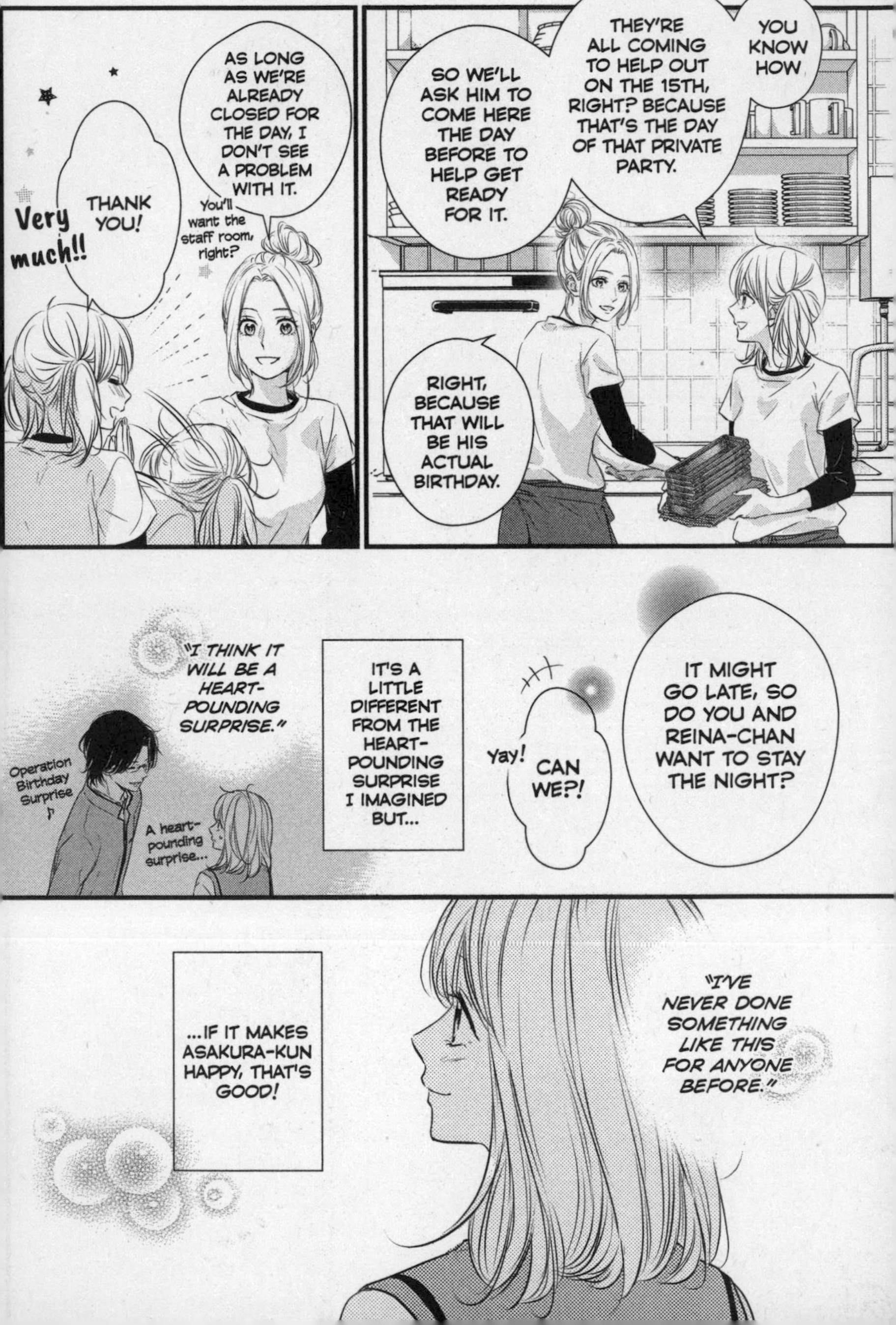
YOU KNOW HOW
THEY'RE ALL COMING TO HELP OUT ON THE 15TH, RIGHT? BECAUSE THAT'S THE DAY OF THAT PRIVATE PARTY.
SO WE'LL ASK HIM TO COME HERE THE DAY BEFORE TO HELP GET READY FOR IT.
RIGHT, BECAUSE THAT WILL BE HIS ACTUAL BIRTHDAY.
AS LONG AS WE'RE ALREADY CLOSED FOR THE DAY, I DON'T SEE A PROBLEM WITH IT.
You'll want the staff room, right?
THANK YOU!
Very much!!
IT MIGHT GO LATE, SO DO YOU AND REINA-CHAN WANT TO STAY THE NIGHT?
CAN WE?!
Yay!
IT'S A LITTLE DIFFERENT FROM THE HEART-POUNDING SURPRISE I IMAGINED BUT...
"I THINK IT WILL BE A HEART-POUNDING SURPRISE."
A heart-pounding surprise...
Operation Birthday Surprise ♪
"I'VE NEVER DONE SOMETHING LIKE THIS FOR ANYONE BEFORE."
...IF IT MAKES ASAKURA-KUN HAPPY, THAT'S GOOD!

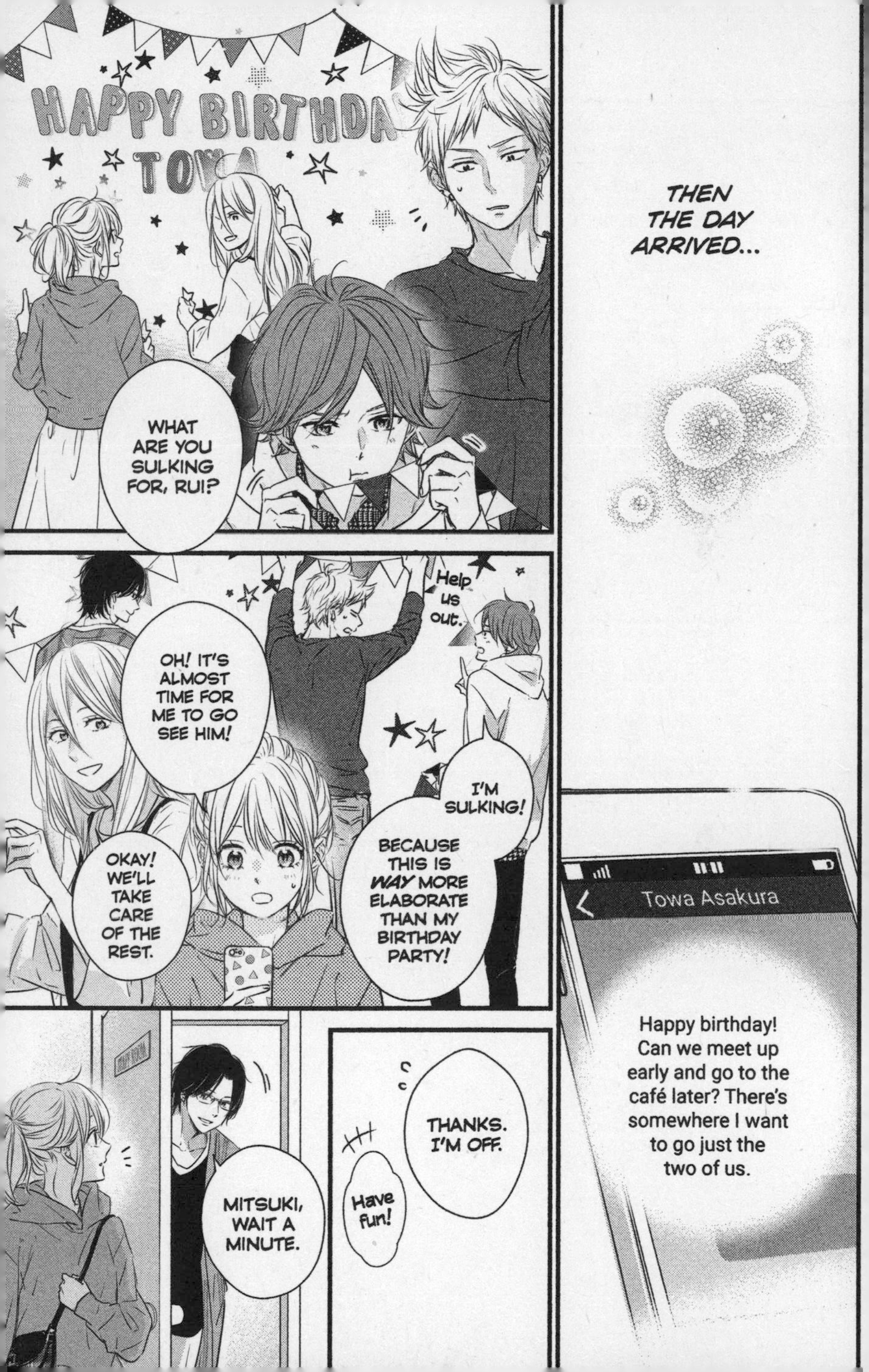
THEN THE DAY ARRIVED...
Towa Asakura
Happy birthday! Can we meet up early and go to the café later? There's somewhere I want to go just the two of us.
HAPPY BIRTHDAY TOWA
WHAT ARE YOU SULKING FOR, RUI?
Help us out.
I'M SULKING!
BECAUSE THIS IS *WAY* MORE ELABORATE THAN MY BIRTHDAY PARTY!
OH! IT'S ALMOST TIME FOR ME TO GO SEE HIM!
OKAY! WE'LL TAKE CARE OF THE REST.
THANKS. I'M OFF.
Have fun!
MITSUKI, WAIT A MINUTE.

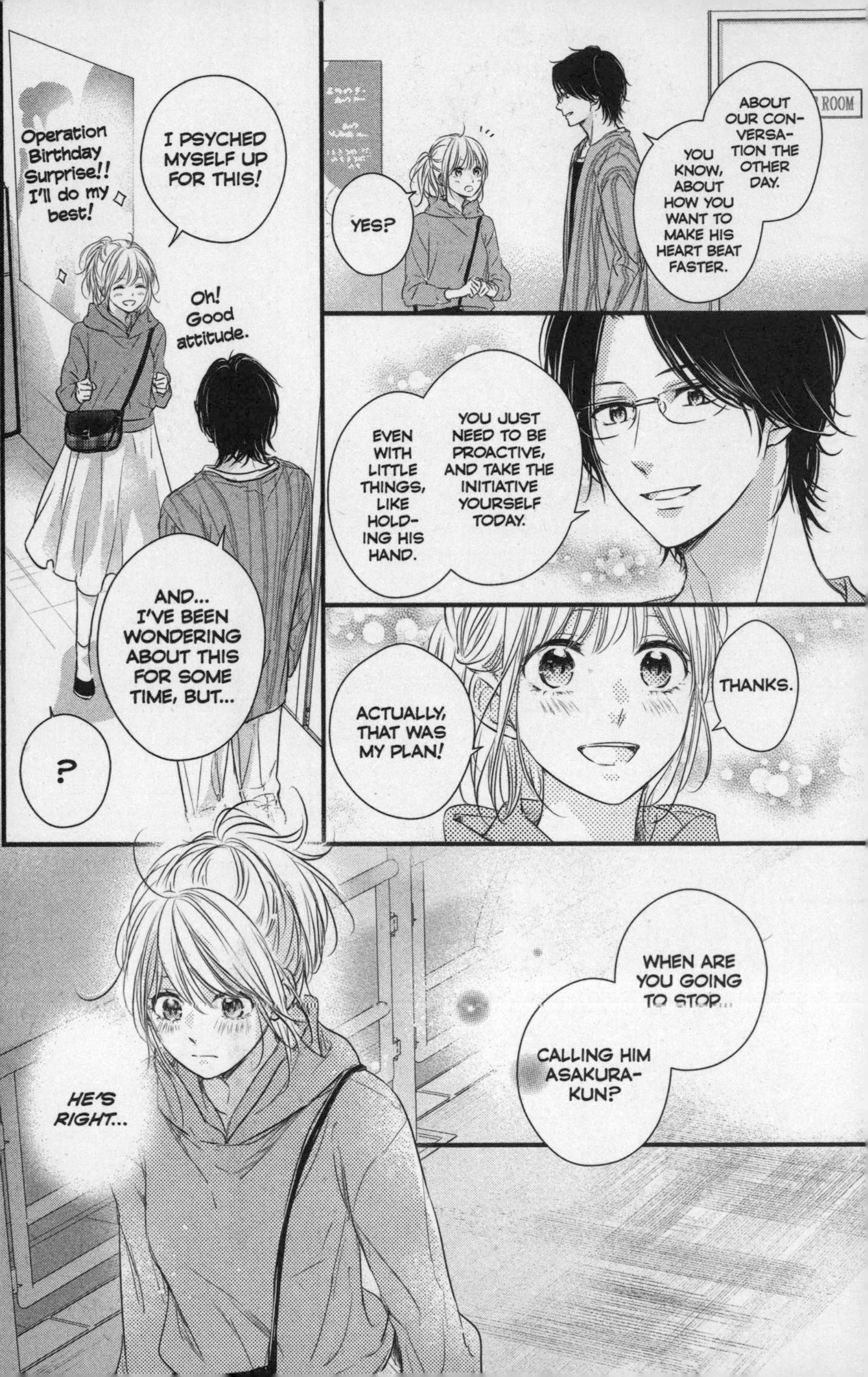
ABOUT OUR CONVERSATION THE OTHER DAY.
YOU KNOW, ABOUT HOW YOU WANT TO MAKE HIS HEART BEAT FASTER.
YES?
YOU JUST NEED TO BE PROACTIVE, AND TAKE THE INITIATIVE YOURSELF TODAY.
EVEN WITH LITTLE THINGS, LIKE HOLDING HIS HAND.
THANKS.
ACTUALLY, THAT WAS MY PLAN!
I PSYCHED MYSELF UP FOR THIS!
Operation Birthday Surprise!! I'll do my best!
Oh! Good attitude.
AND... I'VE BEEN WONDERING ABOUT THIS FOR SOME TIME, BUT...
?
WHEN ARE YOU GOING TO STOP...
CALLING HIM ASAKURA-KUN?
HE'S RIGHT...

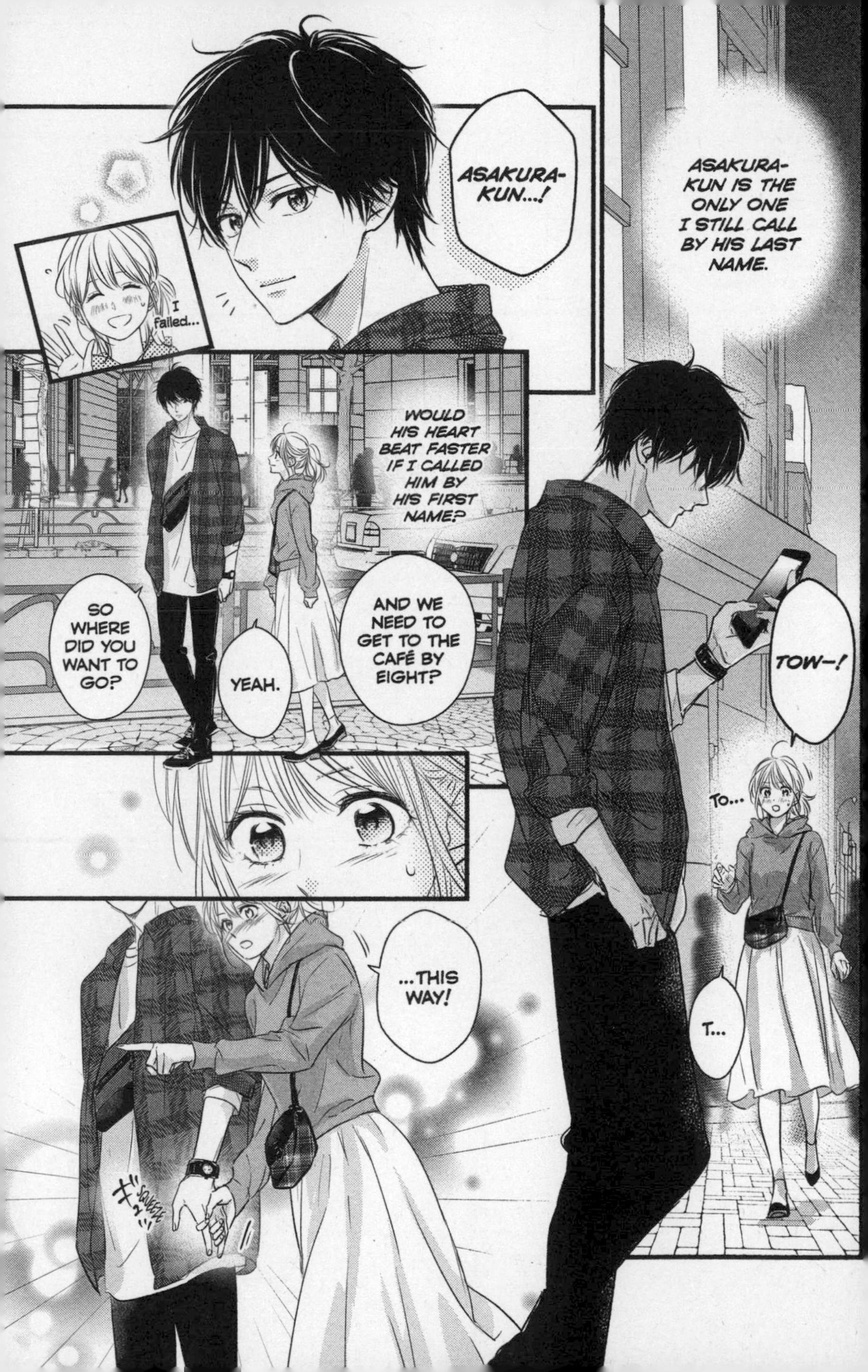
ASAKURA-KUN IS THE ONLY ONE I STILL CALL BY HIS LAST NAME.
TOW-!
TO...
T...
ASAKURA-KUN...!
I failed...
WOULD HIS HEART BEAT FASTER IF I CALLED HIM BY HIS FIRST NAME?
AND WE NEED TO GET TO THE CAFÉ BY EIGHT?
YEAH.
SO WHERE DID YOU WANT TO GO?
...THIS WAY!
SQUEEZE

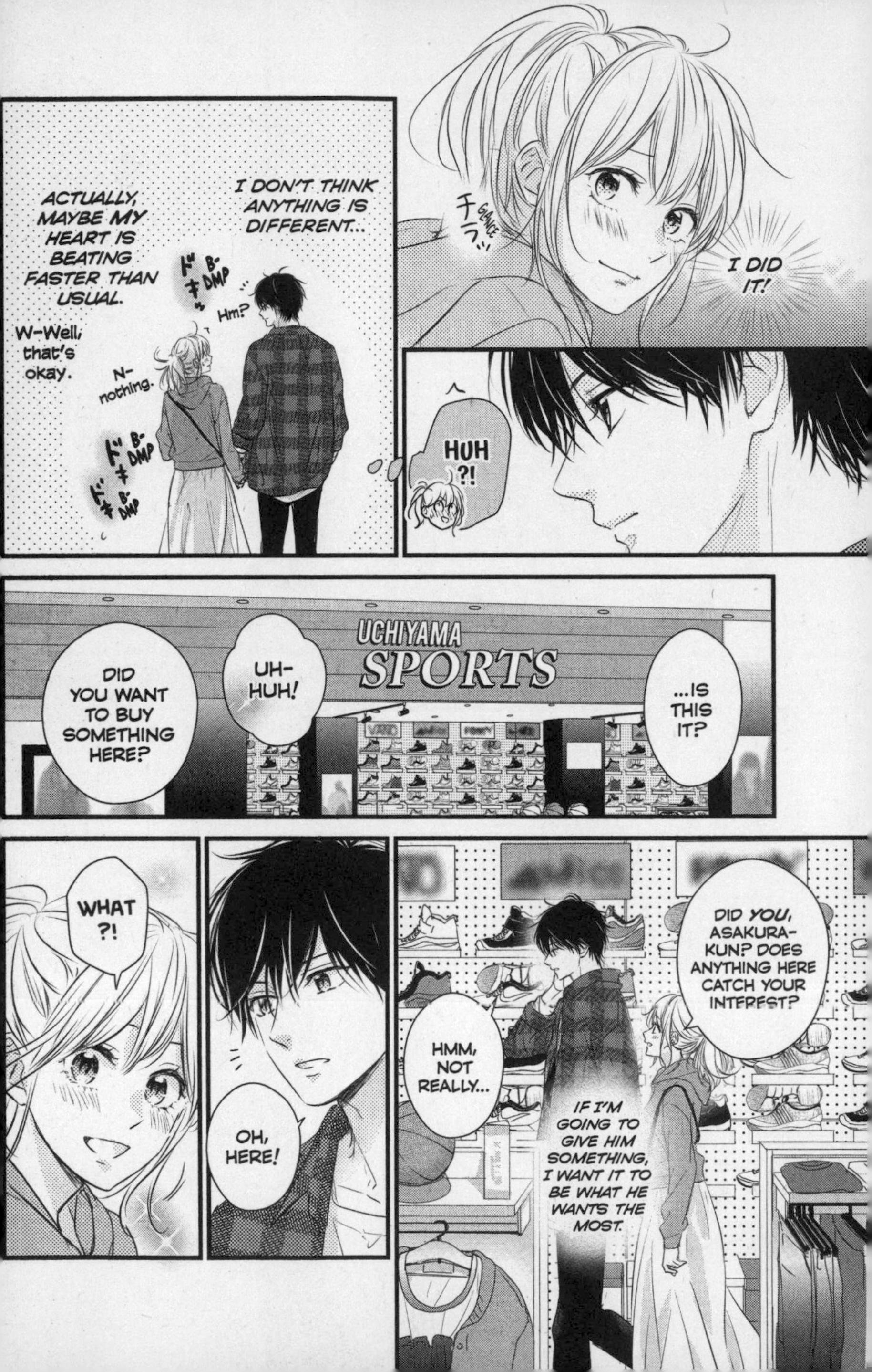
チラッ GLANCE
I DID IT!
HUH ?!
I DON'T THINK ANYTHING IS DIFFERENT...
ACTUALLY, MAYBE MY HEART IS BEATING FASTER THAN USUAL.
ドキ B-DMP
Hm?
N-nothing.
W-Well, that's okay.
ドキ B-DMP
ドキ B-DMP
UCHIYAMA SPORTS
...IS THIS IT?
UH-HUH!
DID YOU WANT TO BUY SOMETHING HERE?
DID YOU, ASAKURA-KUN? DOES ANYTHING HERE CATCH YOUR INTEREST?
HMM, NOT REALLY...
IF I'M GOING TO GIVE HIM SOMETHING, I WANT IT TO BE WHAT HE WANTS THE MOST.
OH, HERE!
WHAT ?!

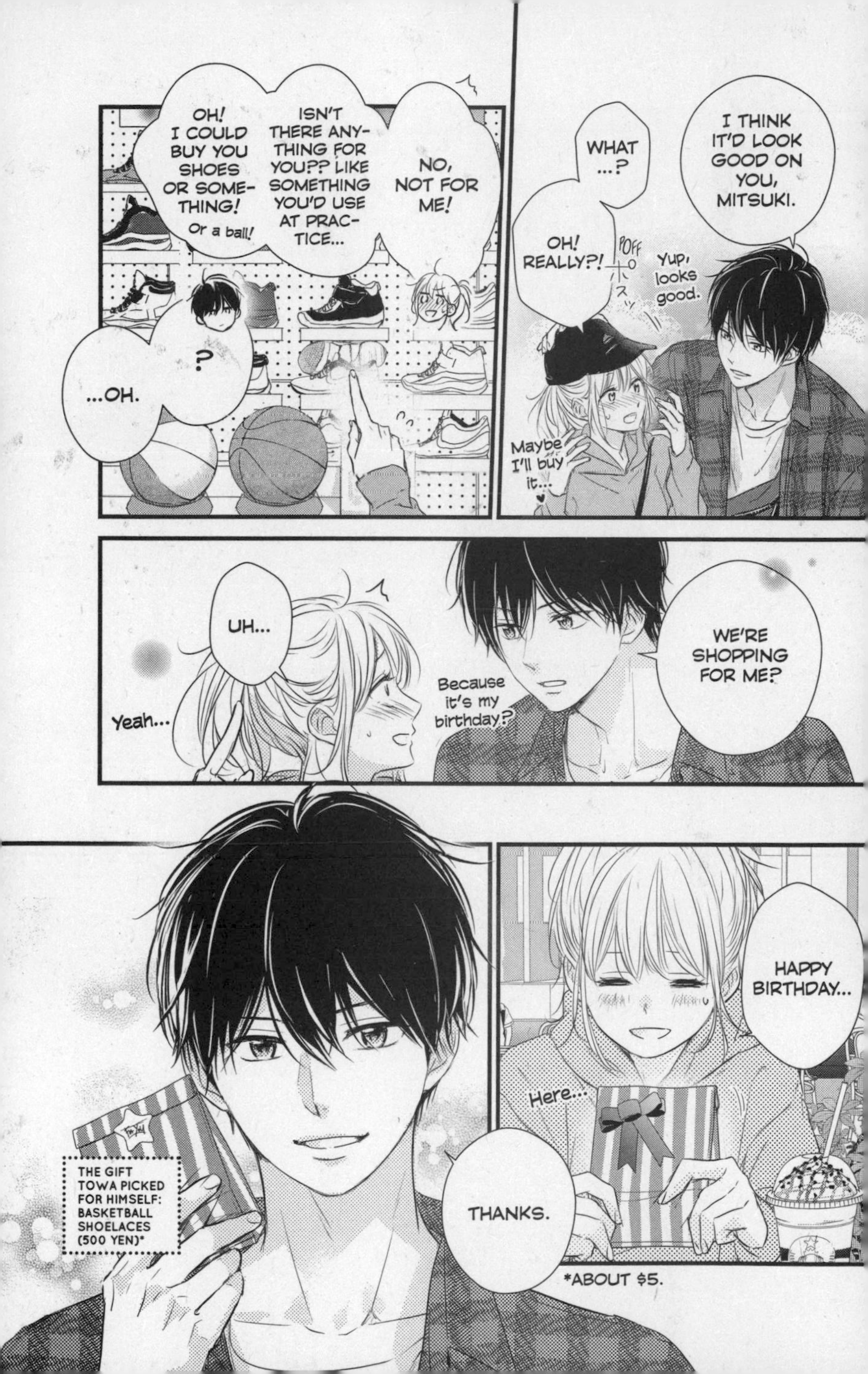
I THINK IT'D LOOK GOOD ON YOU, MITSUKI.
WHAT ...?
OH! REALLY?!
POFF
Yup, looks good.
Maybe I'll buy it...
NO, NOT FOR ME!
ISN'T THERE ANYTHING FOR YOU?? LIKE SOMETHING YOU'D USE AT PRACTICE...
OH! I COULD BUY YOU SHOES OR SOMETHING!
Or a ball!
?
...OH.
WE'RE SHOPPING FOR ME?
Because it's my birthday?
UH...
Yeah...
HAPPY BIRTHDAY...
Here...
THANKS.
THE GIFT TOWA PICKED FOR HIMSELF: BASKETBALL SHOELACES (500 YEN)*
*ABOUT $5.

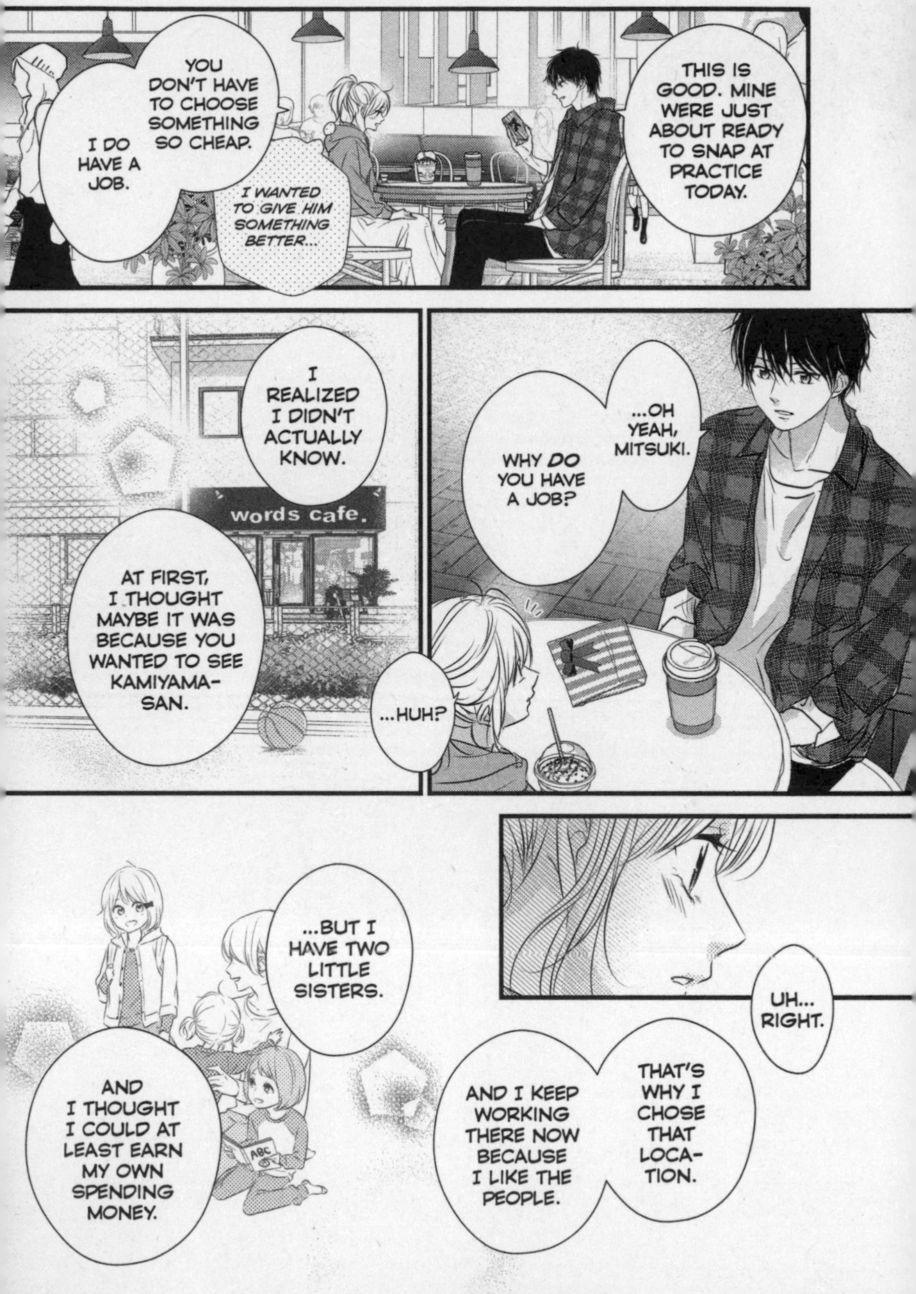
THIS IS GOOD. MINE WERE JUST ABOUT READY TO SNAP AT PRACTICE TODAY.
YOU DON'T HAVE TO CHOOSE SOMETHING SO CHEAP. I DO HAVE A JOB.
I WANTED TO GIVE HIM SOMETHING BETTER...
...OH YEAH, MITSUKI.
WHY DO YOU HAVE A JOB?
...HUH?
I REALIZED I DIDN'T ACTUALLY KNOW.
words cafe.
AT FIRST, I THOUGHT MAYBE IT WAS BECAUSE YOU WANTED TO SEE KAMIYAMA-SAN.
UH... RIGHT.
...BUT I HAVE TWO LITTLE SISTERS.
AND I THOUGHT I COULD AT LEAST EARN MY OWN SPENDING MONEY.
ABC
THAT'S WHY I CHOSE THAT LOCATION.
AND I KEEP WORKING THERE NOW BECAUSE I LIKE THE PEOPLE.

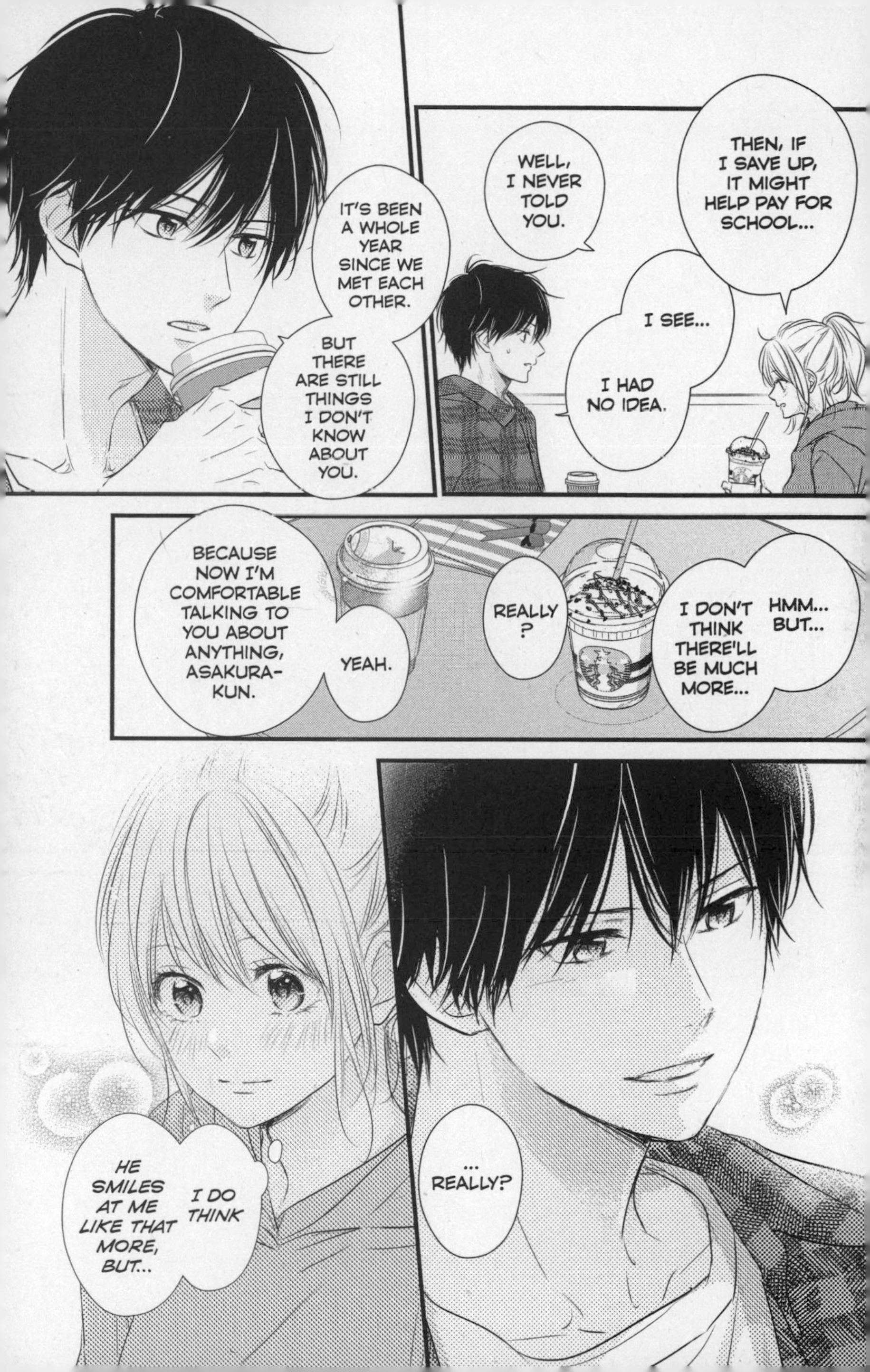
THEN, IF I SAVE UP, IT MIGHT HELP PAY FOR SCHOOL...
WELL, I NEVER TOLD YOU.
I SEE...
I HAD NO IDEA.
IT'S BEEN A WHOLE YEAR SINCE WE MET EACH OTHER.
BUT THERE ARE STILL THINGS I DON'T KNOW ABOUT YOU.
HMM... BUT...
I DON'T THINK THERE'LL BE MUCH MORE...
REALLY?
YEAH.
BECAUSE NOW I'M COMFORTABLE TALKING TO YOU ABOUT ANYTHING, ASAKURA-KUN.
...REALLY?
I DO THINK
HE SMILES AT ME LIKE THAT MORE, BUT...

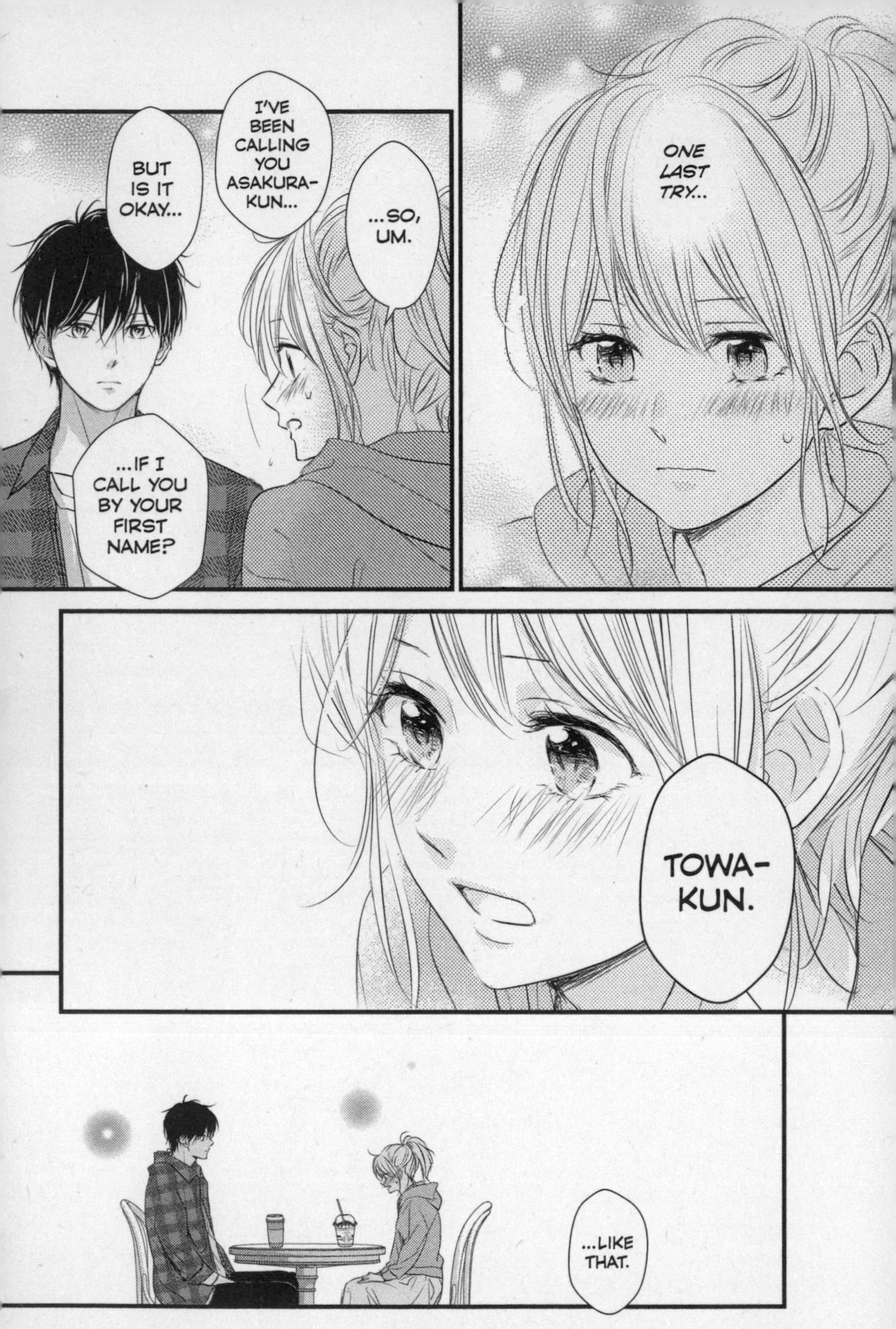
ONE LAST TRY...
...SO, UM.
I'VE BEEN CALLING YOU ASAKURA-KUN...
BUT IS IT OKAY...
...IF I CALL YOU BY YOUR FIRST NAME?
TOWA-KUN.
...LIKE THAT.

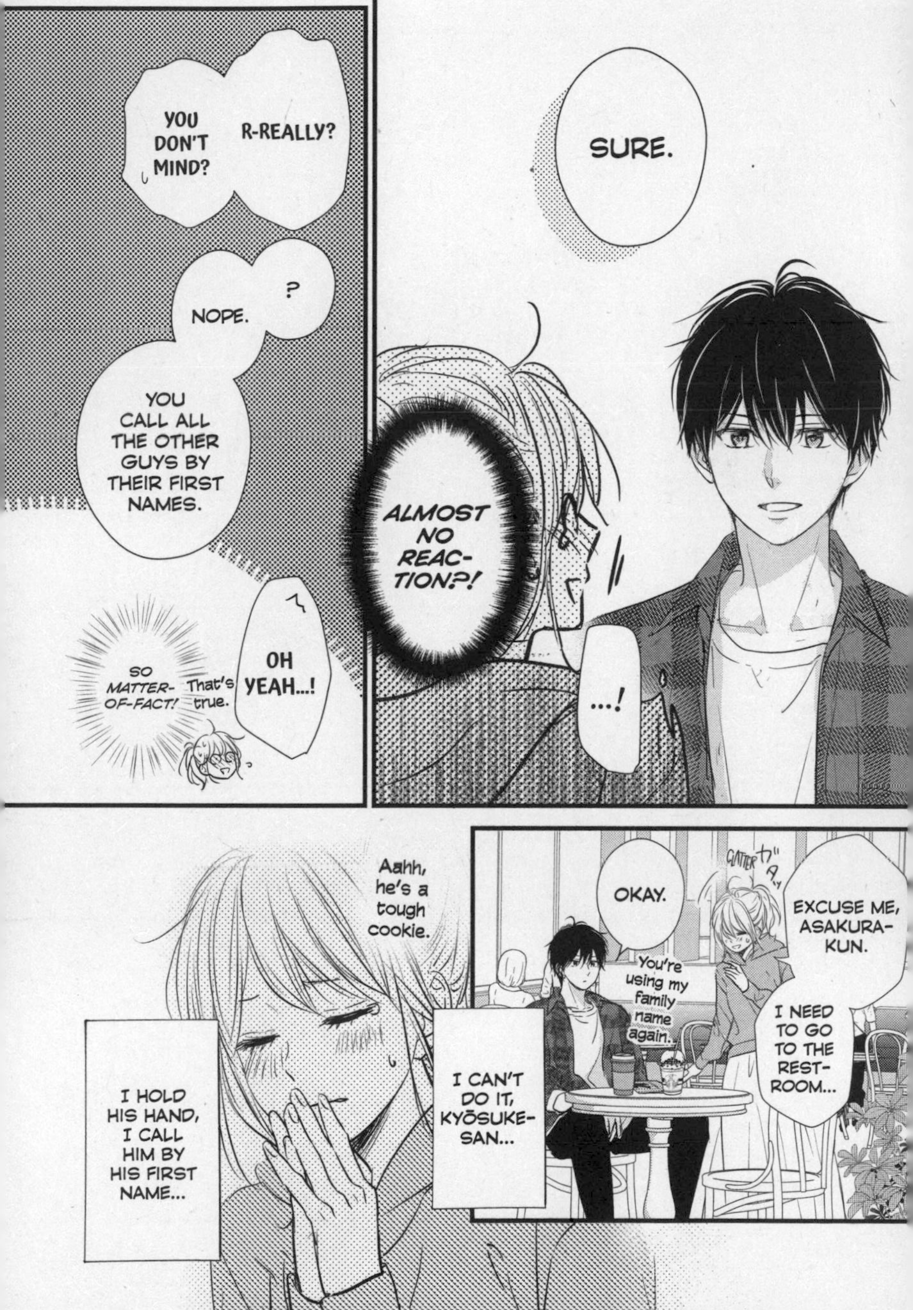
SURE.
...!
ALMOST NO REACTION?!
R-REALLY?
YOU DON'T MIND?
?
NOPE.
YOU CALL ALL THE OTHER GUYS BY THEIR FIRST NAMES.
OH YEAH...!
That's true.
SO MATTER-OF-FACT!
EXCUSE ME, ASAKURA-KUN.
I NEED TO GO TO THE REST-ROOM...
GLITTER
OKAY.
You're using my family name again.
Aahh, he's a tough cookie.
I CAN'T DO IT, KYŌSUKE-SAN...
I HOLD HIS HAND, I CALL HIM BY HIS FIRST NAME...

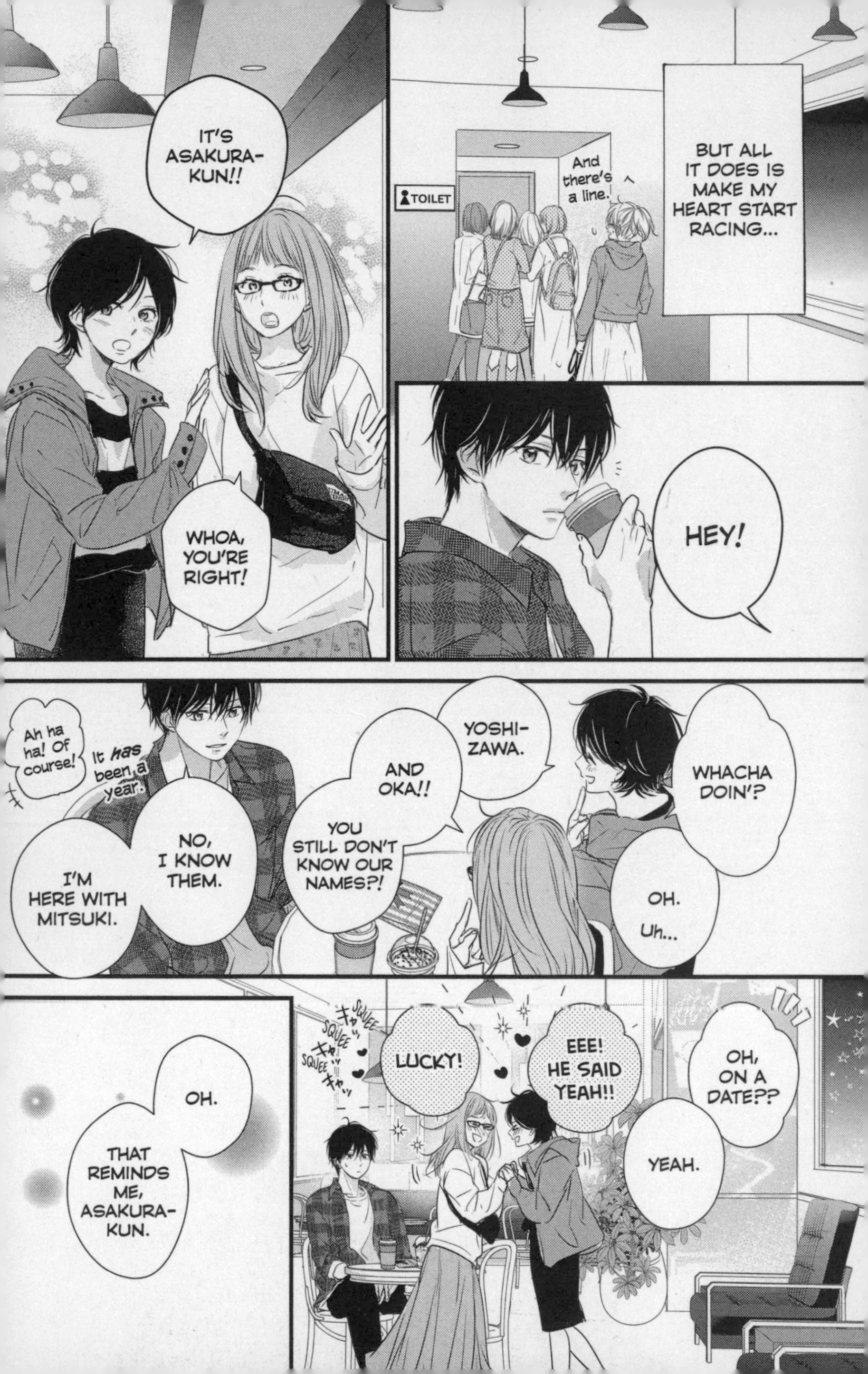
TOILET
BUT ALL IT DOES IS MAKE MY HEART START RACING...
And there's a line.
HEY!
IT'S ASAKURA-KUN!!
WHOA, YOU'RE RIGHT!
WHACHA DOIN'?
YOSHI-ZAWA.
AND OKA!!
OH.
Uh...
YOU STILL DON'T KNOW OUR NAMES?!
NO, I KNOW THEM.
Ah ha ha! Of course!
It *has* been a year.
I'M HERE WITH MITSUKI.
OH, ON A DATE??
YEAH.
EEE! HE SAID YEAH!!
LUCKY!
SQUEE キャッ
SQUEE キャ
SQUEE キャッ
OH.
THAT REMINDS ME, ASAKURA-KUN.

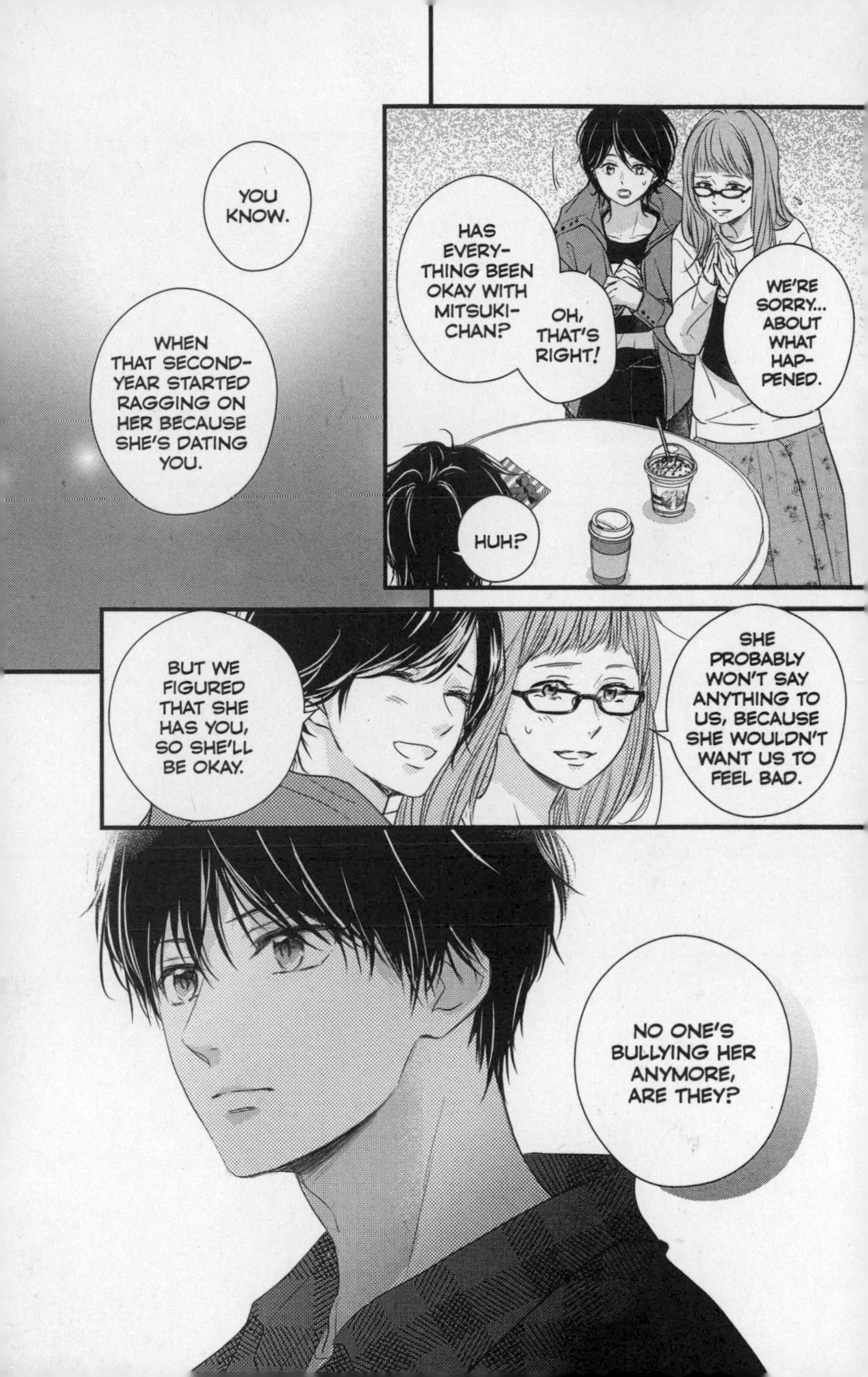
WE'RE SORRY... ABOUT WHAT HAPPENED.
OH, THAT'S RIGHT!
HAS EVERYTHING BEEN OKAY WITH MITSUKI-CHAN?
HUH?
YOU KNOW.
WHEN THAT SECOND-YEAR STARTED RAGGING ON HER BECAUSE SHE'S DATING YOU.
SHE PROBABLY WON'T SAY ANYTHING TO US, BECAUSE SHE WOULDN'T WANT US TO FEEL BAD.
BUT WE FIGURED THAT SHE HAS YOU, SO SHE'LL BE OKAY.
NO ONE'S BULLYING HER ANYMORE, ARE THEY?

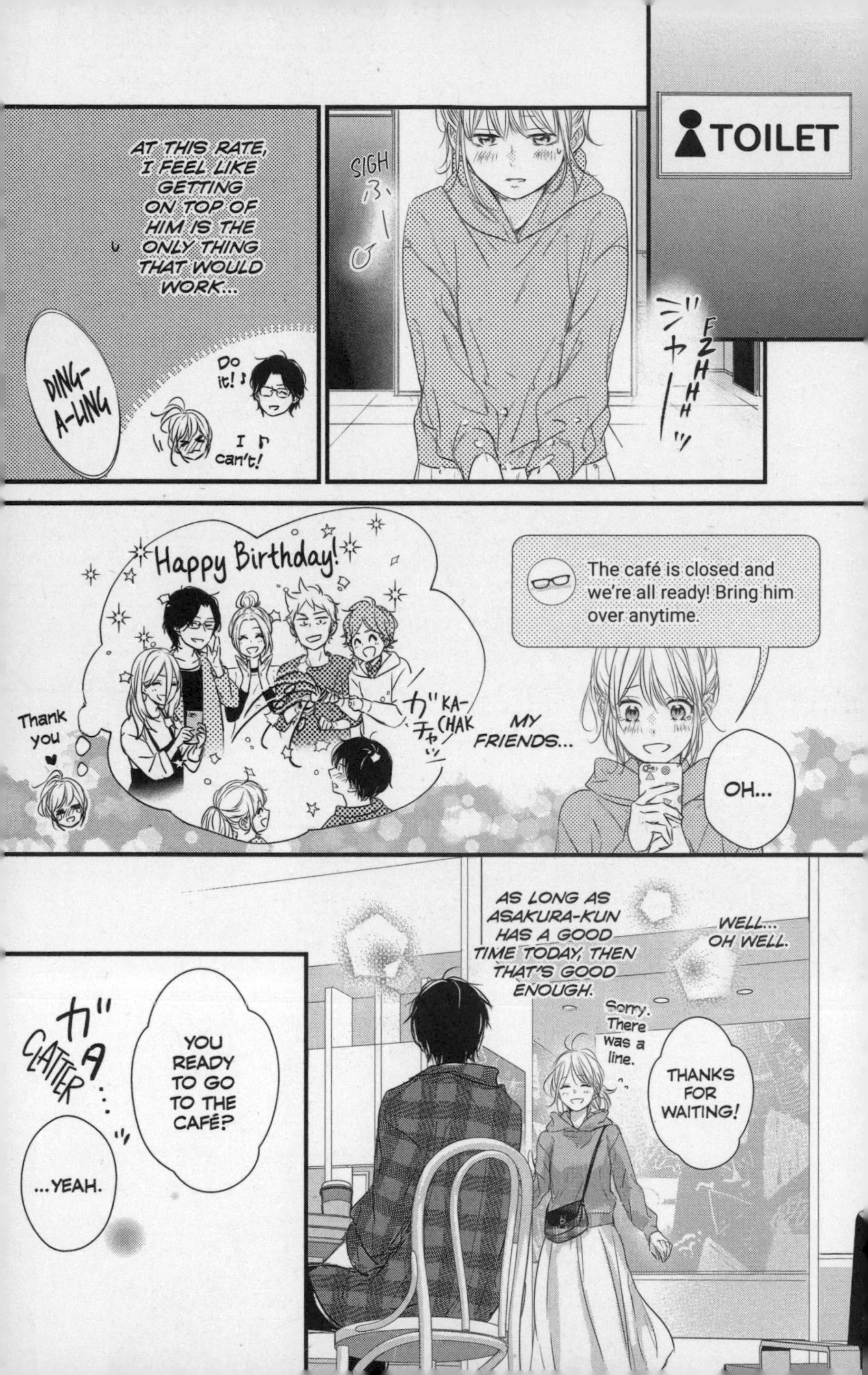
TOILET
ジャーーッ
FZHHHH
SIGH
ふーっ
AT THIS RATE, I FEEL LIKE GETTING ON TOP OF HIM IS THE ONLY THING THAT WOULD WORK...
DING-A-LING
Do it! ♪
I can't! ♪
The café is closed and we're all ready! Bring him over anytime.
OH...
MY FRIENDS...
Happy Birthday!
ガチャッ
KA-CHAK
Thank you ♥
AS LONG AS ASAKURA-KUN HAS A GOOD TIME TODAY, THEN THAT'S GOOD ENOUGH.
WELL... OH WELL.
Sorry. There was a line.
THANKS FOR WAITING!
YOU READY TO GO TO THE CAFÉ?
ガタ
CLATTER
...YEAH.

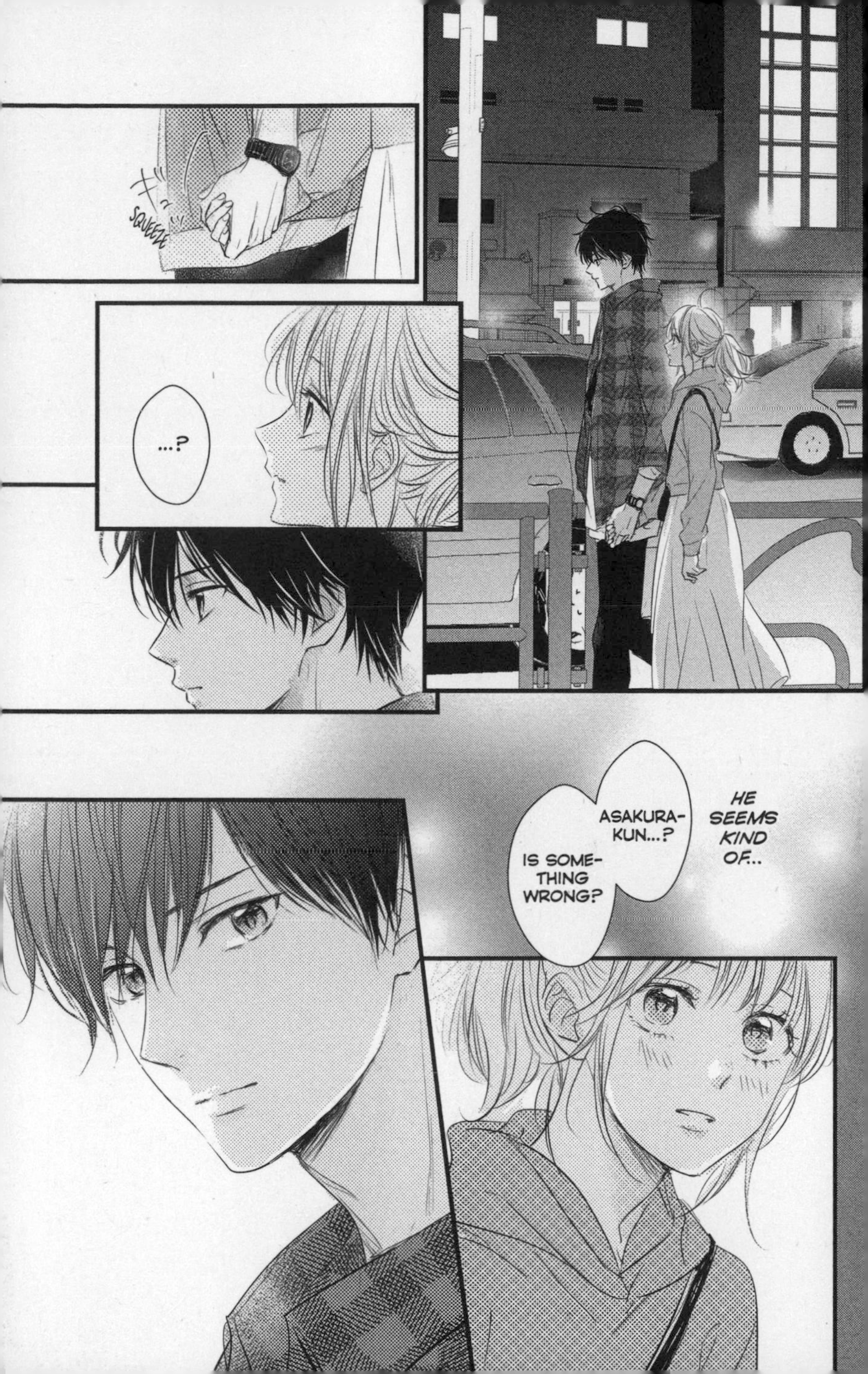
SQUEEZE
...?
HE SEEMS KIND OF...
ASAKURA-KUN...? IS SOMETHING WRONG?

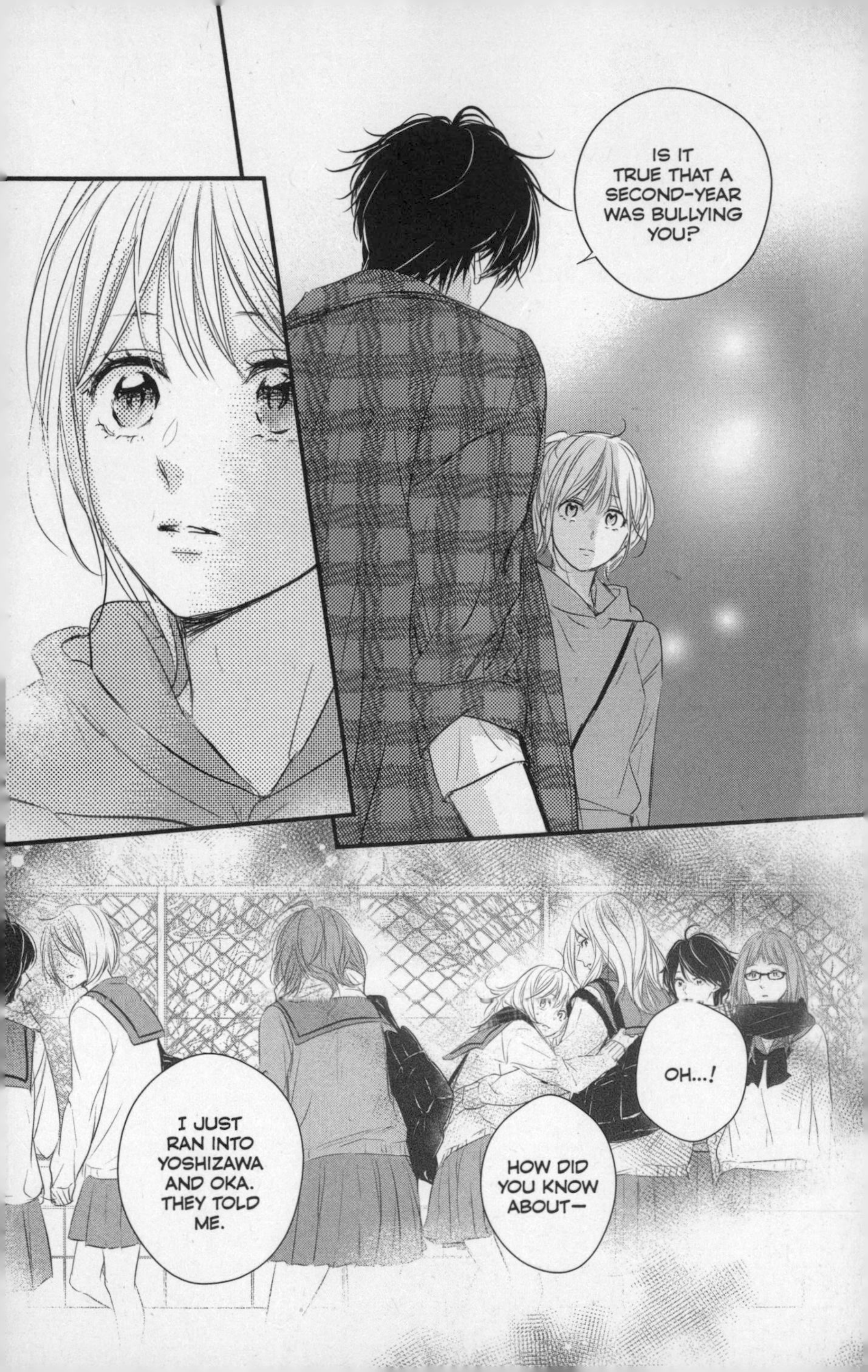
IS IT TRUE THAT A SECOND-YEAR WAS BULLYING YOU?
OH...!
HOW DID YOU KNOW ABOUT—
I JUST RAN INTO YOSHIZAWA AND OKA. THEY TOLD ME.

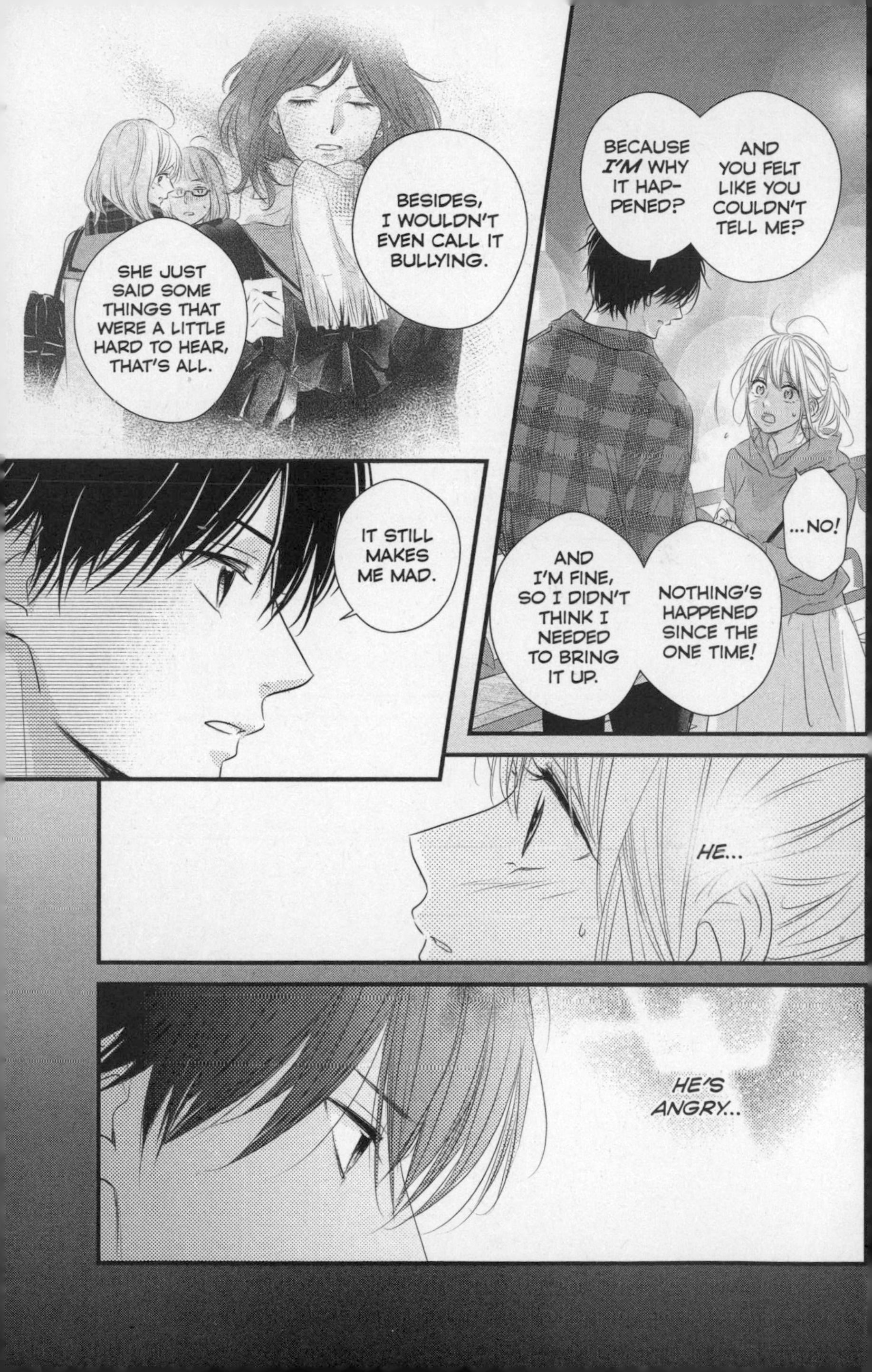
BESIDES, I WOULDN'T EVEN CALL IT BULLYING.
SHE JUST SAID SOME THINGS THAT WERE A LITTLE HARD TO HEAR, THAT'S ALL.
IT STILL MAKES ME MAD.
BECAUSE *I'M* WHY IT HAP-PENED?
AND YOU FELT LIKE YOU COULDN'T TELL ME?
...NO!
NOTHING'S HAPPENED SINCE THE ONE TIME!
AND I'M FINE, SO I DIDN'T THINK I NEEDED TO BRING IT UP.
HE...
HE'S ANGRY...

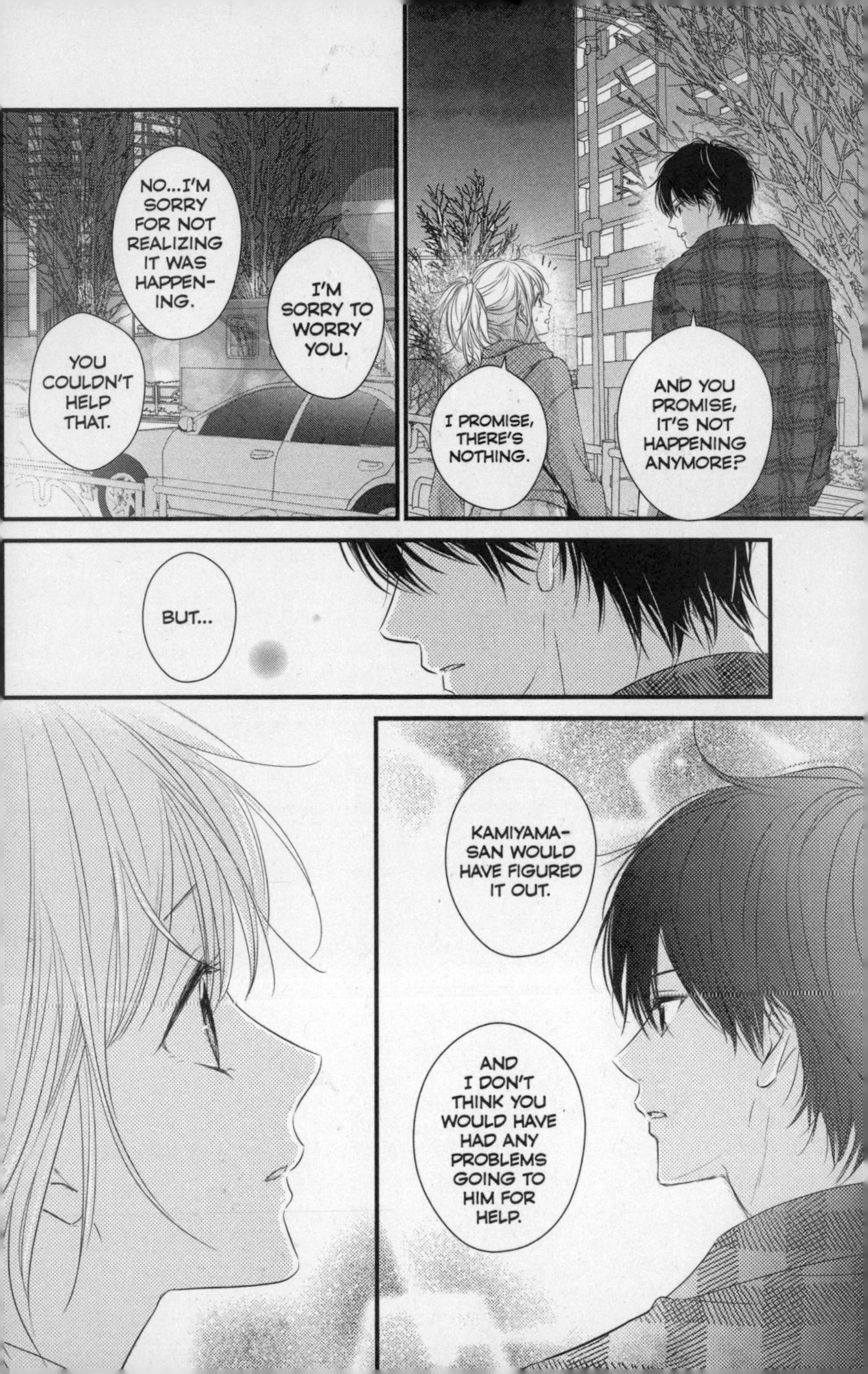
AND YOU PROMISE, IT'S NOT HAPPENING ANYMORE?
I PROMISE, THERE'S NOTHING.
I'M SORRY TO WORRY YOU.
NO...I'M SORRY FOR NOT REALIZING IT WAS HAPPEN-ING.
YOU COULDN'T HELP THAT.
BUT...
KAMIYAMA-SAN WOULD HAVE FIGURED IT OUT.
AND I DON'T THINK YOU WOULD HAVE HAD ANY PROBLEMS GOING TO HIM FOR HELP.

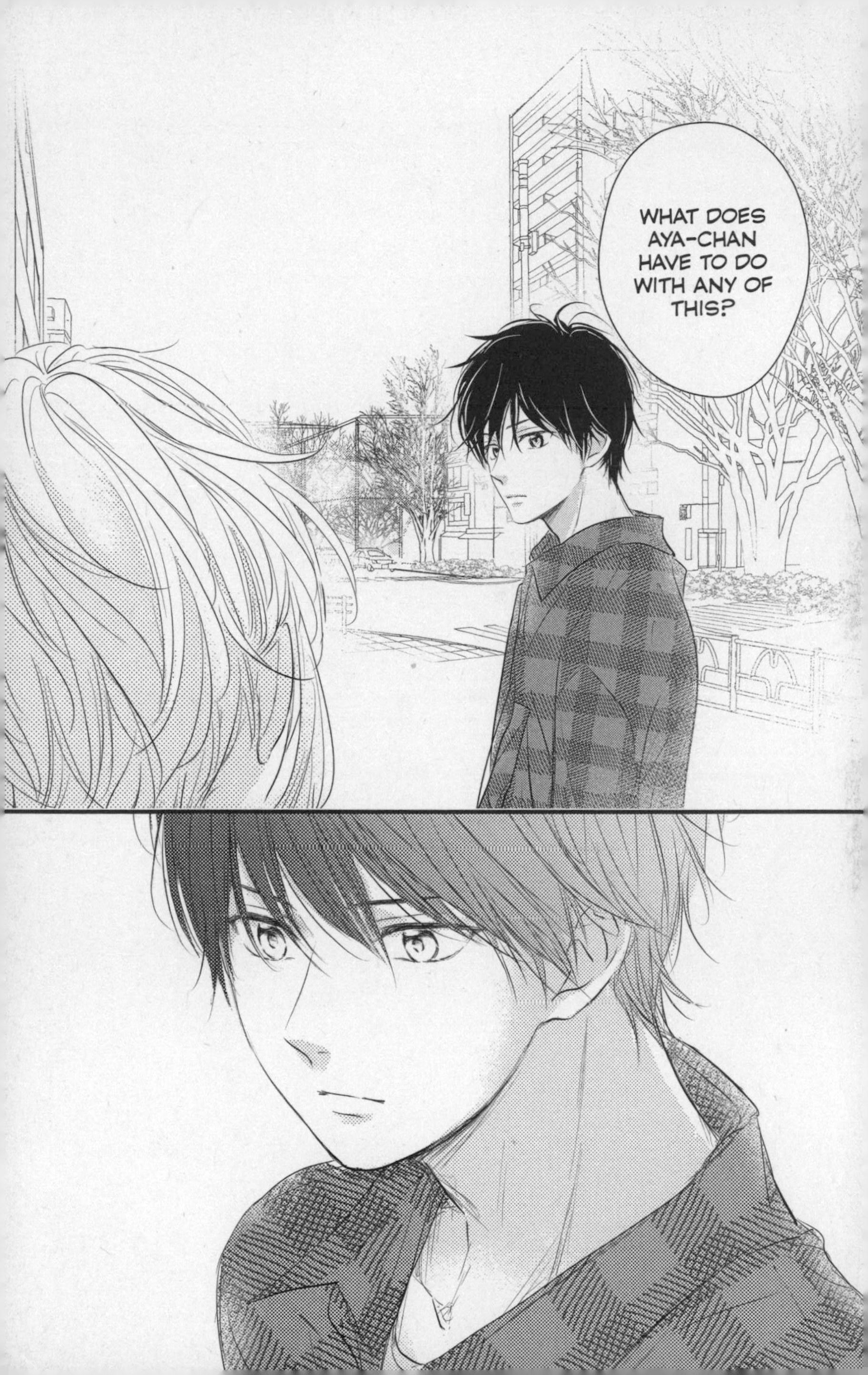
WHAT DOES AYA-CHAN HAVE TO DO WITH ANY OF THIS?

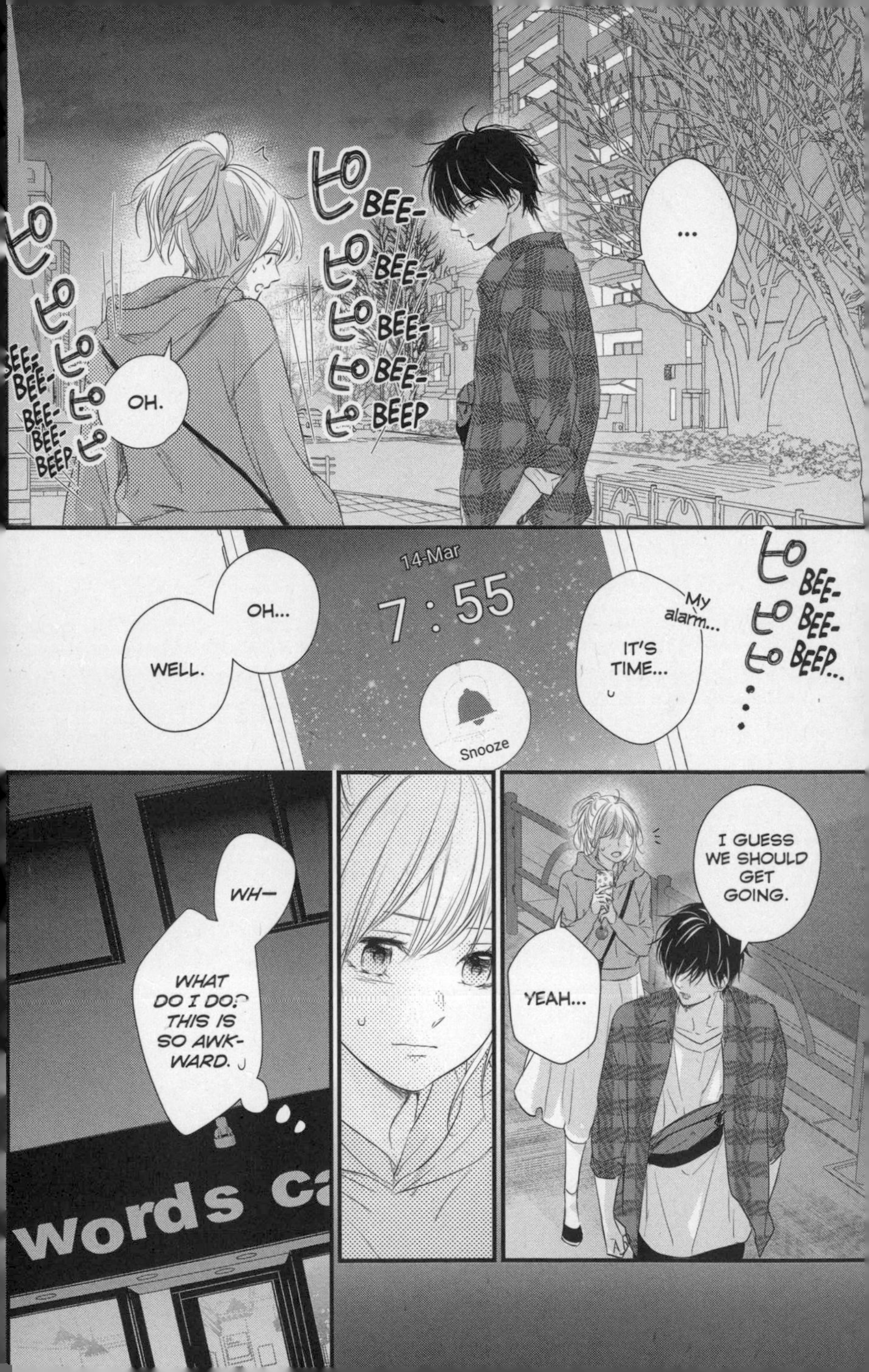
...
ピ BEE- ピ BEE- ピ BEE- ピ BEE- ピ BEEP
OH.
ピピピピピピ BEE- BEE- BEE- BEE- BEEP
ピ BEE- ピ BEE- ピ BEEP...
My alarm...
IT'S TIME...
14-Mar
7:55
Snooze
OH... WELL.
I GUESS WE SHOULD GET GOING.
YEAH...
WH—
WHAT DO I DO? THIS IS SO AWK-WARD.
words ca

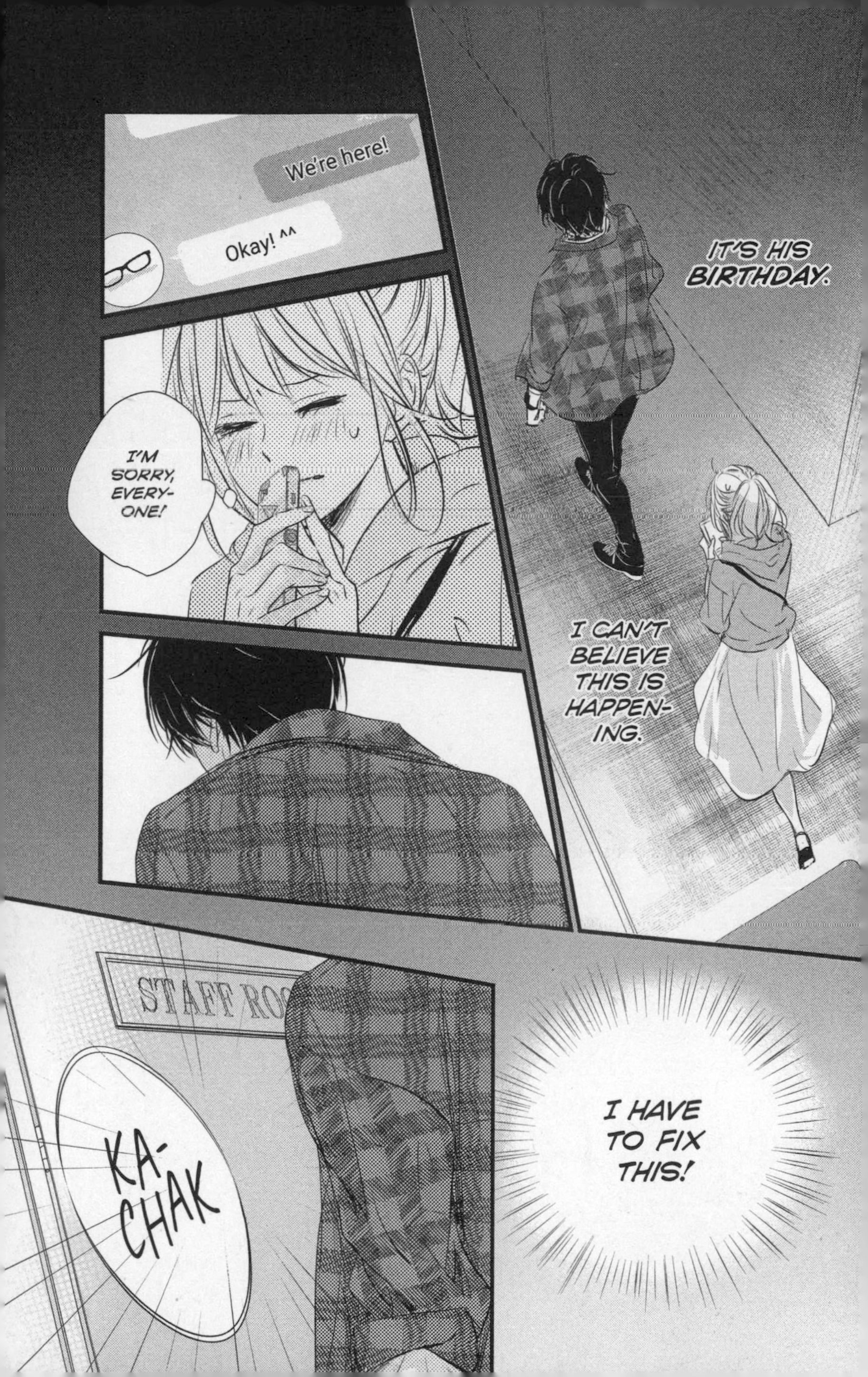

IT'S HIS BIRTHDAY.
I CAN'T BELIEVE THIS IS HAPPEN-ING.
We're here!
Okay! ^^
I'M SORRY, EVERY-ONE!
I HAVE TO FIX THIS!
STAFF RO
KA-CHAK

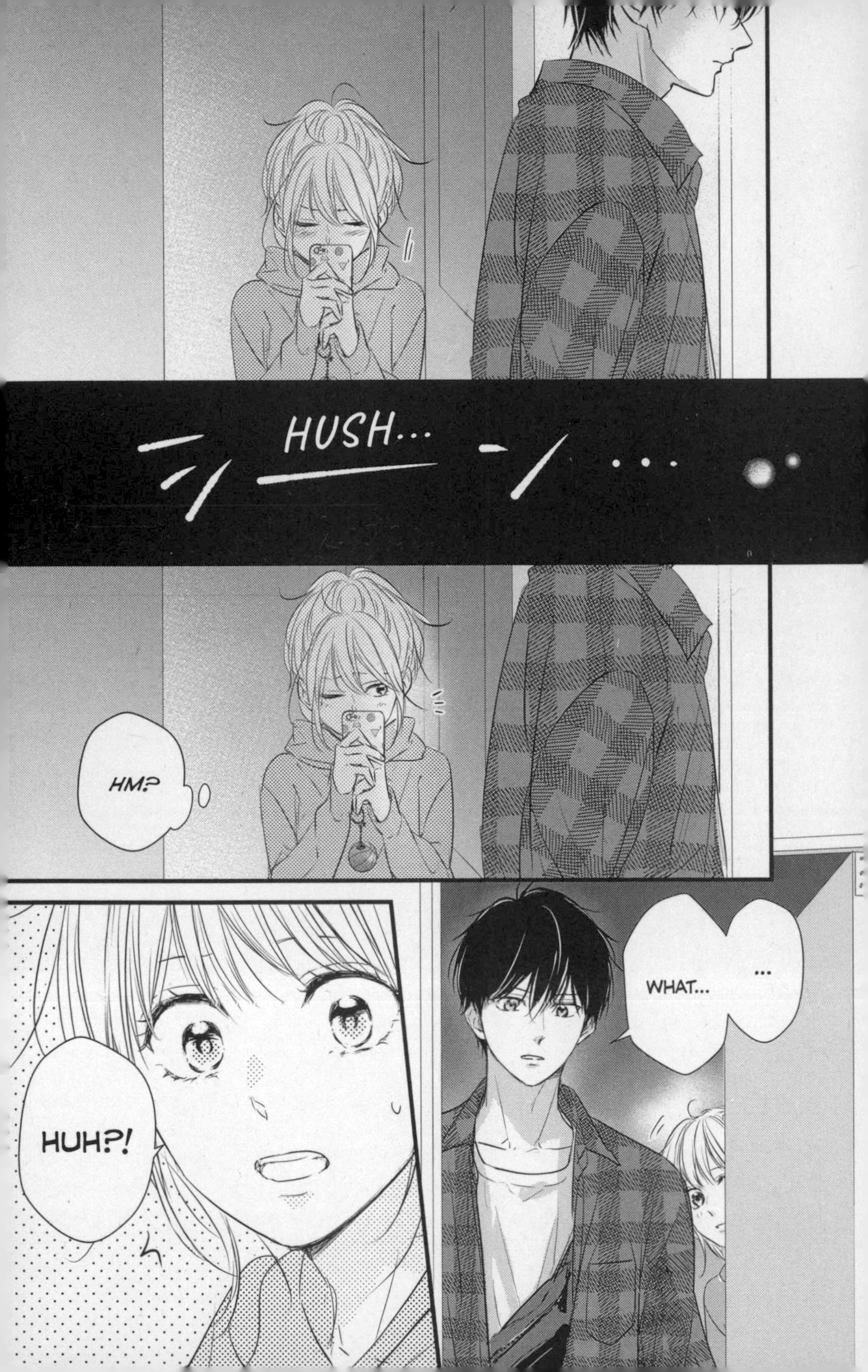
HUSH...
HM?
WHAT...
...
HUH?!

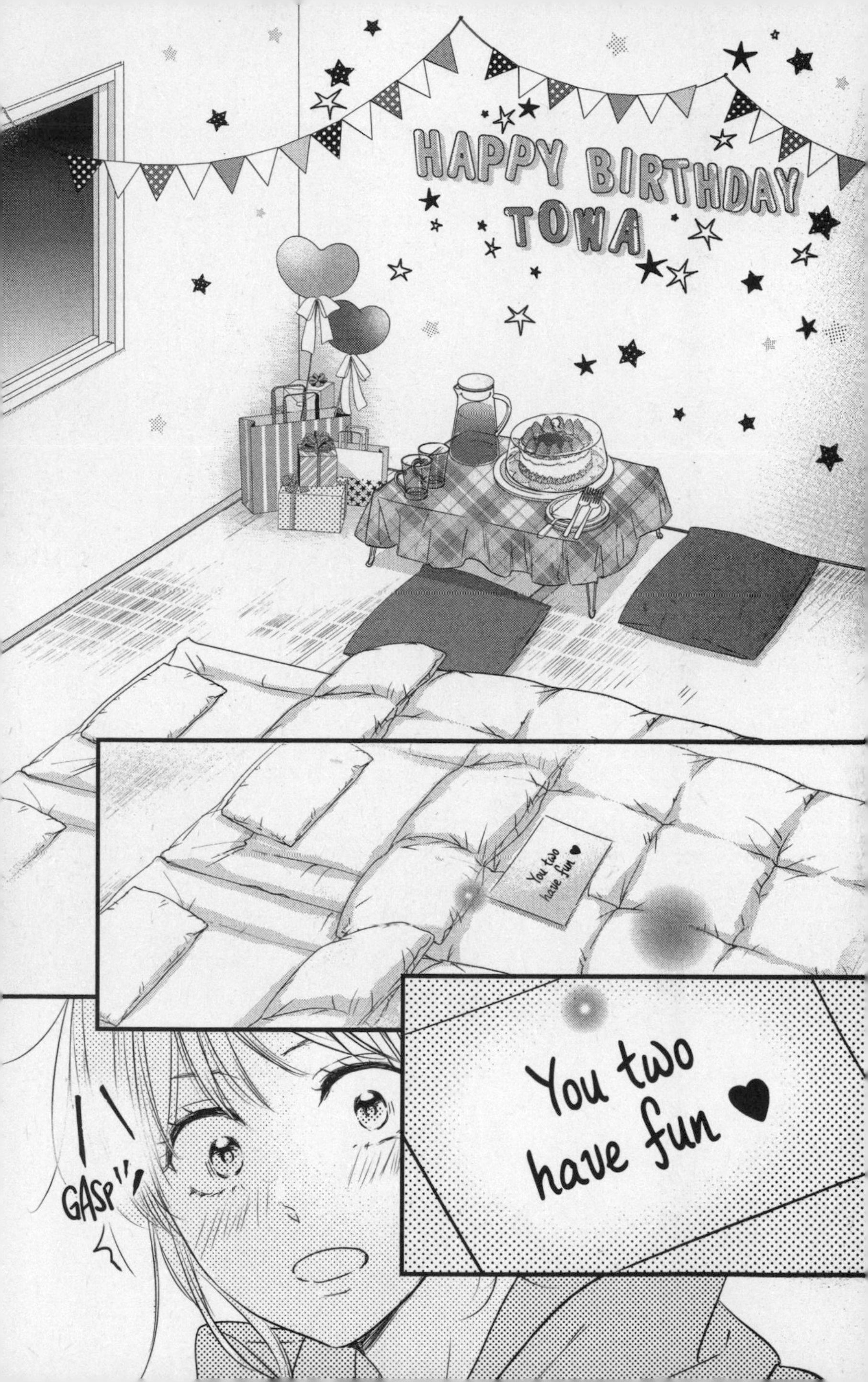
HAPPY BIRTHDAY TOWA
You two have fun ♥
You two have fun ♥
GASP

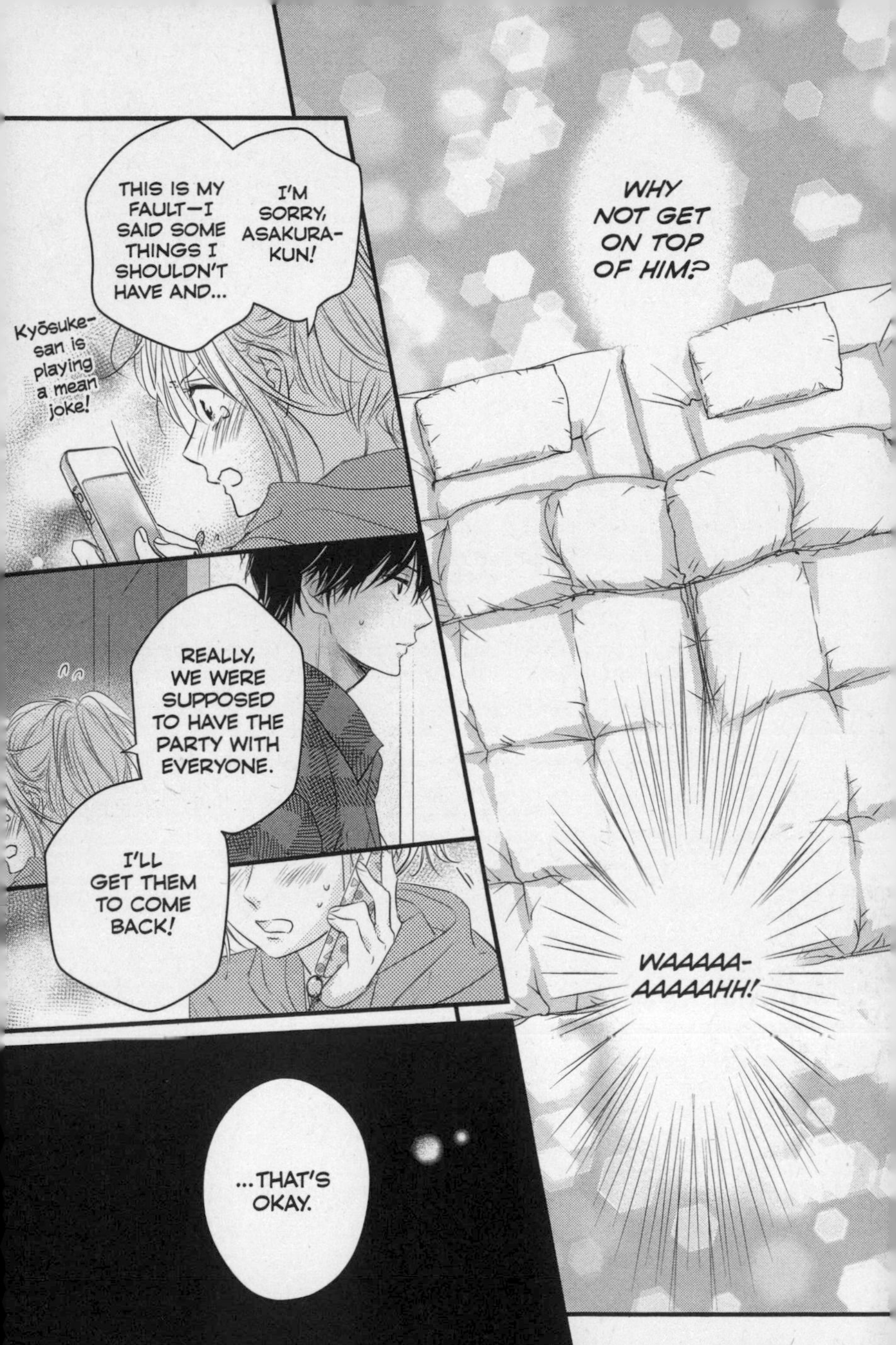
WHY NOT GET ON TOP OF HIM?
WAAAAA-AAAAAHH!
I'M SORRY, ASAKURA-KUN!
THIS IS MY FAULT—I SAID SOME THINGS I SHOULDN'T HAVE AND...
Kyōsuke-san is playing a mean joke!
REALLY, WE WERE SUPPOSED TO HAVE THE PARTY WITH EVERYONE.
I'LL GET THEM TO COME BACK!
...THAT'S OKAY.

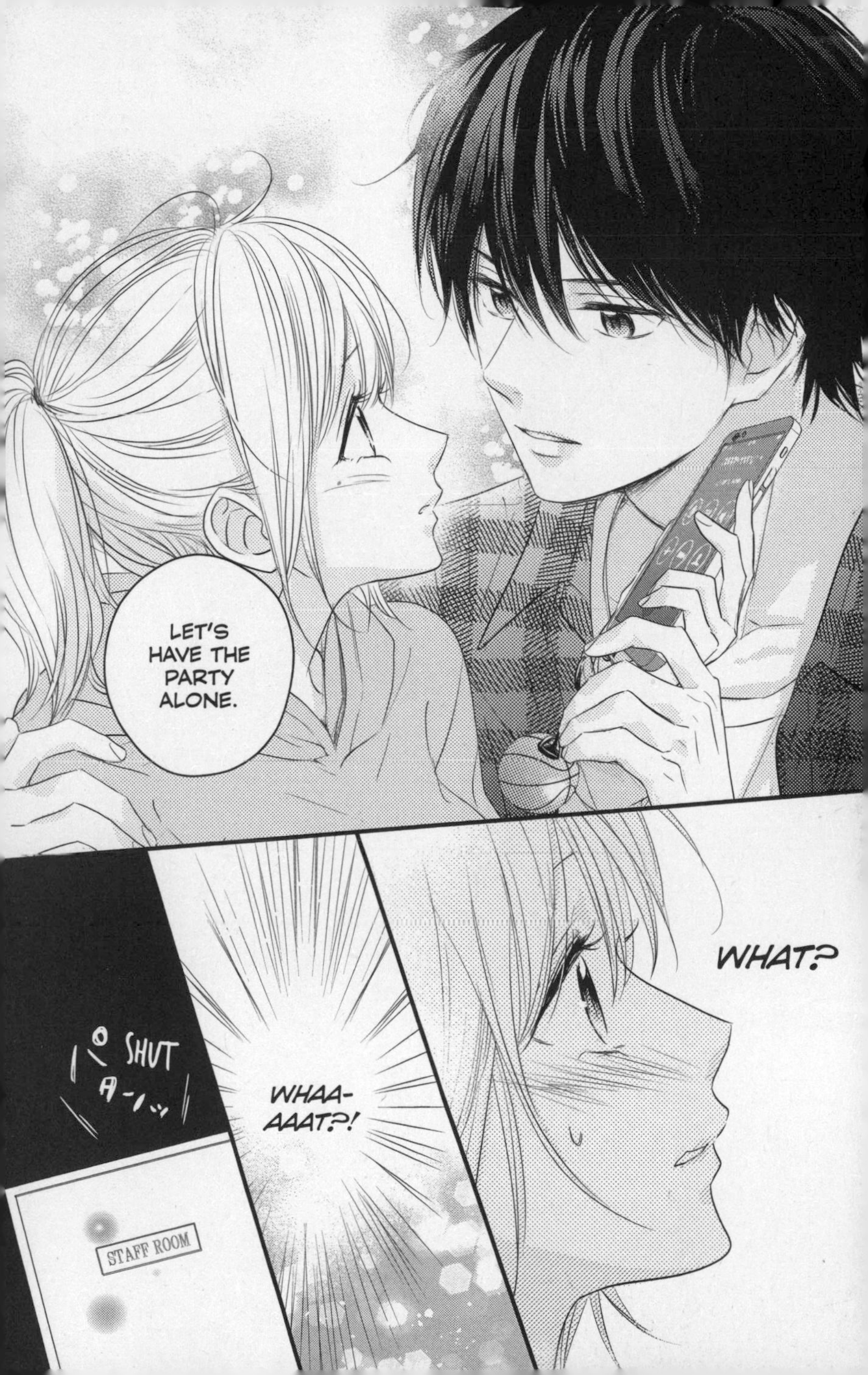
LET'S HAVE THE PARTY ALONE.
WHAT?
WHAA-AAAT?!
SHUT
STAFF ROOM

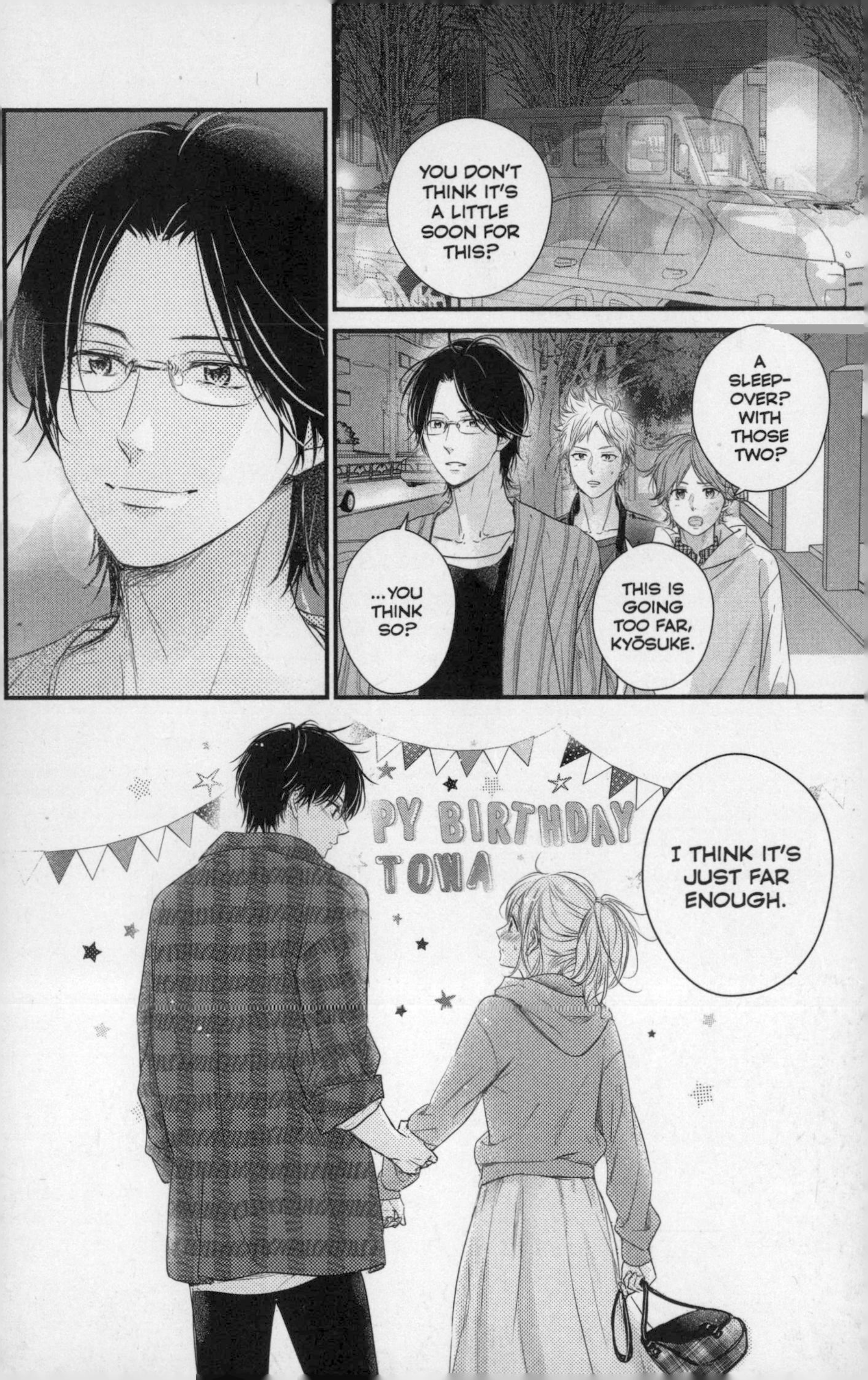
YOU DON'T THINK IT'S A LITTLE SOON FOR THIS?
A SLEEP-OVER? WITH THOSE TWO?
THIS IS GOING TOO FAR, KYŌSUKE.
...YOU THINK SO?
PY BIRTHDAY TOWA
I THINK IT'S JUST FAR ENOUGH.

period 55:
"Wholesome Birthday Night"

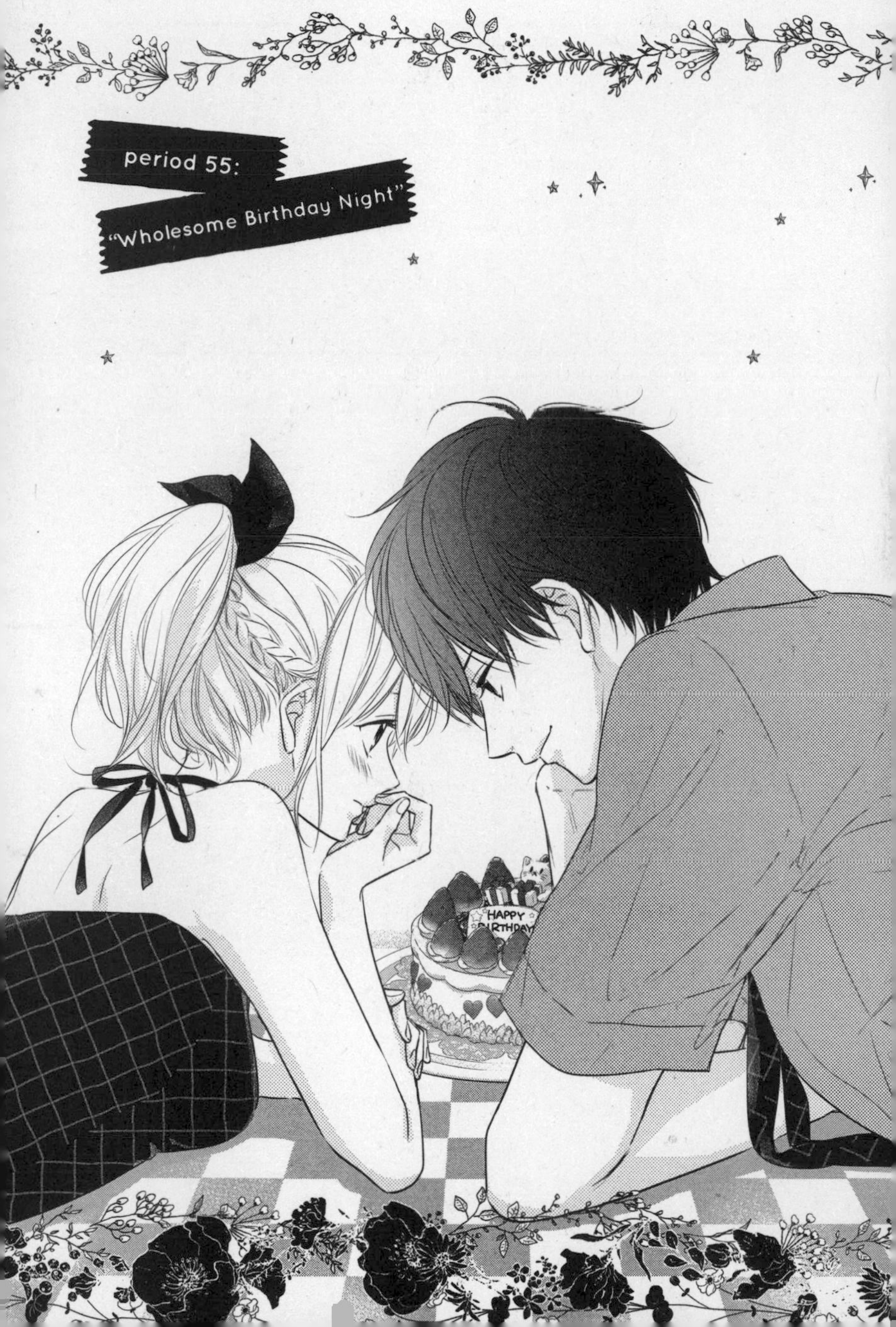
HAPPY BIRTHDAY

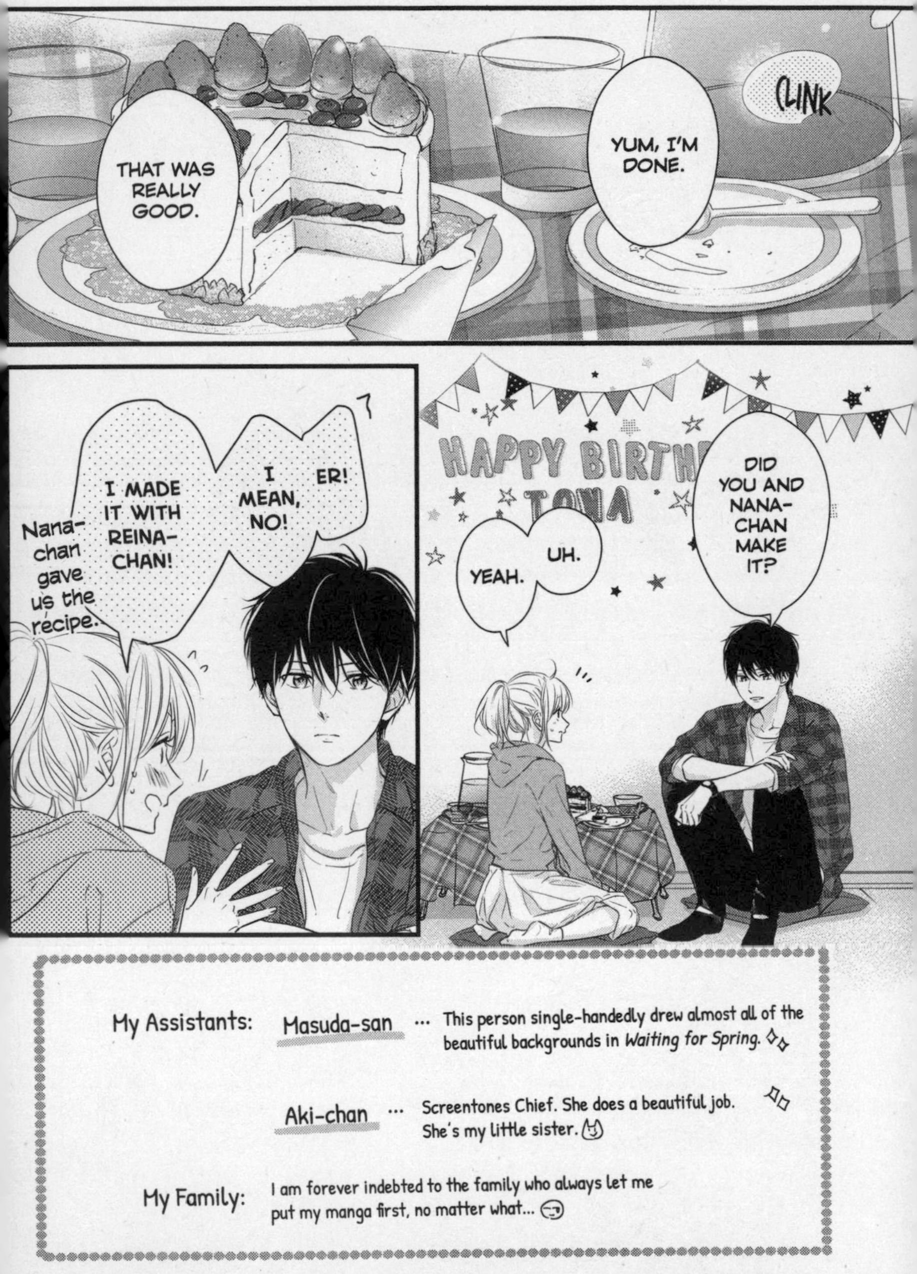
CLINK
YUM, I'M DONE.
THAT WAS REALLY GOOD.
DID YOU AND NANA-CHAN MAKE IT?
UH.
YEAH.
ER! I MEAN, NO!
I MADE IT WITH REINA-CHAN!
Nana-chan gave us the recipe.

My Assistants: Masuda-san ... This person single-handedly drew almost all of the beautiful backgrounds in *Waiting for Spring*.

Aki-chan ... Screentones Chief. She does a beautiful job. She's my little sister.

My Family: I am forever indebted to the family who always let me put my manga first, no matter what...

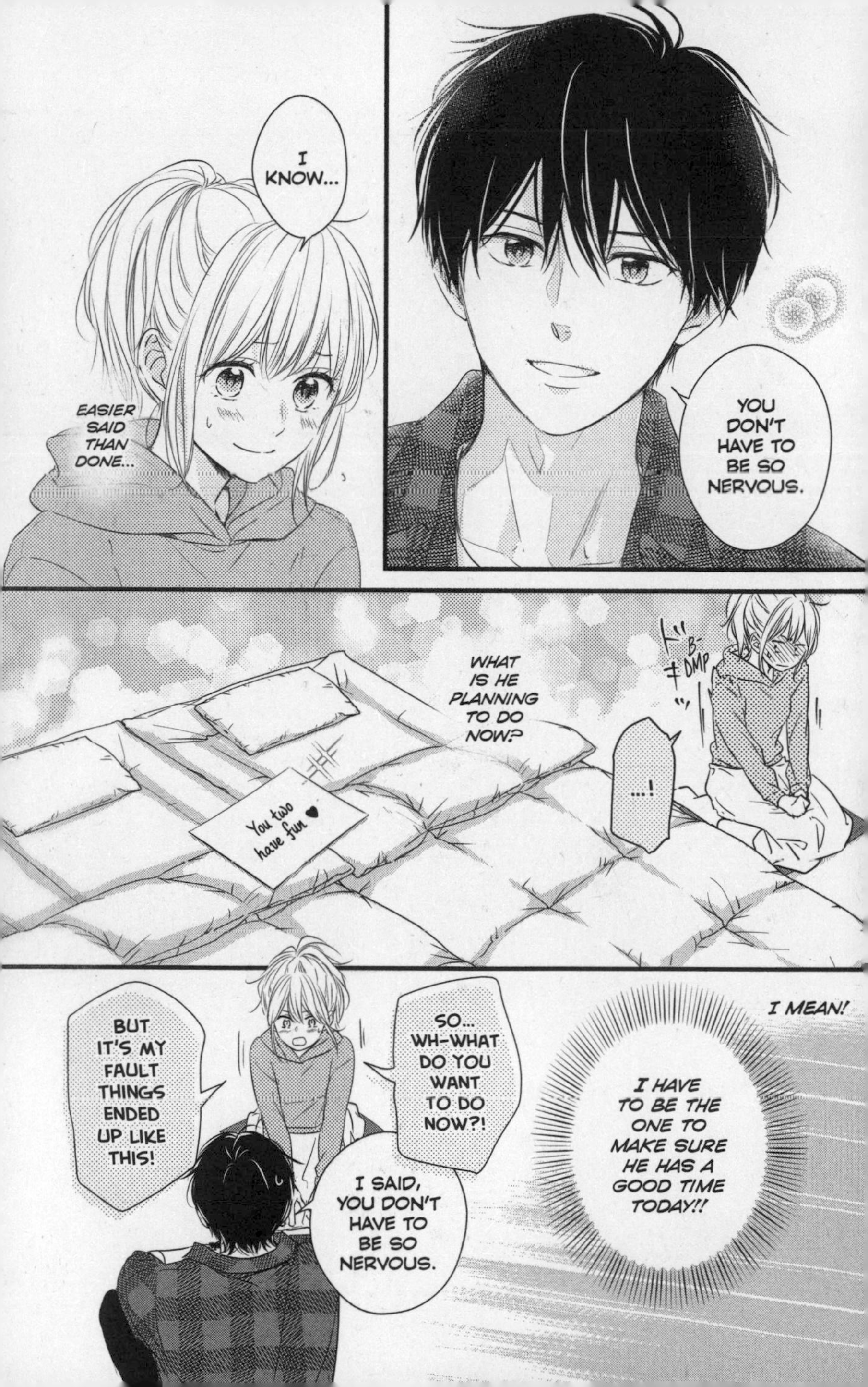
YOU DON'T HAVE TO BE SO NERVOUS.
I KNOW...
EASIER SAID THAN DONE...
B-DMP
...!
WHAT IS HE PLANNING TO DO NOW?
You two have fun ♥
I MEAN!
I HAVE TO BE THE ONE TO MAKE SURE HE HAS A GOOD TIME TODAY!!
SO... WH-WHAT DO YOU WANT TO DO NOW?!
BUT IT'S MY FAULT THINGS ENDED UP LIKE THIS!
I SAID, YOU DON'T HAVE TO BE SO NERVOUS.

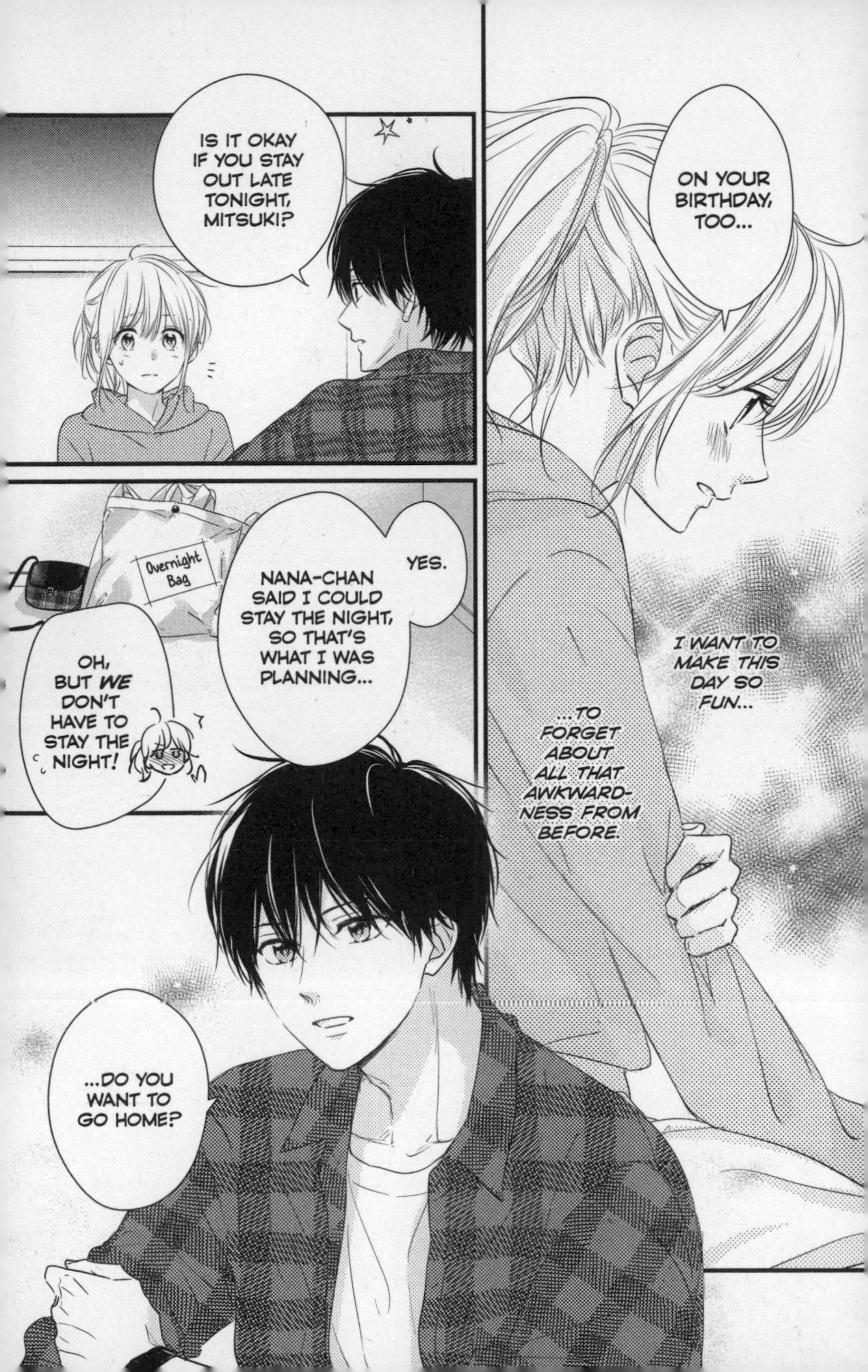
ON YOUR BIRTHDAY, TOO...
I WANT TO MAKE THIS DAY SO FUN...
...TO FORGET ABOUT ALL THAT AWKWARDNESS FROM BEFORE.
IS IT OKAY IF YOU STAY OUT LATE TONIGHT, MITSUKI?
YES.
NANA-CHAN SAID I COULD STAY THE NIGHT, SO THAT'S WHAT I WAS PLANNING...
Overnight Bag
OH, BUT WE DON'T HAVE TO STAY THE NIGHT!
...DO YOU WANT TO GO HOME?

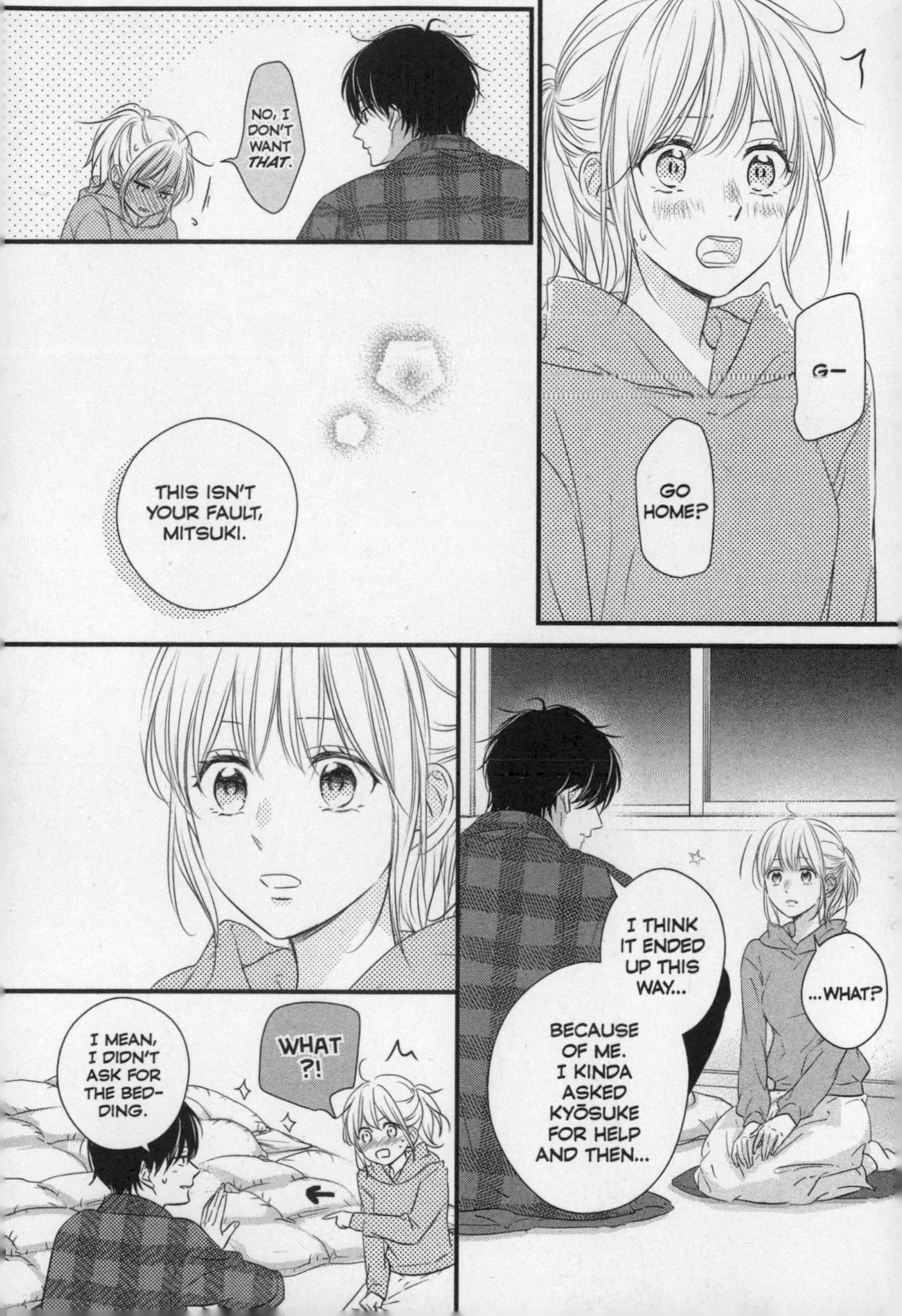
G—
GO HOME?
NO, I DON'T WANT THAT.
THIS ISN'T YOUR FAULT, MITSUKI.
I THINK IT ENDED UP THIS WAY...
BECAUSE OF ME. I KINDA ASKED KYŌSUKE FOR HELP AND THEN...
...WHAT?
WHAT ?!
I MEAN, I DIDN'T ASK FOR THE BED-DING.

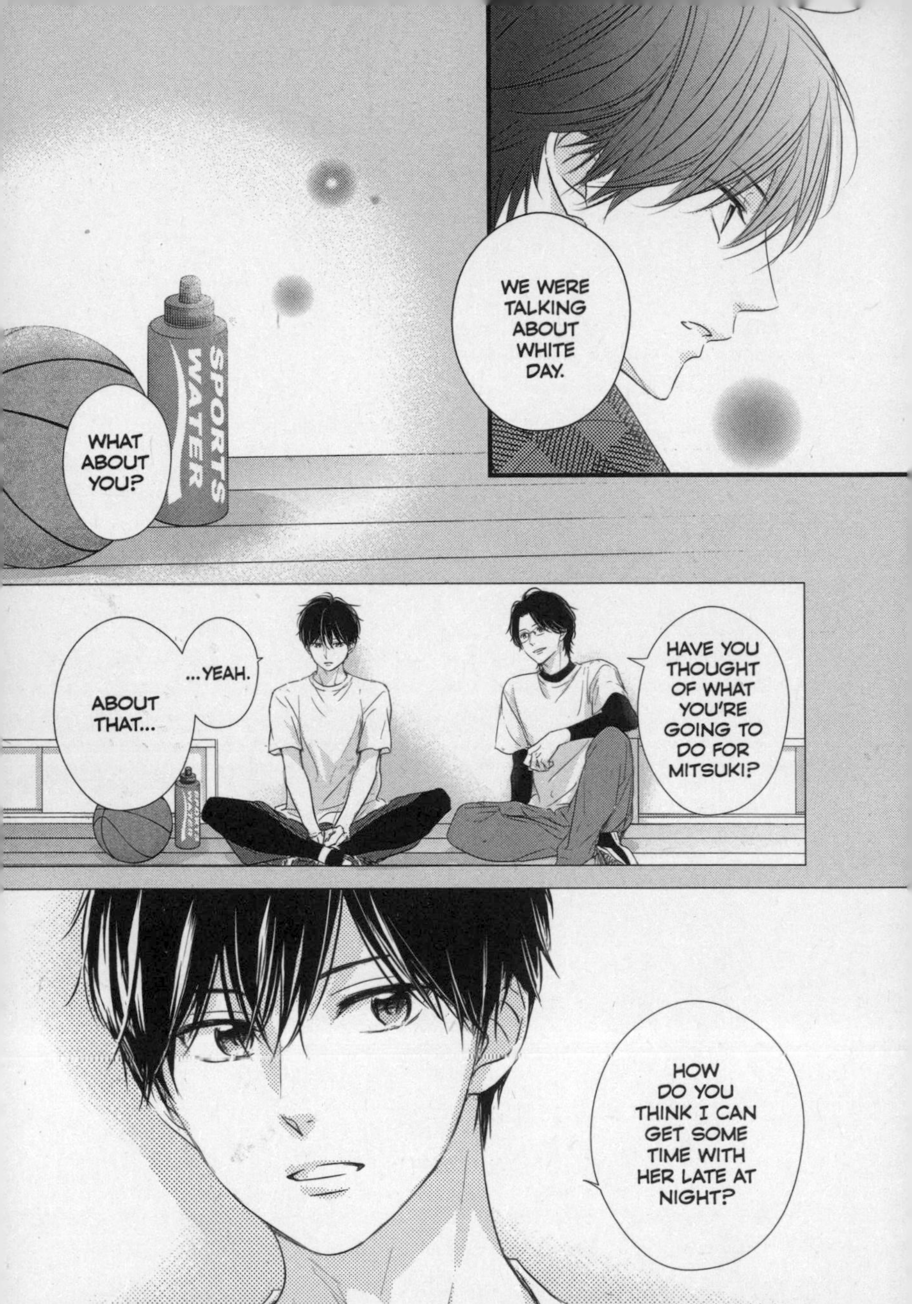
WE WERE TALKING ABOUT WHITE DAY.
WHAT ABOUT YOU?
SPORTS WATER
HAVE YOU THOUGHT OF WHAT YOU'RE GOING TO DO FOR MITSUKI?
...YEAH.
ABOUT THAT...
HOW DO YOU THINK I CAN GET SOME TIME WITH HER LATE AT NIGHT?

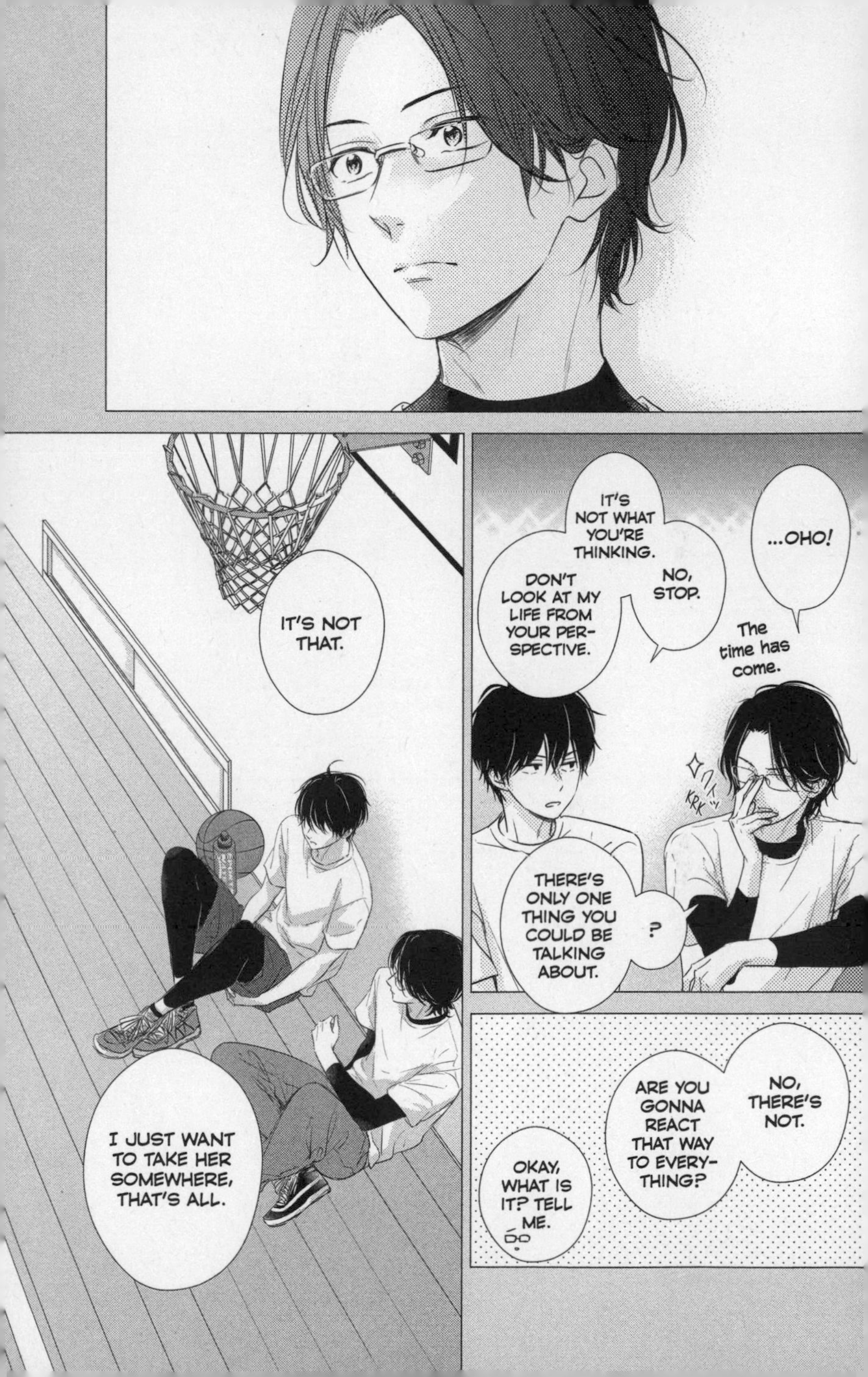
...OHO!
The time has come.
NO, STOP.
IT'S NOT WHAT YOU'RE THINKING.
DON'T LOOK AT MY LIFE FROM YOUR PER-SPECTIVE.
KRK
?
THERE'S ONLY ONE THING YOU COULD BE TALKING ABOUT.
NO, THERE'S NOT.
ARE YOU GONNA REACT THAT WAY TO EVERY-THING?
OKAY, WHAT IS IT? TELL ME.
IT'S NOT THAT.
I JUST WANT TO TAKE HER SOMEWHERE, THAT'S ALL.

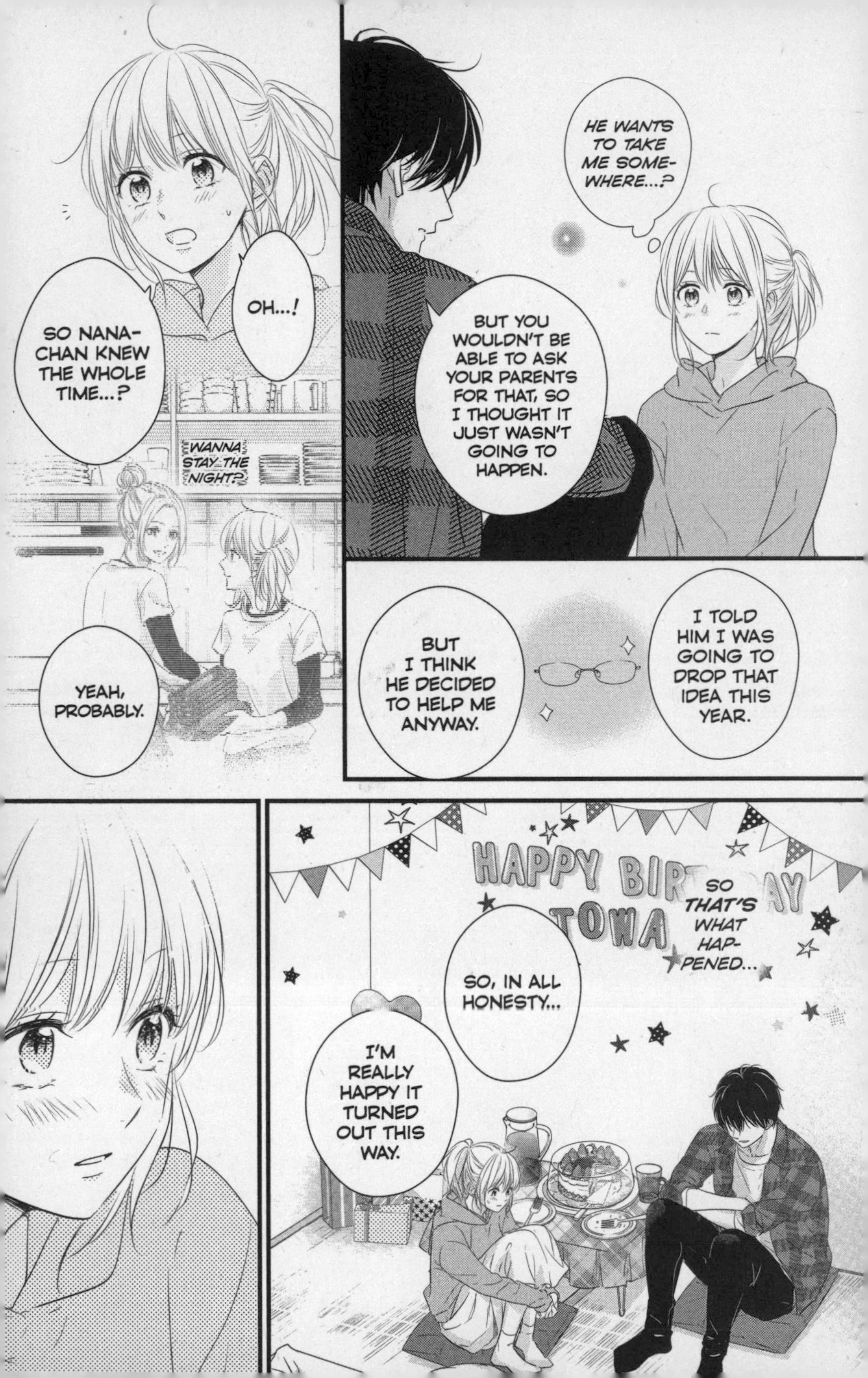
HE WANTS TO TAKE ME SOME-WHERE...?
BUT YOU WOULDN'T BE ABLE TO ASK YOUR PARENTS FOR THAT, SO I THOUGHT IT JUST WASN'T GOING TO HAPPEN.
I TOLD HIM I WAS GOING TO DROP THAT IDEA THIS YEAR.
BUT I THINK HE DECIDED TO HELP ME ANYWAY.
OH...!
SO NANA-CHAN KNEW THE WHOLE TIME...?
WANNA STAY THE NIGHT?
YEAH, PROBABLY.
HAPPY BIR AY
TOWA
SO THAT'S WHAT HAP-PENED...
SO, IN ALL HONESTY...
I'M REALLY HAPPY IT TURNED OUT THIS WAY.

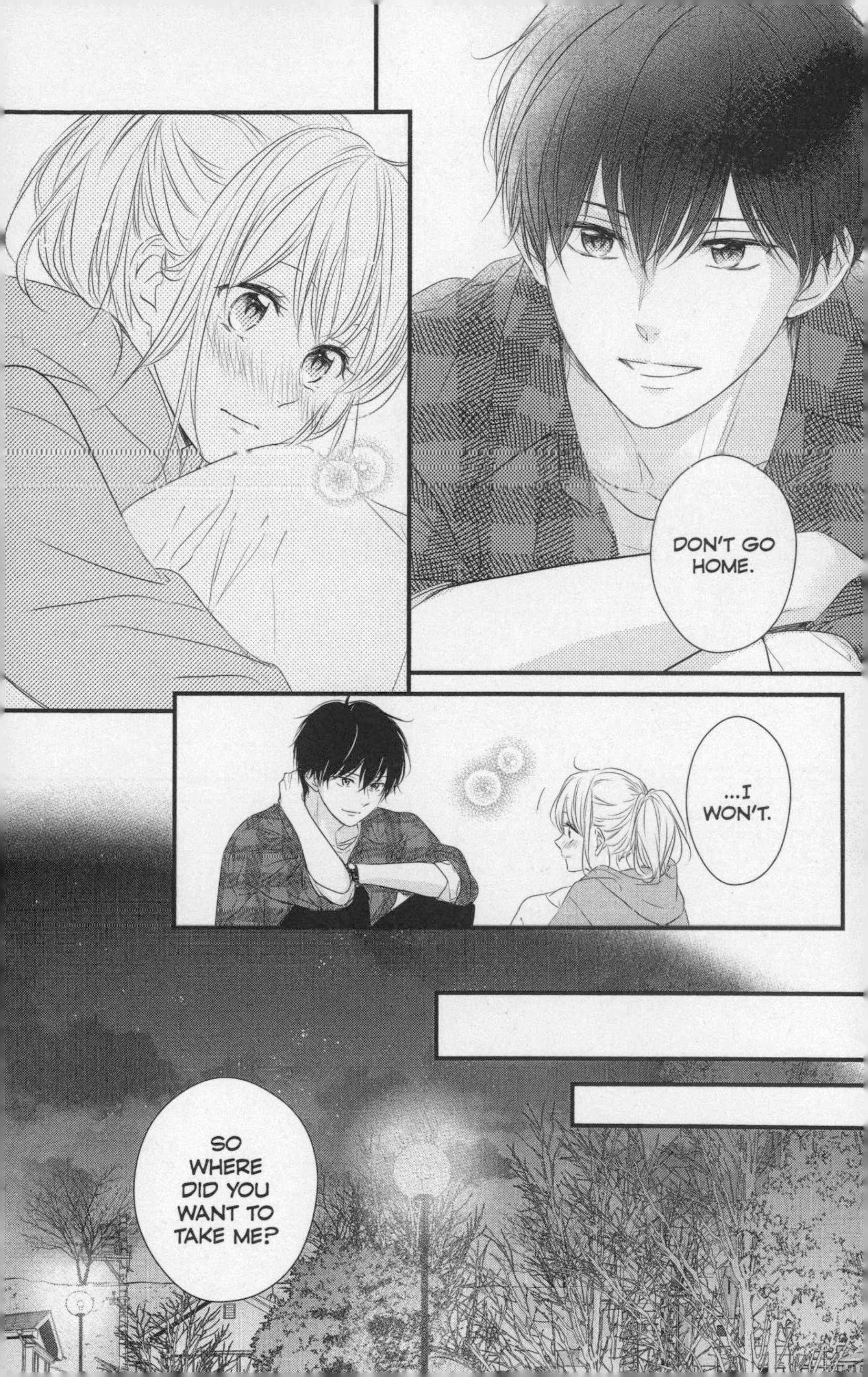
DON'T GO HOME.
...I WON'T.
SO WHERE DID YOU WANT TO TAKE ME?

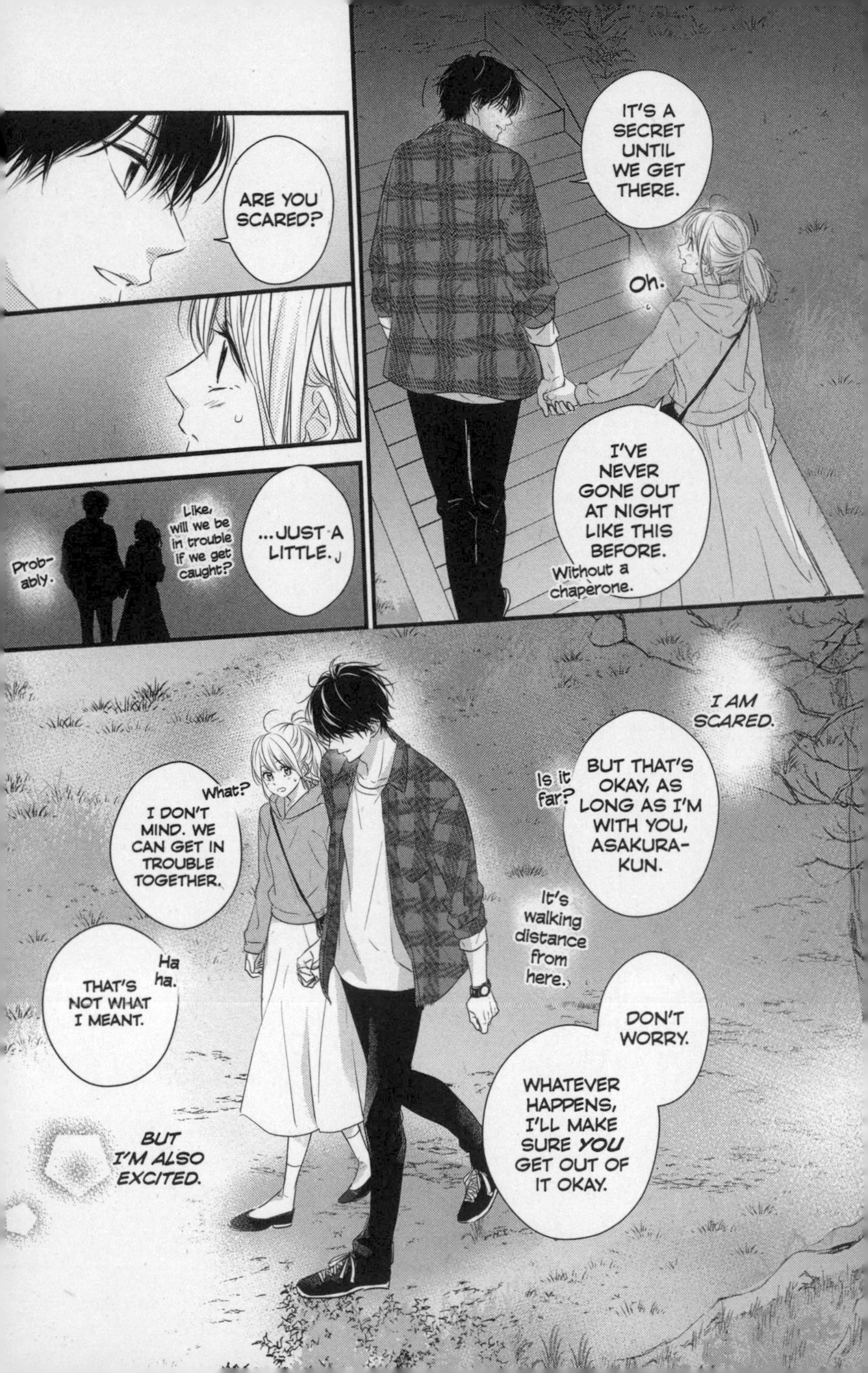
IT'S A SECRET UNTIL WE GET THERE.
Oh.
I'VE NEVER GONE OUT AT NIGHT LIKE THIS BEFORE.
Without a chaperone.
ARE YOU SCARED?
...JUST A LITTLE.
Like, will we be in trouble if we get caught?
Prob-ably.
I AM SCARED.
BUT THAT'S OKAY, AS LONG AS I'M WITH YOU, ASAKURA-KUN.
Is it far?
It's walking distance from here.
DON'T WORRY.
WHATEVER HAPPENS, I'LL MAKE SURE YOU GET OUT OF IT OKAY.
What?
I DON'T MIND. WE CAN GET IN TROUBLE TOGETHER.
Ha ha.
THAT'S NOT WHAT I MEANT.
BUT I'M ALSO EXCITED.

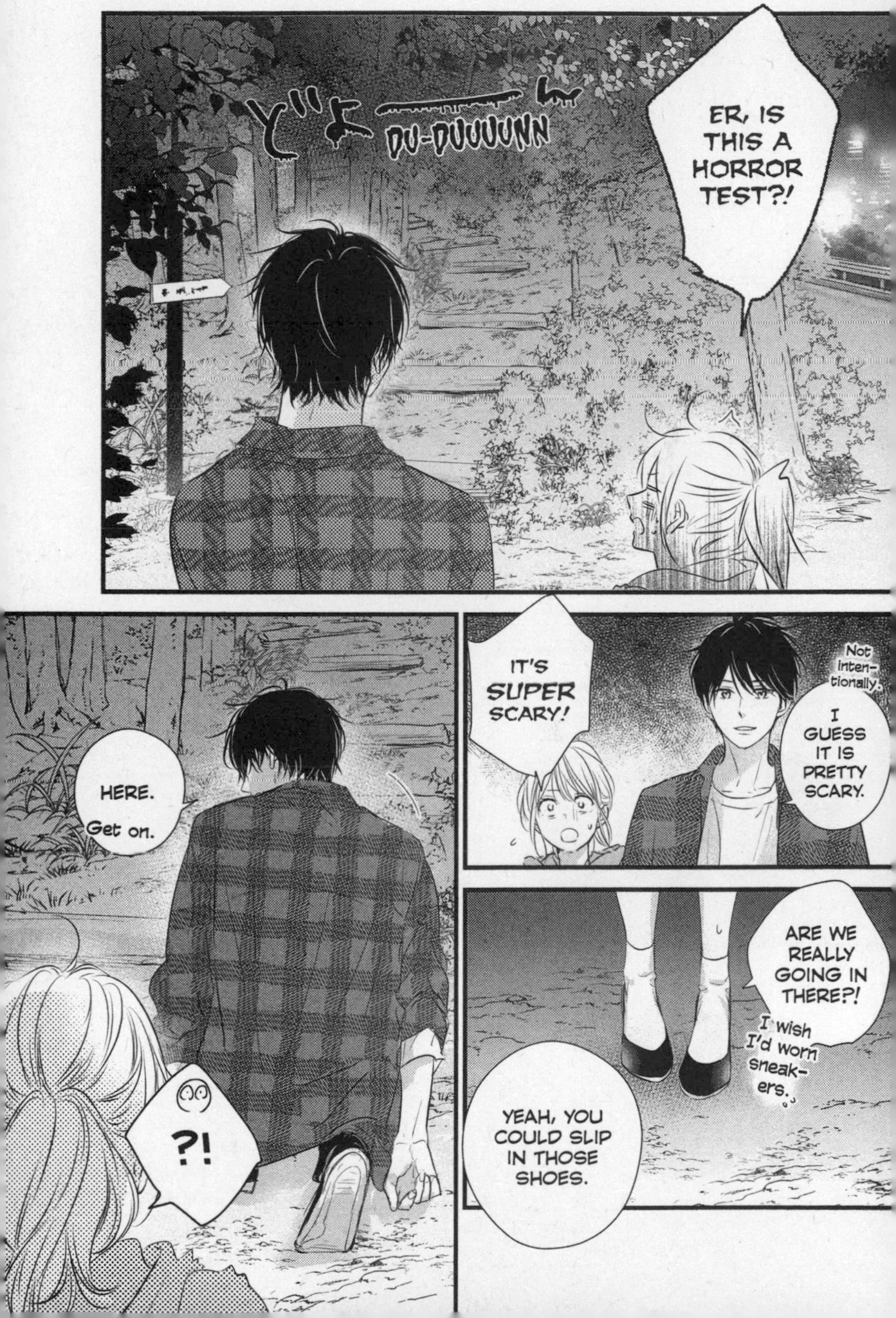
DU-DUUUUNN
ER, IS THIS A HORROR TEST?!
Not intentionally.
I GUESS IT IS PRETTY SCARY.
IT'S SUPER SCARY!
ARE WE REALLY GOING IN THERE?!
I wish I'd worn sneakers.
YEAH, YOU COULD SLIP IN THOSE SHOES.
HERE. Get on.
?!

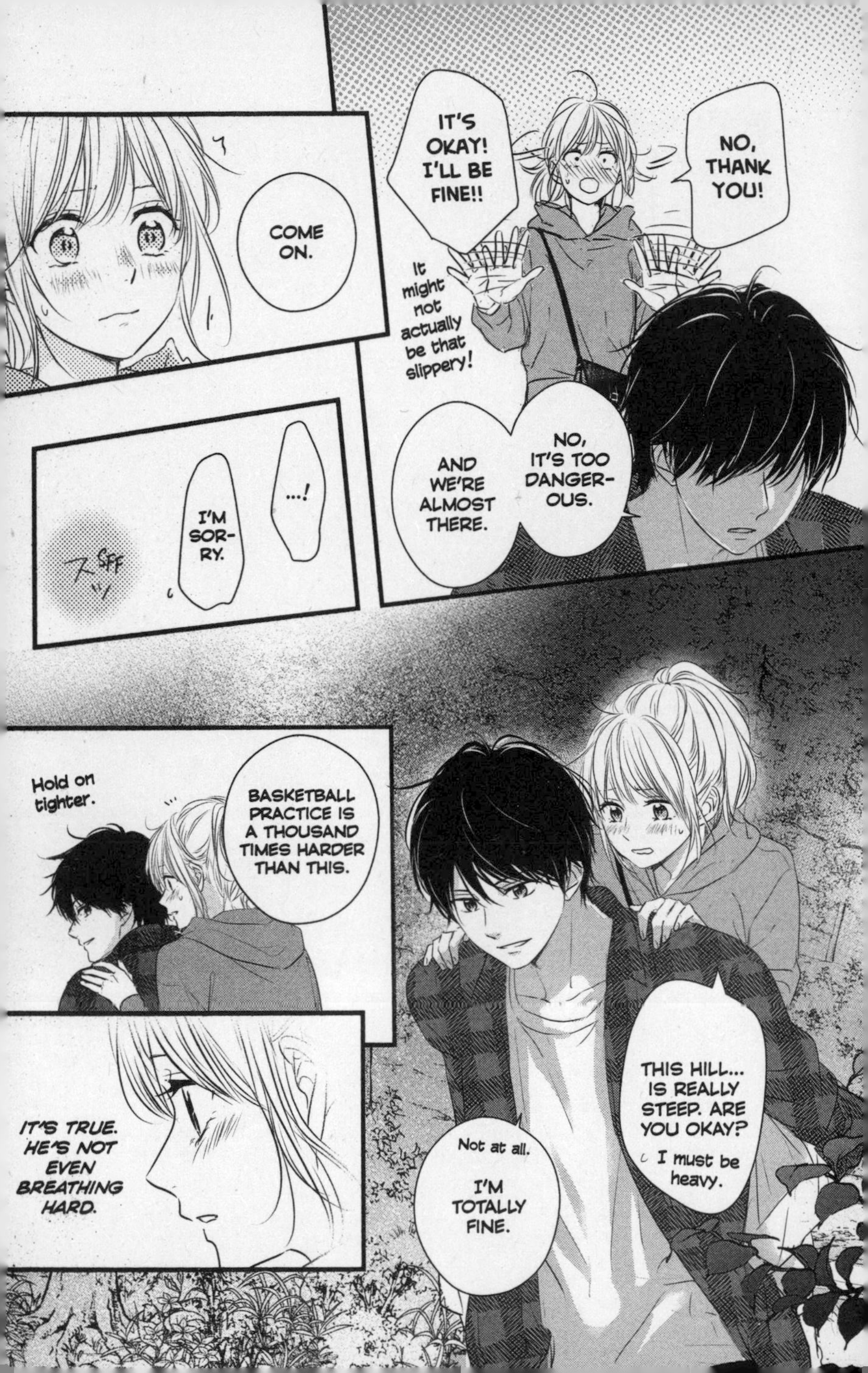
IT'S OKAY! I'LL BE FINE!!
NO, THANK YOU!
It might not actually be that slippery!
NO, IT'S TOO DANGER-OUS.
AND WE'RE ALMOST THERE.
COME ON.
...!
I'M SOR-RY.
SFF
THIS HILL... IS REALLY STEEP. ARE YOU OKAY?
I must be heavy.
Not at all.
I'M TOTALLY FINE.
BASKETBALL PRACTICE IS A THOUSAND TIMES HARDER THAN THIS.
Hold on tighter.
IT'S TRUE. HE'S NOT EVEN BREATHING HARD.

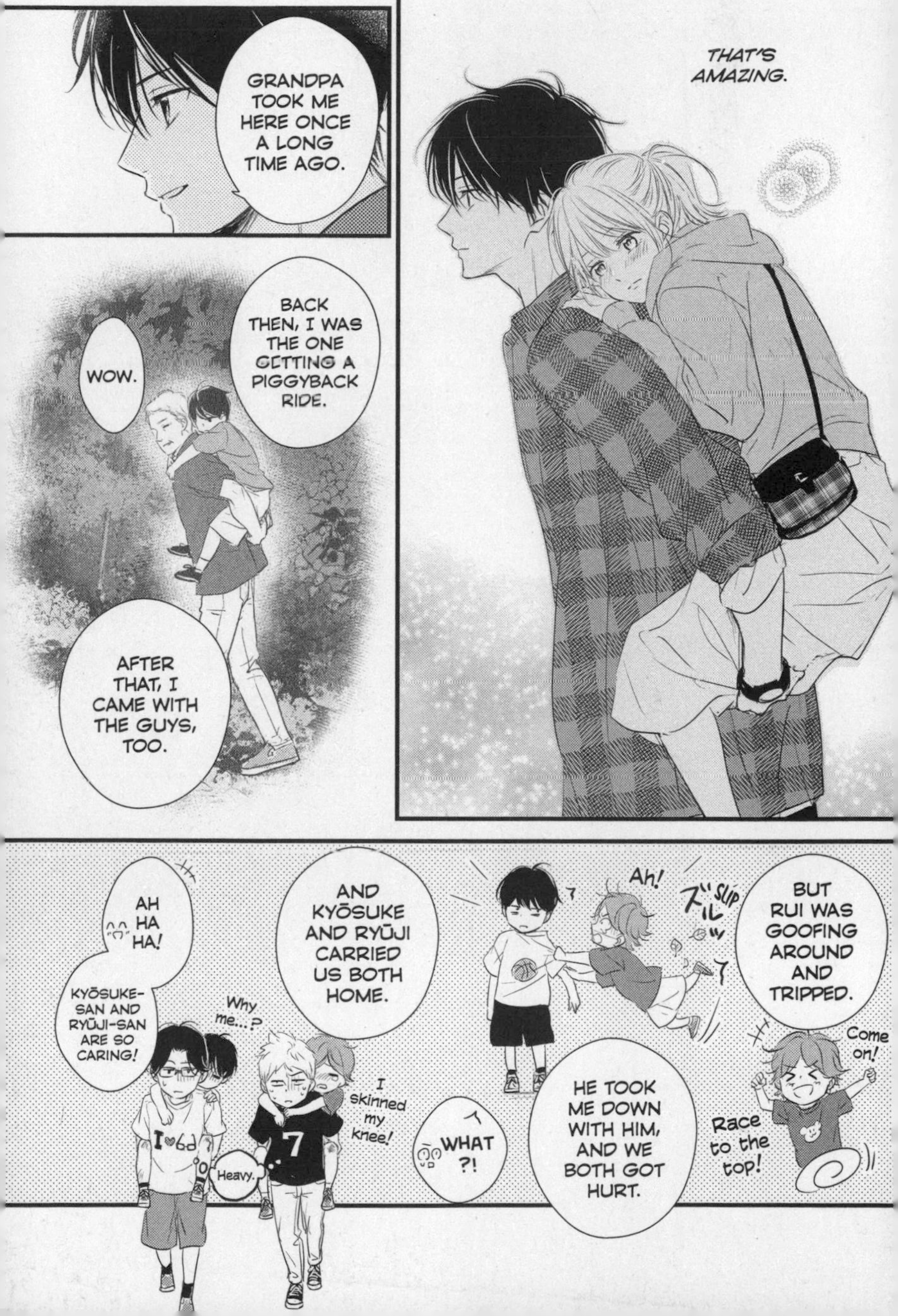
THAT'S AMAZING.
GRANDPA TOOK ME HERE ONCE A LONG TIME AGO.
BACK THEN, I WAS THE ONE GETTING A PIGGYBACK RIDE.
WOW.
AFTER THAT, I CAME WITH THE GUYS, TOO.
BUT RUI WAS GOOFING AROUND AND TRIPPED.
Come on!
Race to the top!
Ah!
SLIP
HE TOOK ME DOWN WITH HIM, AND WE BOTH GOT HURT.
WHAT?!
AND KYŌSUKE AND RYŪJI CARRIED US BOTH HOME.
I skinned my knee!
Why me...?
Heavy.
AH HA HA!
KYŌSUKE-SAN AND RYŪJI-SAN ARE SO CARING!

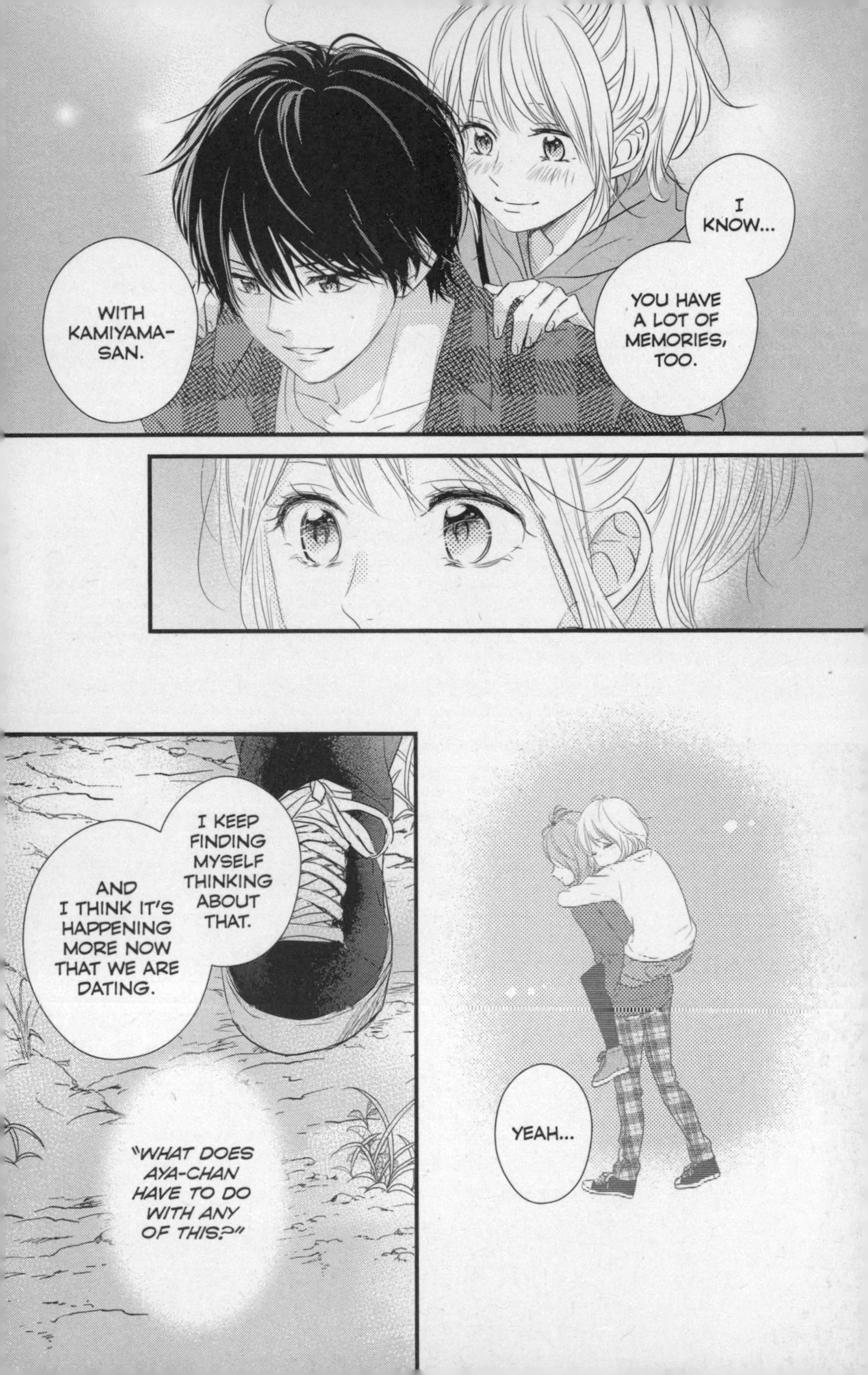
I KNOW...
YOU HAVE A LOT OF MEMORIES, TOO.
WITH KAMIYAMA-SAN.
YEAH...
I KEEP FINDING MYSELF THINKING ABOUT THAT.
AND I THINK IT'S HAPPENING MORE NOW THAT WE ARE DATING.
"WHAT DOES AYA-CHAN HAVE TO DO WITH ANY OF THIS?"

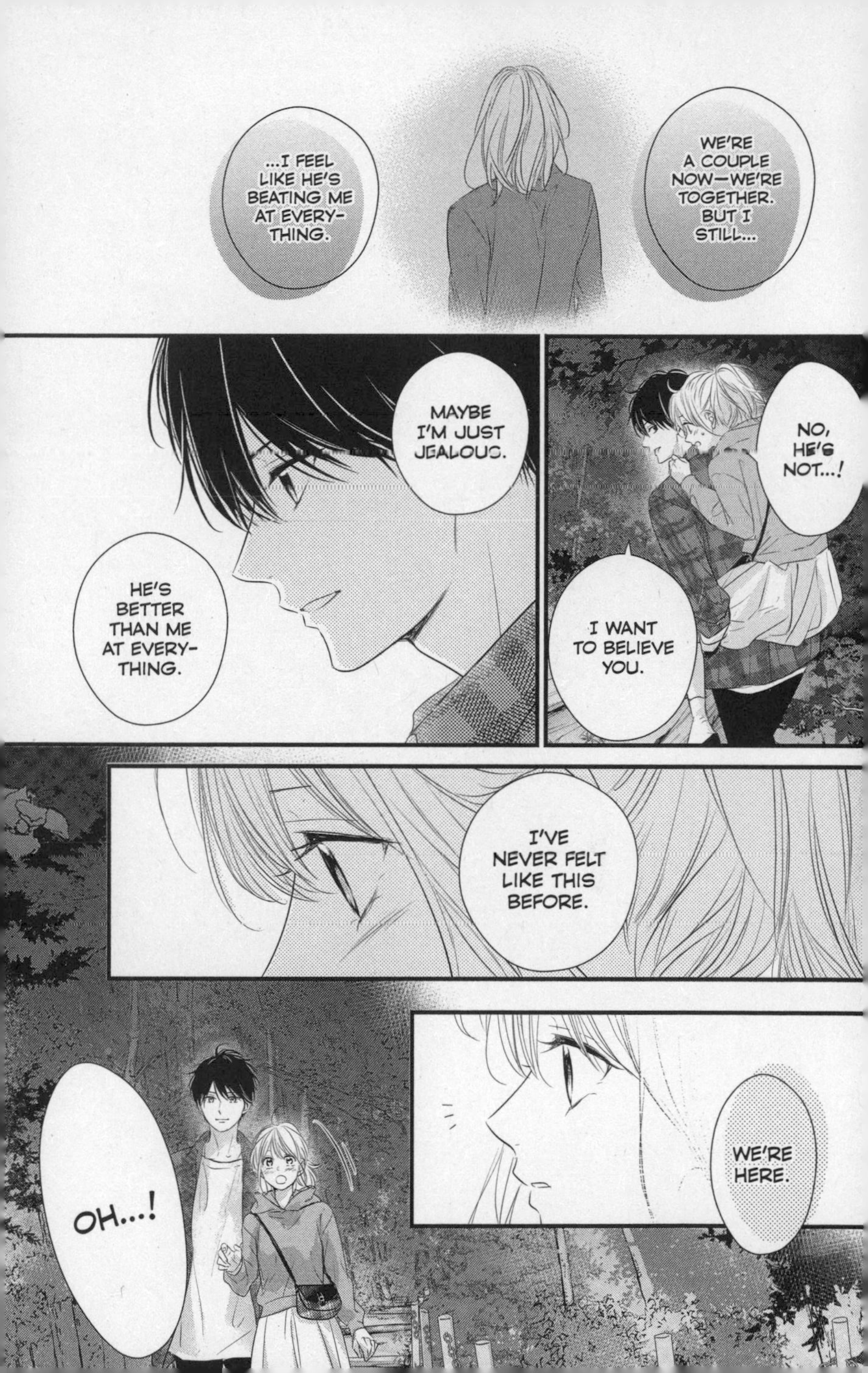
WE'RE A COUPLE NOW—WE'RE TOGETHER. BUT I STILL...
...I FEEL LIKE HE'S BEATING ME AT EVERYTHING.
NO, HE'S NOT...!
I WANT TO BELIEVE YOU.
MAYBE I'M JUST JEALOUS.
HE'S BETTER THAN ME AT EVERYTHING.
I'VE NEVER FELT LIKE THIS BEFORE.
WE'RE HERE.
OH...!

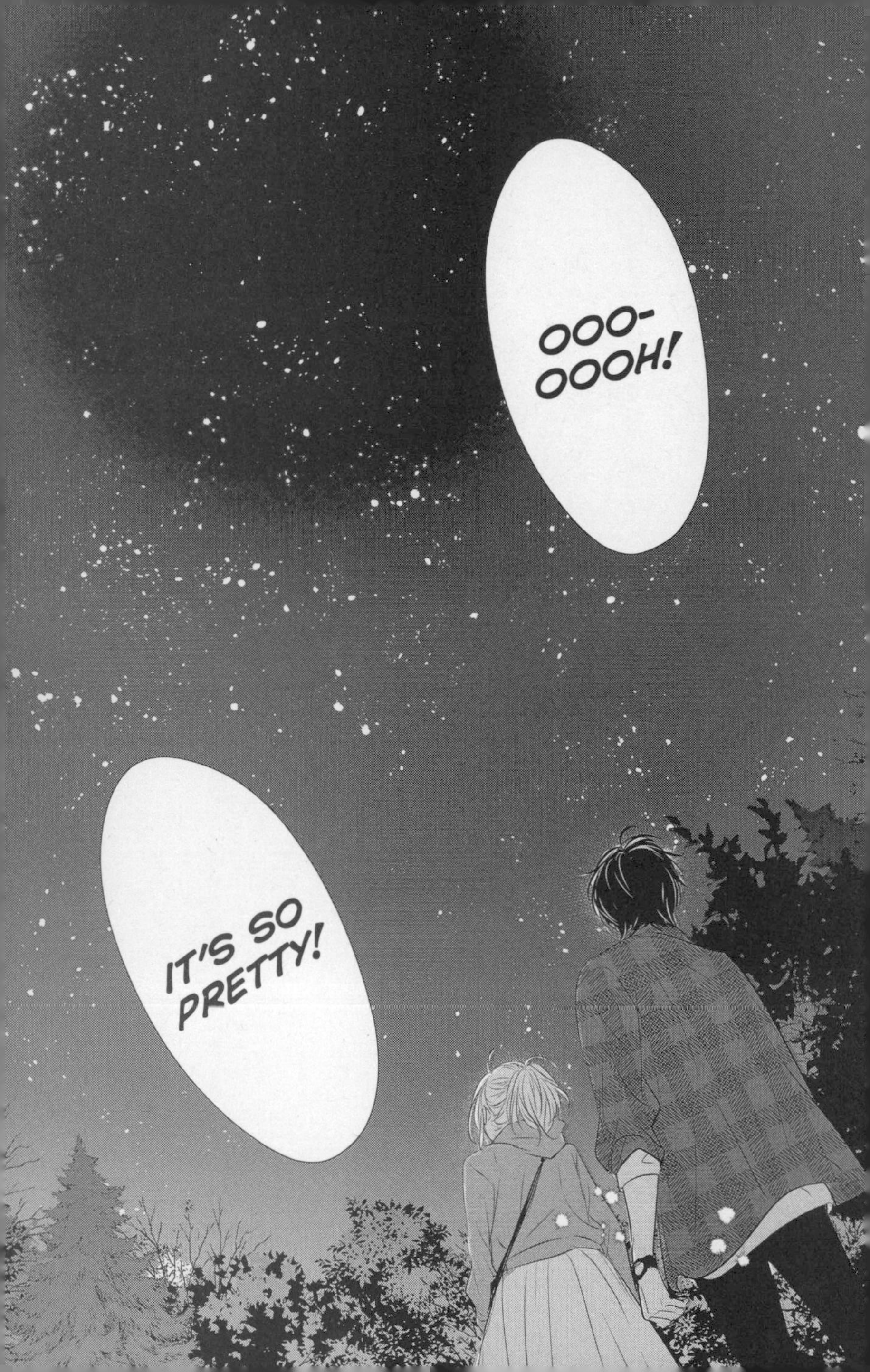
OOO-OOOH!
IT'S SO PRETTY!

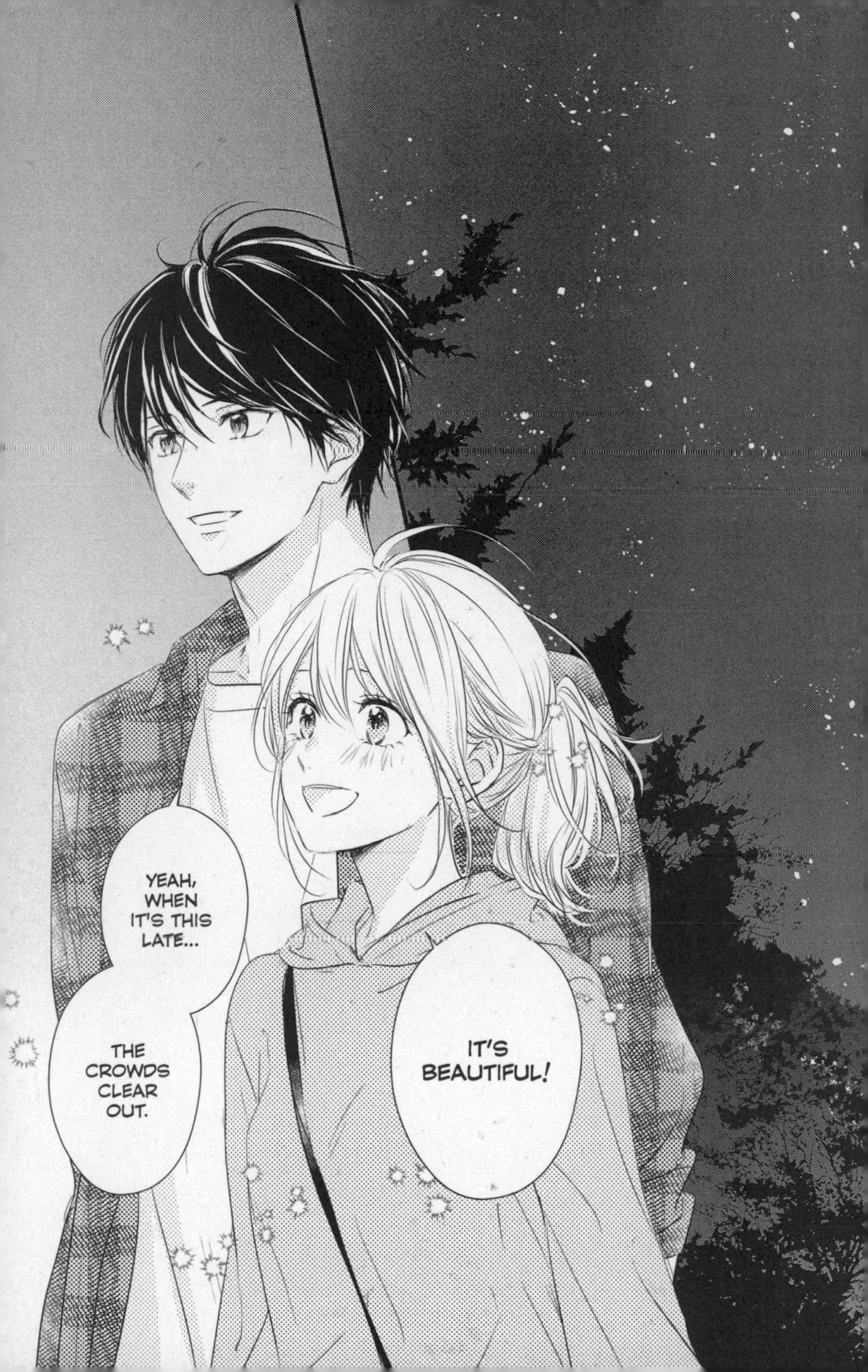
IT'S BEAUTIFUL!
YEAH, WHEN IT'S THIS LATE...
THE CROWDS CLEAR OUT.

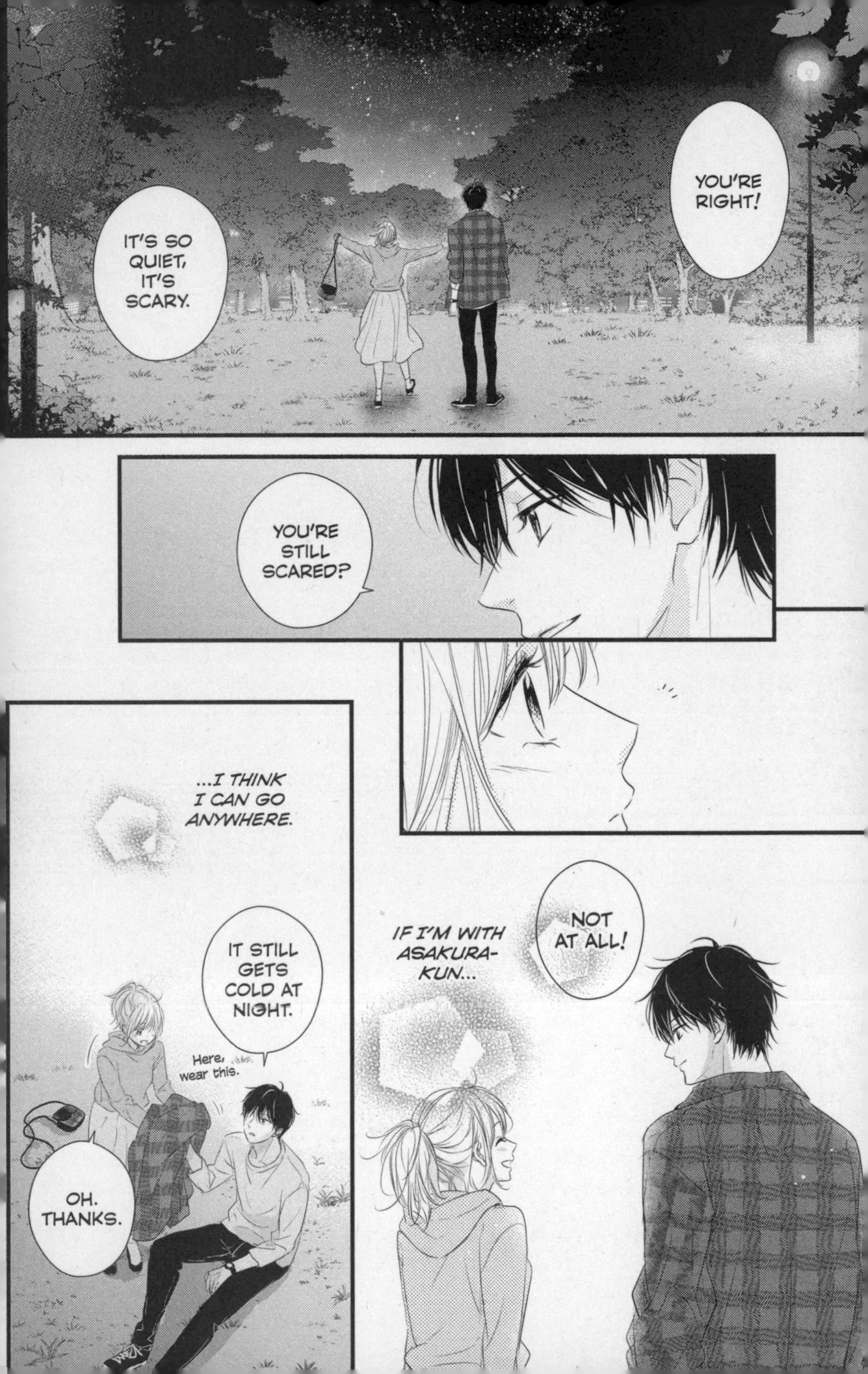
YOU'RE RIGHT!
IT'S SO QUIET, IT'S SCARY.
YOU'RE STILL SCARED?
NOT AT ALL!
IF I'M WITH ASAKURA-KUN...
...I THINK I CAN GO ANYWHERE.
IT STILL GETS COLD AT NIGHT.
Here, wear this.
OH. THANKS.

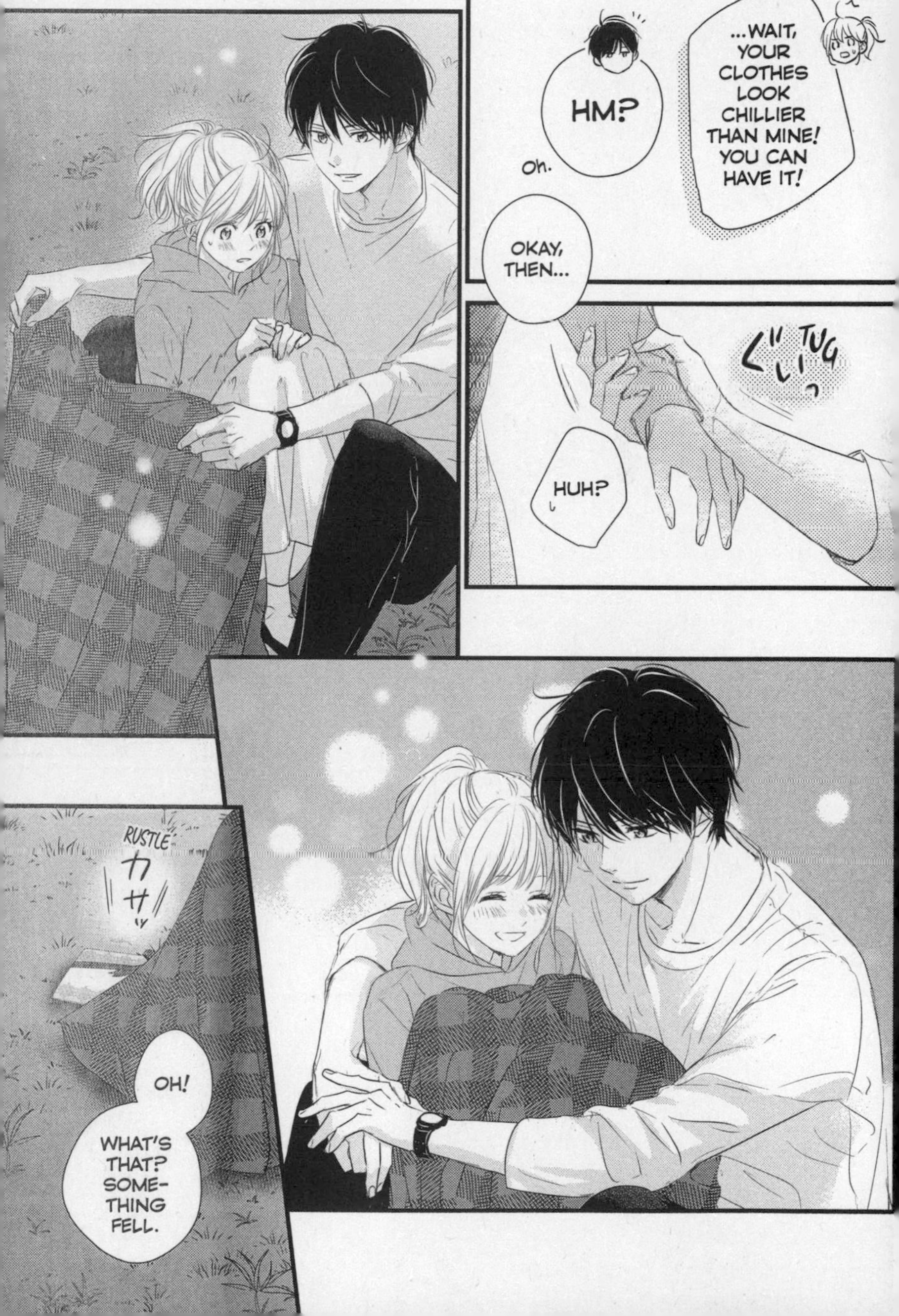
...WAIT, YOUR CLOTHES LOOK CHILLIER THAN MINE! YOU CAN HAVE IT!
HM?
Oh.
OKAY, THEN...
TUG
HUH?
RUSTLE
OH!
WHAT'S THAT? SOME-THING FELL.

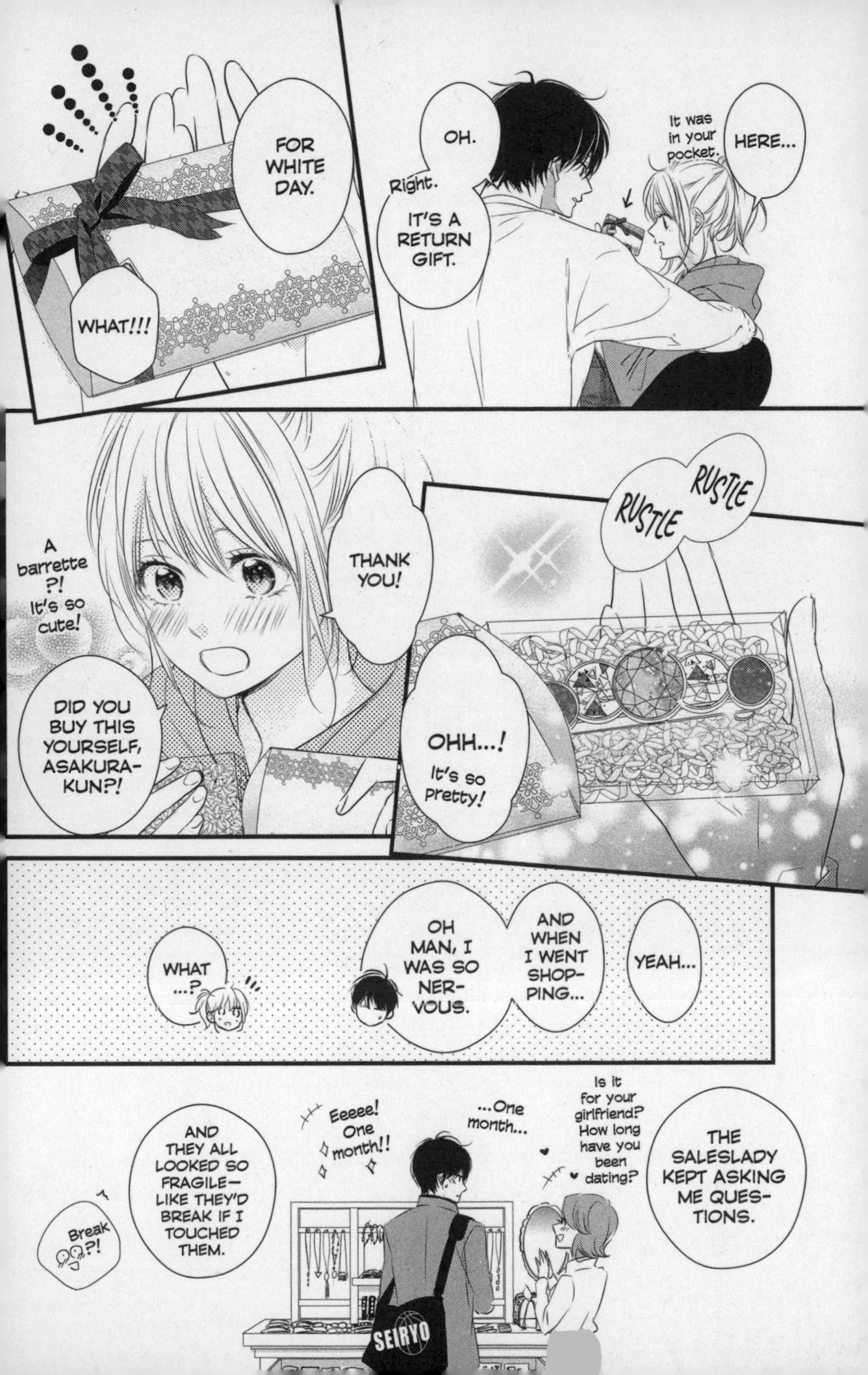
HERE...
It was in your pocket.
OH.
Right.
IT'S A RETURN GIFT.
FOR WHITE DAY.
WHAT!!!
RUSTLE
RUSTLE
OHH...! It's so pretty!
THANK YOU!
A barrette?! It's so cute!
DID YOU BUY THIS YOURSELF, ASAKURA-KUN?!
YEAH...
AND WHEN I WENT SHOP-PING...
OH MAN, I WAS SO NER-VOUS.
WHAT...?
THE SALESLADY KEPT ASKING ME QUES-TIONS.
Is it for your girlfriend? How long have you been dating?
...One month...
Eeeee! One month!!
SEIRYO
AND THEY ALL LOOKED SO FRAGILE—LIKE THEY'D BREAK IF I TOUCHED THEM.
Break?!

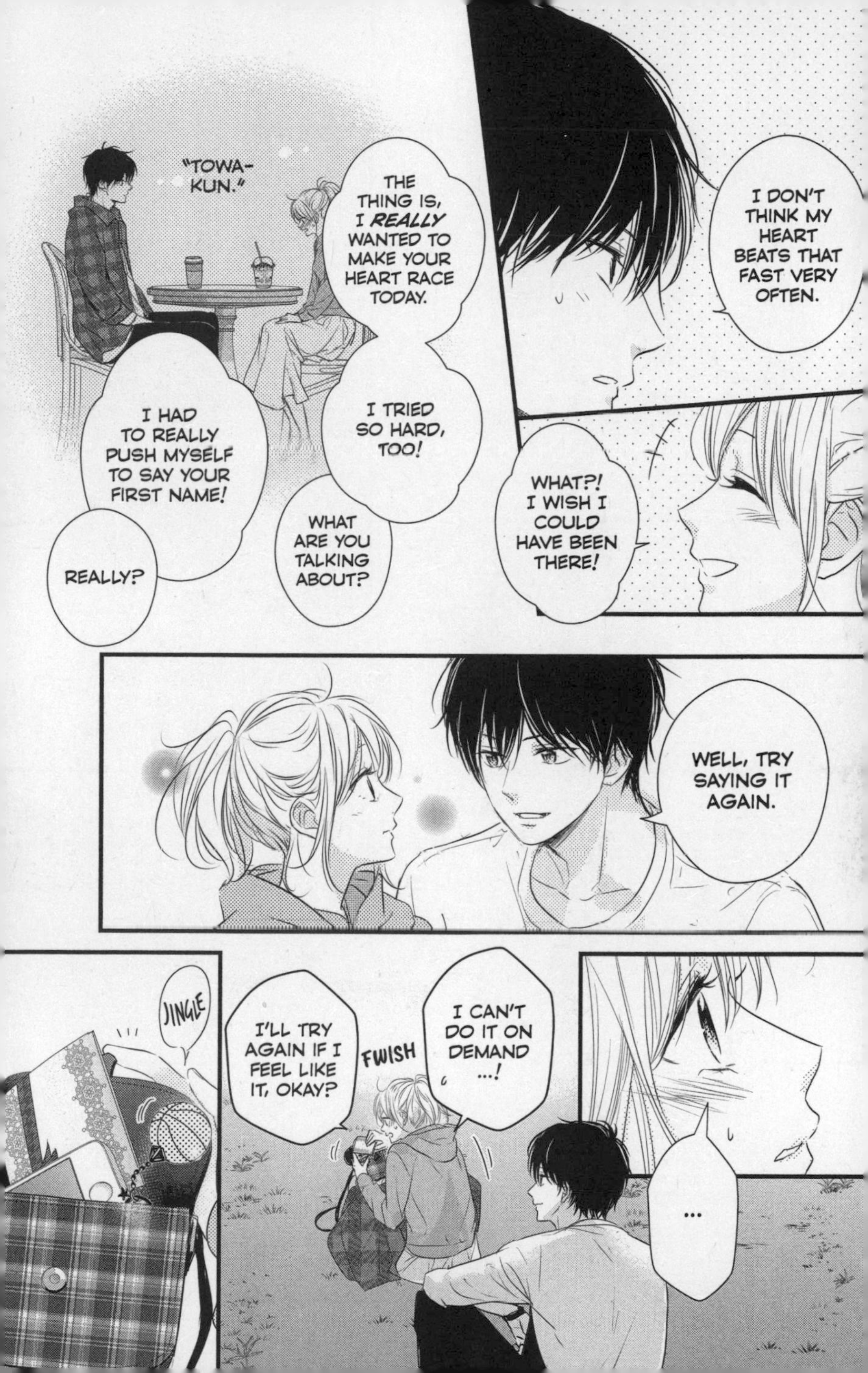
I DON'T THINK MY HEART BEATS THAT FAST VERY OFTEN.
WHAT?! I WISH I COULD HAVE BEEN THERE!
"TOWA-KUN."
THE THING IS, I *REALLY* WANTED TO MAKE YOUR HEART RACE TODAY.
I TRIED SO HARD, TOO!
I HAD TO REALLY PUSH MYSELF TO SAY YOUR FIRST NAME!
WHAT ARE YOU TALKING ABOUT?
REALLY?
WELL, TRY SAYING IT AGAIN.
...
I CAN'T DO IT ON DEMAND ...!
FWISH
I'LL TRY AGAIN IF I FEEL LIKE IT, OKAY?
JINGLE

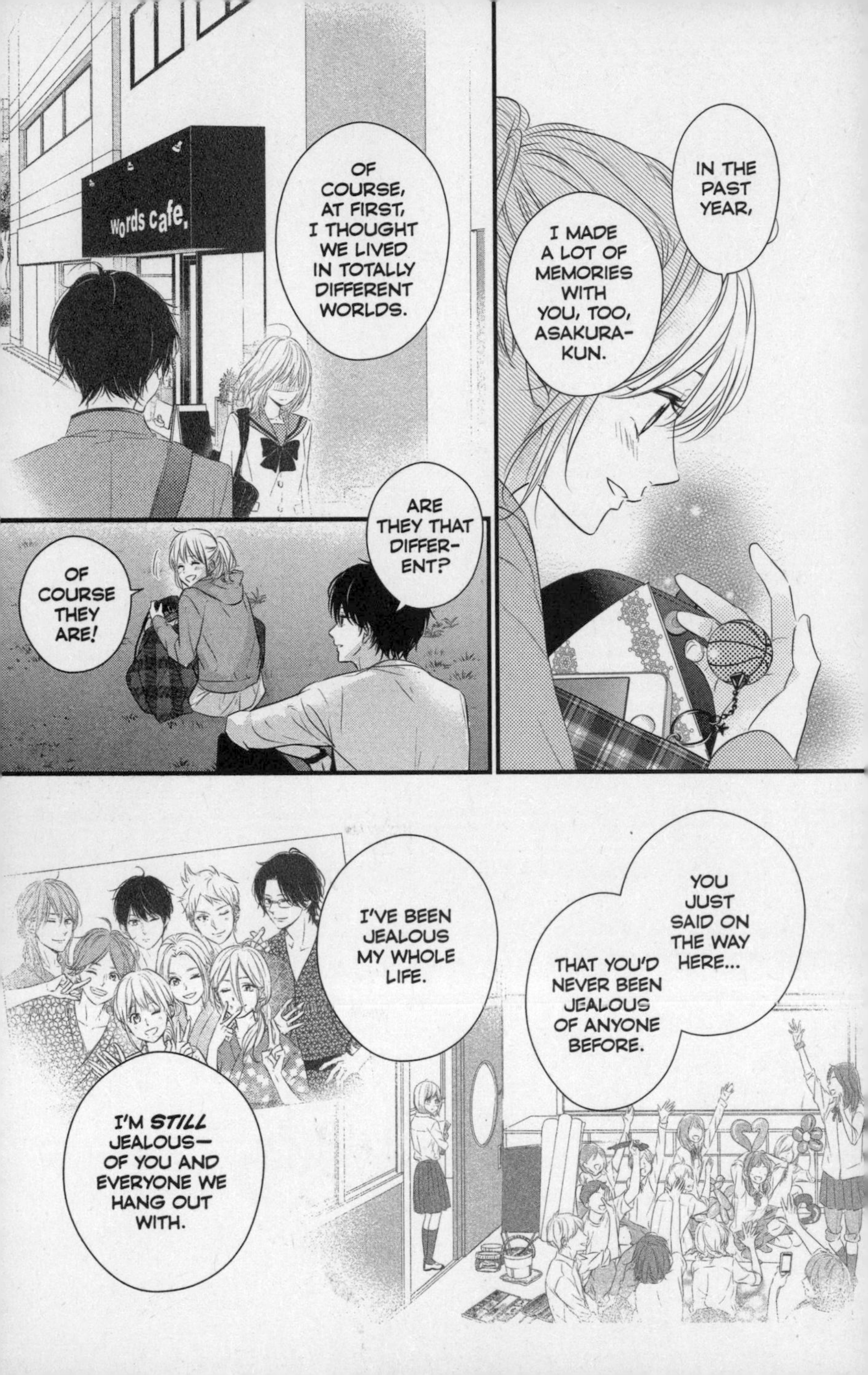
IN THE PAST YEAR,
I MADE A LOT OF MEMORIES WITH YOU, TOO, ASAKURA-KUN.
OF COURSE, AT FIRST, I THOUGHT WE LIVED IN TOTALLY DIFFERENT WORLDS.
Words cafe,
ARE THEY THAT DIFFER-ENT?
OF COURSE THEY ARE!
YOU JUST SAID ON THE WAY HERE...
THAT YOU'D NEVER BEEN JEALOUS OF ANYONE BEFORE.
I'VE BEEN JEALOUS MY WHOLE LIFE.
I'M *STILL* JEALOUS— OF YOU AND EVERYONE WE HANG OUT WITH.

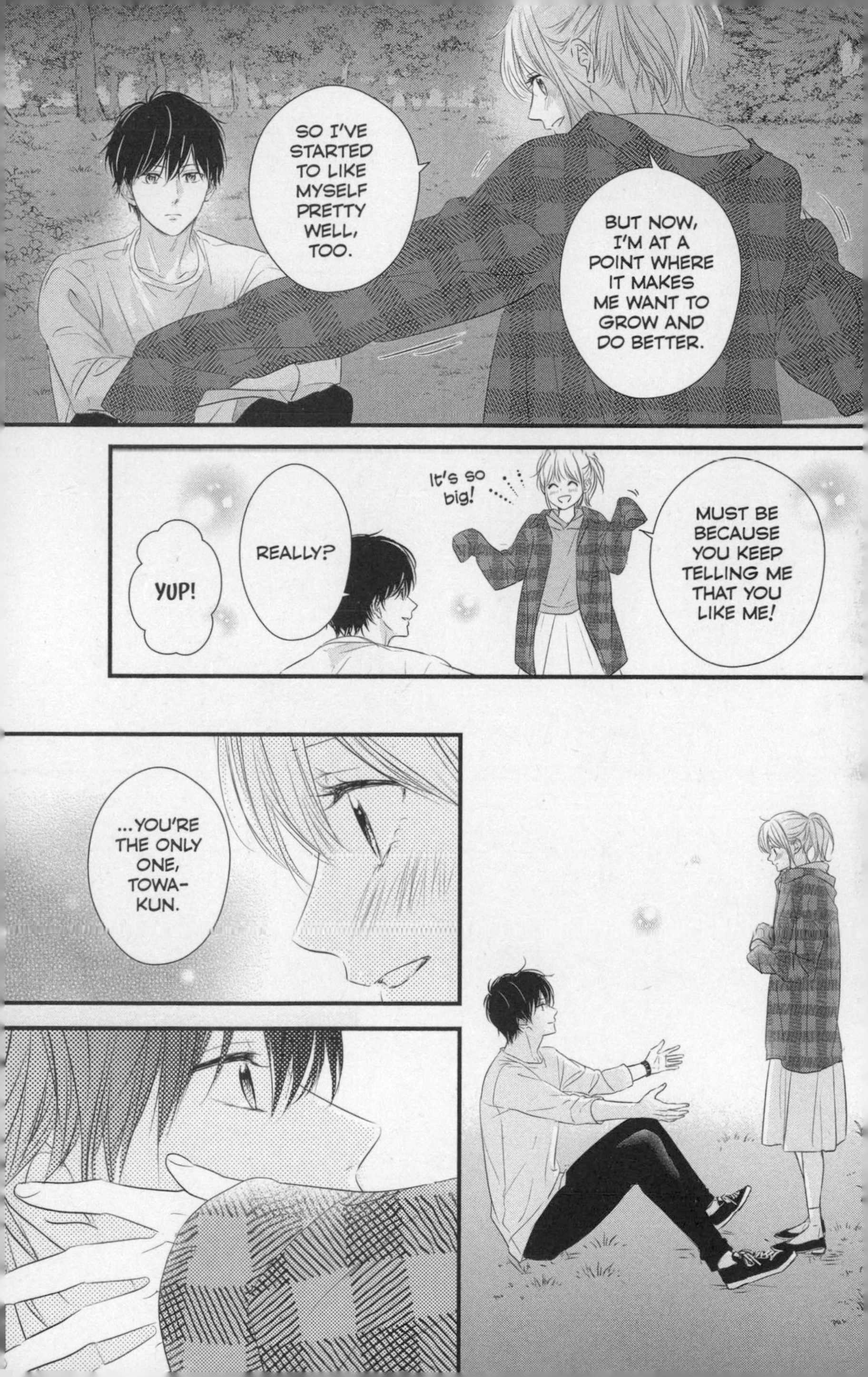
SO I'VE STARTED TO LIKE MYSELF PRETTY WELL, TOO.
BUT NOW, I'M AT A POINT WHERE IT MAKES ME WANT TO GROW AND DO BETTER.
MUST BE BECAUSE YOU KEEP TELLING ME THAT YOU LIKE ME!
It's so big!
REALLY?
YUP!
...YOU'RE THE ONLY ONE, TOWA-KUN.

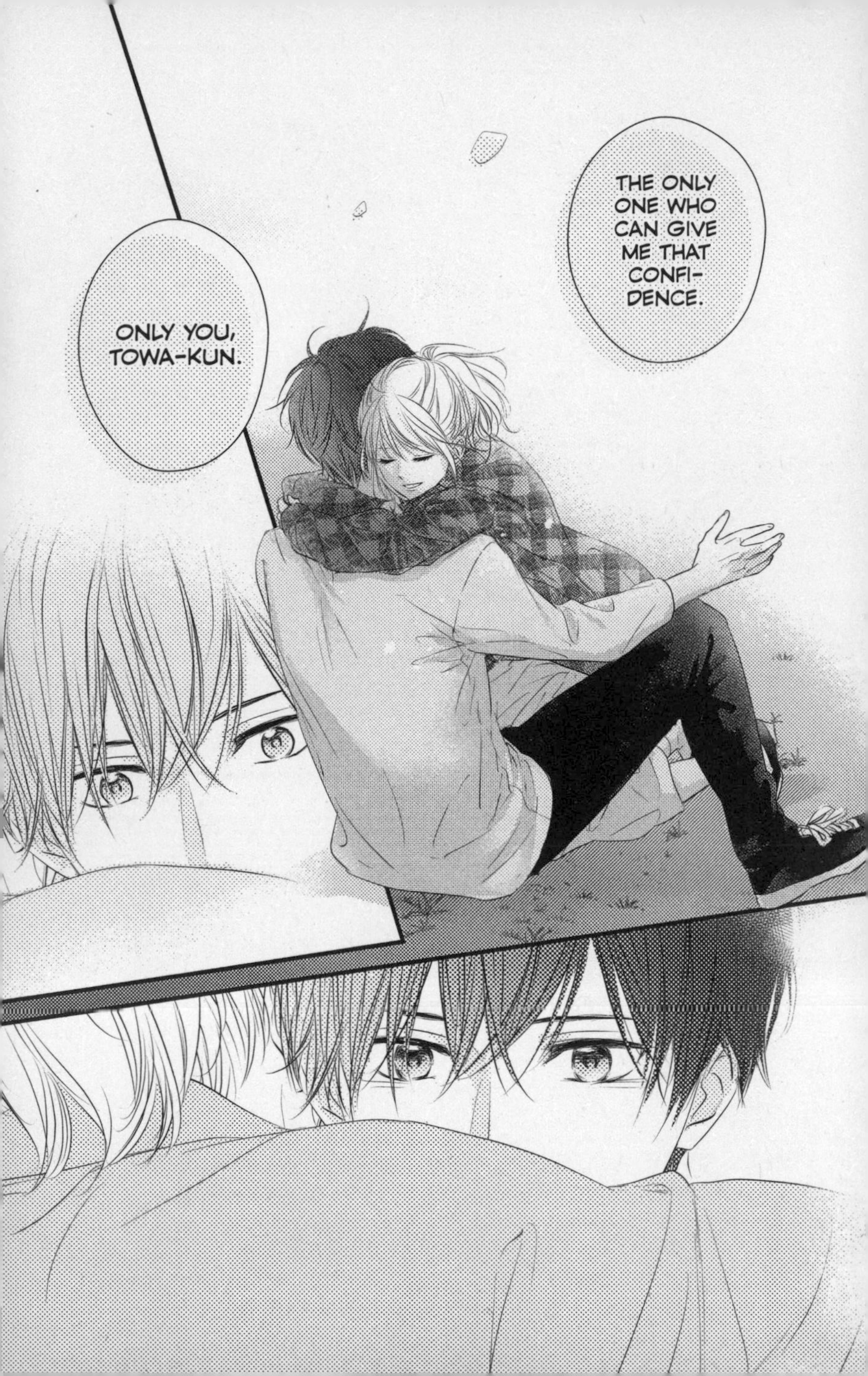
THE ONLY ONE WHO CAN GIVE ME THAT CONFI- DENCE.
ONLY YOU, TOWA-KUN.

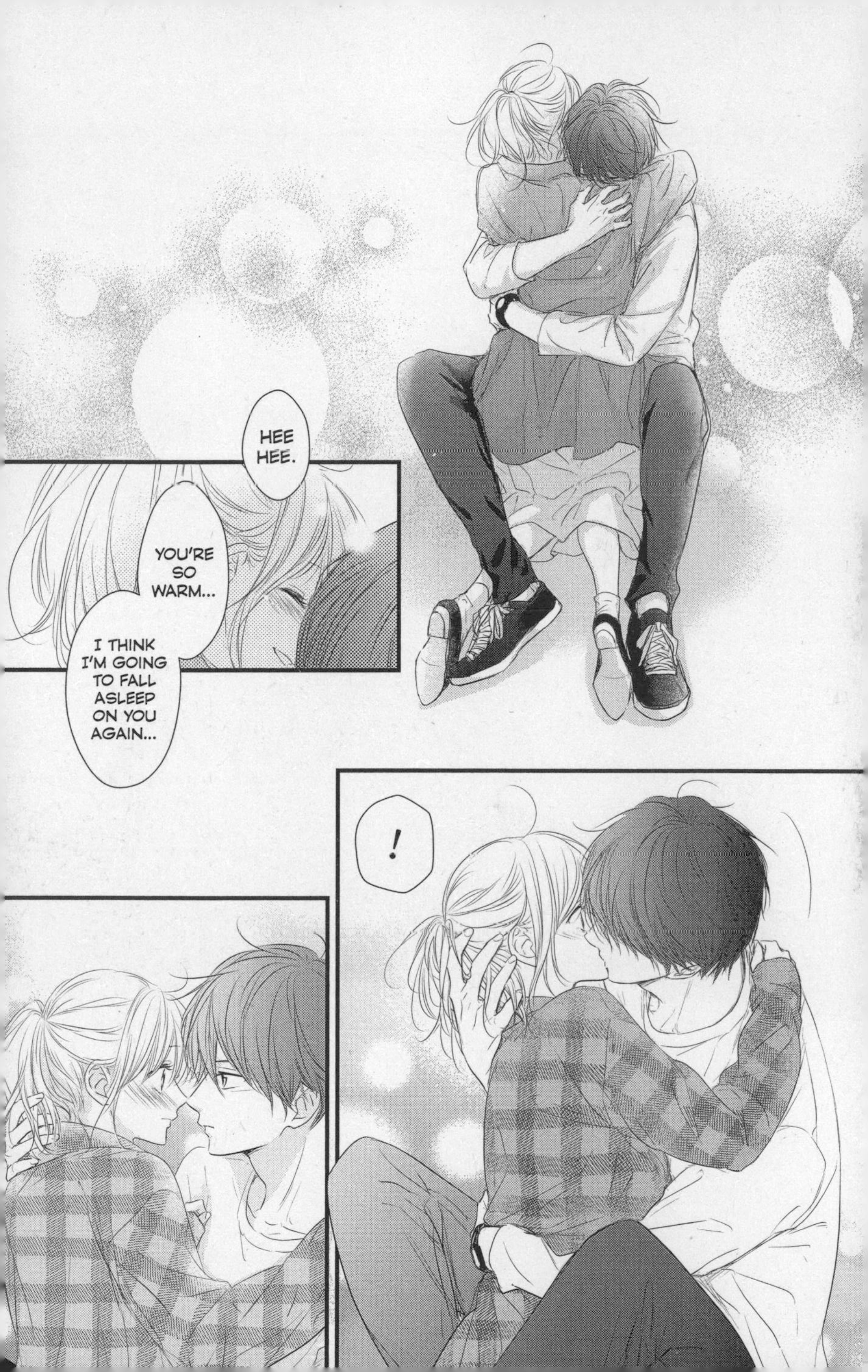
HEE HEE.
YOU'RE SO WARM...
I THINK I'M GOING TO FALL ASLEEP ON YOU AGAIN...
!

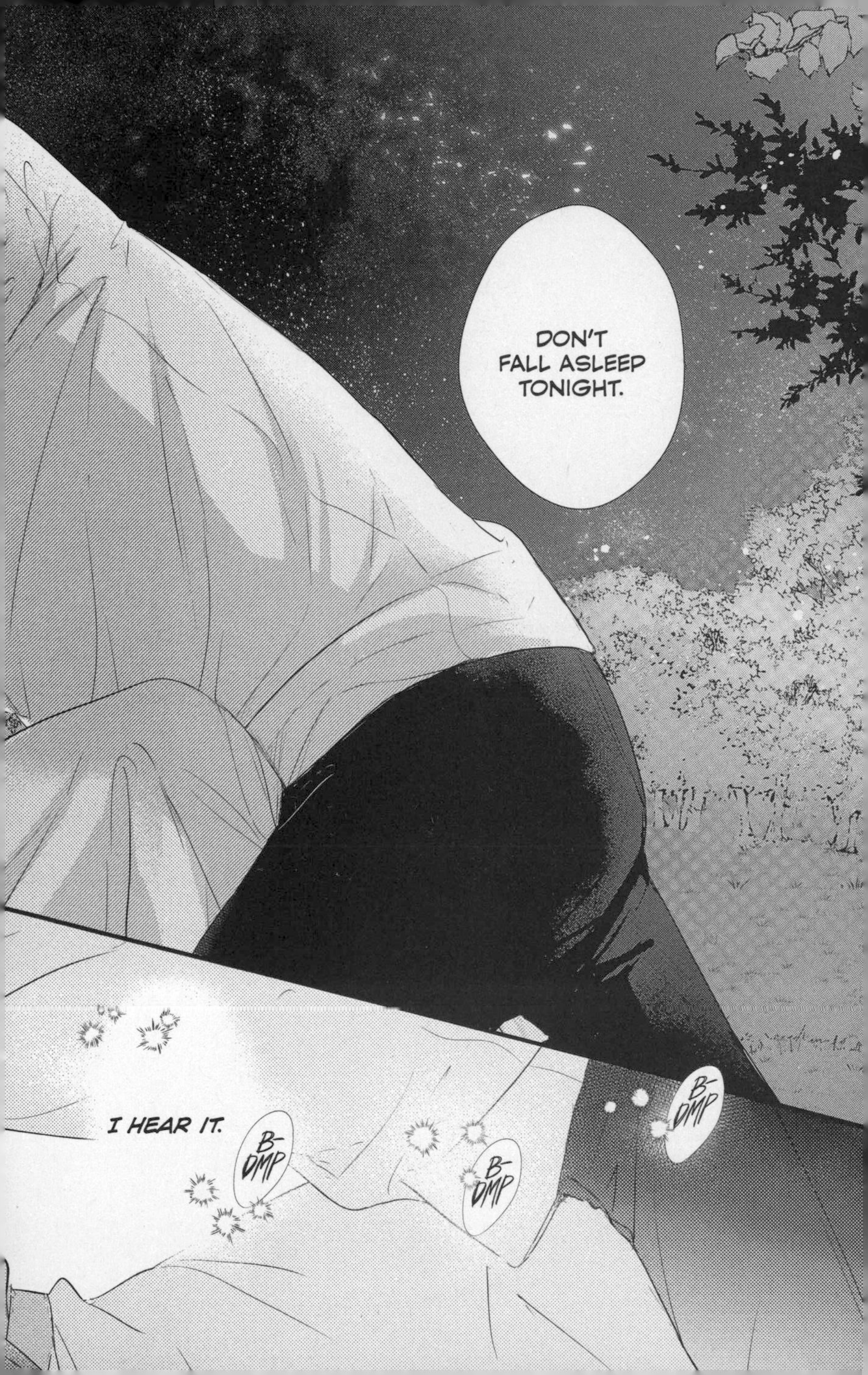
DON'T FALL ASLEEP TONIGHT.
B-DMP
B-DMP
I HEAR IT.
B-DMP

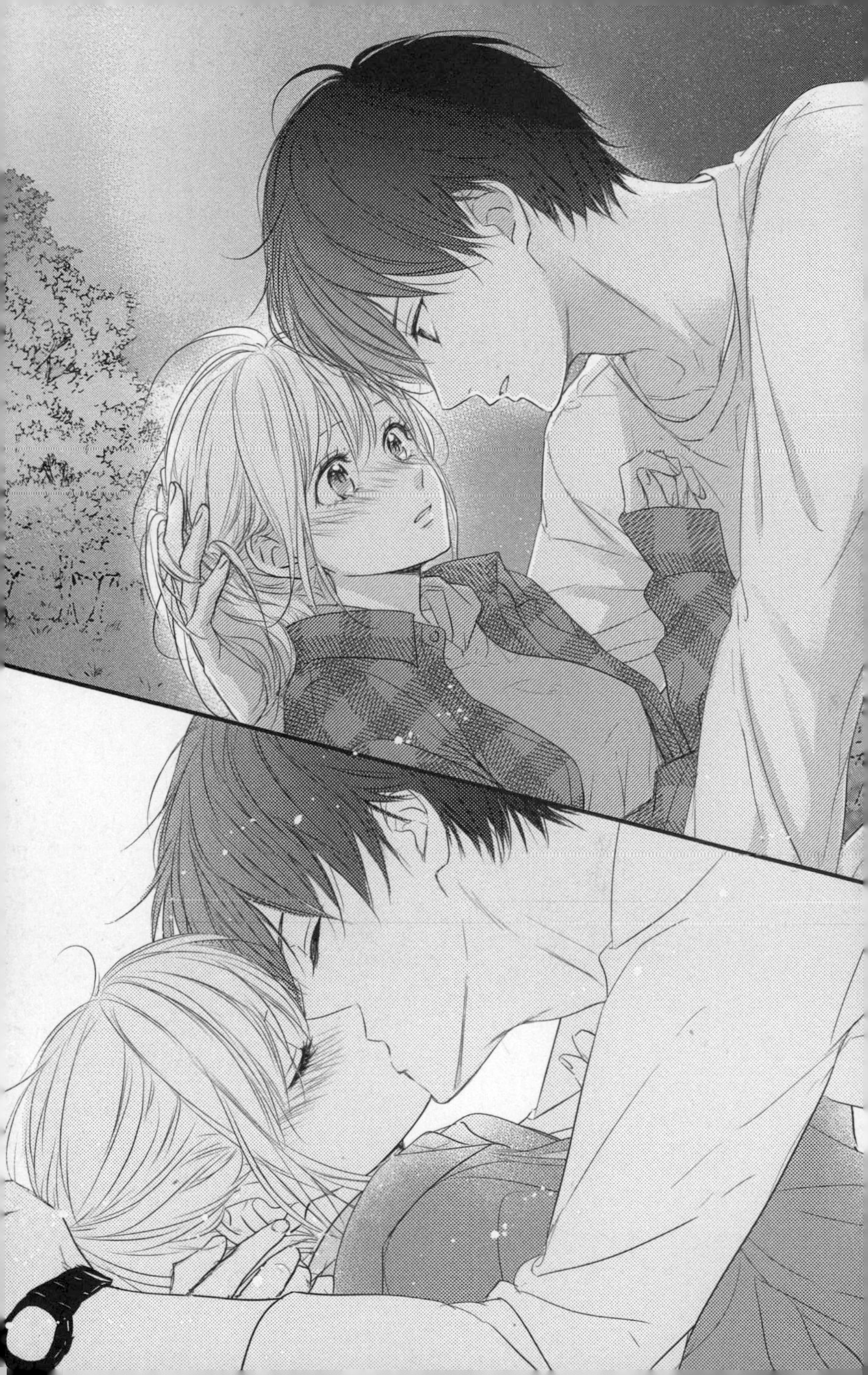

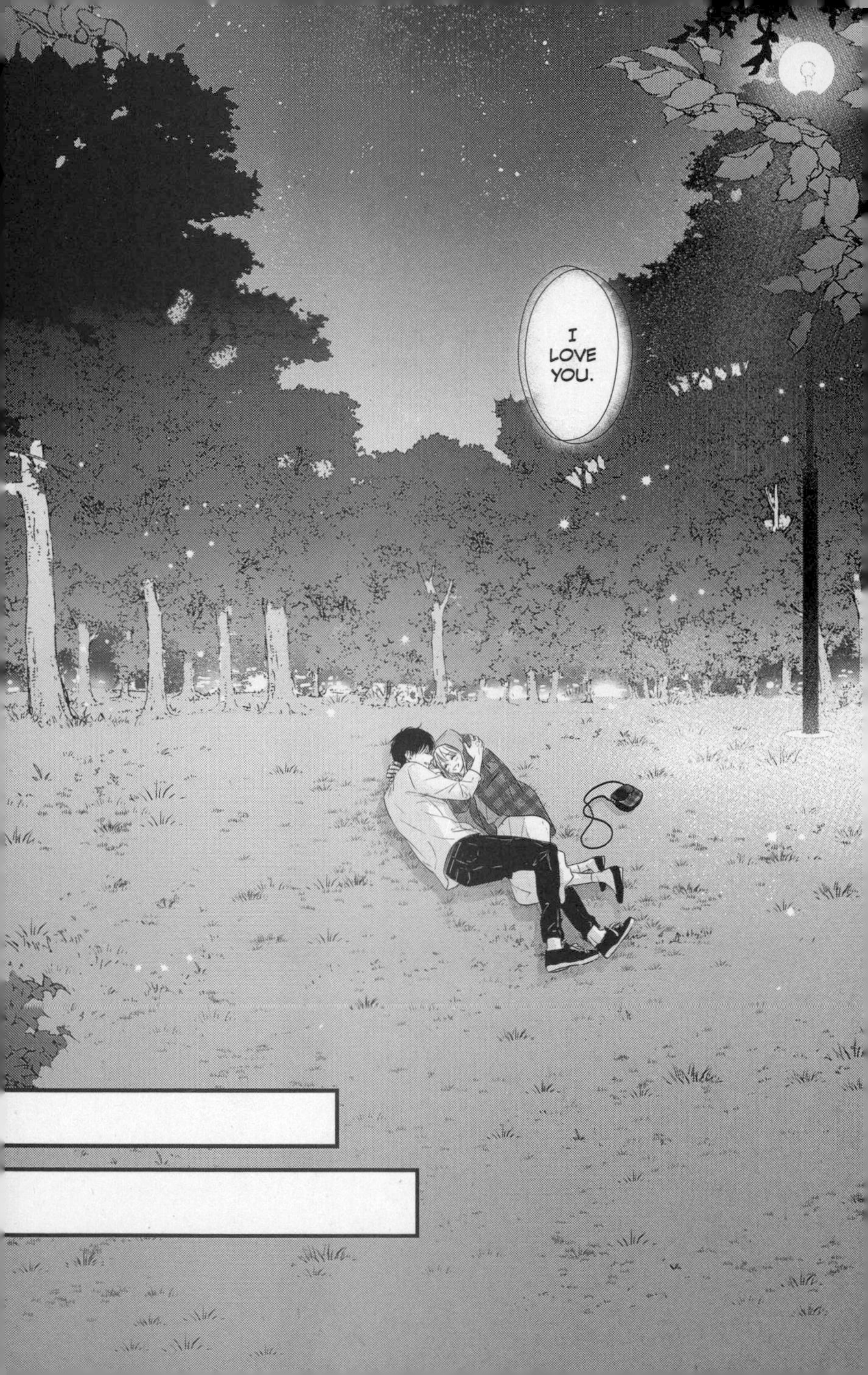
I LOVE YOU.

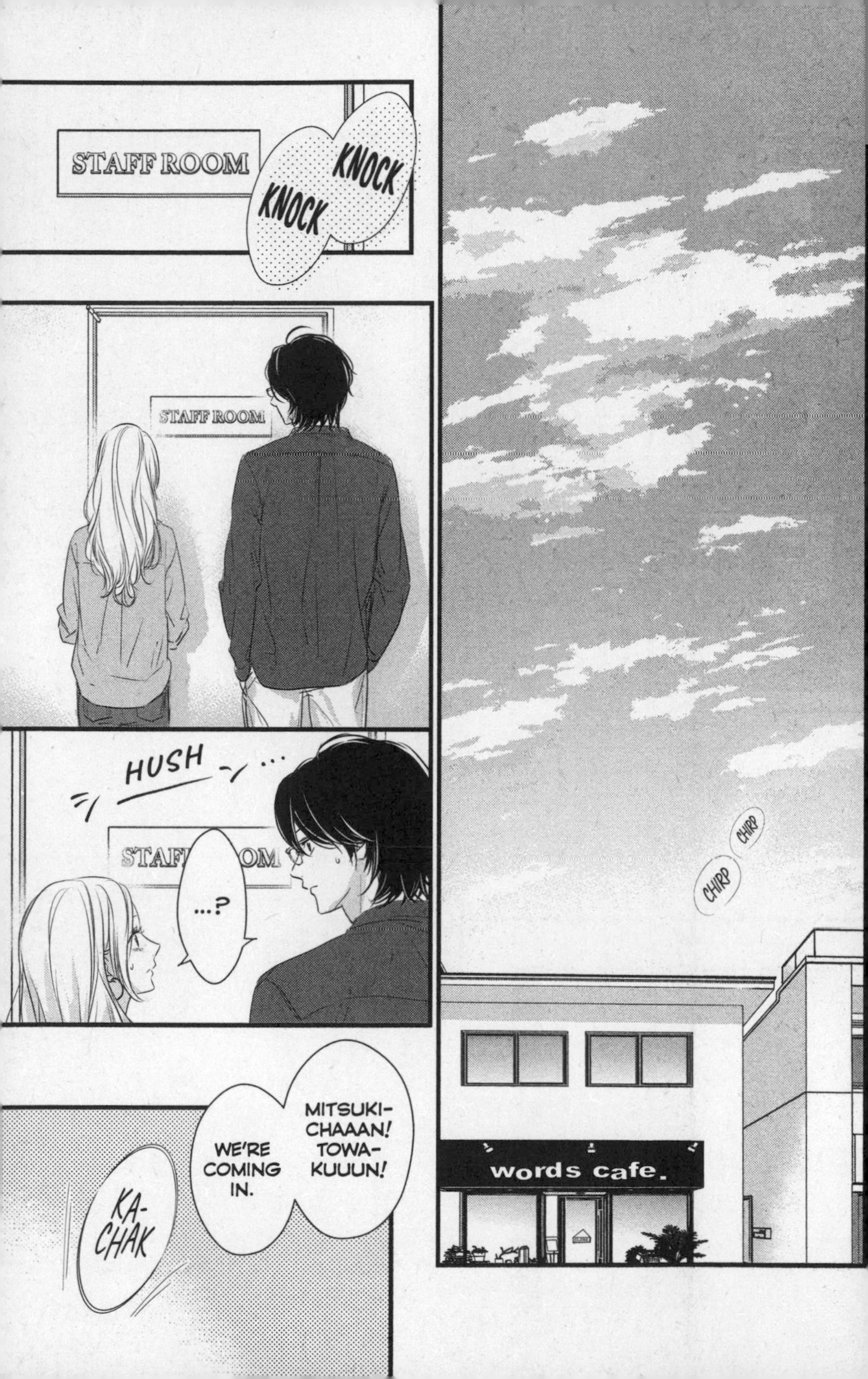
CHIRP
CHIRP
words cafe.
STAFF ROOM
KNOCK
KNOCK
STAFF ROOM
HUSH
...?
MITSUKI-CHAAAN! TOWA-KUUUN!
WE'RE COMING IN.
KA-CHAK

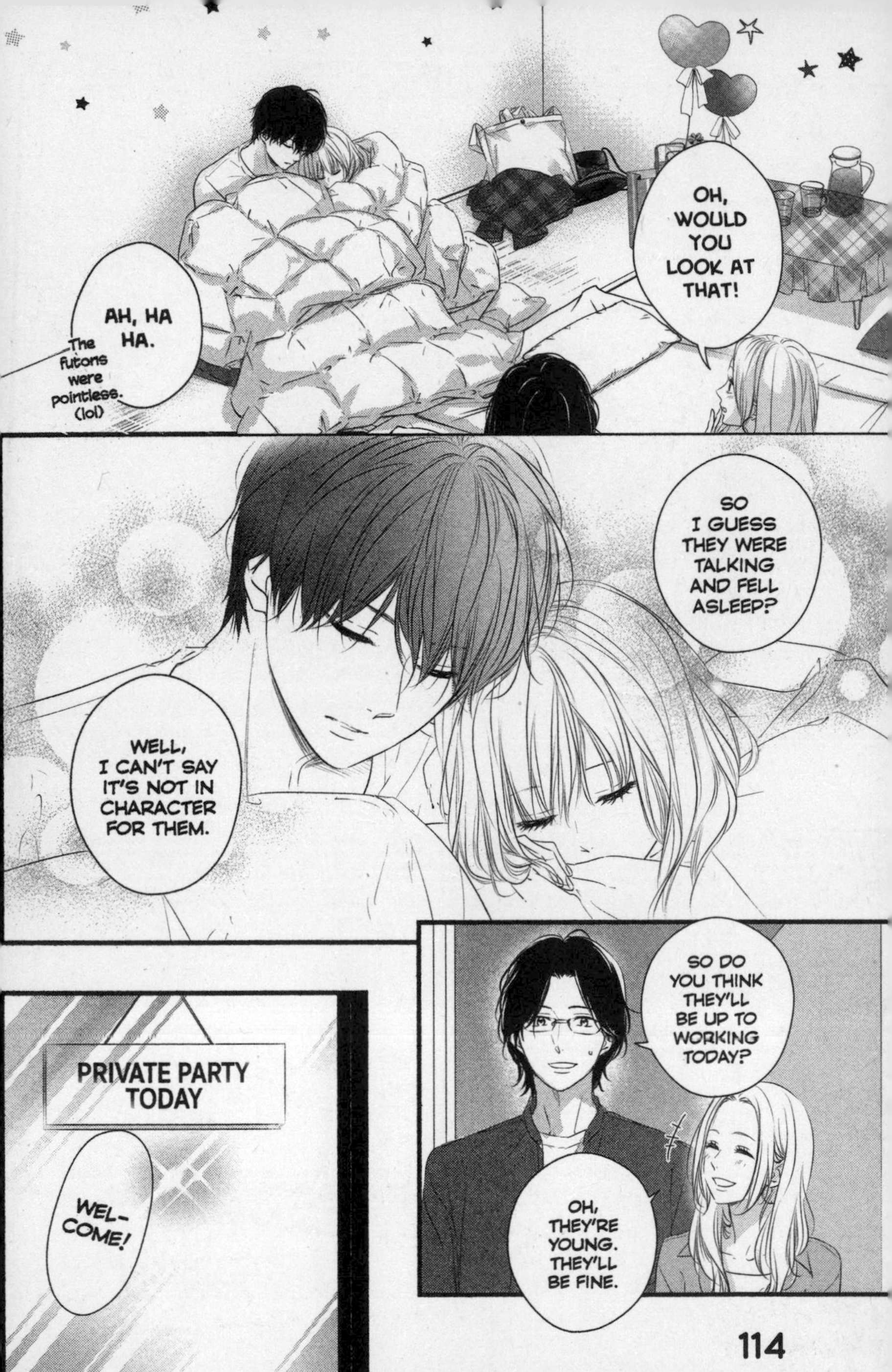
OH, WOULD YOU LOOK AT THAT!
AH, HA HA.
The futons were pointless. (lol)
SO I GUESS THEY WERE TALKING AND FELL ASLEEP?
WELL, I CAN'T SAY IT'S NOT IN CHARACTER FOR THEM.
SO DO YOU THINK THEY'LL BE UP TO WORKING TODAY?
OH, THEY'RE YOUNG. THEY'LL BE FINE.
PRIVATE PARTY TODAY
WEL-COME!

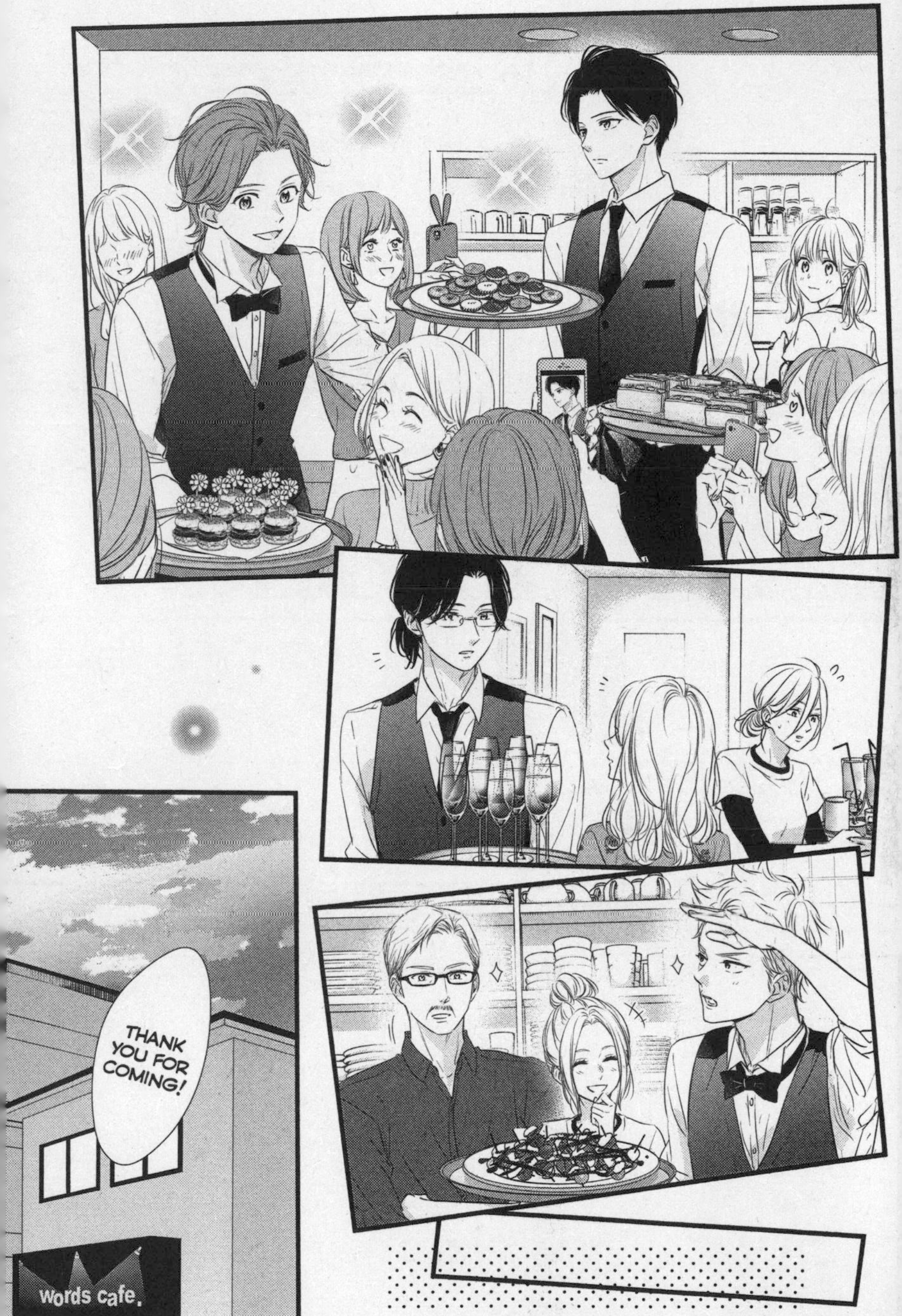
THANK YOU FOR COMING!
Words cafe.

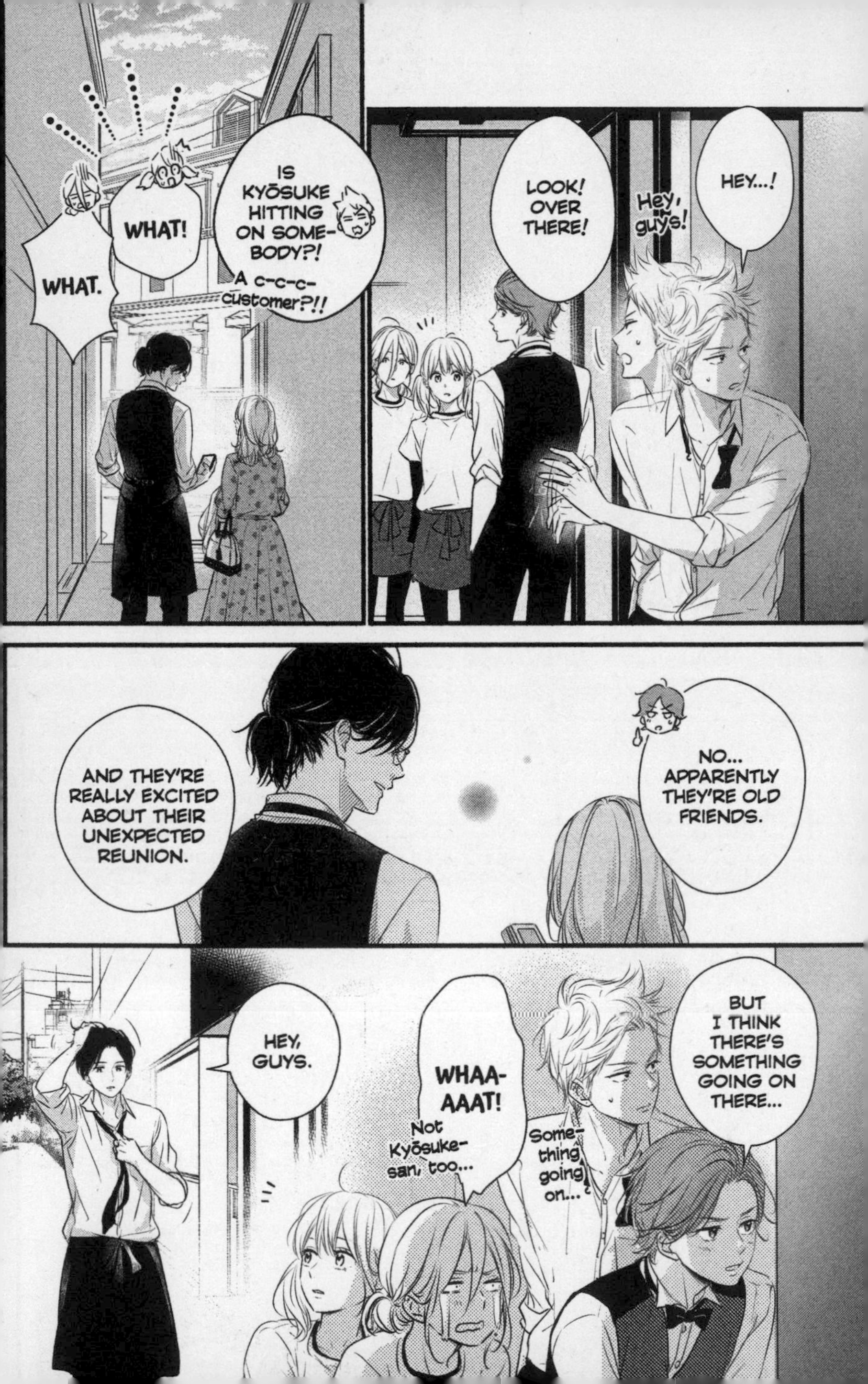
HEY...!
Hey, guys!
LOOK! OVER THERE!
IS KYŌSUKE HITTING ON SOMEBODY?!
A c-c-c-customer?!!
WHAT!
WHAT.
NO... APPARENTLY THEY'RE OLD FRIENDS.
AND THEY'RE REALLY EXCITED ABOUT THEIR UNEXPECTED REUNION.
BUT I THINK THERE'S SOMETHING GOING ON THERE...
Something going on...
WHAAAAAT!
Not Kyōsuke-san, too...
HEY, GUYS.

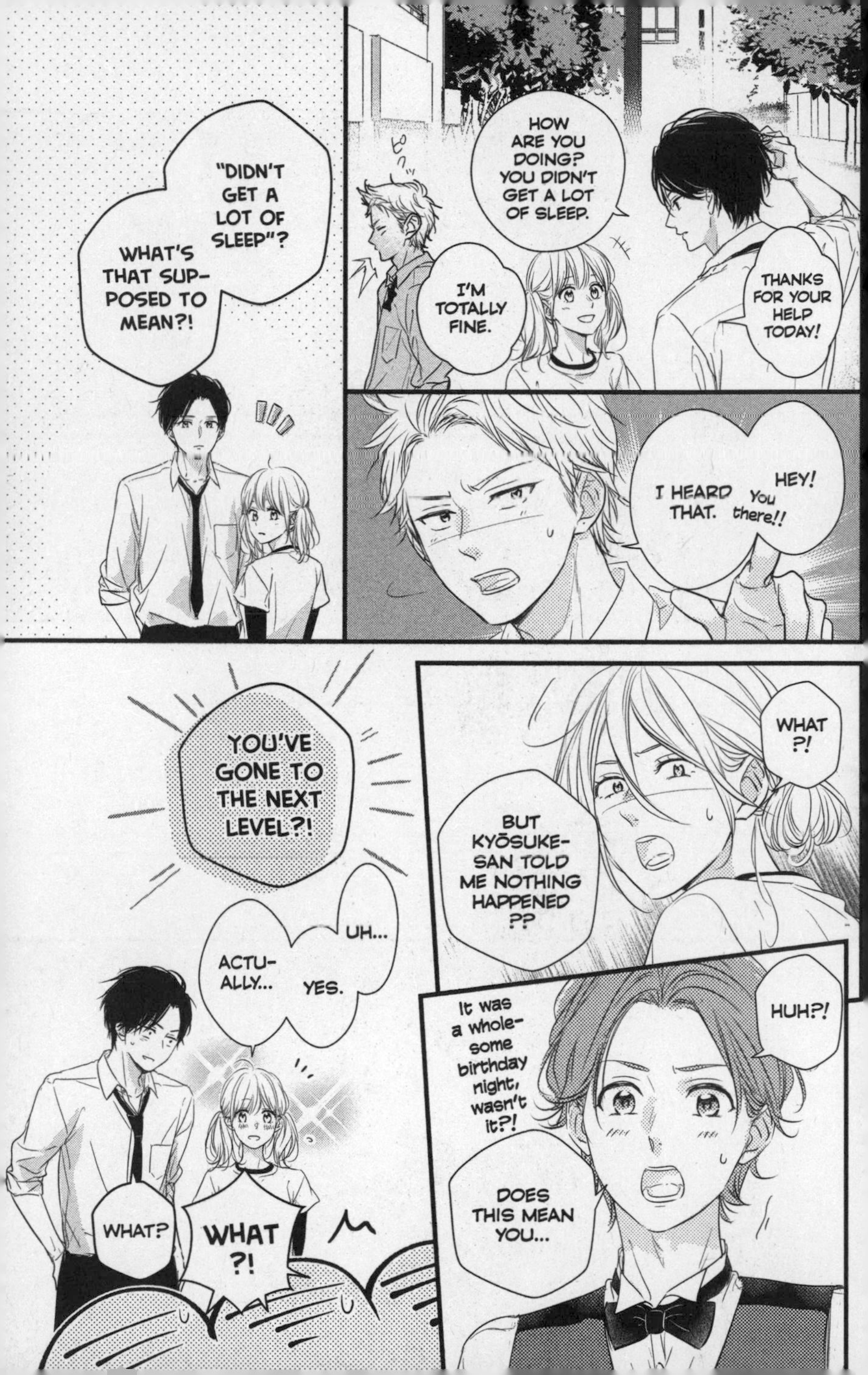
THANKS FOR YOUR HELP TODAY!
HOW ARE YOU DOING? YOU DIDN'T GET A LOT OF SLEEP.
I'M TOTALLY FINE.
HEY! You there!!
I HEARD THAT.
"DIDN'T GET A LOT OF SLEEP"?
WHAT'S THAT SUP-POSED TO MEAN?!
WHAT?!
BUT KYŌSUKE-SAN TOLD ME NOTHING HAPPENED??
HUH?!
It was a whole-some birthday night, wasn't it?!
DOES THIS MEAN YOU...
YOU'VE GONE TO THE NEXT LEVEL?!
UH...
ACTU-ALLY...
YES.
WHAT?!
WHAT?

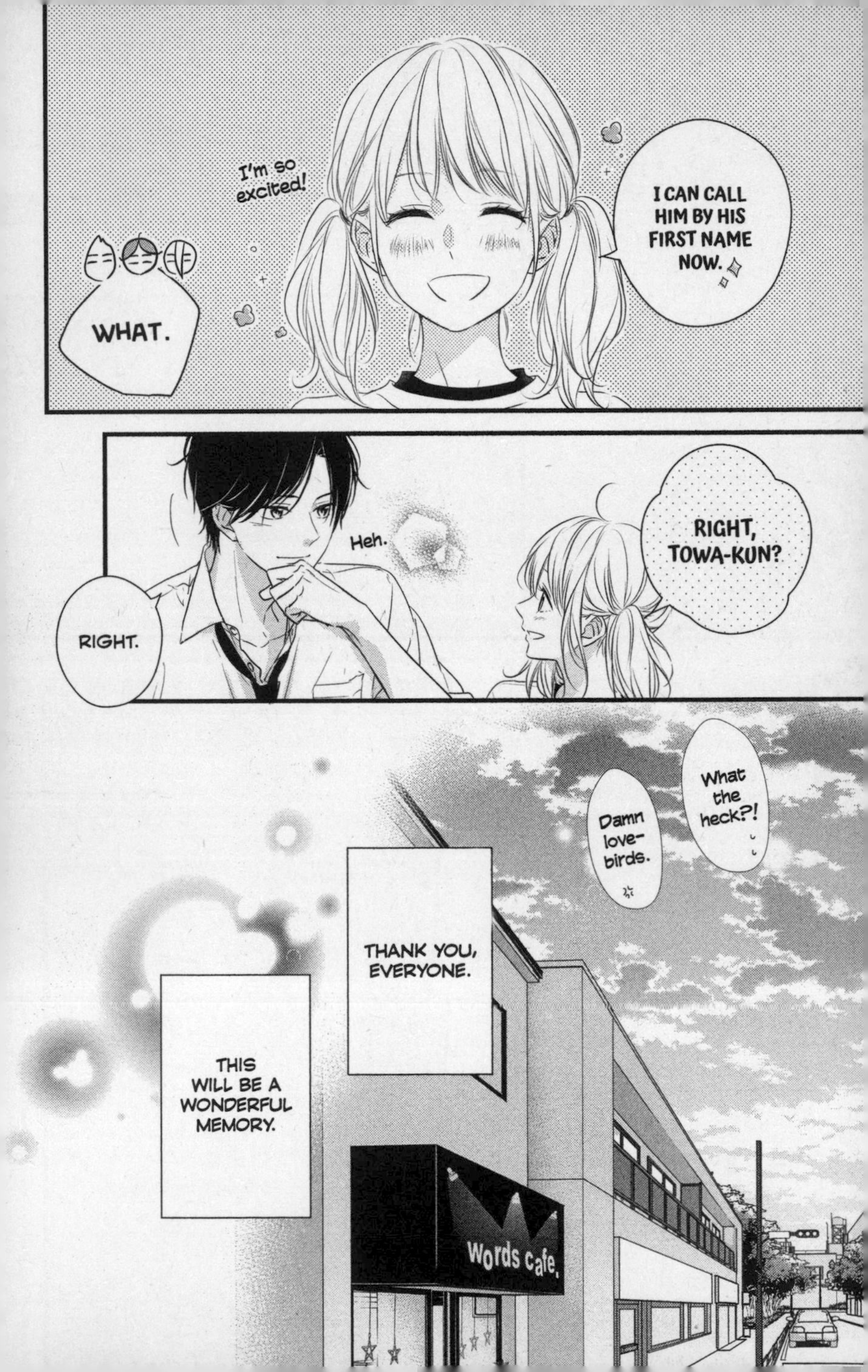
I CAN CALL HIM BY HIS FIRST NAME NOW.
I'm so excited!
WHAT.
RIGHT, TOWA-KUN?
Heh.
RIGHT.
What the heck?!
Damn love-birds.
THANK YOU, EVERYONE.
THIS WILL BE A WONDERFUL MEMORY.
Words cafe.

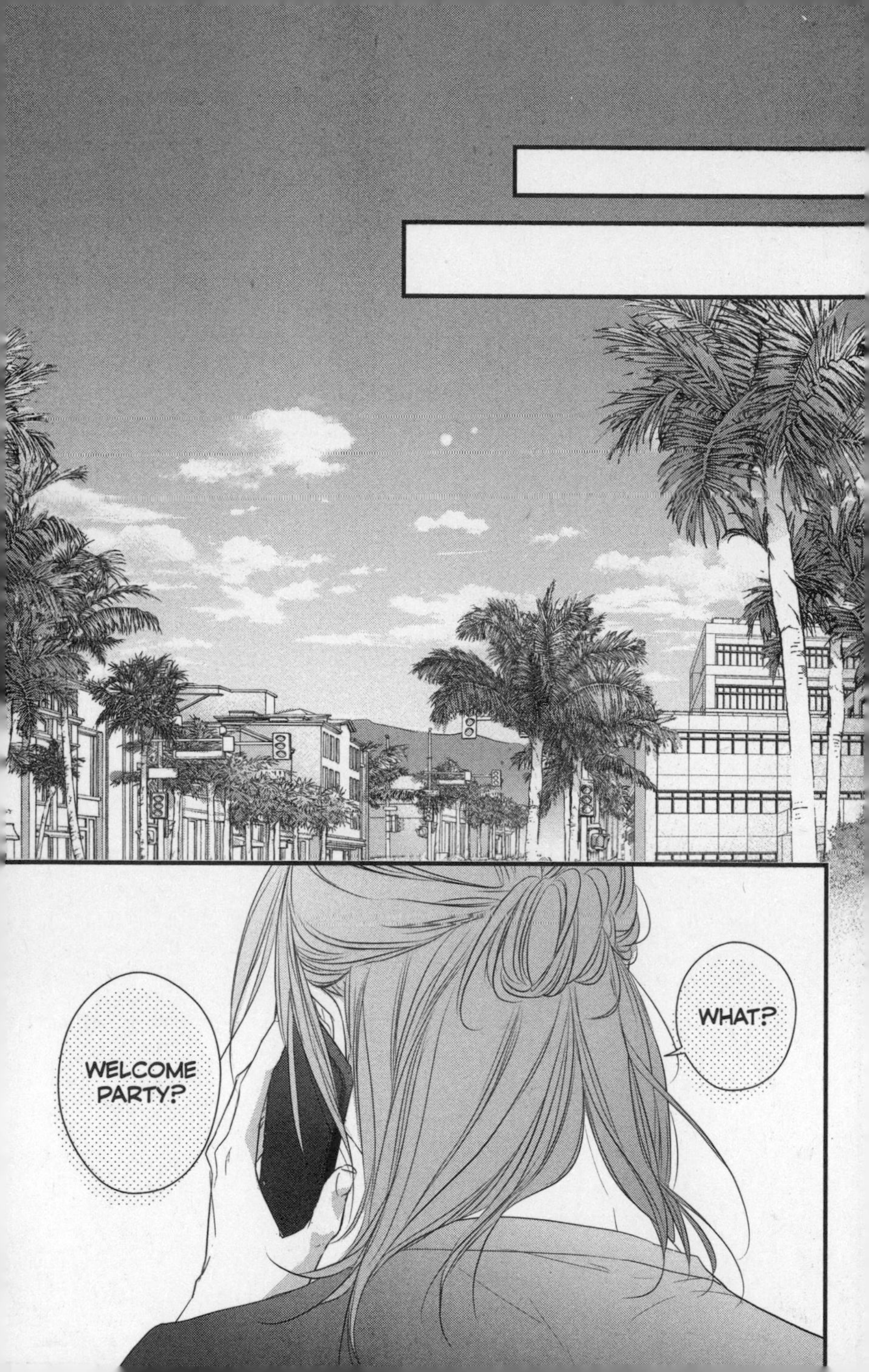
WHAT?
WELCOME PARTY?

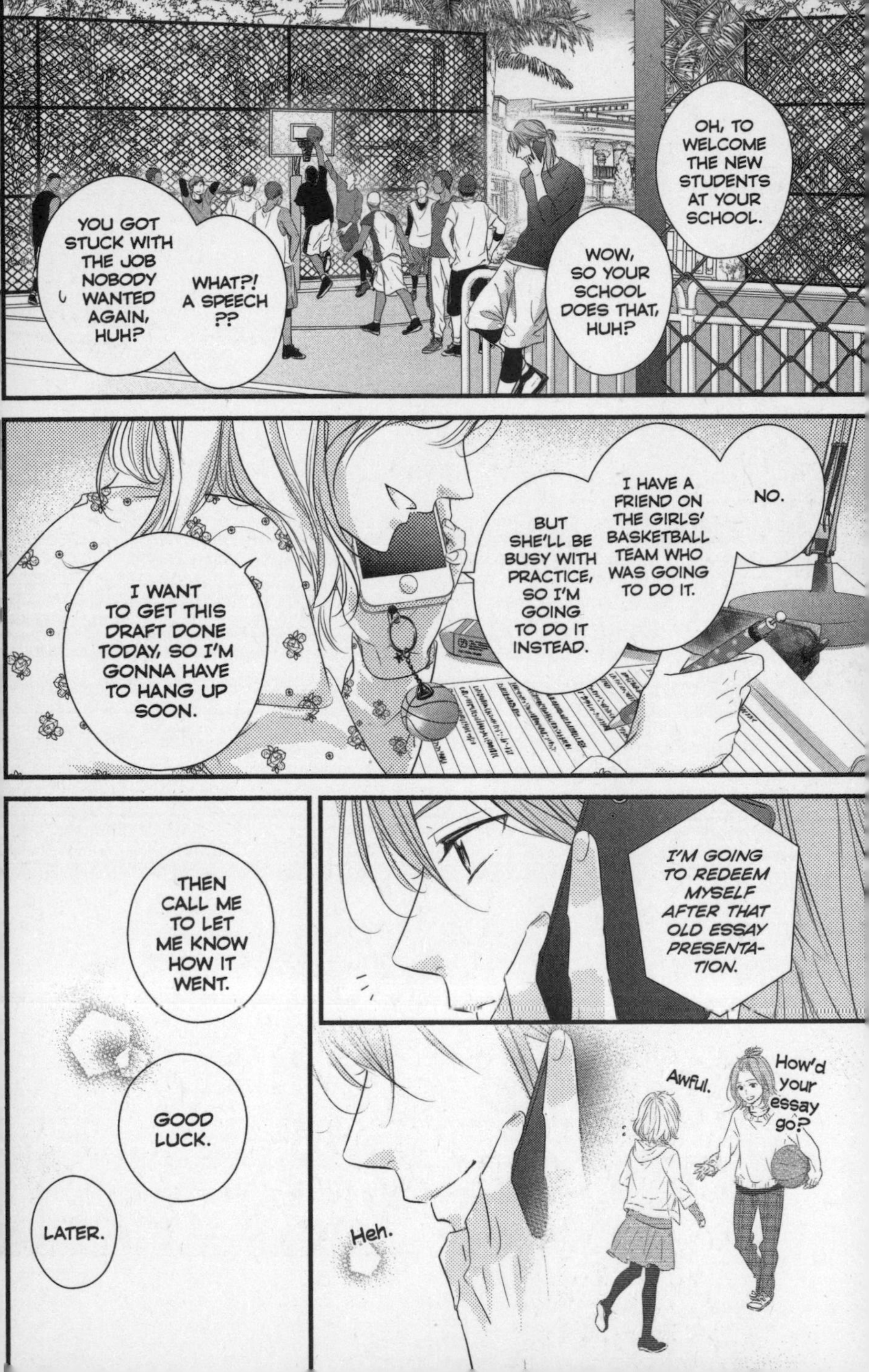
OH, TO WELCOME THE NEW STUDENTS AT YOUR SCHOOL.
WOW, SO YOUR SCHOOL DOES THAT, HUH?
WHAT?! A SPEECH ??
YOU GOT STUCK WITH THE JOB NOBODY WANTED AGAIN, HUH?
NO.
I HAVE A FRIEND ON THE GIRLS' BASKETBALL TEAM WHO WAS GOING TO DO IT.
BUT SHE'LL BE BUSY WITH PRACTICE, SO I'M GOING TO DO IT INSTEAD.
I WANT TO GET THIS DRAFT DONE TODAY, SO I'M GONNA HAVE TO HANG UP SOON.
I'M GOING TO REDEEM MYSELF AFTER THAT OLD ESSAY PRESENTATION.
How'd your essay go?
Awful.
Heh.
THEN CALL ME TO LET ME KNOW HOW IT WENT.
GOOD LUCK.
LATER.

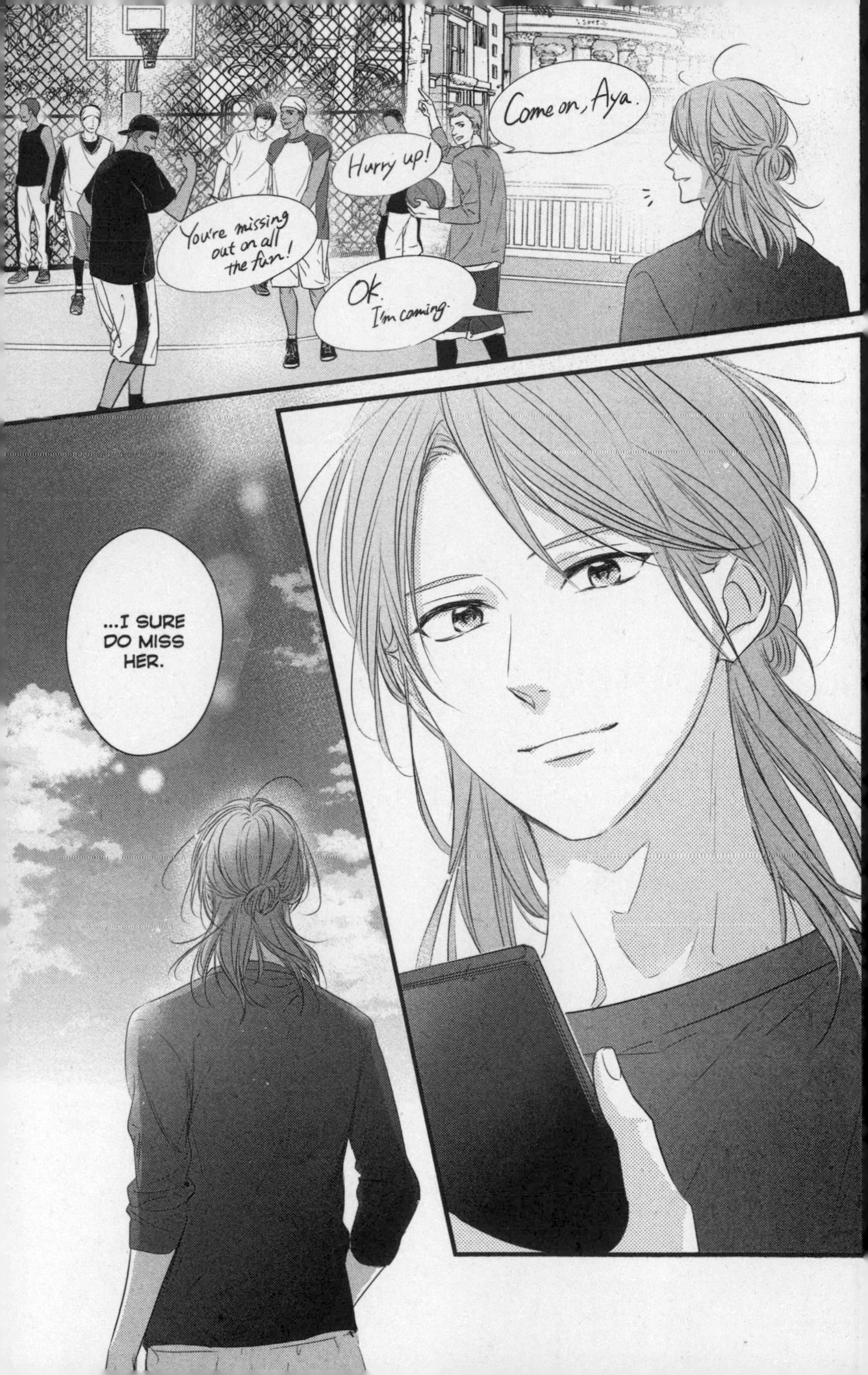
Come on, Aya.
Hurry up!
You're missing out on all the fun!
OK. I'm coming.
...I SURE DO MISS HER.

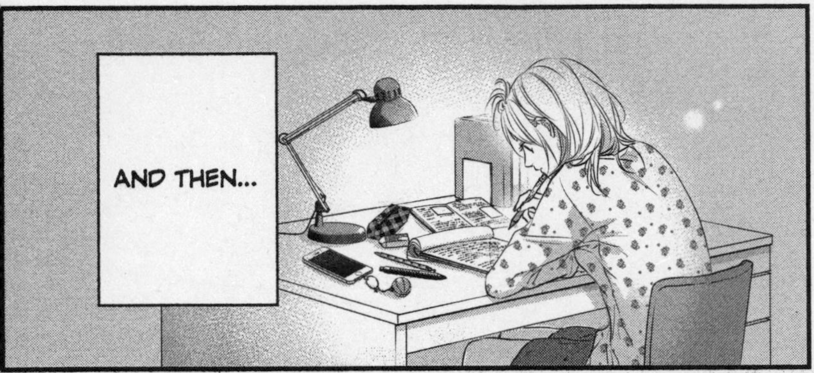
AND THEN...

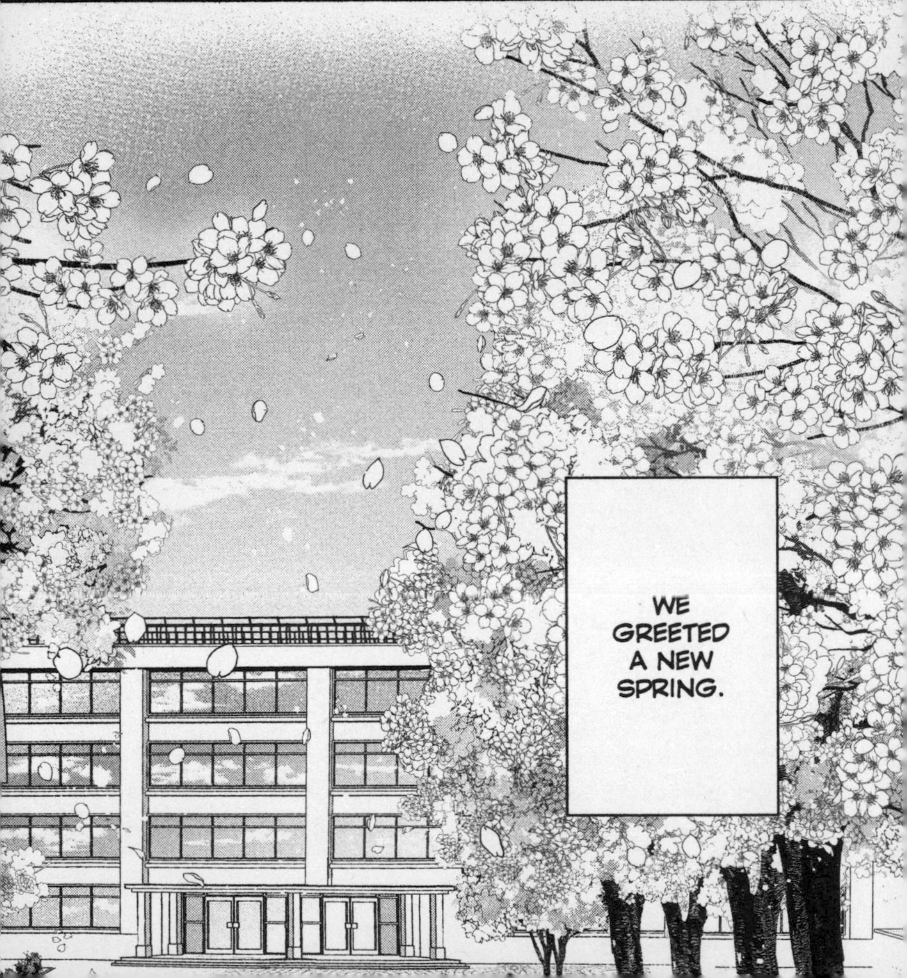
WE GREETED A NEW SPRING.

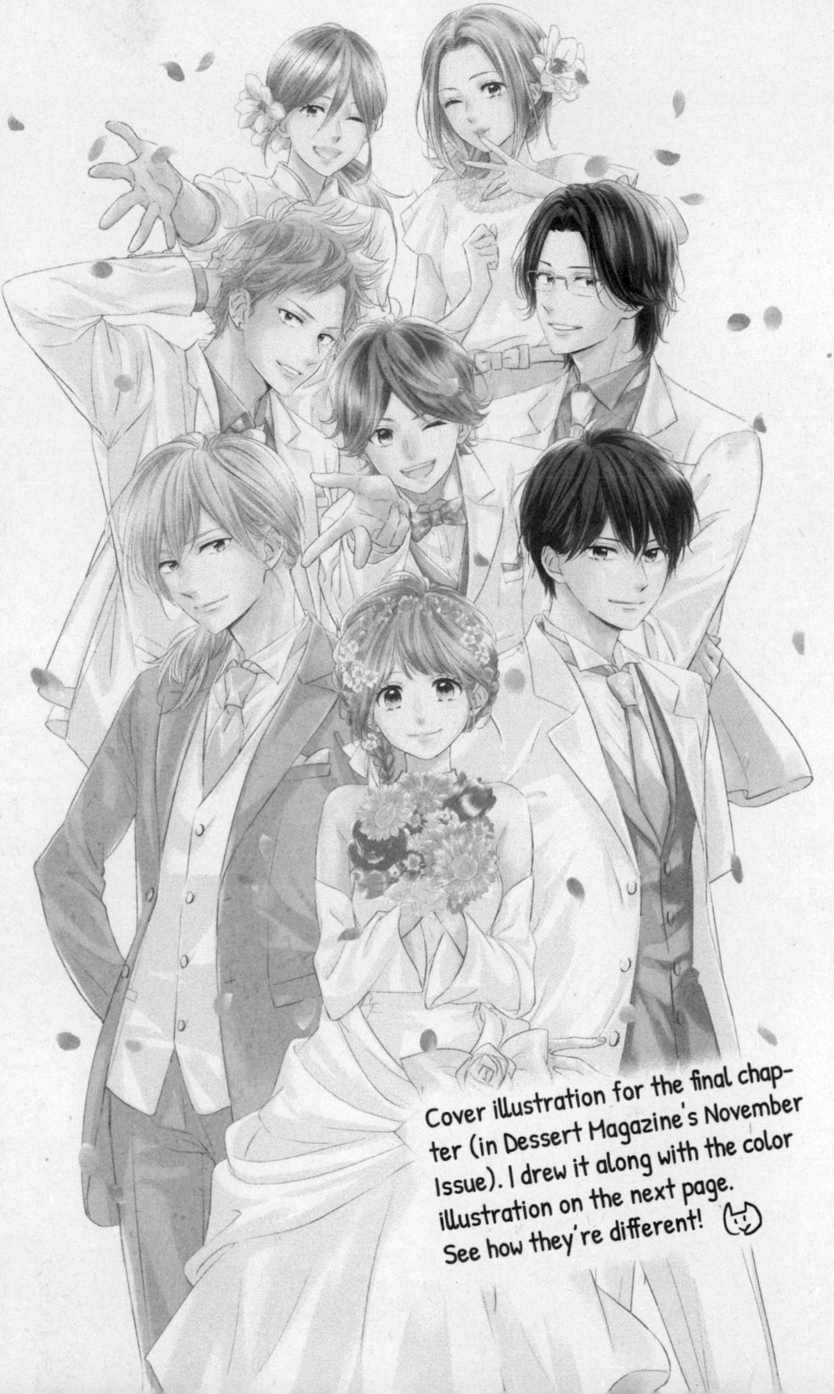
Cover illustration for the final chap-
ter (in Dessert Magazine's November
Issue). I drew it along with the color
illustration on the next page.
See how they're different!

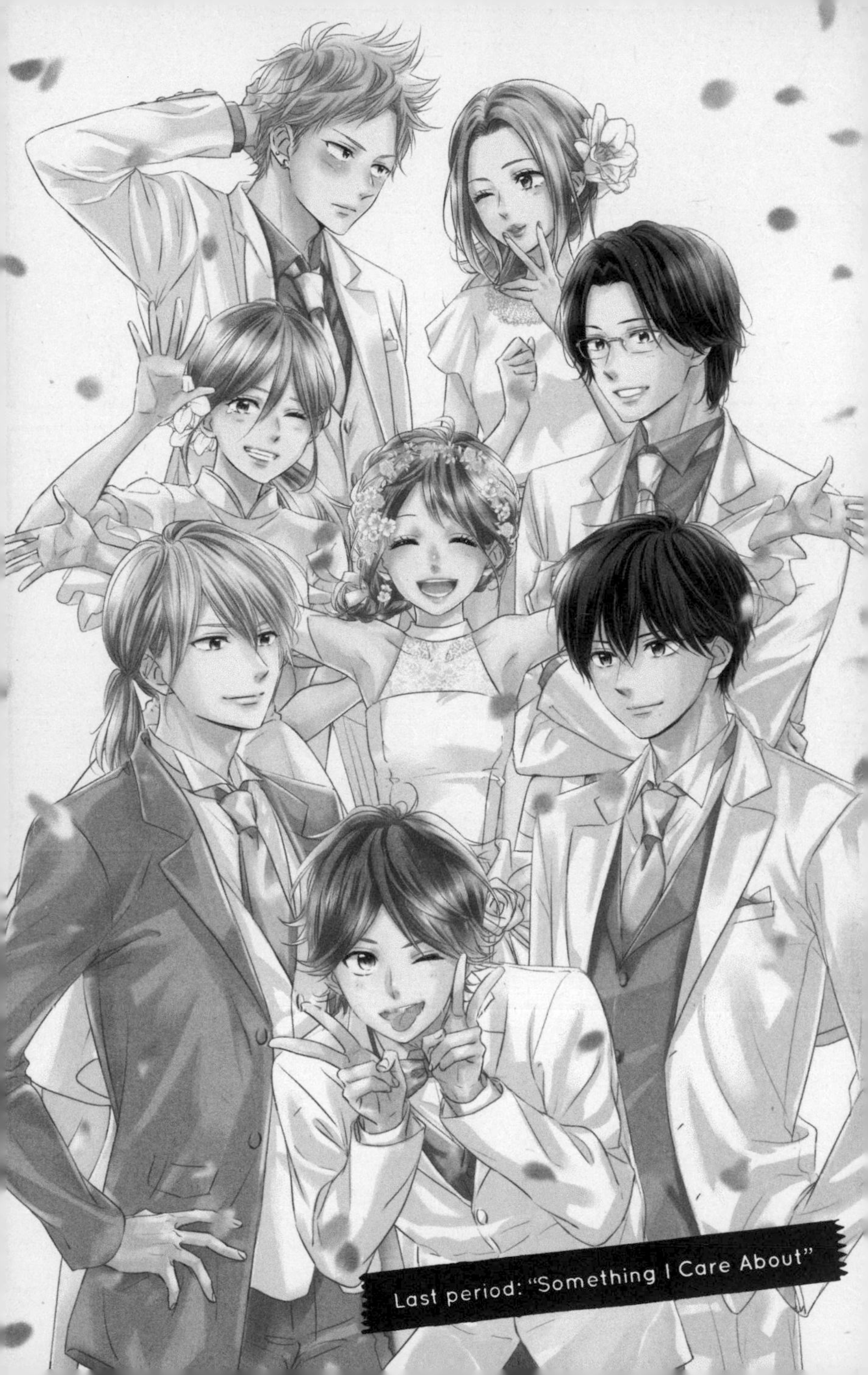
Last period: "Something I Care About"

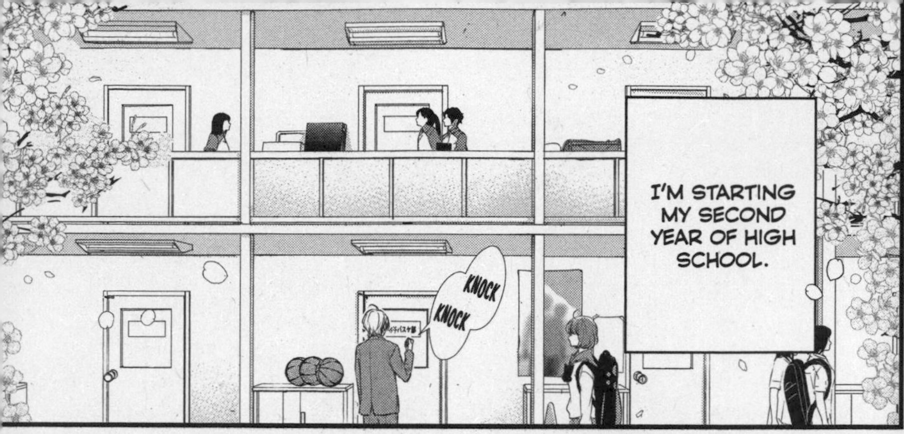
I'M STARTING MY SECOND YEAR OF HIGH SCHOOL.
KNOCK KNOCK

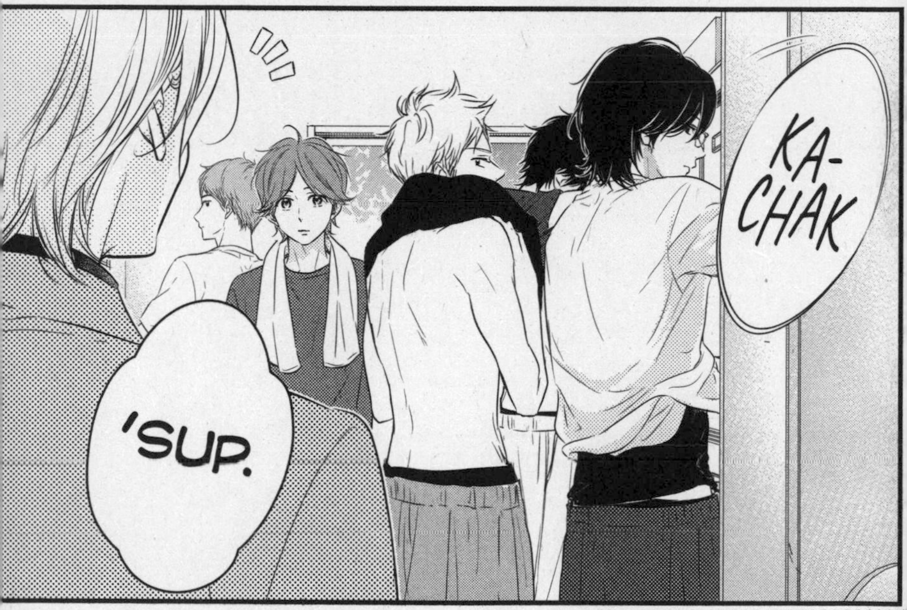
KA-CHAK
'SUP.

With a lot of help from a lot of people, we made it to volume 13.

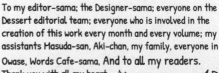

SPECIAL THANKS

To my editor-sama; the Designer-sama; everyone on the Dessert editorial team; everyone who is involved in the creation of this work every month and every volume; my assistants Masuda-san, Aki-chan, my family, everyone in Owase, Words Cafe-sama, And to all my readers. Thank you with all my heart... ✧✧

あなしん
Anashin 11/2019

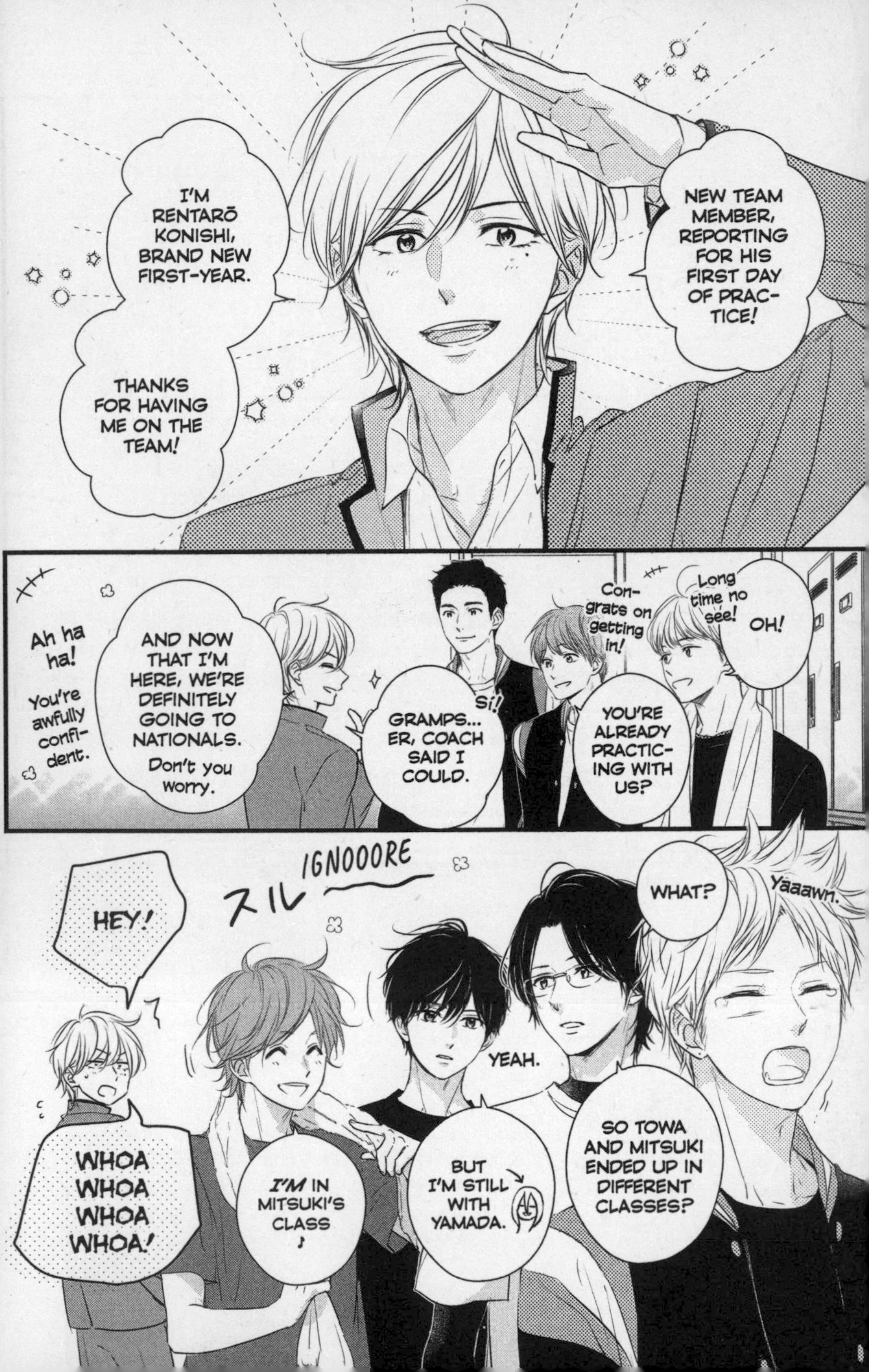
NEW TEAM MEMBER, REPORTING FOR HIS FIRST DAY OF PRAC-TICE!
I'M RENTARŌ KONISHI, BRAND NEW FIRST-YEAR.
THANKS FOR HAVING ME ON THE TEAM!
OH!
Long time no see!
Con-grats on getting in!
YOU'RE ALREADY PRACTIC-ING WITH US?
Sí!
GRAMPS... ER, COACH SAID I COULD.
AND NOW THAT I'M HERE, WE'RE DEFINITELY GOING TO NATIONALS.
Don't you worry.
Ah ha ha!
You're awfully confi-dent.
Yaaawn.
WHAT?
SO TOWA AND MITSUKI ENDED UP IN DIFFERENT CLASSES?
YEAH.
BUT I'M STILL WITH YAMADA.
I'M IN MITSUKI'S CLASS ♪
スル IGNOOORE
HEY!
WHOA WHOA WHOA WHOA!

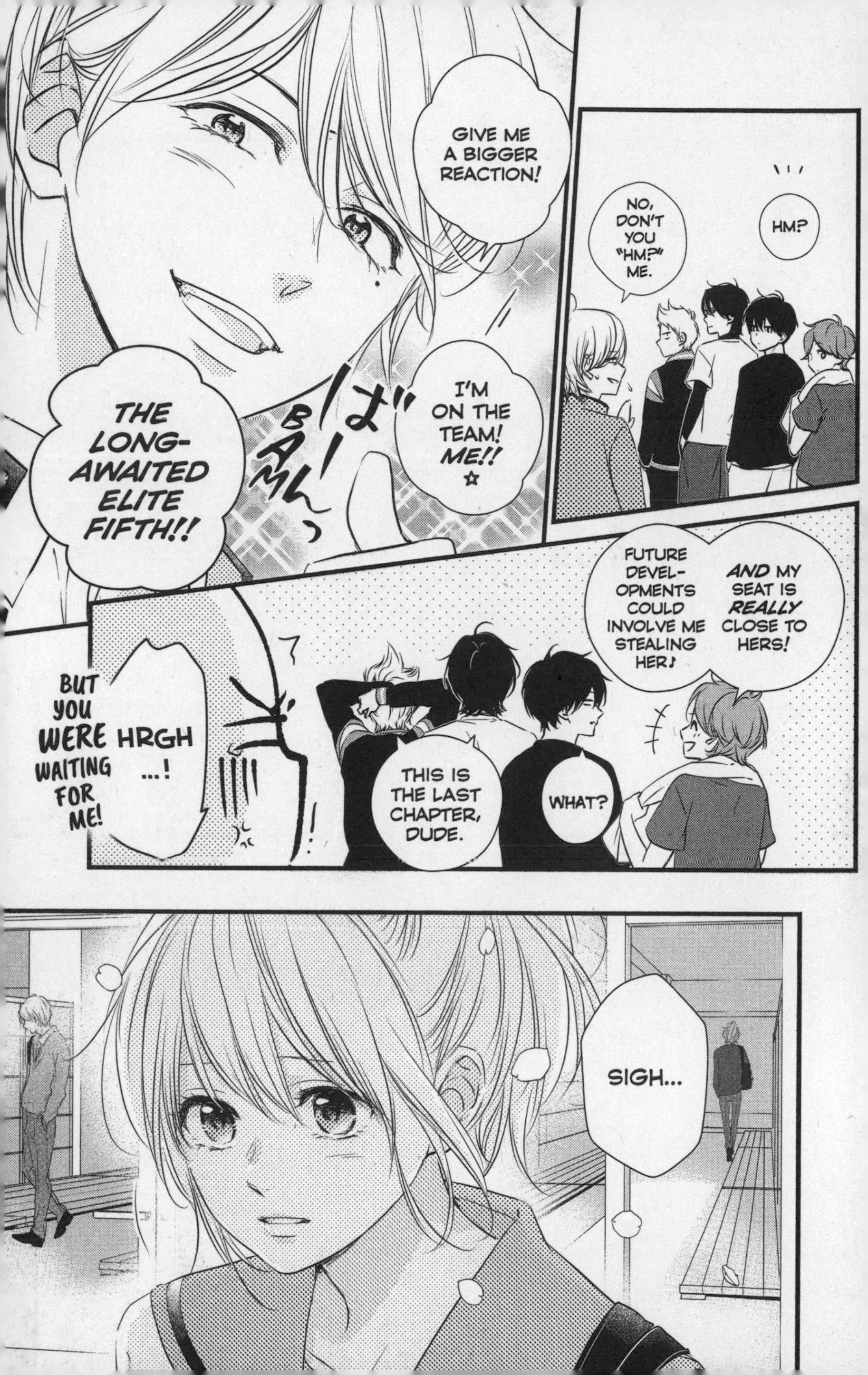
I'M ON THE TEAM! ME!! ☆
ばーん BAM
THE LONG-AWAITED ELITE FIFTH!!
GIVE ME A BIGGER REACTION!
HM?
NO, DON'T YOU "HM?" ME.
FUTURE DEVEL-OPMENTS COULD INVOLVE ME STEALING HER♪
AND MY SEAT IS REALLY CLOSE TO HERS!
WHAT?
THIS IS THE LAST CHAPTER, DUDE.
HRGH ...!
BUT YOU WERE WAITING FOR ME!
SIGH...

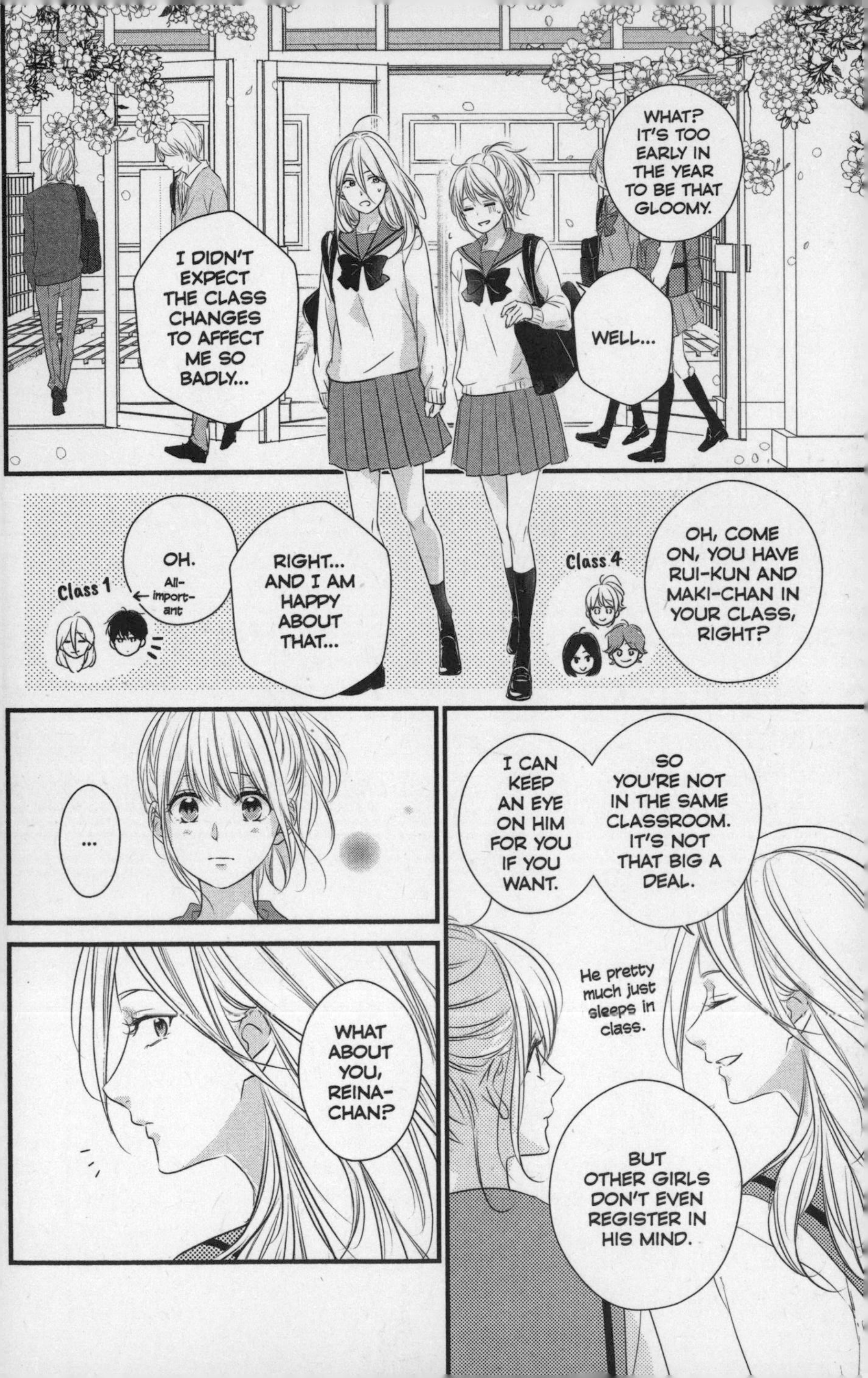
WHAT? IT'S TOO EARLY IN THE YEAR TO BE THAT GLOOMY.
WELL...
I DIDN'T EXPECT THE CLASS CHANGES TO AFFECT ME SO BADLY...
OH, COME ON, YOU HAVE RUI-KUN AND MAKI-CHAN IN YOUR CLASS, RIGHT?
Class 4
RIGHT... AND I AM HAPPY ABOUT THAT...
OH.
All-important
Class 1
SO YOU'RE NOT IN THE SAME CLASSROOM. IT'S NOT THAT BIG A DEAL.
I CAN KEEP AN EYE ON HIM FOR YOU IF YOU WANT.
He pretty much just sleeps in class.
BUT OTHER GIRLS DON'T EVEN REGISTER IN HIS MIND.
...
WHAT ABOUT YOU, REINA-CHAN?

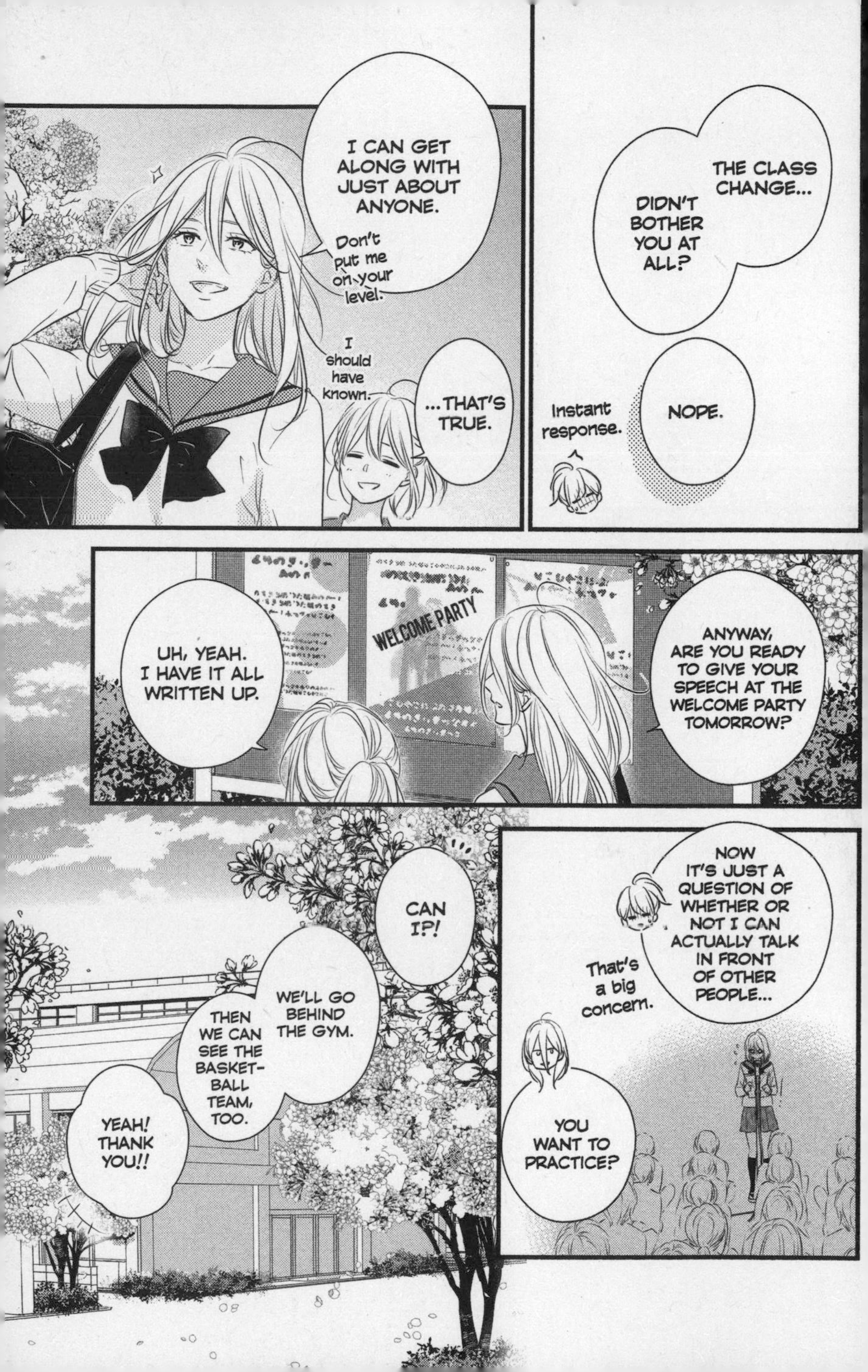
THE CLASS CHANGE... DIDN'T BOTHER YOU AT ALL?
NOPE.
Instant response.
I CAN GET ALONG WITH JUST ABOUT ANYONE.
Don't put me on your level.
I should have known.
...THAT'S TRUE.
ANYWAY, ARE YOU READY TO GIVE YOUR SPEECH AT THE WELCOME PARTY TOMORROW?
WELCOME PARTY
UH, YEAH. I HAVE IT ALL WRITTEN UP.
NOW IT'S JUST A QUESTION OF WHETHER OR NOT I CAN ACTUALLY TALK IN FRONT OF OTHER PEOPLE...
That's a big concern.
YOU WANT TO PRACTICE?
CAN I?!
WE'LL GO BEHIND THE GYM.
THEN WE CAN SEE THE BASKET-BALL TEAM, TOO.
YEAH! THANK YOU!!

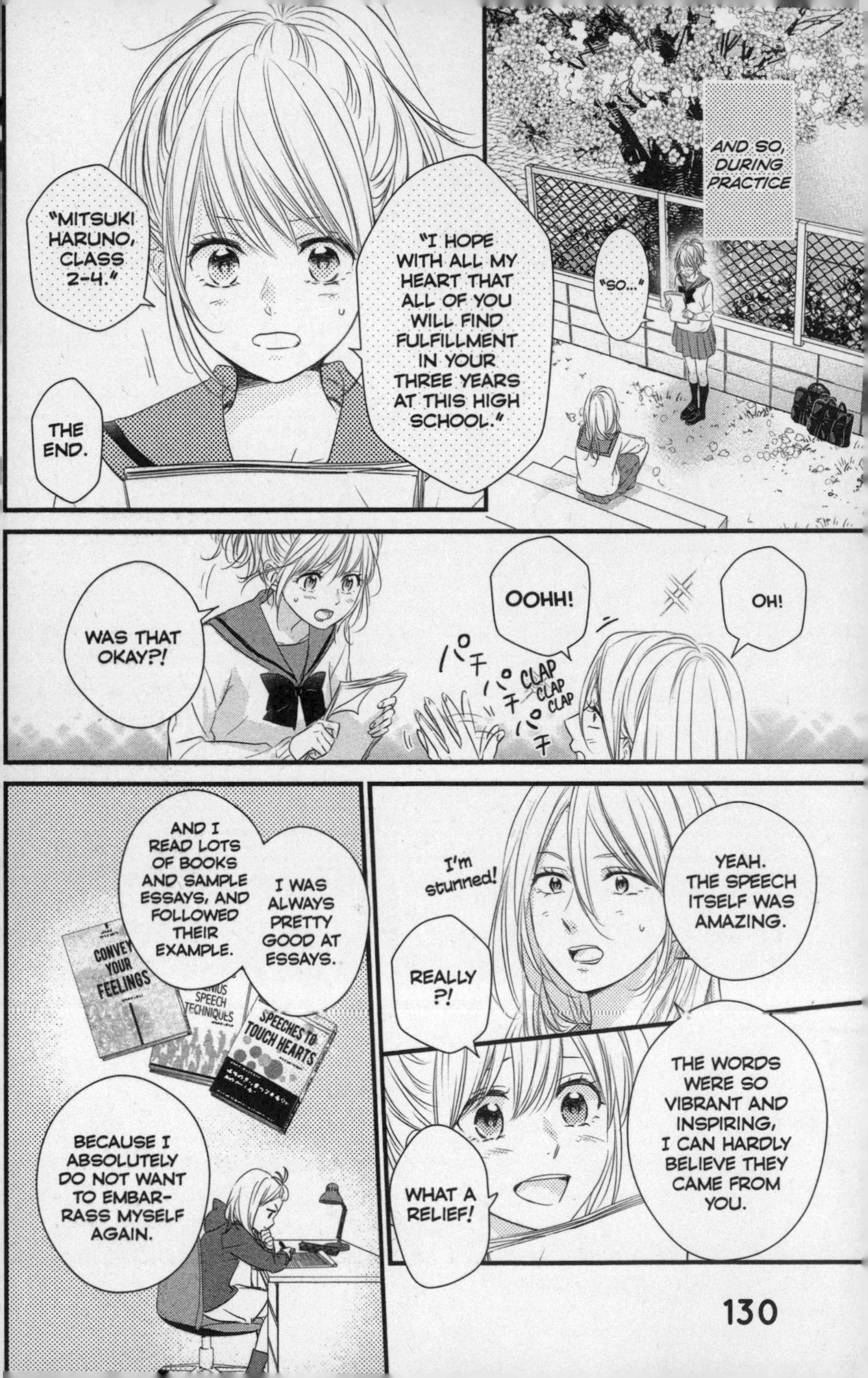
AND SO, DURING PRACTICE
"SO..."
"I HOPE WITH ALL MY HEART THAT ALL OF YOU WILL FIND FULFILLMENT IN YOUR THREE YEARS AT THIS HIGH SCHOOL."
"MITSUKI HARUNO, CLASS 2-4."
THE END.
OH!
OOHH!
CLAP CLAP CLAP
WAS THAT OKAY?!
YEAH. THE SPEECH ITSELF WAS AMAZING.
I'm stunned!
REALLY?!
THE WORDS WERE SO VIBRANT AND INSPIRING, I CAN HARDLY BELIEVE THEY CAME FROM YOU.
WHAT A RELIEF!
I WAS ALWAYS PRETTY GOOD AT ESSAYS.
AND I READ LOTS OF BOOKS AND SAMPLE ESSAYS, AND FOLLOWED THEIR EXAMPLE.
CONVEY YOUR FEELINGS
SPEECH TECHNIQUES
SPEECHES TO TOUCH HEARTS
BECAUSE I ABSOLUTELY DO NOT WANT TO EMBARRASS MYSELF AGAIN.

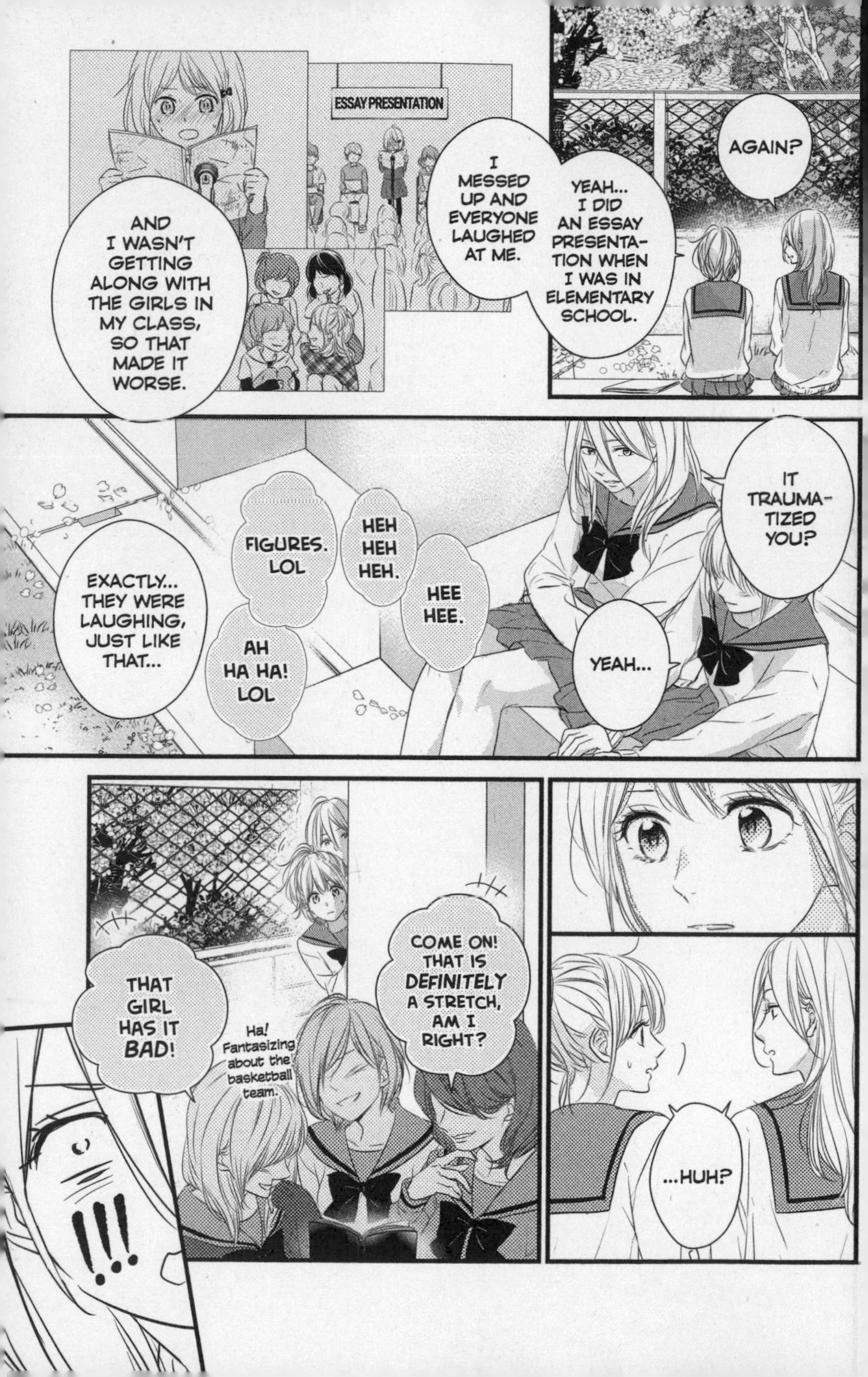
AGAIN?
YEAH... I DID AN ESSAY PRESENTATION WHEN I WAS IN ELEMENTARY SCHOOL.
I MESSED UP AND EVERYONE LAUGHED AT ME.
ESSAY PRESENTATION
AND I WASN'T GETTING ALONG WITH THE GIRLS IN MY CLASS, SO THAT MADE IT WORSE.
IT TRAUMATIZED YOU?
YEAH...
HEE HEE.
HEH HEH HEH.
FIGURES. LOL
AH HA HA! LOL
EXACTLY... THEY WERE LAUGHING, JUST LIKE THAT...
...HUH?
COME ON! THAT IS DEFINITELY A STRETCH, AM I RIGHT?
Ha! Fantasizing about the basketball team.
THAT GIRL HAS IT BAD!
!!!

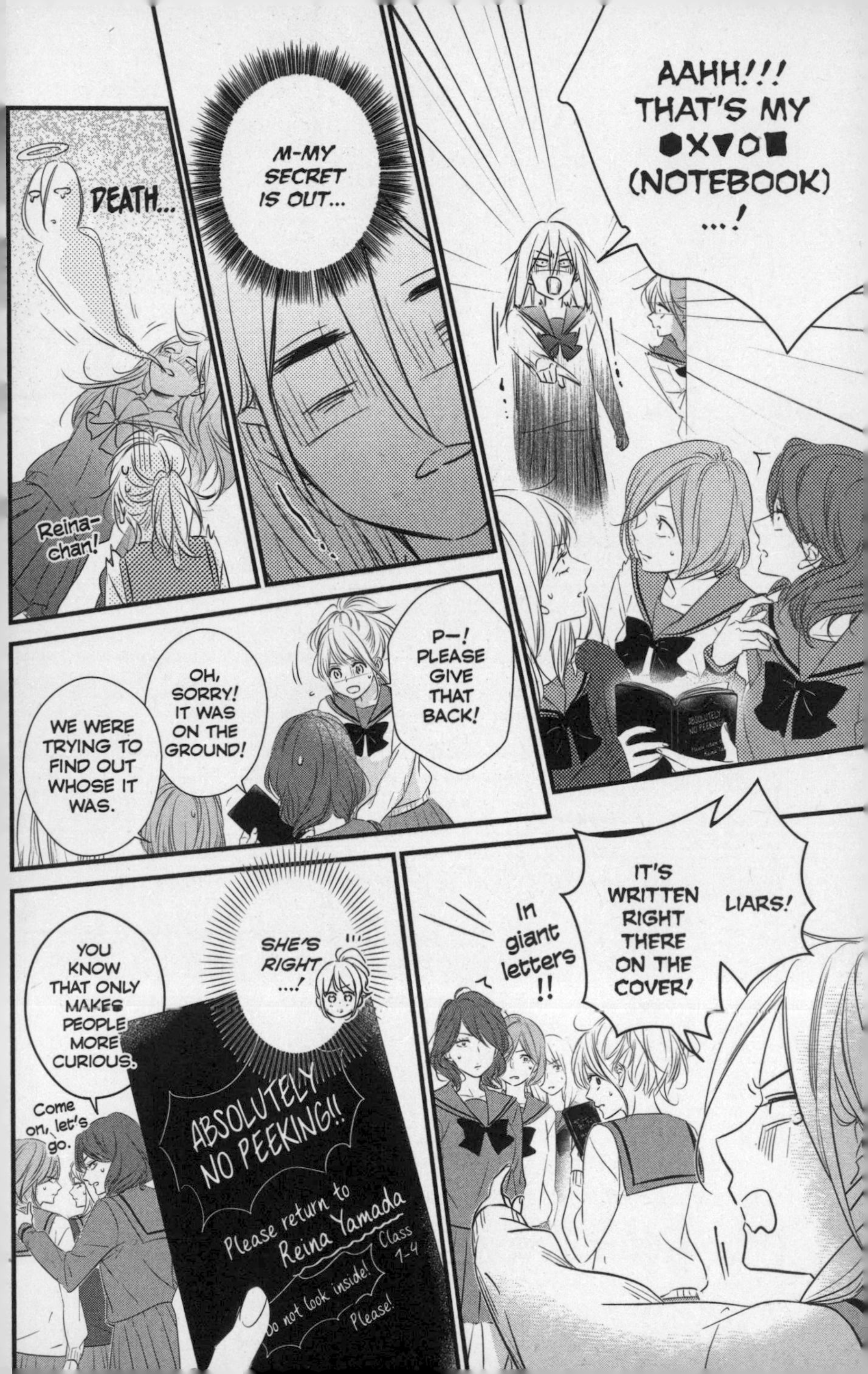
AAHH!!! THAT'S MY ●X▼O■ (NOTEBOOK) ...!
M-MY SECRET IS OUT...
DEATH...
Reina-chan!
P—! PLEASE GIVE THAT BACK!
OH, SORRY! IT WAS ON THE GROUND!
WE WERE TRYING TO FIND OUT WHOSE IT WAS.
LIARS!
IT'S WRITTEN RIGHT THERE ON THE COVER!
In giant letters!!
SHE'S RIGHT ...!
YOU KNOW THAT ONLY MAKES PEOPLE MORE CURIOUS.
Come on, let's go.
ABSOLUTELY NO PEEKING!!
Please return to Reina Yamada
Class 1-4
Do not look inside! Please!

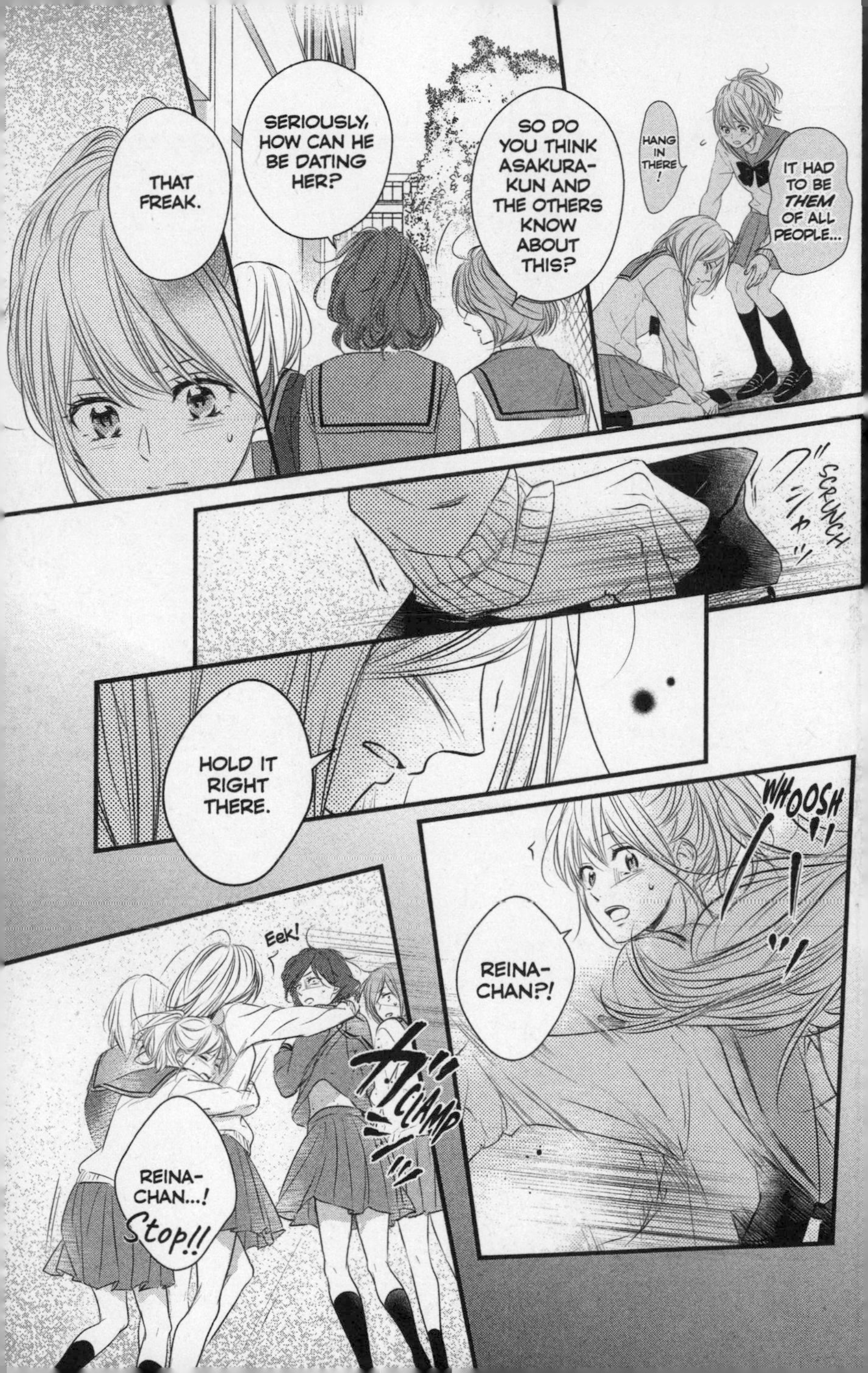
HANG IN THERE!
IT HAD TO BE *THEM* OF ALL PEOPLE...
SO DO YOU THINK ASAKURA-KUN AND THE OTHERS KNOW ABOUT THIS?
SERIOUSLY, HOW CAN HE BE DATING HER?
THAT FREAK.
SCRUNCH
HOLD IT RIGHT THERE.
WHOOSH
REINA-CHAN?!
Eek!
CLAMP
REINA-CHAN...! Stop!!

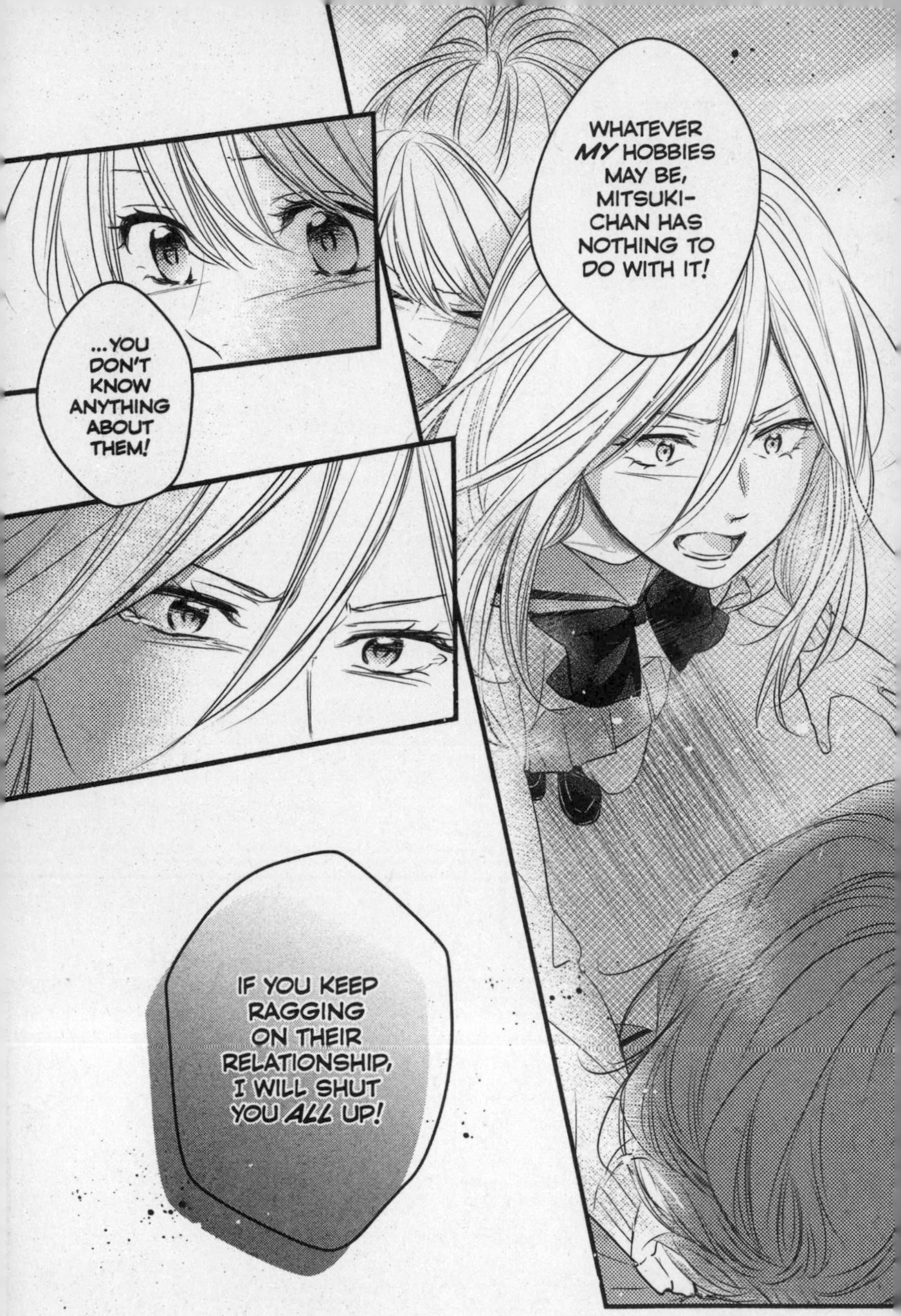
WHATEVER *MY* HOBBIES MAY BE, MITSUKI-CHAN HAS NOTHING TO DO WITH IT!
...YOU DON'T KNOW ANYTHING ABOUT THEM!
IF YOU KEEP RAGGING ON THEIR RELATIONSHIP, I WILL SHUT YOU *ALL* UP!

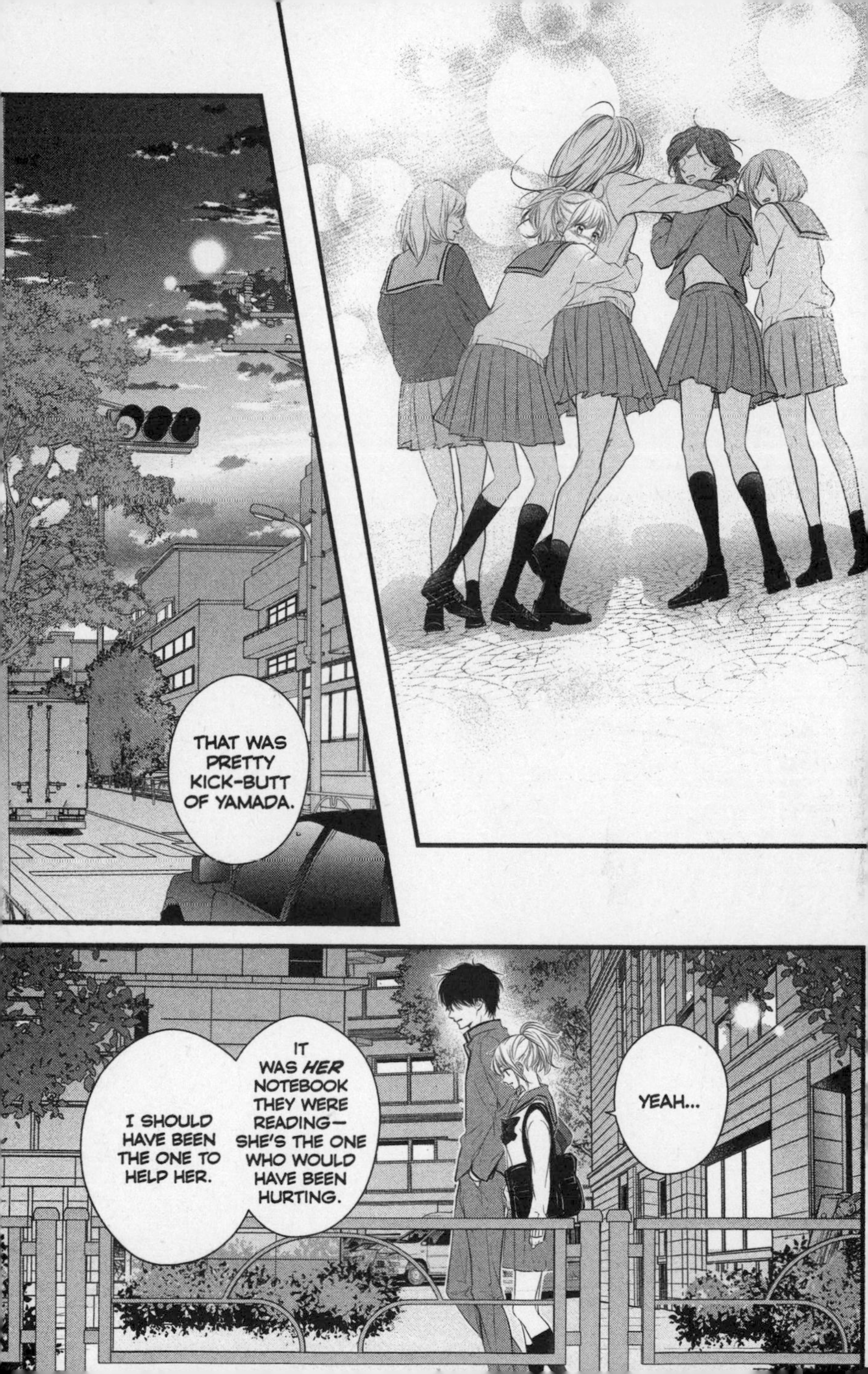
THAT WAS PRETTY KICK-BUTT OF YAMADA.
YEAH...
IT WAS *HER* NOTEBOOK THEY WERE READING— SHE'S THE ONE WHO WOULD HAVE BEEN HURTING.
I SHOULD HAVE BEEN THE ONE TO HELP HER.

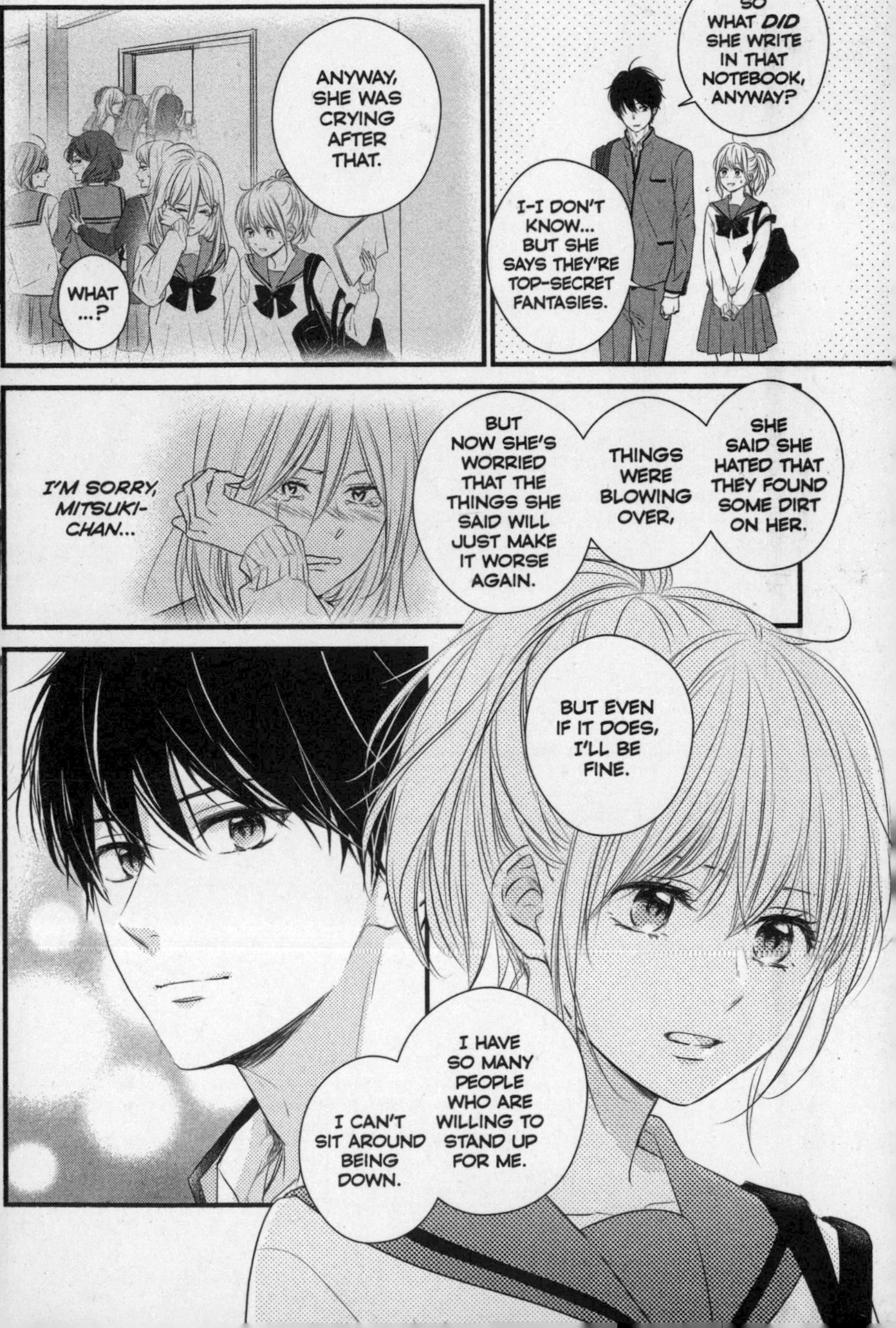
SO WHAT *DID* SHE WRITE IN THAT NOTEBOOK, ANYWAY?
I-I DON'T KNOW... BUT SHE SAYS THEY'RE TOP-SECRET FANTASIES.
ANYWAY, SHE WAS CRYING AFTER THAT.
WHAT ...?
SHE SAID SHE HATED THAT THEY FOUND SOME DIRT ON HER.
THINGS WERE BLOWING OVER,
BUT NOW SHE'S WORRIED THAT THE THINGS SHE SAID WILL JUST MAKE IT WORSE AGAIN.
I'M SORRY, MITSUKI-CHAN...
BUT EVEN IF IT DOES, I'LL BE FINE.
I HAVE SO MANY PEOPLE WHO ARE WILLING TO STAND UP FOR ME.
I CAN'T SIT AROUND BEING DOWN.

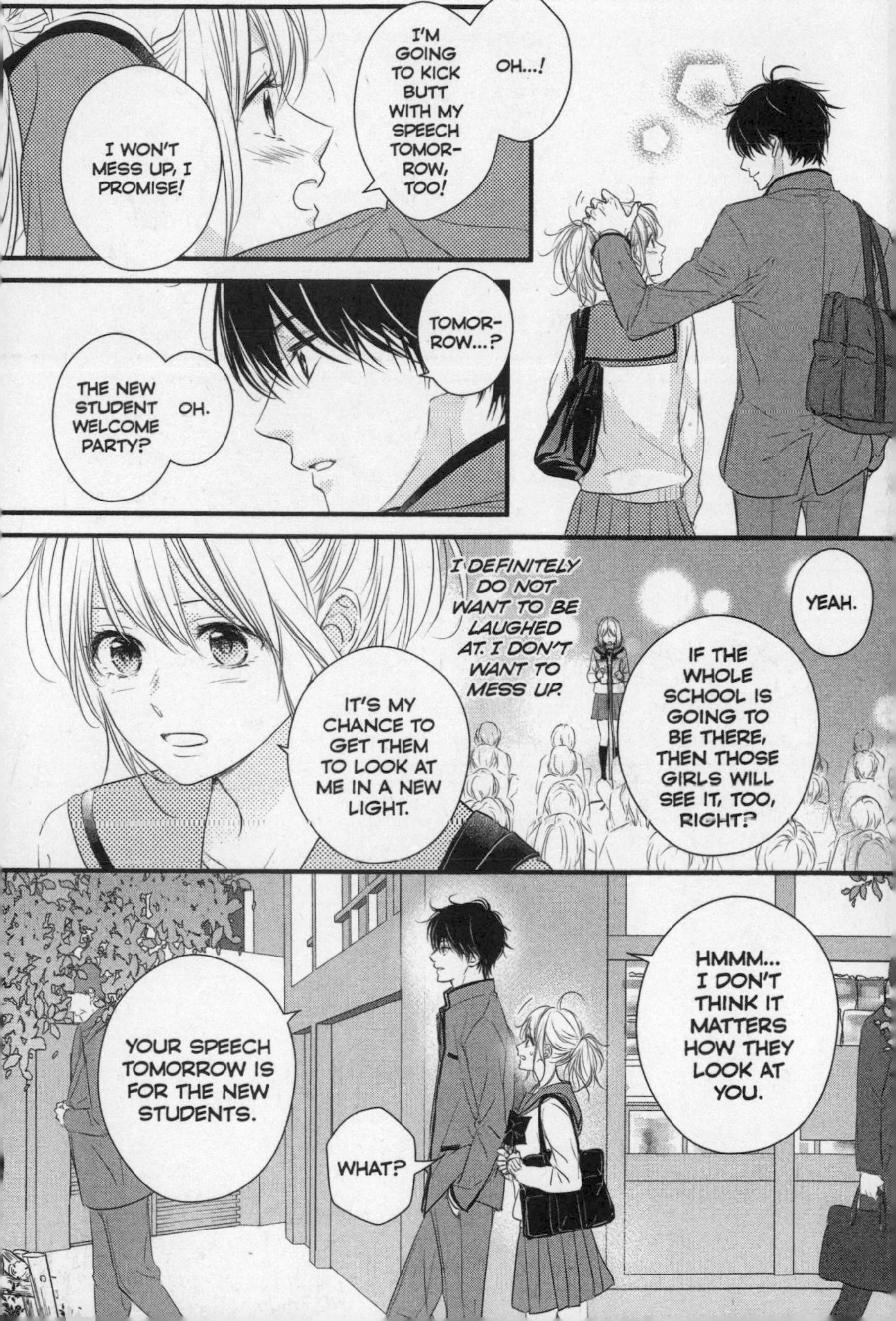
OH...!
I'M GOING TO KICK BUTT WITH MY SPEECH TOMORROW, TOO!
I WON'T MESS UP, I PROMISE!
TOMORROW...?
OH.
THE NEW STUDENT WELCOME PARTY?
YEAH.
IF THE WHOLE SCHOOL IS GOING TO BE THERE, THEN THOSE GIRLS WILL SEE IT, TOO, RIGHT?
I DEFINITELY DO NOT WANT TO BE LAUGHED AT. I DON'T WANT TO MESS UP.
IT'S MY CHANCE TO GET THEM TO LOOK AT ME IN A NEW LIGHT.
HMMM... I DON'T THINK IT MATTERS HOW THEY LOOK AT YOU.
WHAT?
YOUR SPEECH TOMORROW IS FOR THE NEW STUDENTS.

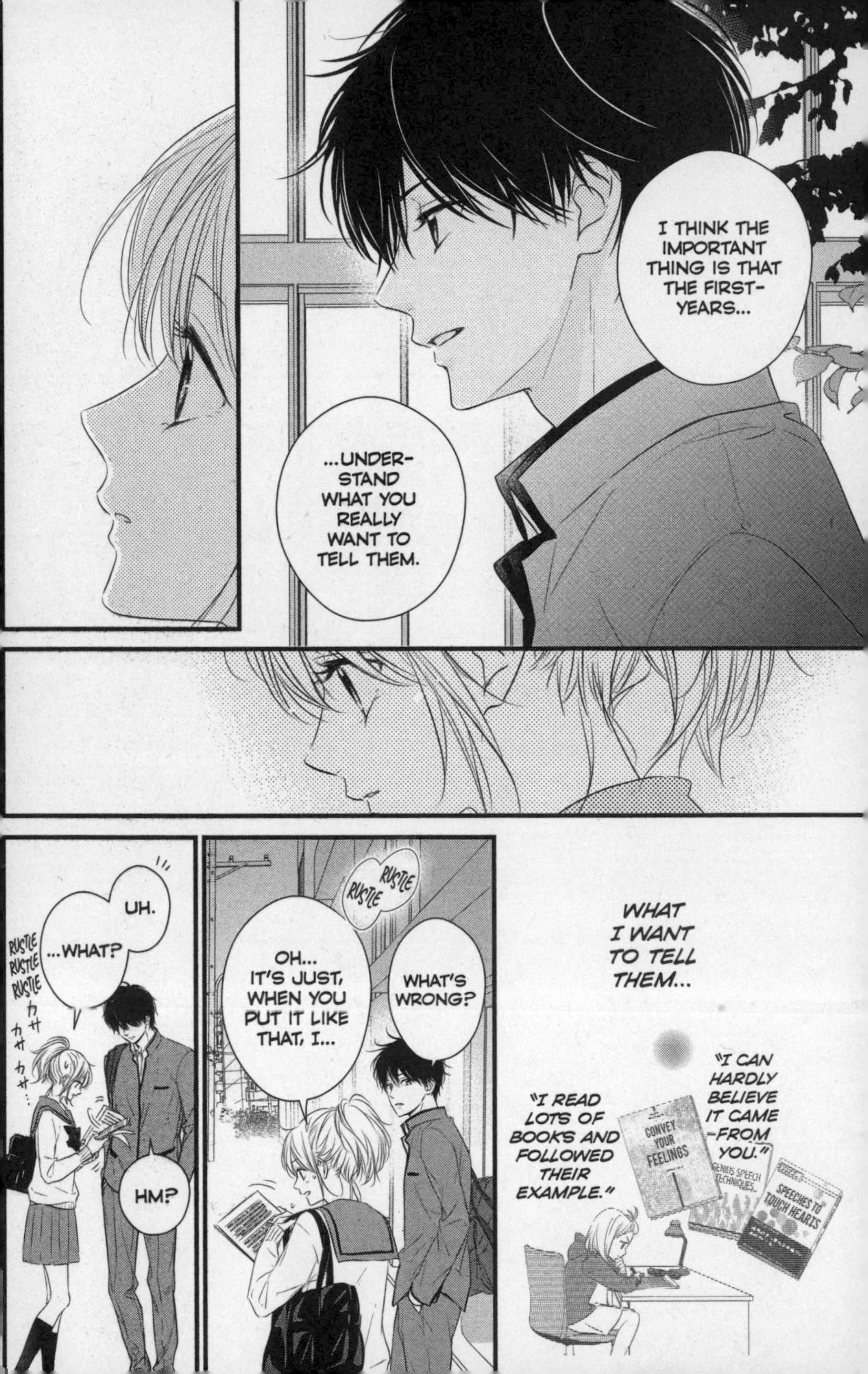
I THINK THE IMPORTANT THING IS THAT THE FIRST-YEARS...
...UNDER-STAND WHAT YOU REALLY WANT TO TELL THEM.
WHAT I WANT TO TELL THEM...
"I CAN HARDLY BELIEVE IT CAME FROM YOU."
"I READ LOTS OF BOOKS AND FOLLOWED THEIR EXAMPLE."
CONVEY YOUR FEELINGS
GENIUS SPEECH TECHNIQUES...
SPEECHES TO TOUCH HEARTS
RUSTLE RUSTLE
WHAT'S WRONG?
OH... IT'S JUST, WHEN YOU PUT IT LIKE THAT, I...
UH.
...WHAT?
RUSTLE RUSTLE RUSTLE
カサカサカサ…
HM?

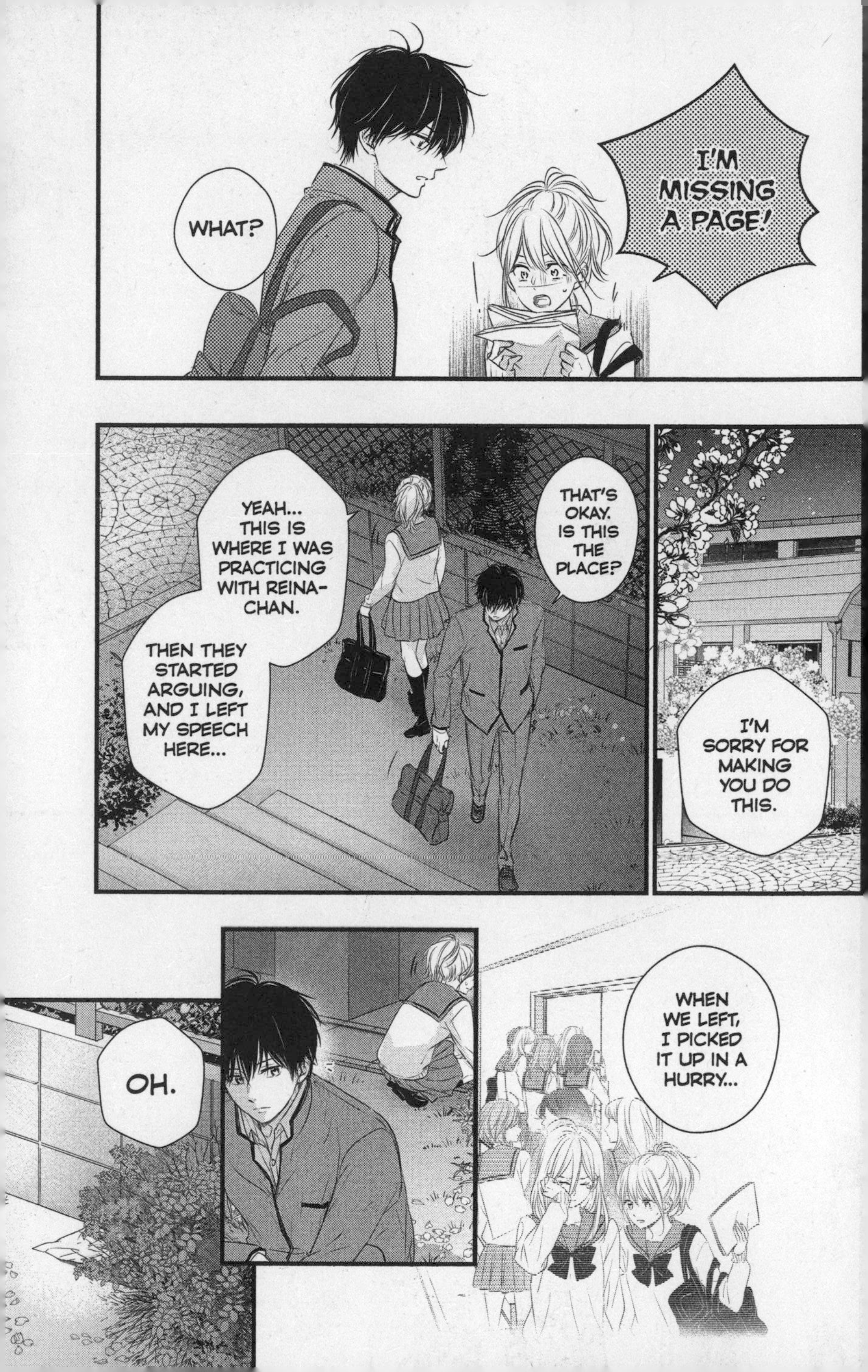
I'M MISSING A PAGE!
WHAT?
I'M SORRY FOR MAKING YOU DO THIS.
THAT'S OKAY. IS THIS THE PLACE?
YEAH... THIS IS WHERE I WAS PRACTICING WITH REINA-CHAN.
THEN THEY STARTED ARGUING, AND I LEFT MY SPEECH HERE...
WHEN WE LEFT, I PICKED IT UP IN A HURRY...
OH.

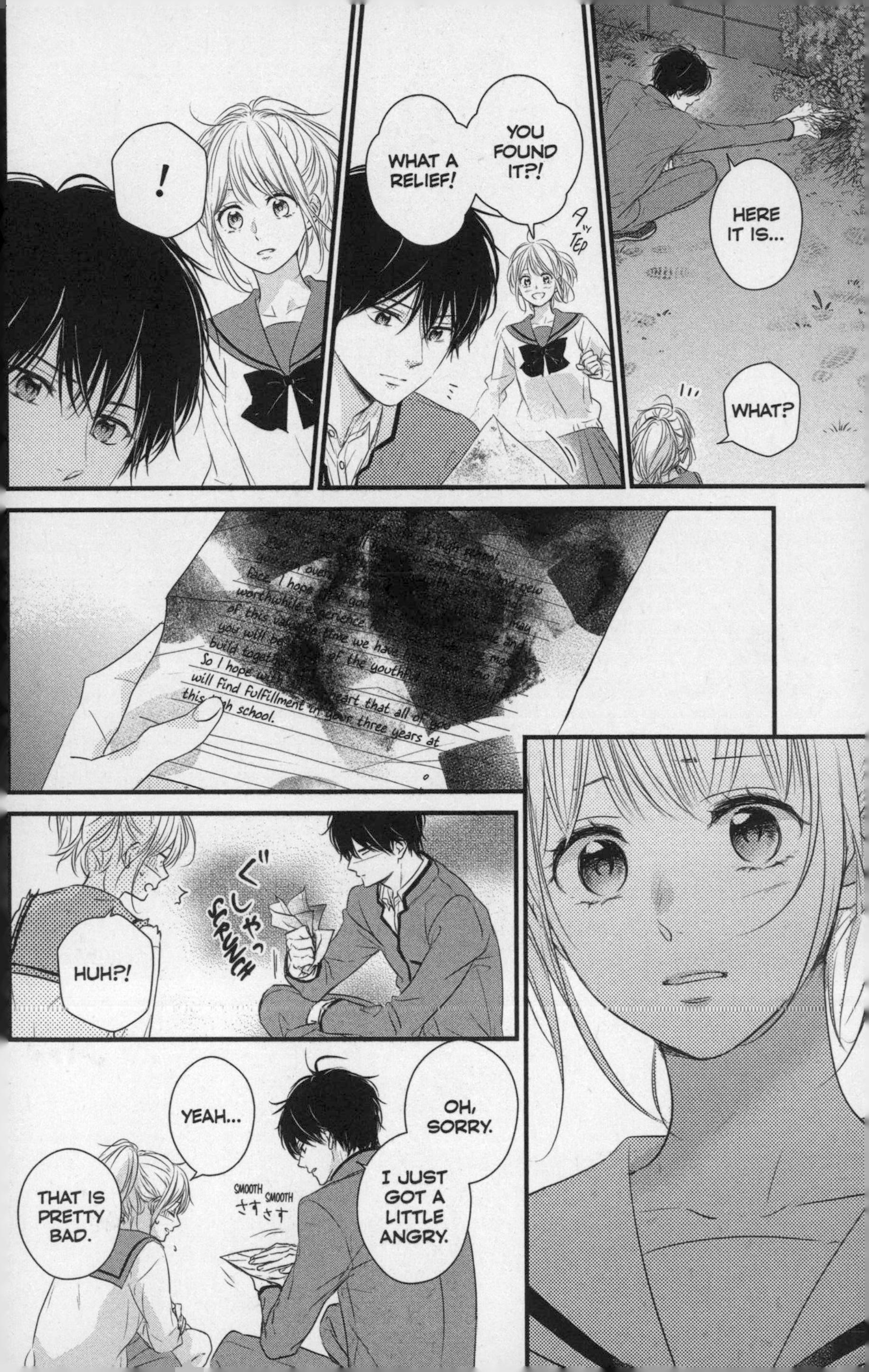
HERE IT IS...
WHAT?
YOU FOUND IT?!
TEP
WHAT A RELIEF!
!
So I hope
will find fulfillment in your three years at
heart that all of you
HUH?!
SCRUNCH
OH, SORRY.
I JUST GOT A LITTLE ANGRY.
YEAH...
SMOOTH SMOOTH
THAT IS PRETTY BAD.

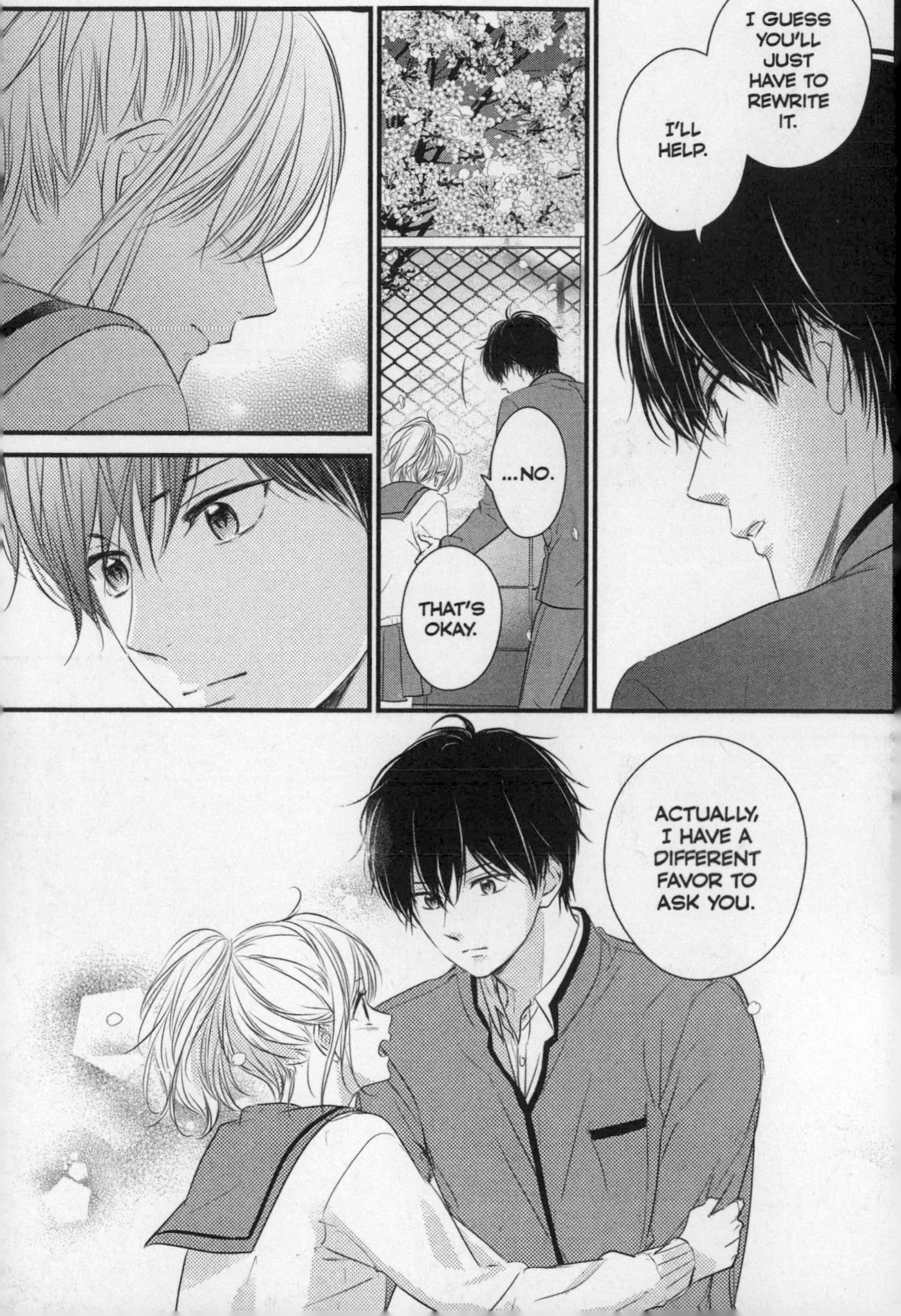
I GUESS YOU'LL JUST HAVE TO REWRITE IT.
I'LL HELP.
...NO.
THAT'S OKAY.
ACTUALLY, I HAVE A DIFFERENT FAVOR TO ASK YOU.

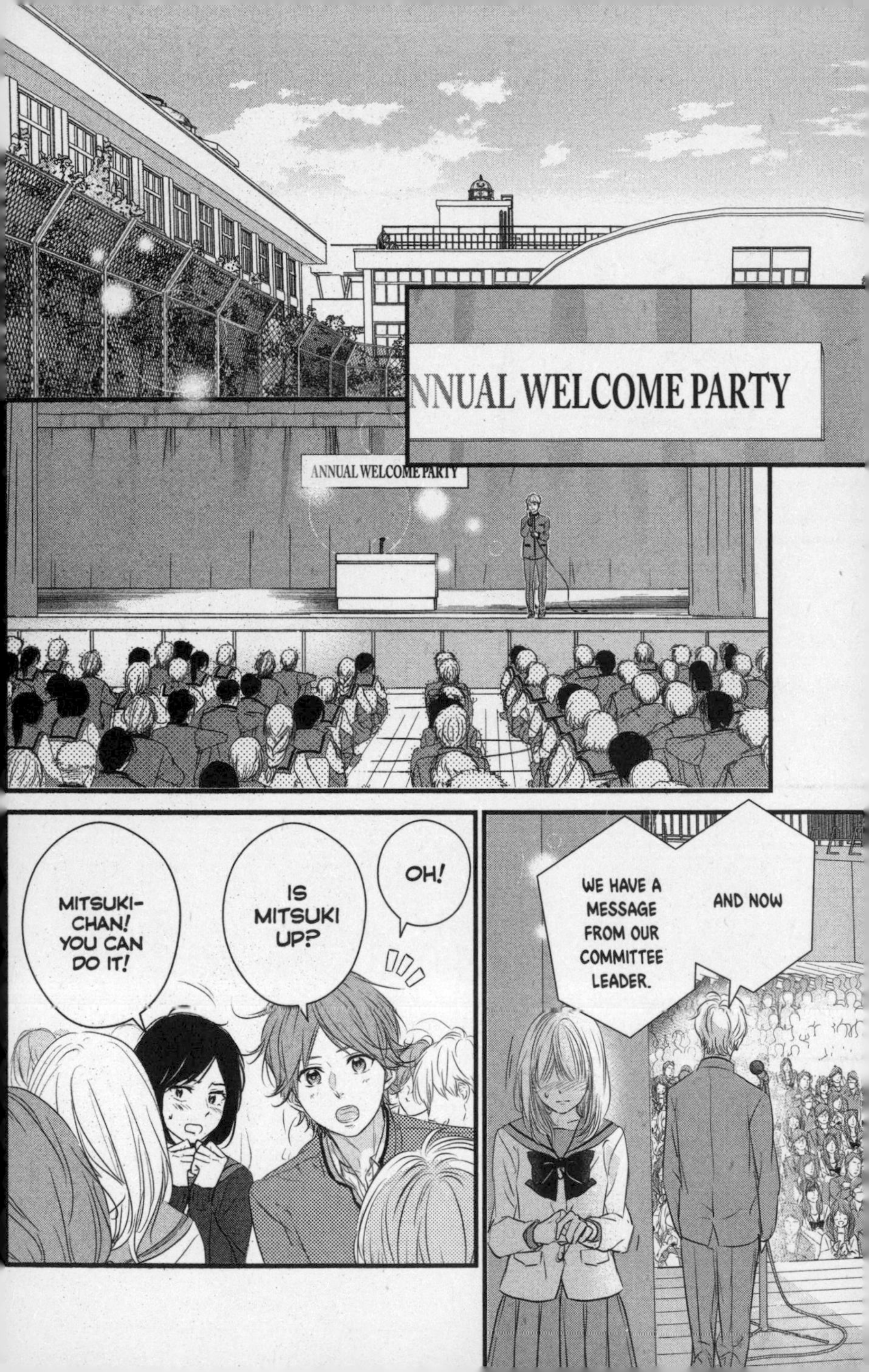
NNUAL WELCOME PARTY
ANNUAL WELCOME PARTY
AND NOW
WE HAVE A MESSAGE FROM OUR COMMITTEE LEADER.
OH!
IS MITSUKI UP?
MITSUKI-CHAN! YOU CAN DO IT!

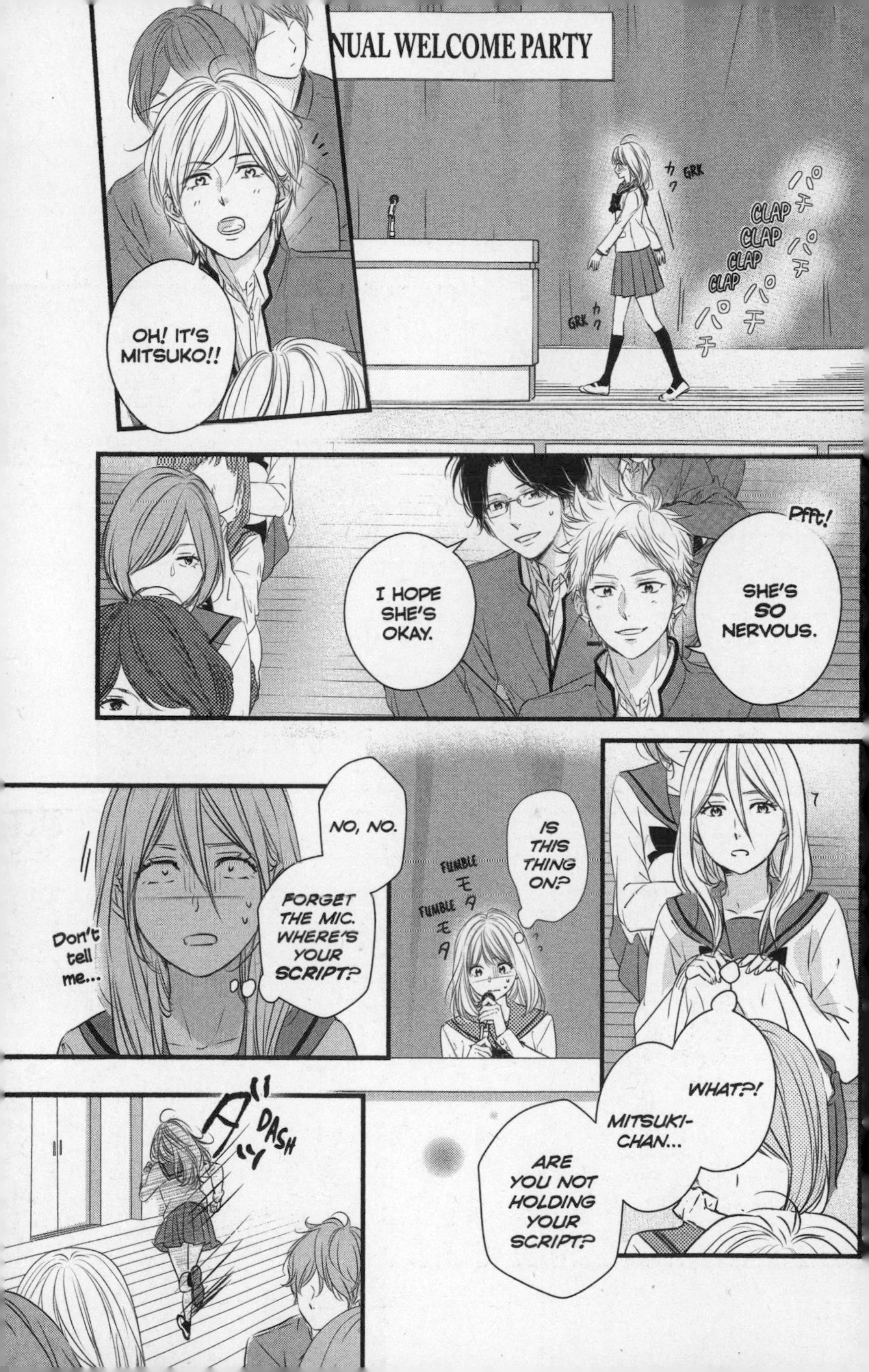
NUAL WELCOME PARTY
GRK
CLAP
CLAP
CLAP
CLAP
GRK
OH! IT'S MITSUKO!!
Pfft!
SHE'S SO NERVOUS.
I HOPE SHE'S OKAY.
WHAT?!
MITSUKI-CHAN...
ARE YOU NOT HOLDING YOUR SCRIPT?
IS THIS THING ON?
FUMBLE
FUMBLE
NO, NO.
FORGET THE MIC. WHERE'S YOUR SCRIPT?
Don't tell me...
DASH

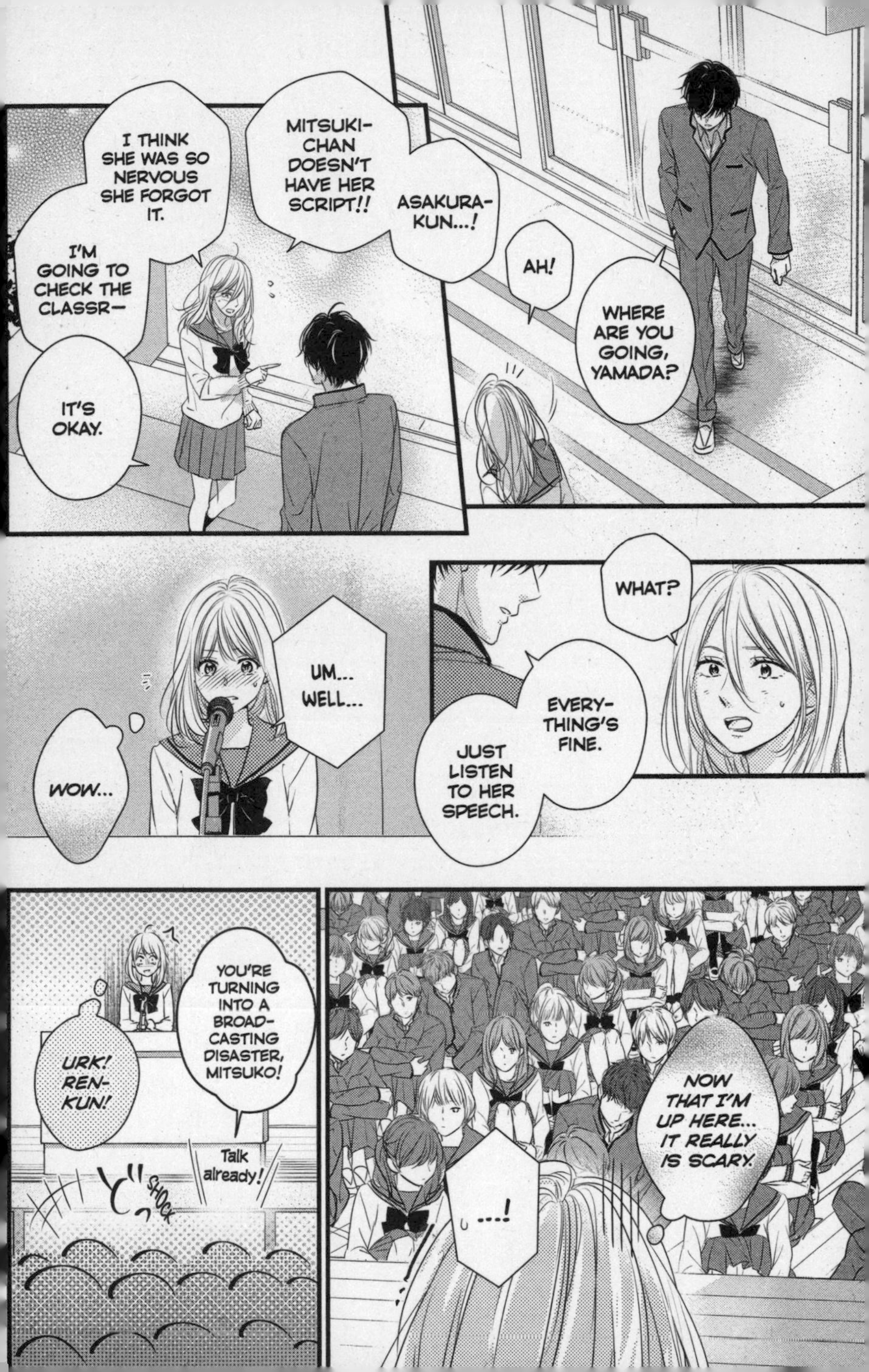
AH!
WHERE ARE YOU GOING, YAMADA?
ASAKURA-KUN...!
MITSUKI-CHAN DOESN'T HAVE HER SCRIPT!!
I THINK SHE WAS SO NERVOUS SHE FORGOT IT.
I'M GOING TO CHECK THE CLASSR—
IT'S OKAY.
WHAT?
EVERY-THING'S FINE.
JUST LISTEN TO HER SPEECH.
UM... WELL...
WOW...
NOW THAT I'M UP HERE... IT REALLY IS SCARY.
...!
YOU'RE TURNING INTO A BROAD-CASTING DISASTER, MITSUKO!
Talk already!
URK! REN-KUN!
SHOCK

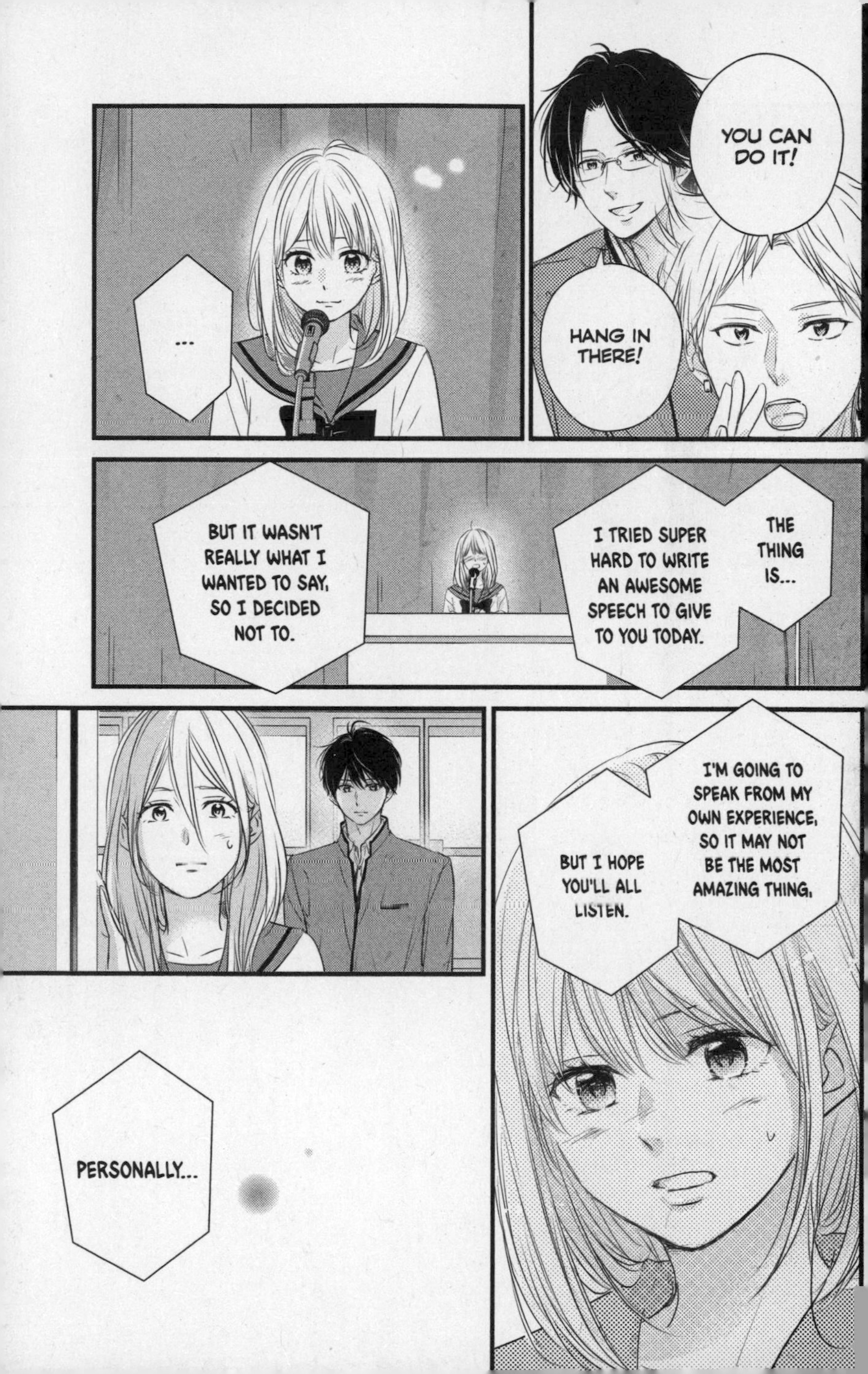
YOU CAN DO IT!
HANG IN THERE!
...
THE THING IS...
I TRIED SUPER HARD TO WRITE AN AWESOME SPEECH TO GIVE TO YOU TODAY.
BUT IT WASN'T REALLY WHAT I WANTED TO SAY, SO I DECIDED NOT TO.
I'M GOING TO SPEAK FROM MY OWN EXPERIENCE, SO IT MAY NOT BE THE MOST AMAZING THING,
BUT I HOPE YOU'LL ALL LISTEN.
PERSONALLY...

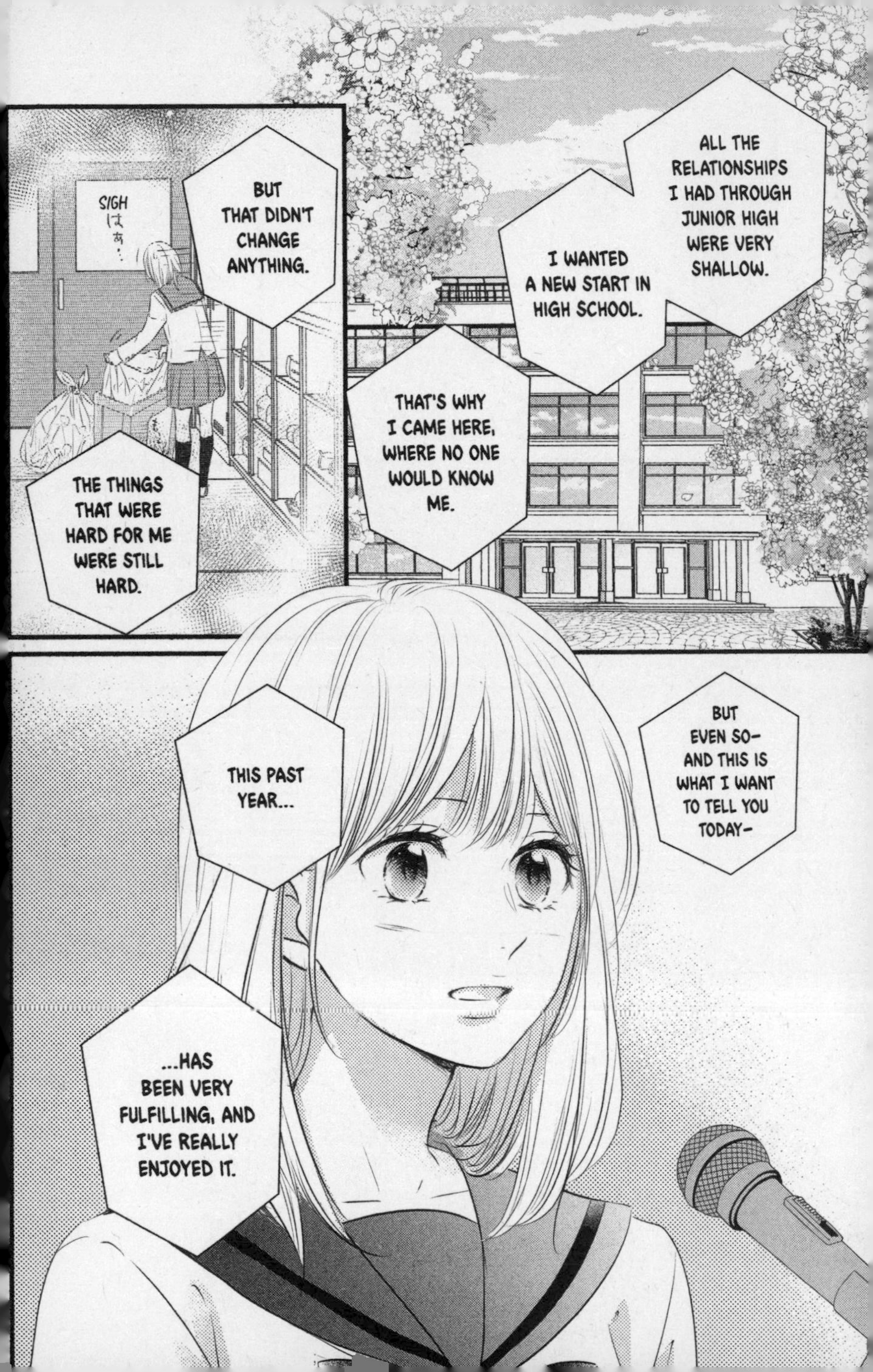
ALL THE RELATIONSHIPS I HAD THROUGH JUNIOR HIGH WERE VERY SHALLOW.
I WANTED A NEW START IN HIGH SCHOOL.
THAT'S WHY I CAME HERE, WHERE NO ONE WOULD KNOW ME.
BUT THAT DIDN'T CHANGE ANYTHING.
SIGH
はあ・・・
THE THINGS THAT WERE HARD FOR ME WERE STILL HARD.
BUT EVEN SO—AND THIS IS WHAT I WANT TO TELL YOU TODAY—
THIS PAST YEAR...
...HAS BEEN VERY FULFILLING, AND I'VE REALLY ENJOYED IT.

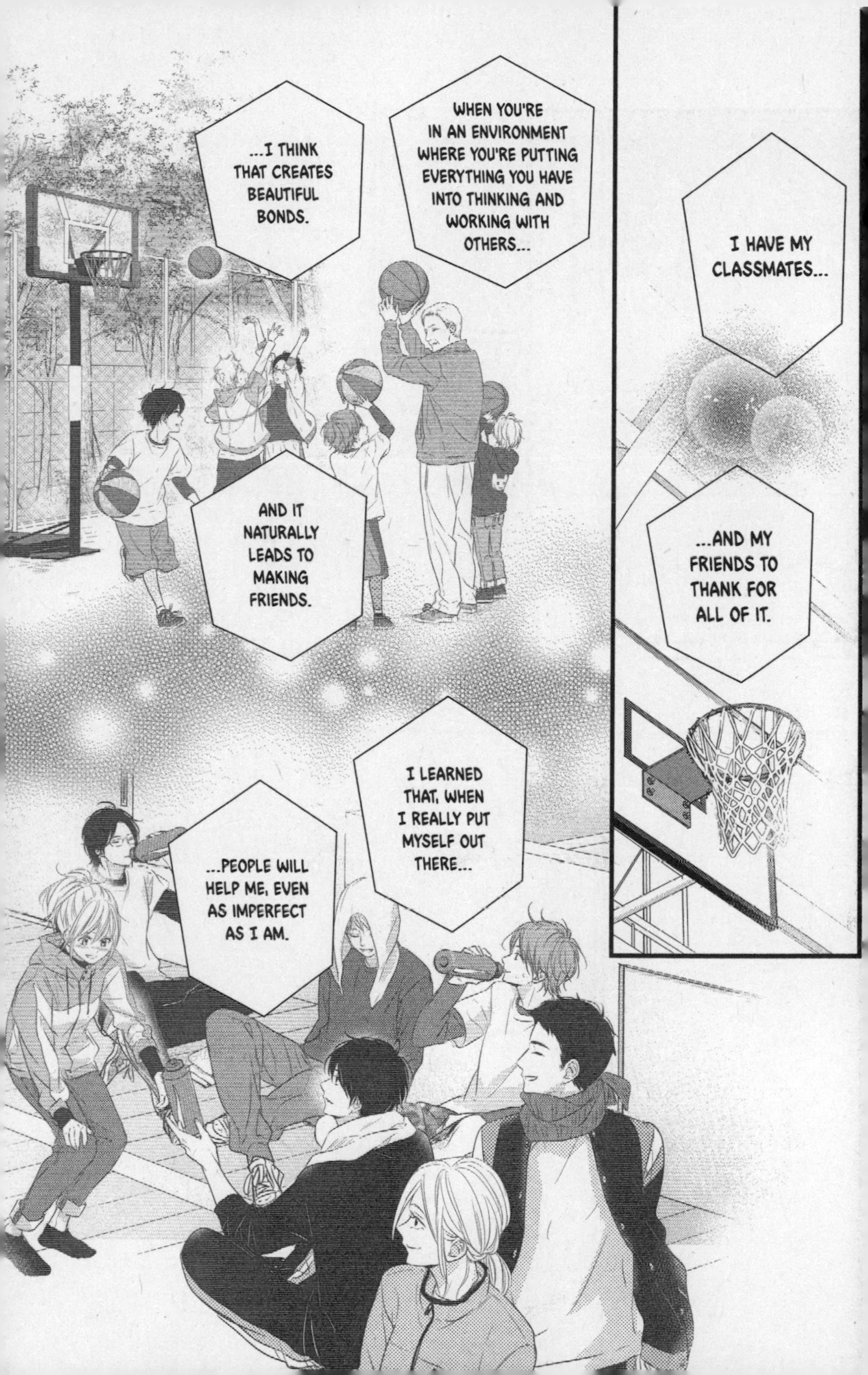
WHEN YOU'RE IN AN ENVIRONMENT WHERE YOU'RE PUTTING EVERYTHING YOU HAVE INTO THINKING AND WORKING WITH OTHERS...
...I THINK THAT CREATES BEAUTIFUL BONDS.
AND IT NATURALLY LEADS TO MAKING FRIENDS.
I LEARNED THAT, WHEN I REALLY PUT MYSELF OUT THERE...
...PEOPLE WILL HELP ME, EVEN AS IMPERFECT AS I AM.
I HAVE MY CLASSMATES...
...AND MY FRIENDS TO THANK FOR ALL OF IT.

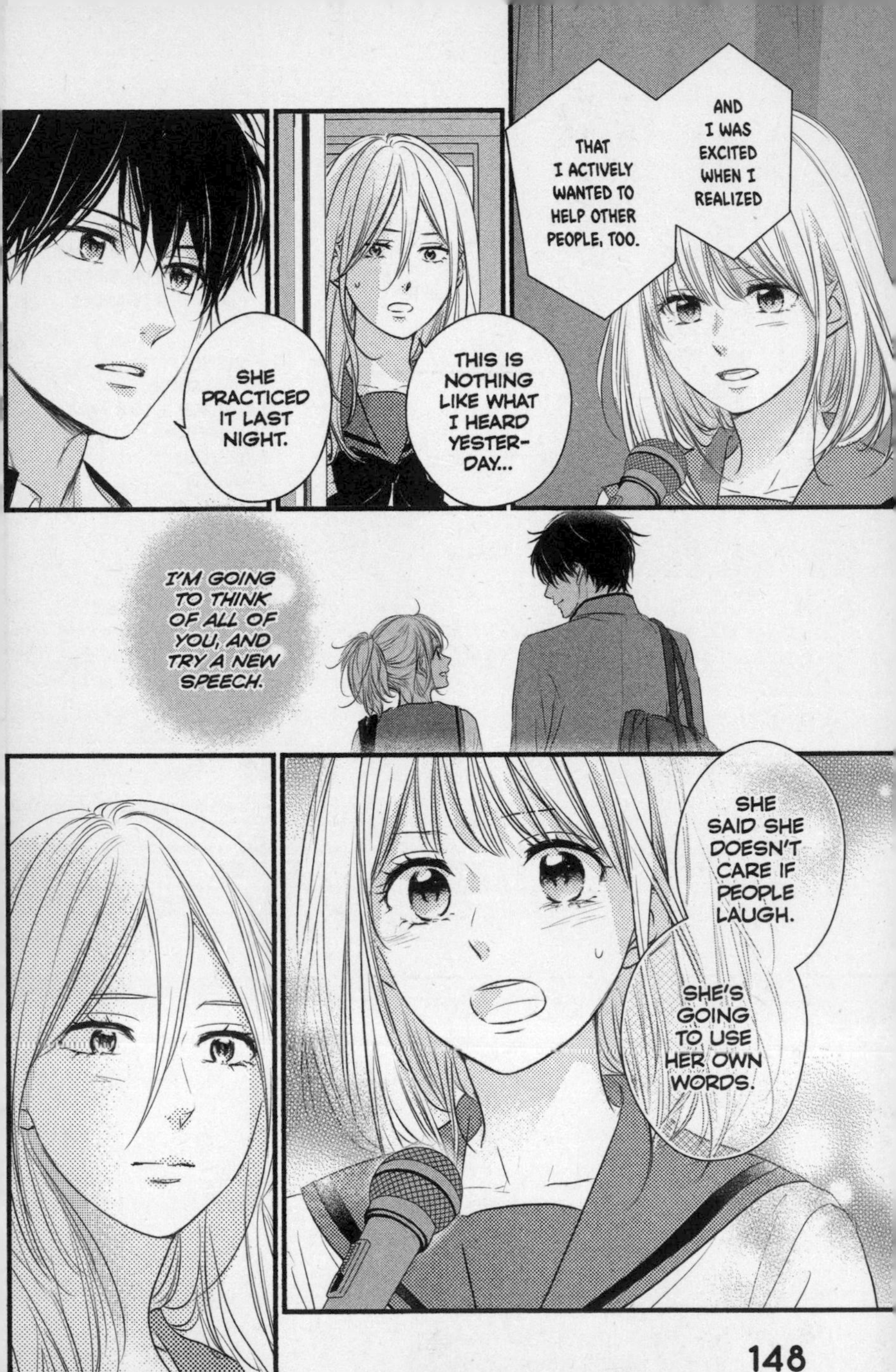
AND I WAS EXCITED WHEN I REALIZED
THAT I ACTIVELY WANTED TO HELP OTHER PEOPLE, TOO.
THIS IS NOTHING LIKE WHAT I HEARD YESTER-DAY...
SHE PRACTICED IT LAST NIGHT.
I'M GOING TO THINK OF ALL OF YOU, AND TRY A NEW SPEECH.
SHE SAID SHE DOESN'T CARE IF PEOPLE LAUGH.
SHE'S GOING TO USE HER OWN WORDS.

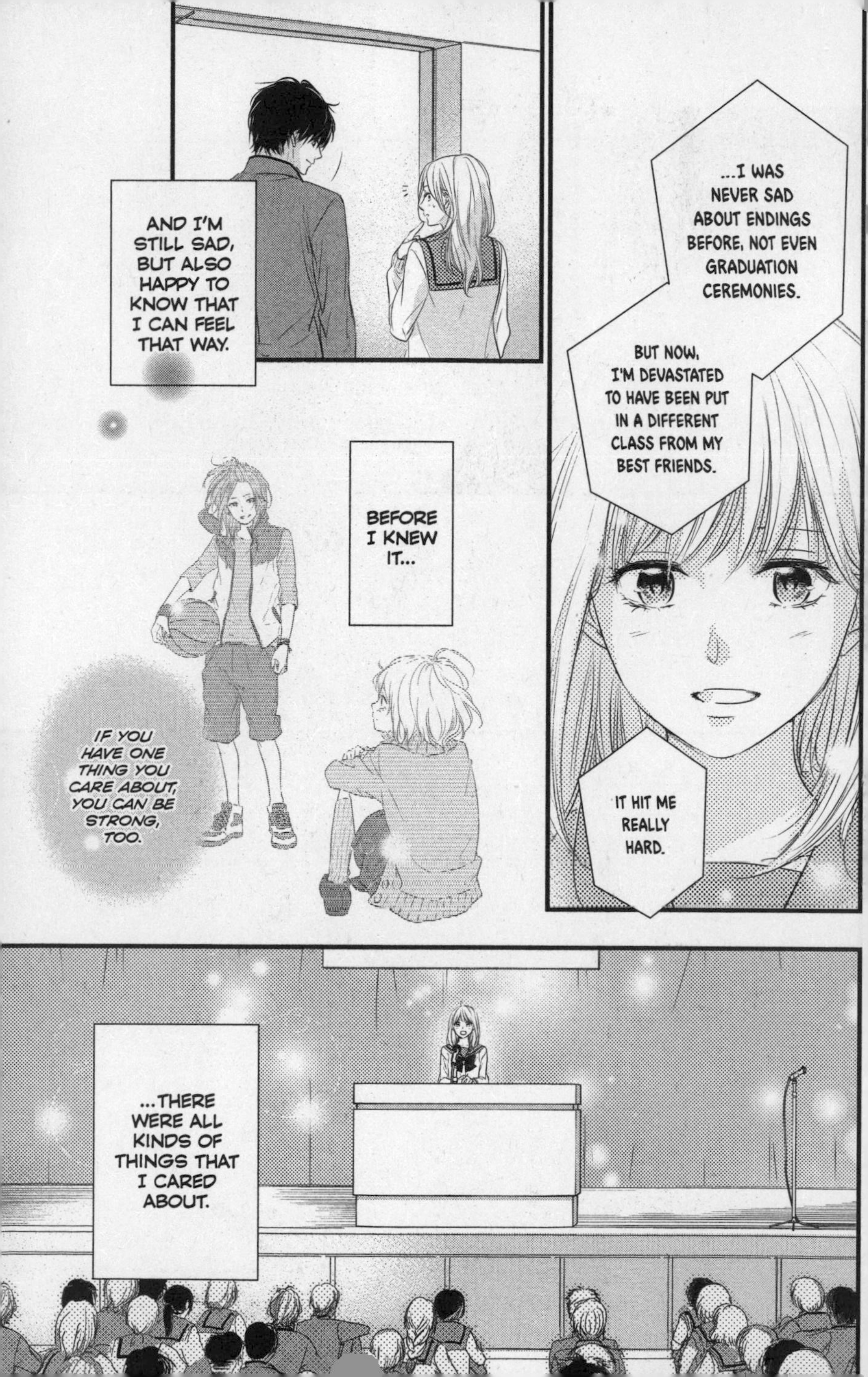
...I WAS NEVER SAD ABOUT ENDINGS BEFORE, NOT EVEN GRADUATION CEREMONIES.
BUT NOW, I'M DEVASTATED TO HAVE BEEN PUT IN A DIFFERENT CLASS FROM MY BEST FRIENDS.
IT HIT ME REALLY HARD.
AND I'M STILL SAD, BUT ALSO HAPPY TO KNOW THAT I CAN FEEL THAT WAY.
BEFORE I KNEW IT...
IF YOU HAVE ONE THING YOU CARE ABOUT, YOU CAN BE STRONG, TOO.
...THERE WERE ALL KINDS OF THINGS THAT I CARED ABOUT.

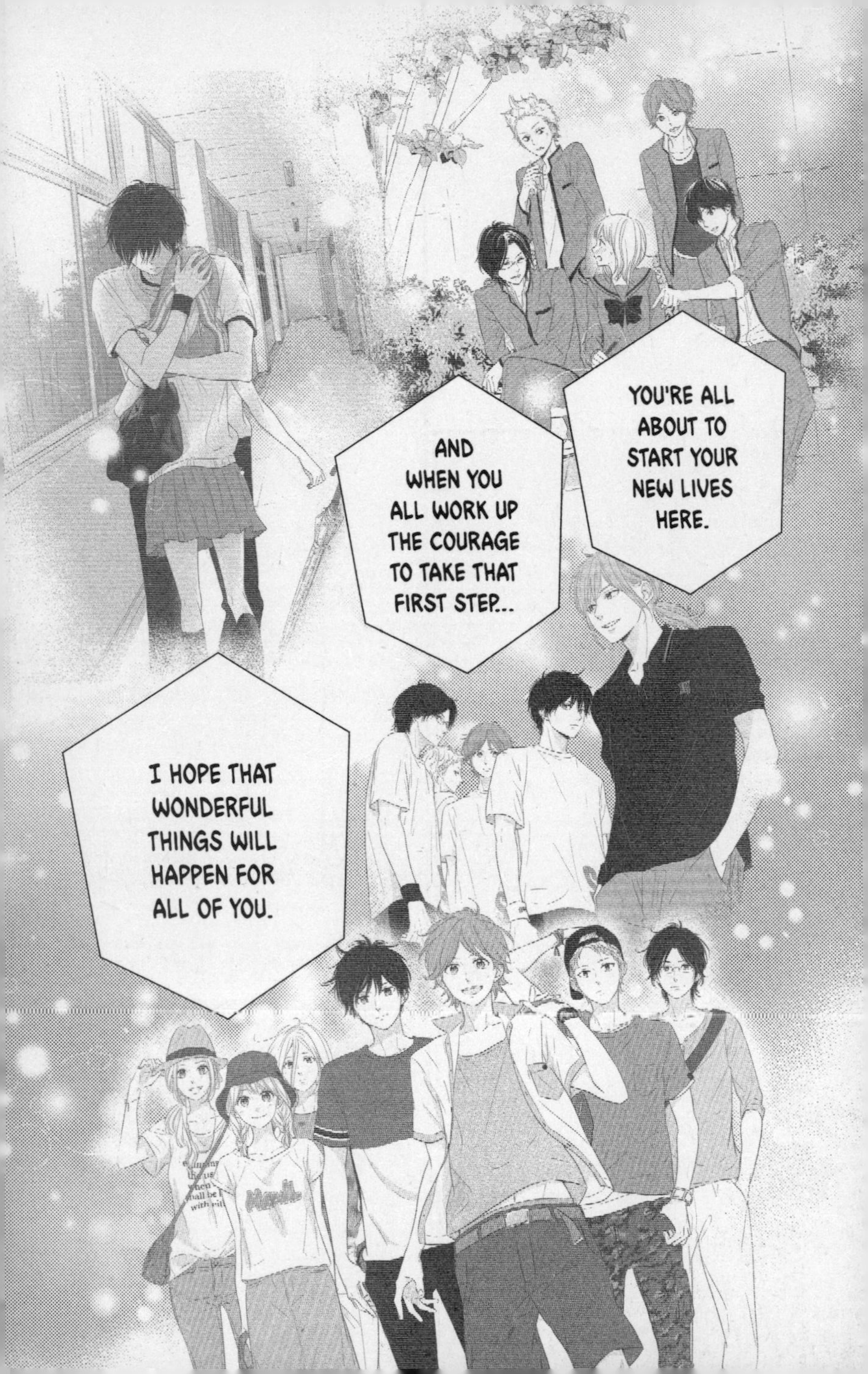
YOU'RE ALL ABOUT TO START YOUR NEW LIVES HERE.
AND WHEN YOU ALL WORK UP THE COURAGE TO TAKE THAT FIRST STEP...
I HOPE THAT WONDERFUL THINGS WILL HAPPEN FOR ALL OF YOU.

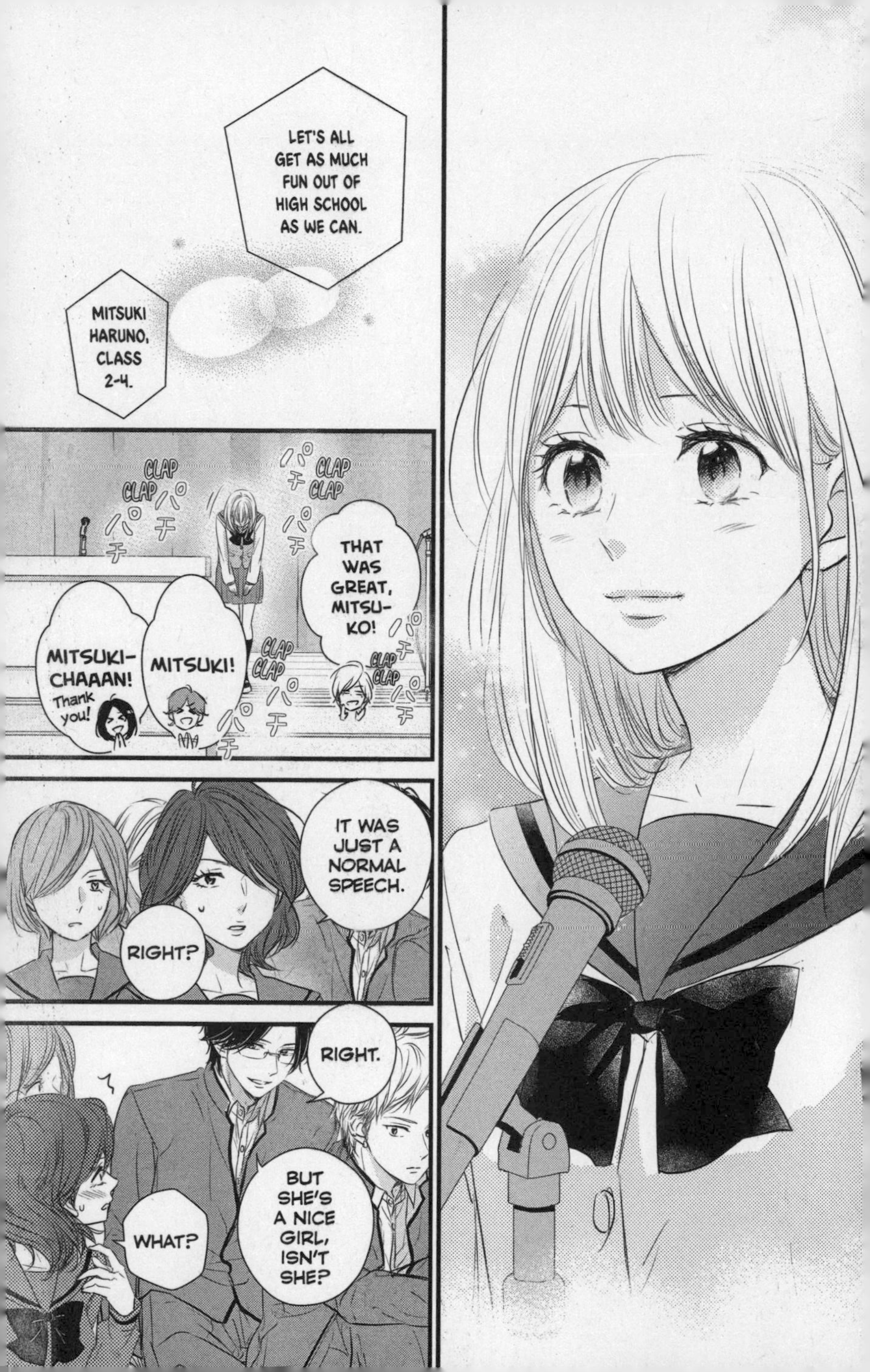
LET'S ALL GET AS MUCH FUN OUT OF HIGH SCHOOL AS WE CAN.
MITSUKI HARUNO, CLASS 2-4.
CLAP CLAP
パチ パチ
THAT WAS GREAT, MITSU-KO!
CLAP CLAP
パチ パチ
CLAP CLAP
パチ パチ
MITSUKI!
MITSUKI-CHAAAN! Thank you!
CLAP CLAP
パチ パチ
IT WAS JUST A NORMAL SPEECH.
RIGHT?
RIGHT.
BUT SHE'S A NICE GIRL, ISN'T SHE?
WHAT?

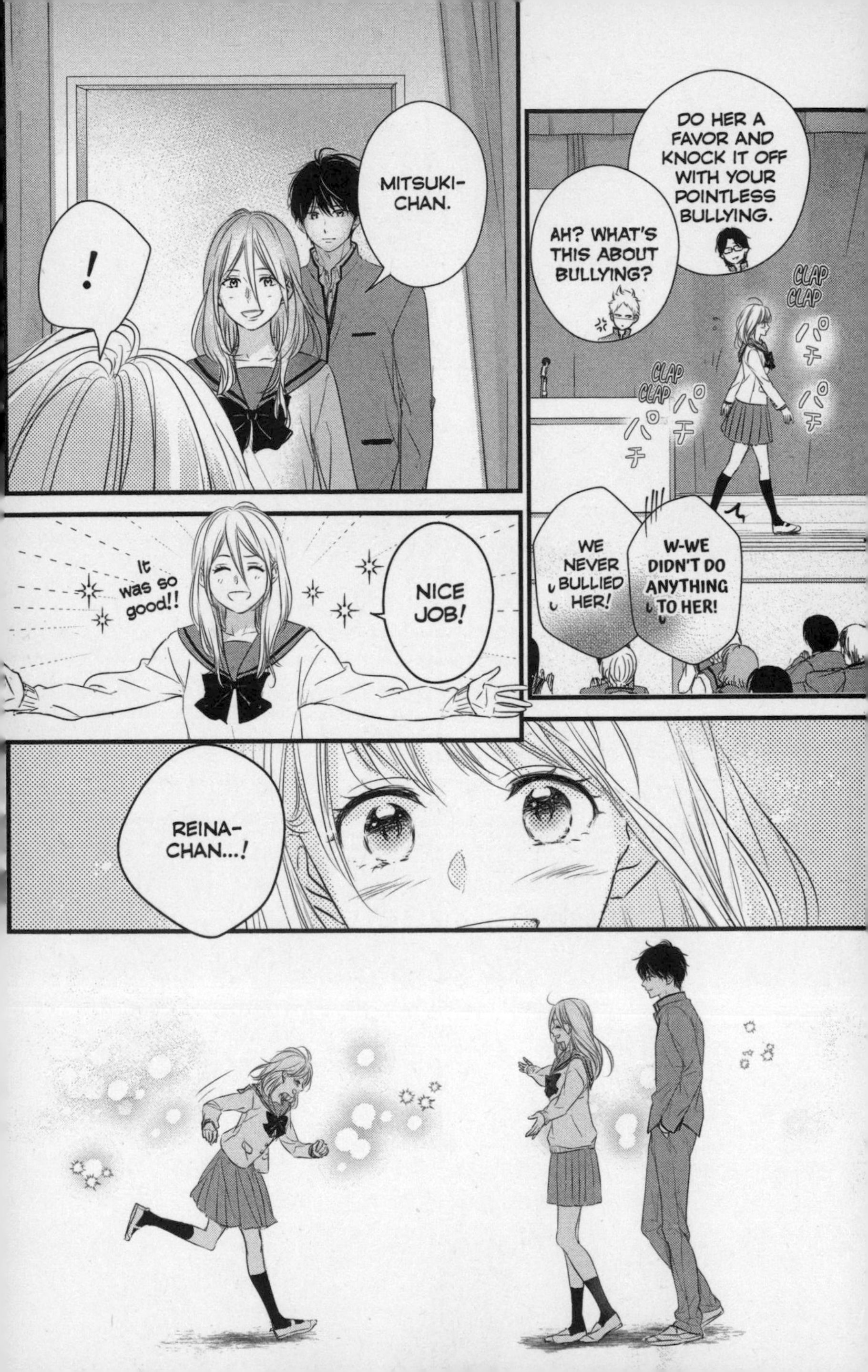
DO HER A FAVOR AND KNOCK IT OFF WITH YOUR POINTLESS BULLYING.
AH? WHAT'S THIS ABOUT BULLYING?
CLAP CLAP
パチ パチ
CLAP CLAP
パチ パチ
W-WE DIDN'T DO ANYTHING TO HER!
WE NEVER BULLIED HER!
MITSUKI-CHAN.
!
NICE JOB!
It was so good!!
REINA-CHAN...!

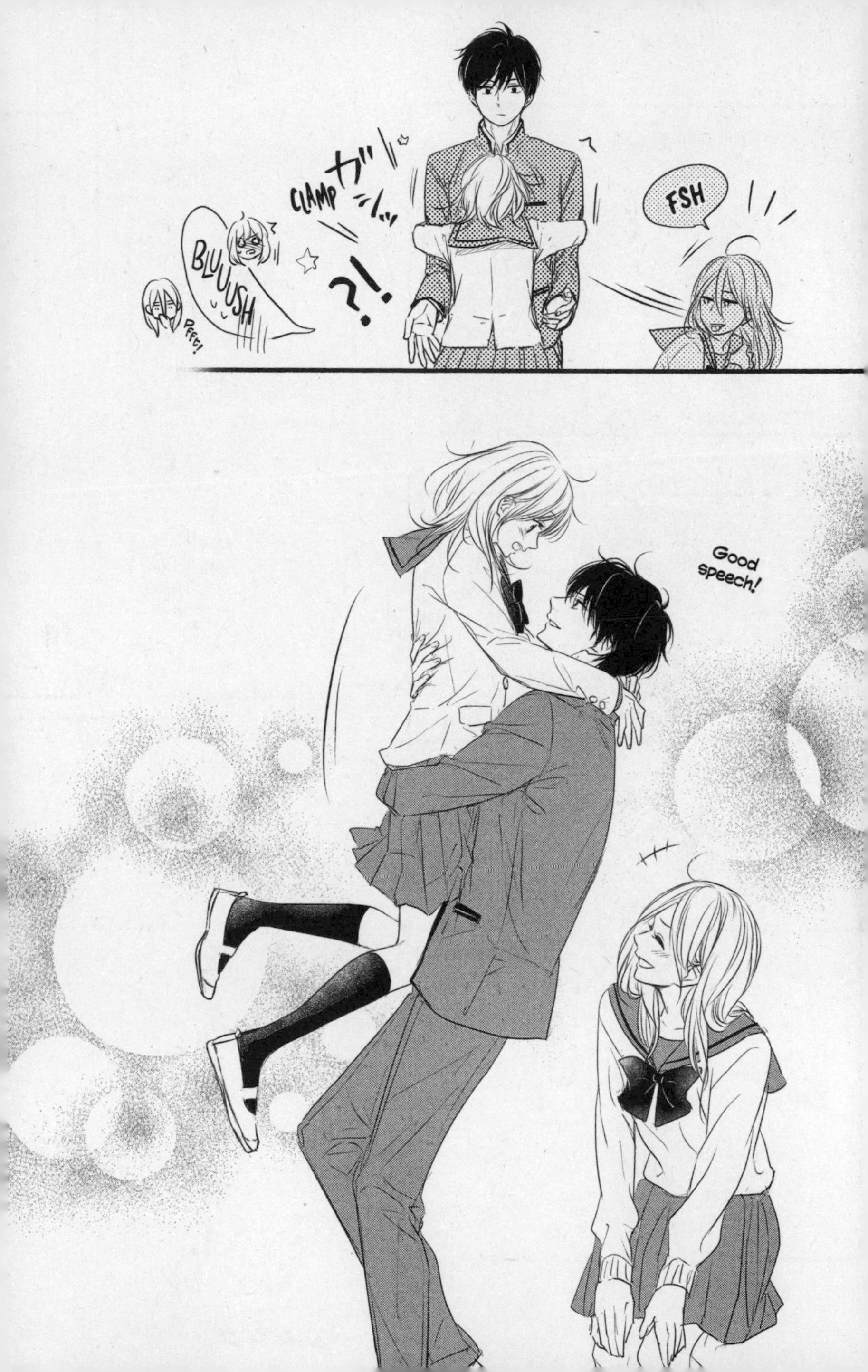
FSH
CLAMP
ガッ
?!
BLUUUSH
Pfft!
Good speech!

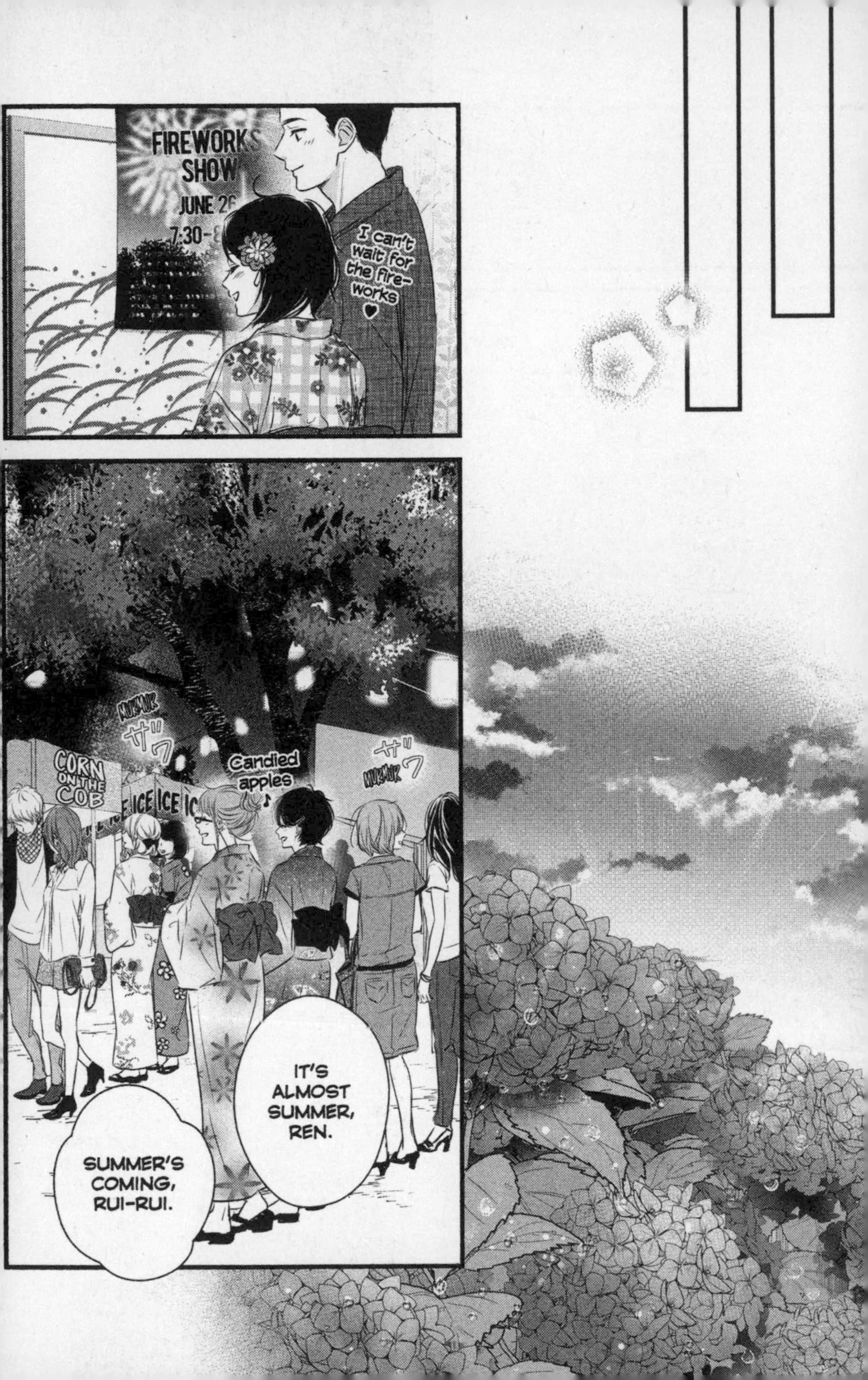
FIREWORKS SHOW
JUNE 2
7:30-
I can't wait for the fire-works ♥
MURMUR ザワ
Candied apples ♪
CORN ON THE COB
ICE ICE IC
MURMUR ザワ
IT'S ALMOST SUMMER, REN.
SUMMER'S COMING, RUI-RUI.

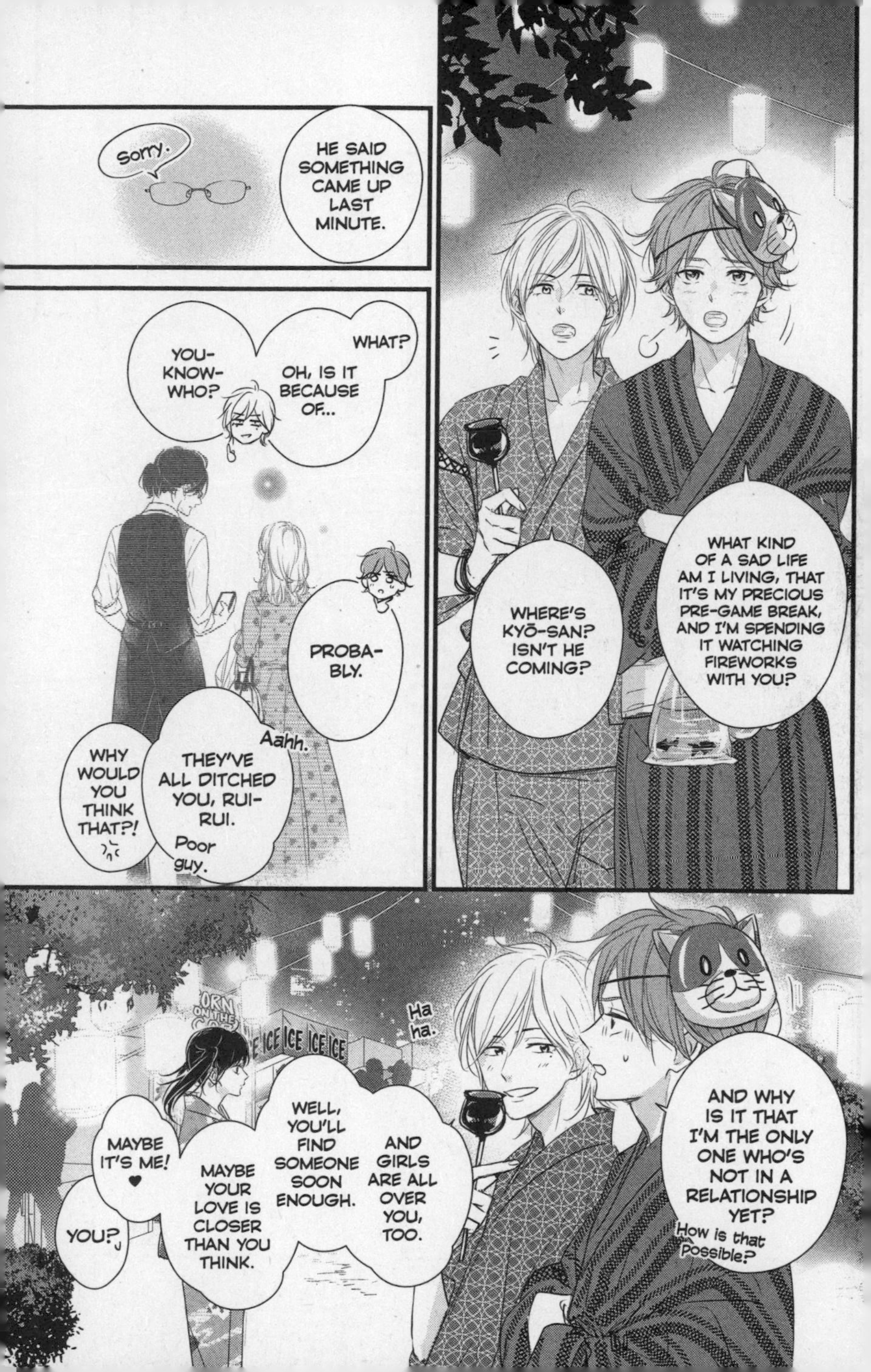
WHAT KIND OF A SAD LIFE AM I LIVING, THAT IT'S MY PRECIOUS PRE-GAME BREAK, AND I'M SPENDING IT WATCHING FIREWORKS WITH YOU?
WHERE'S KYŌ-SAN? ISN'T HE COMING?
HE SAID SOMETHING CAME UP LAST MINUTE.
Sorry.
WHAT?
OH, IS IT BECAUSE OF...
YOU-KNOW-WHO?
PROBA-BLY.
Aahh.
THEY'VE ALL DITCHED YOU, RUI-RUI.
Poor guy.
WHY WOULD YOU THINK THAT?!
AND WHY IS IT THAT I'M THE ONLY ONE WHO'S NOT IN A RELATIONSHIP YET?
How is that possible?
Ha ha.
ICE ICE ICE ICE
AND GIRLS ARE ALL OVER YOU, TOO.
WELL, YOU'LL FIND SOMEONE SOON ENOUGH.
MAYBE YOUR LOVE IS CLOSER THAN YOU THINK.
MAYBE IT'S ME! ♥
YOU?

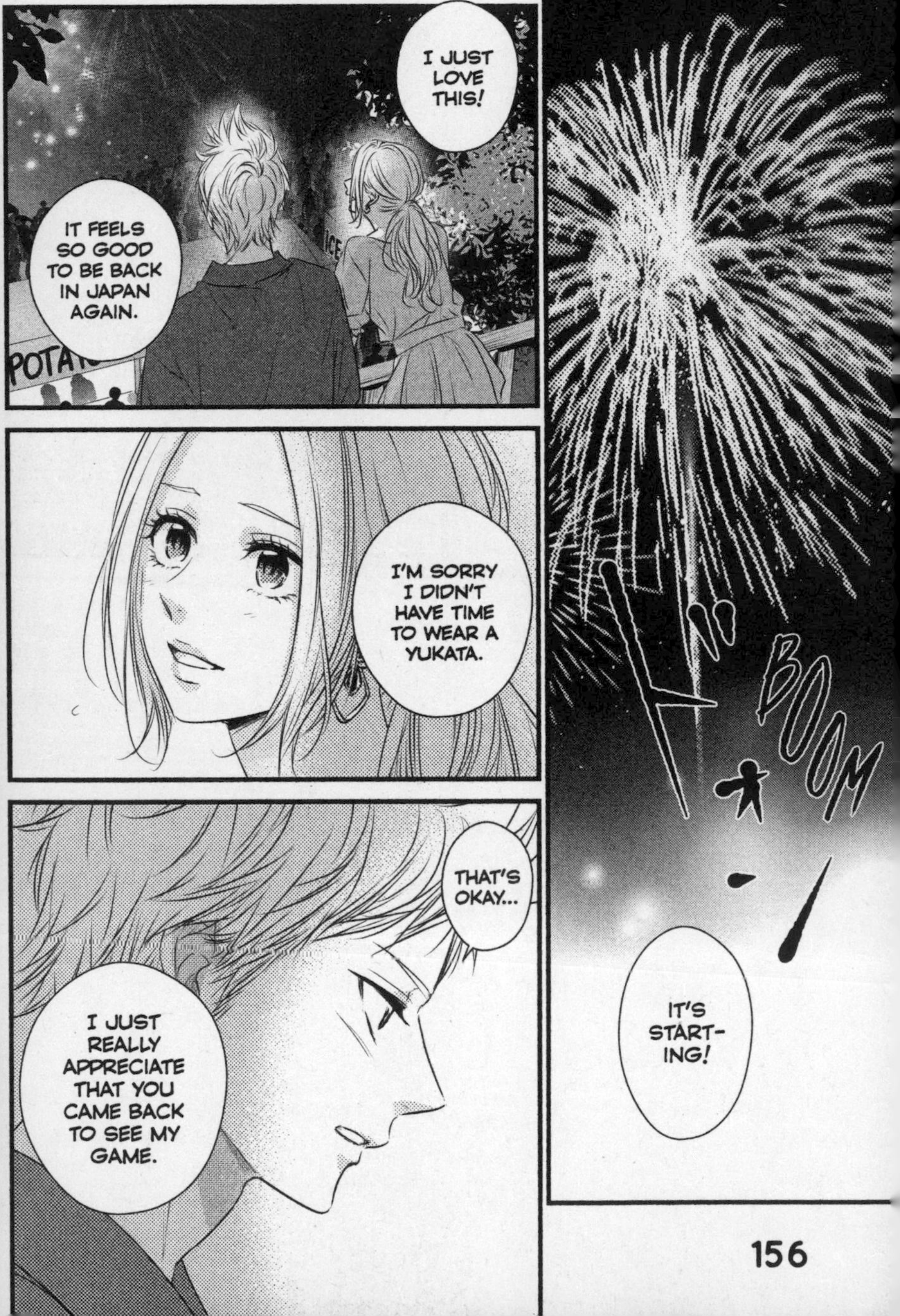
BOOM
IT'S START-ING!
I JUST LOVE THIS!
IT FEELS SO GOOD TO BE BACK IN JAPAN AGAIN.
I'M SORRY I DIDN'T HAVE TIME TO WEAR A YUKATA.
THAT'S OKAY...
I JUST REALLY APPRECIATE THAT YOU CAME BACK TO SEE MY GAME.

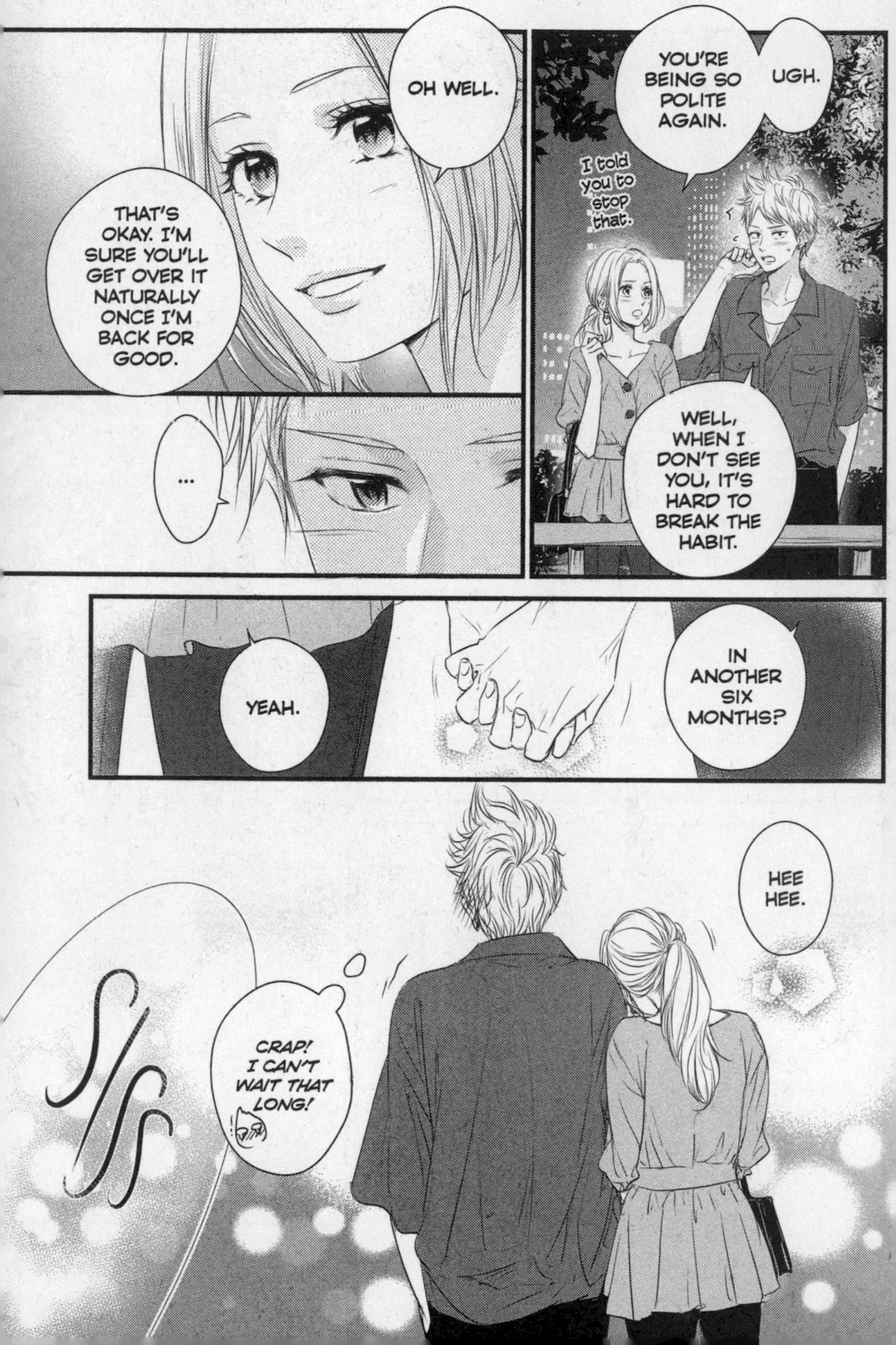
UGH.
YOU'RE BEING SO POLITE AGAIN.
I told you to stop that.
WELL, WHEN I DON'T SEE YOU, IT'S HARD TO BREAK THE HABIT.
OH WELL.
THAT'S OKAY. I'M SURE YOU'LL GET OVER IT NATURALLY ONCE I'M BACK FOR GOOD.
...
IN ANOTHER SIX MONTHS?
YEAH.
HEE HEE.
CRAP! I CAN'T WAIT THAT LONG!

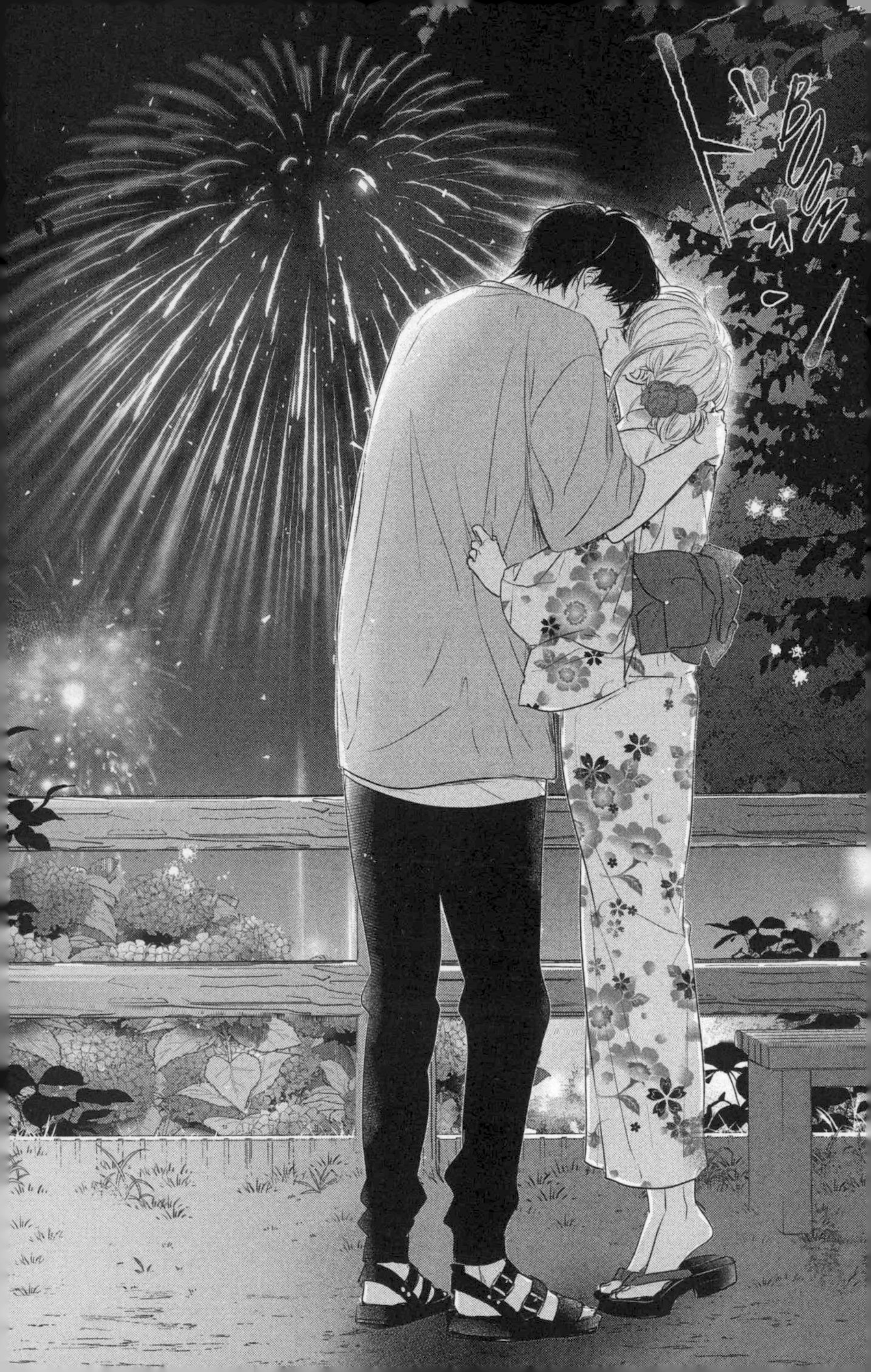
BOOM

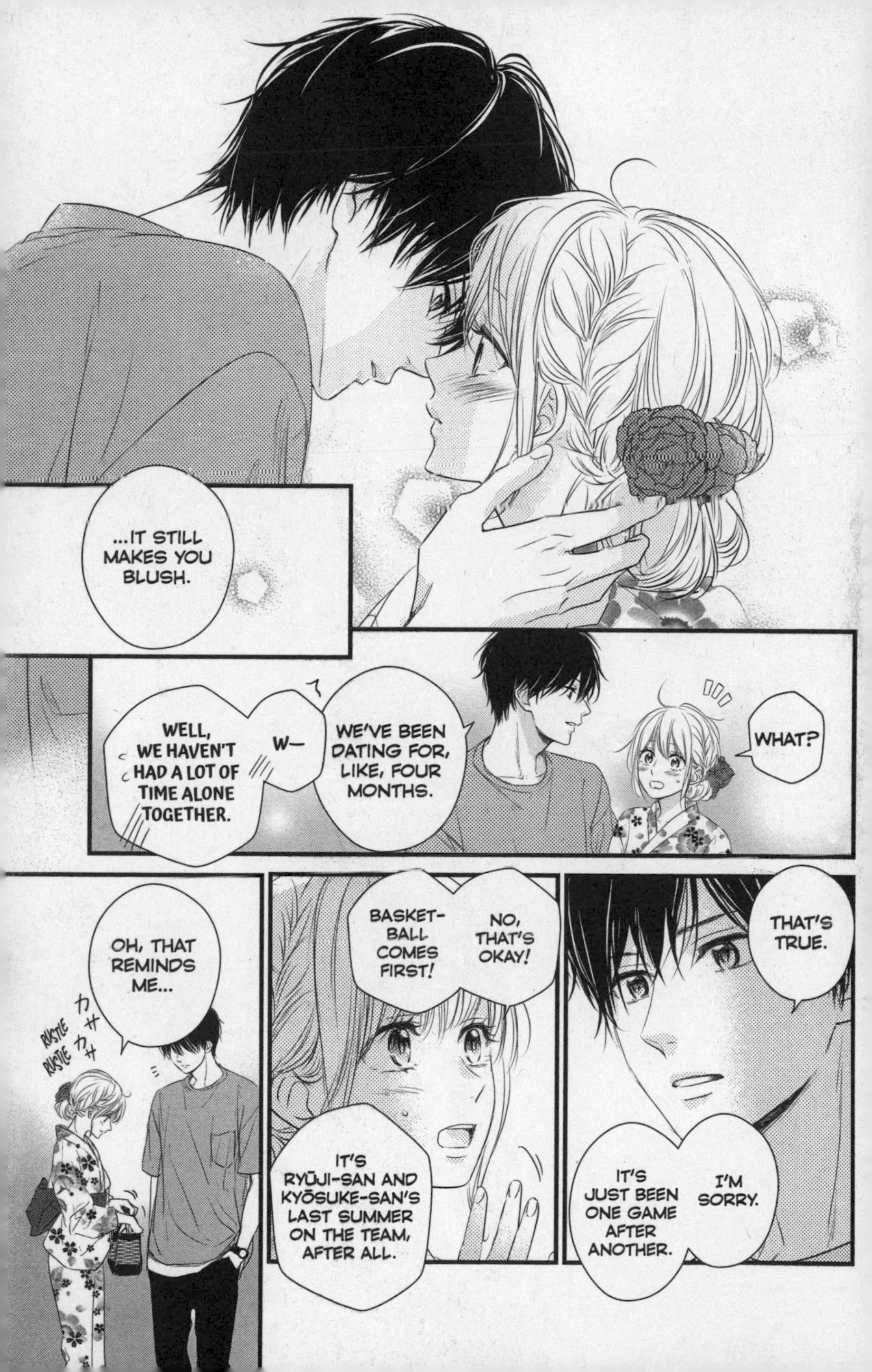
...IT STILL MAKES YOU BLUSH.
WHAT?
WE'VE BEEN DATING FOR, LIKE, FOUR MONTHS.
W—
WELL, WE HAVEN'T HAD A LOT OF TIME ALONE TOGETHER.
THAT'S TRUE.
I'M SORRY.
IT'S JUST BEEN ONE GAME AFTER ANOTHER.
NO, THAT'S OKAY!
BASKET-BALL COMES FIRST!
IT'S RYŪJI-SAN AND KYŌSUKE-SAN'S LAST SUMMER ON THE TEAM, AFTER ALL.
OH, THAT REMINDS ME...
カサ カサ
RUSTLE RUSTLE

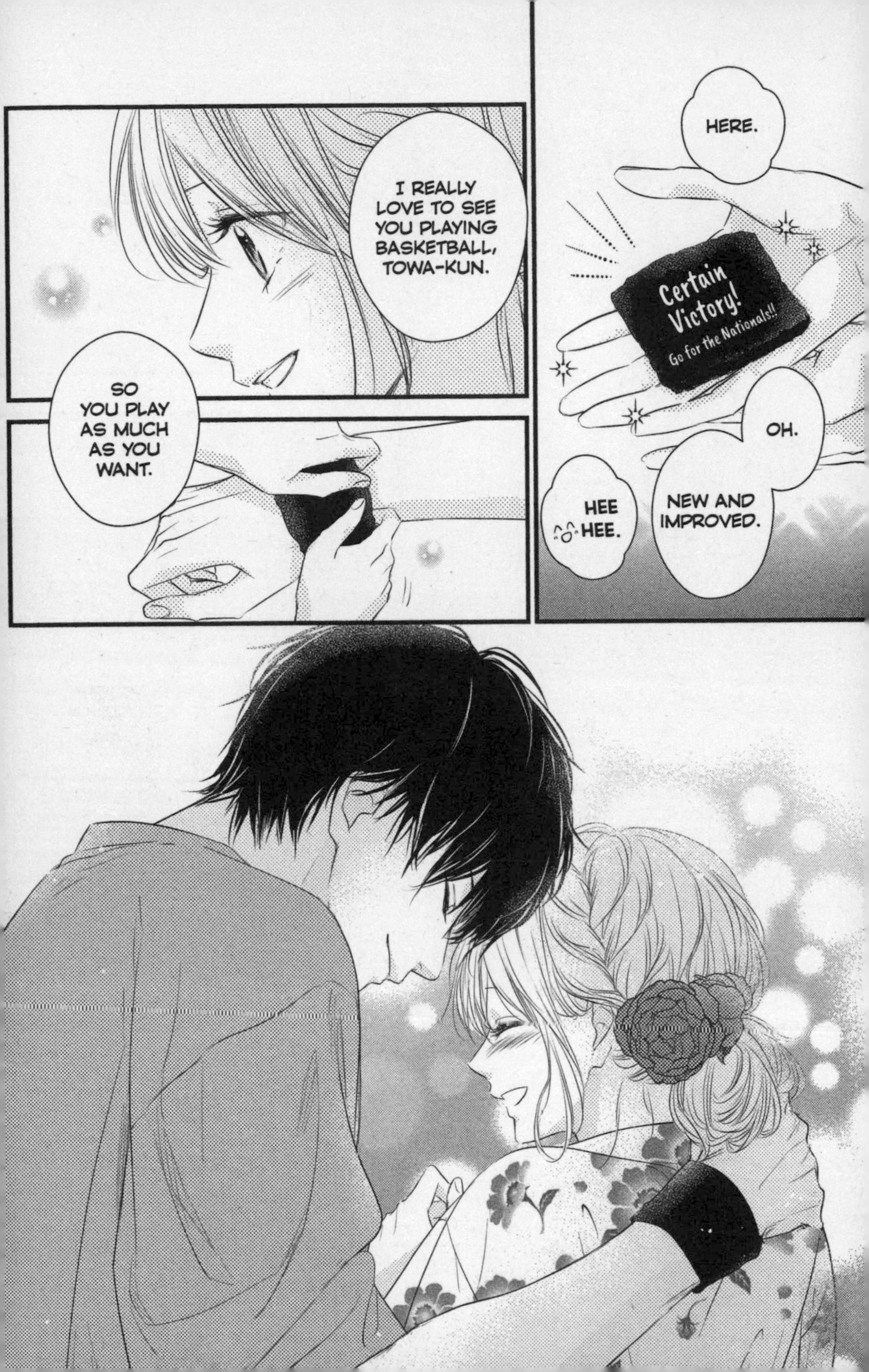
HERE.
Certain Victory!
Go for the Nationals!!
OH.
NEW AND IMPROVED.
HEE HEE.
I REALLY LOVE TO SEE YOU PLAYING BASKETBALL, TOWA-KUN.
SO YOU PLAY AS MUCH AS YOU WANT.

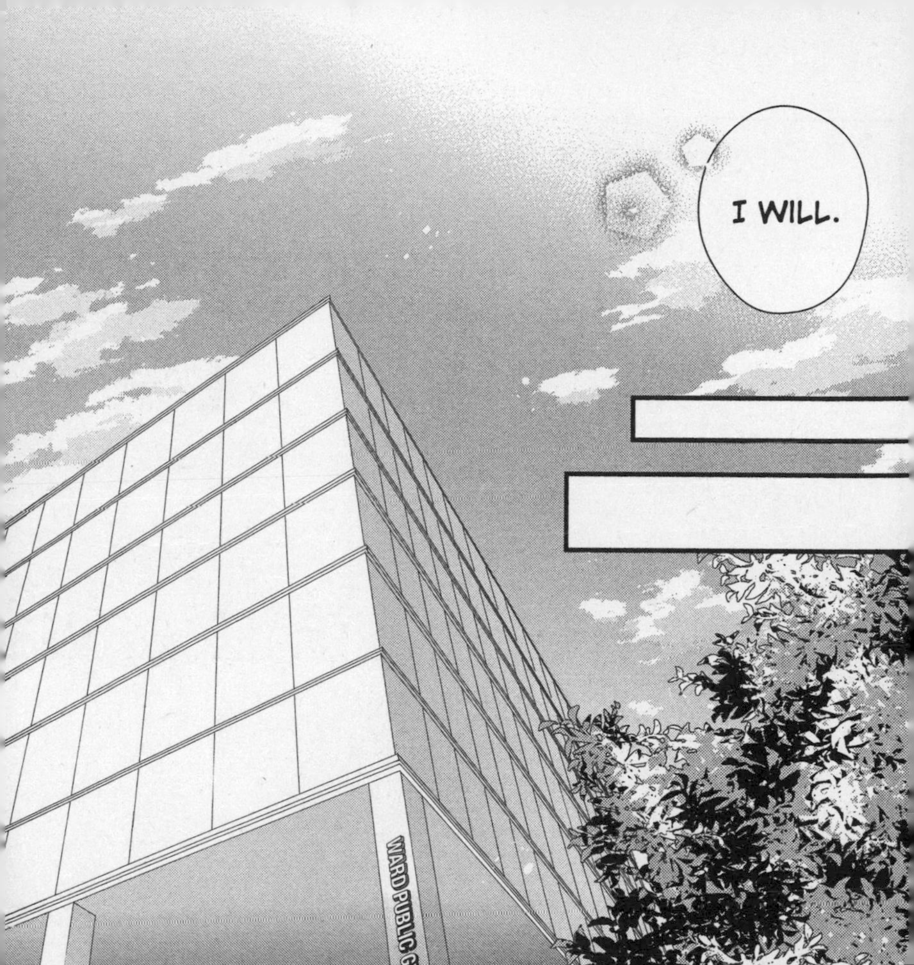
I WILL.
WARD PUBLIC GYMNASIUM
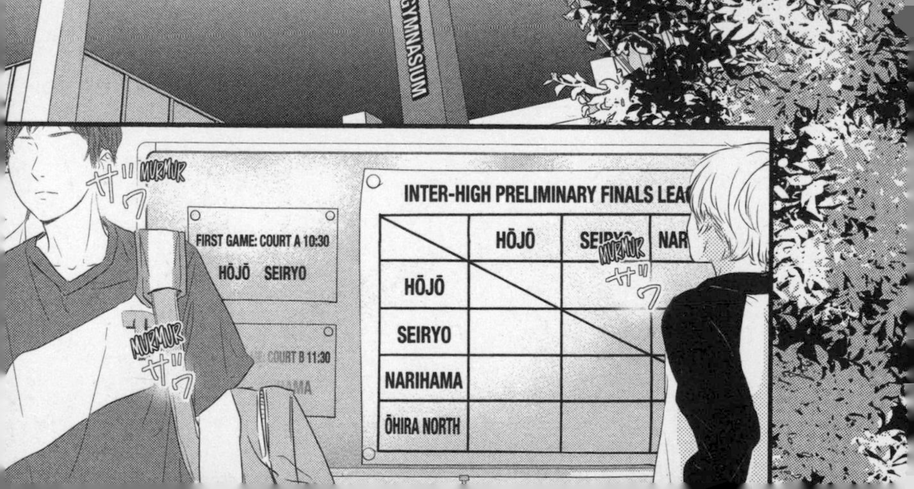
MURMUR
INTER-HIGH PRELIMINARY FINALS
HŌJŌ
NARIHAMA
ŌHIRA NORTH
FIRST GAME: COURT A 10:30
HŌJŌ SEIRYO
COURT B 11:30
MURMUR
MURMUR

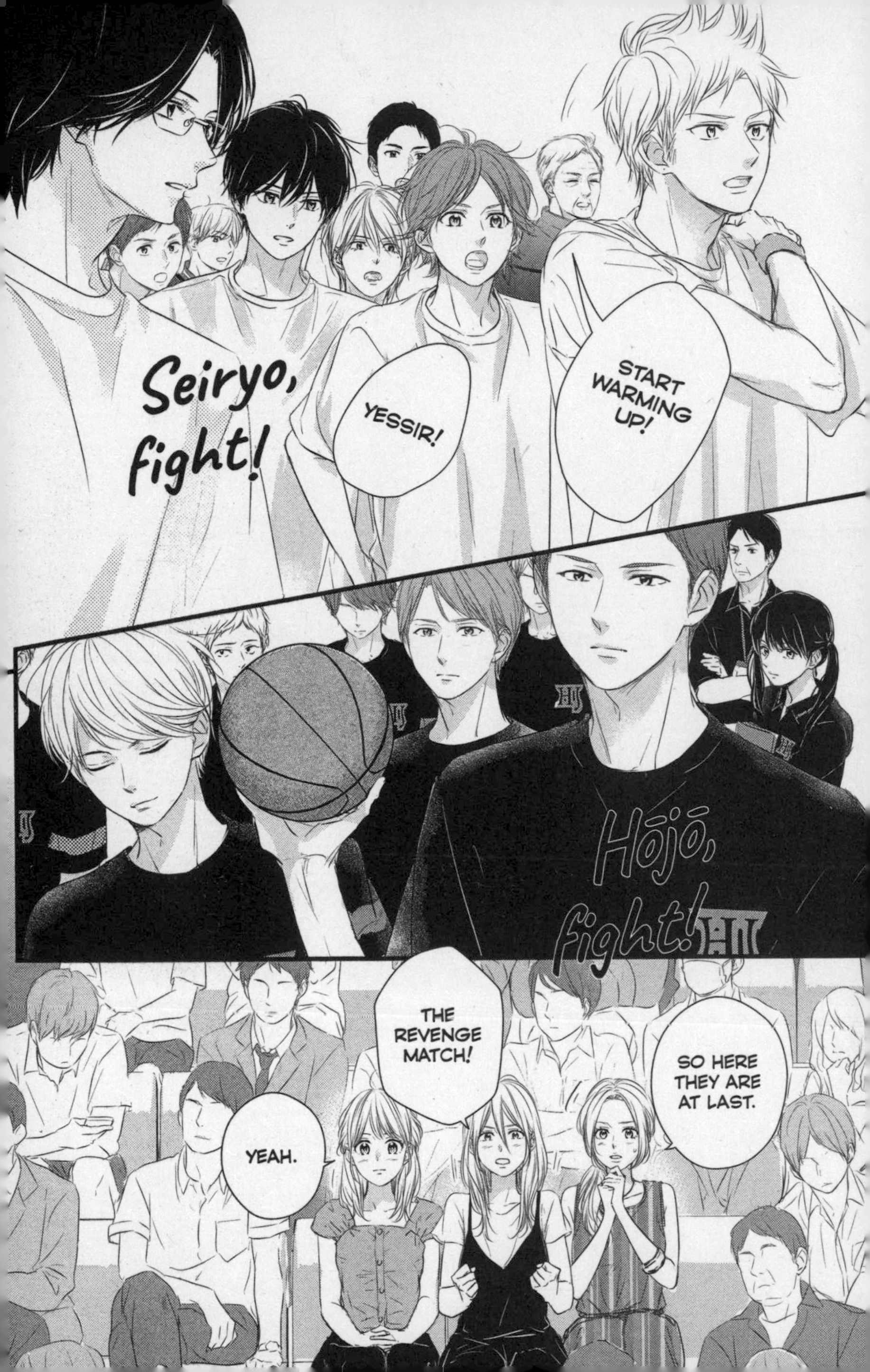
START WARMING UP!
YESSIR!
Seiryo, fight!
Hōjō, fight!
SO HERE THEY ARE AT LAST.
THE REVENGE MATCH!
YEAH.

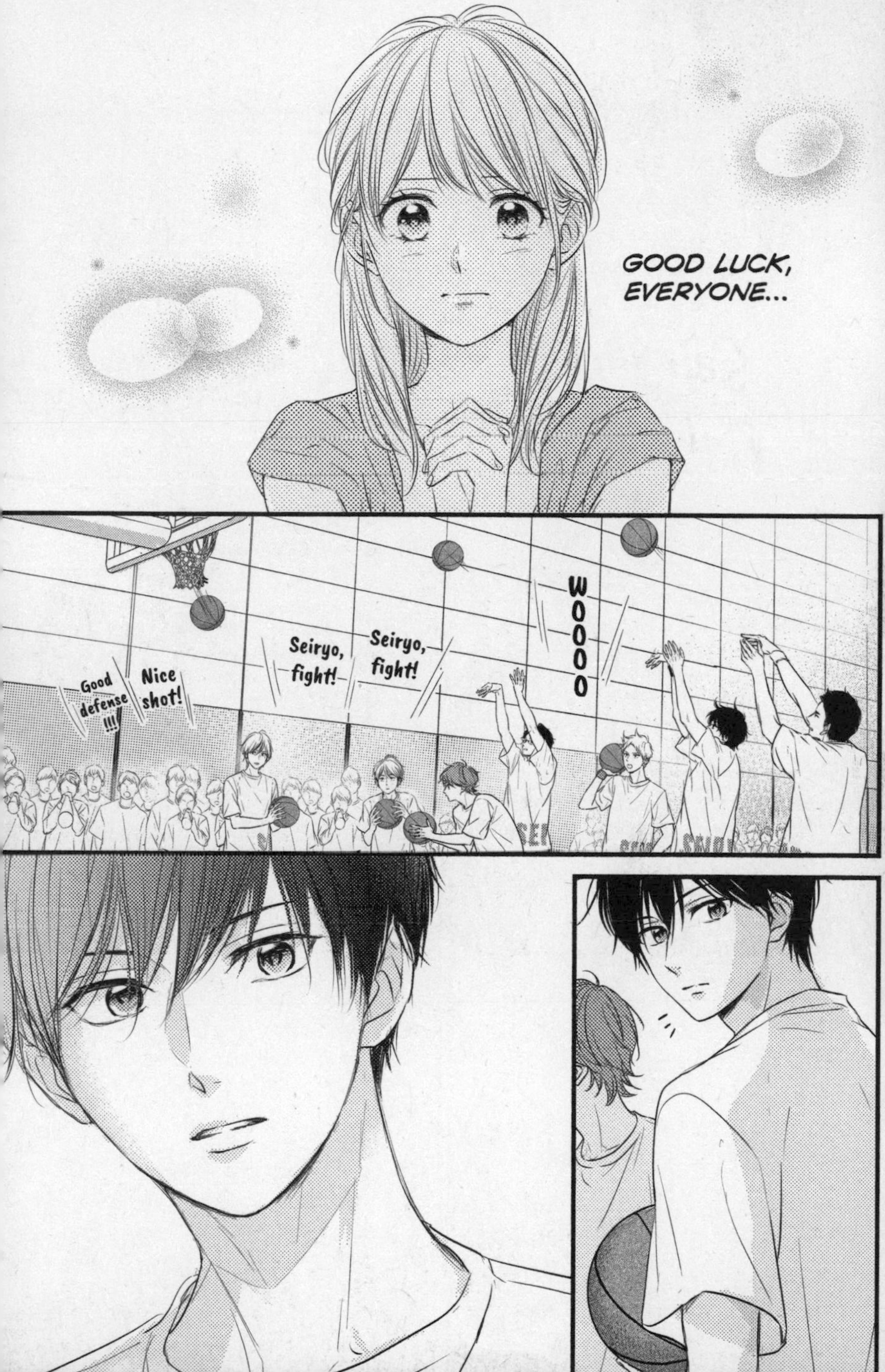
GOOD LUCK, EVERYONE...
WOOOOO
Seiryo, fight!
Seiryo, fight!
Nice shot!
Good defense!!!

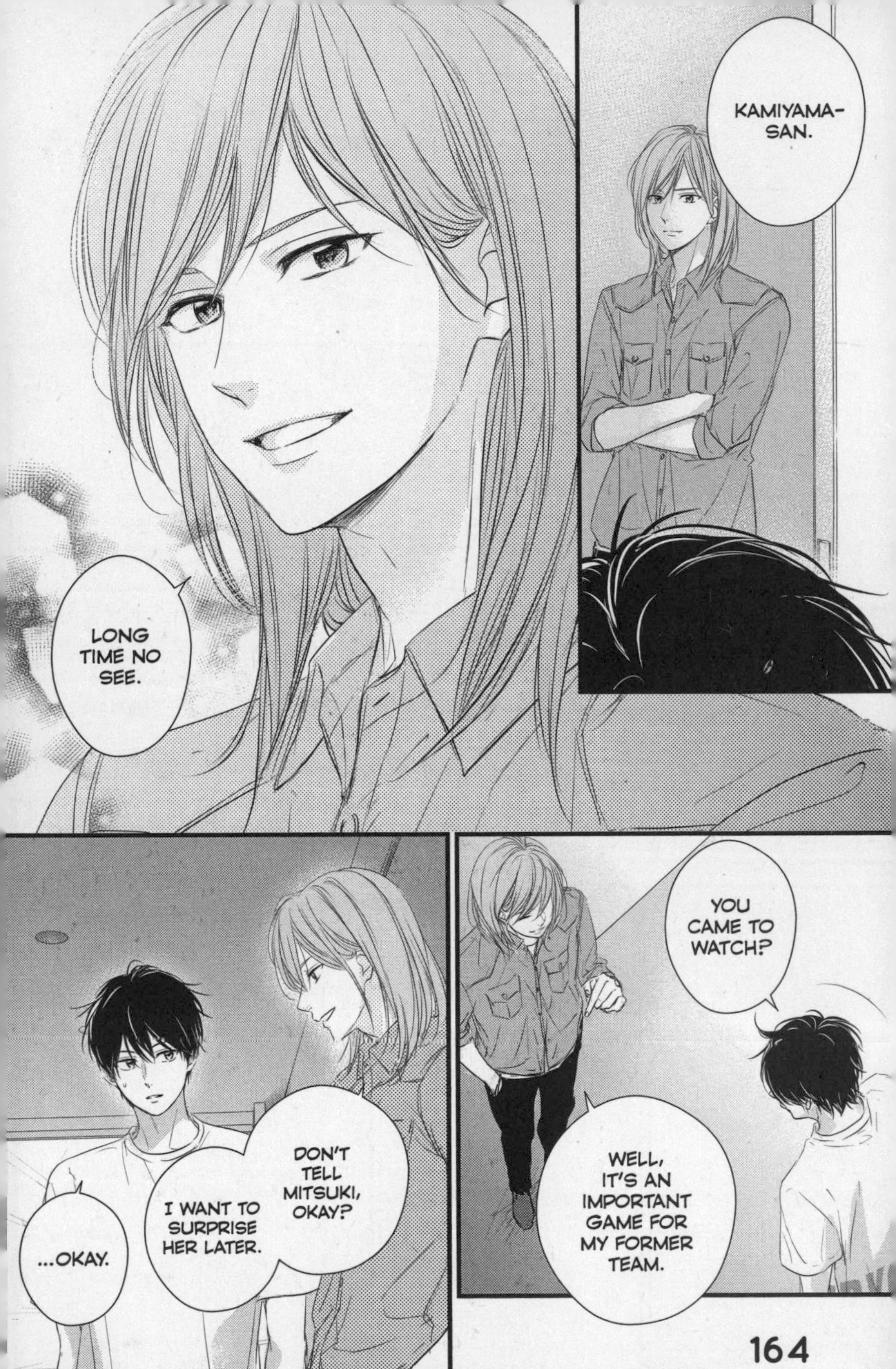
KAMIYAMA-SAN.
LONG TIME NO SEE.
YOU CAME TO WATCH?
WELL, IT'S AN IMPORTANT GAME FOR MY FORMER TEAM.
DON'T TELL MITSUKI, OKAY?
I WANT TO SURPRISE HER LATER.
...OKAY.

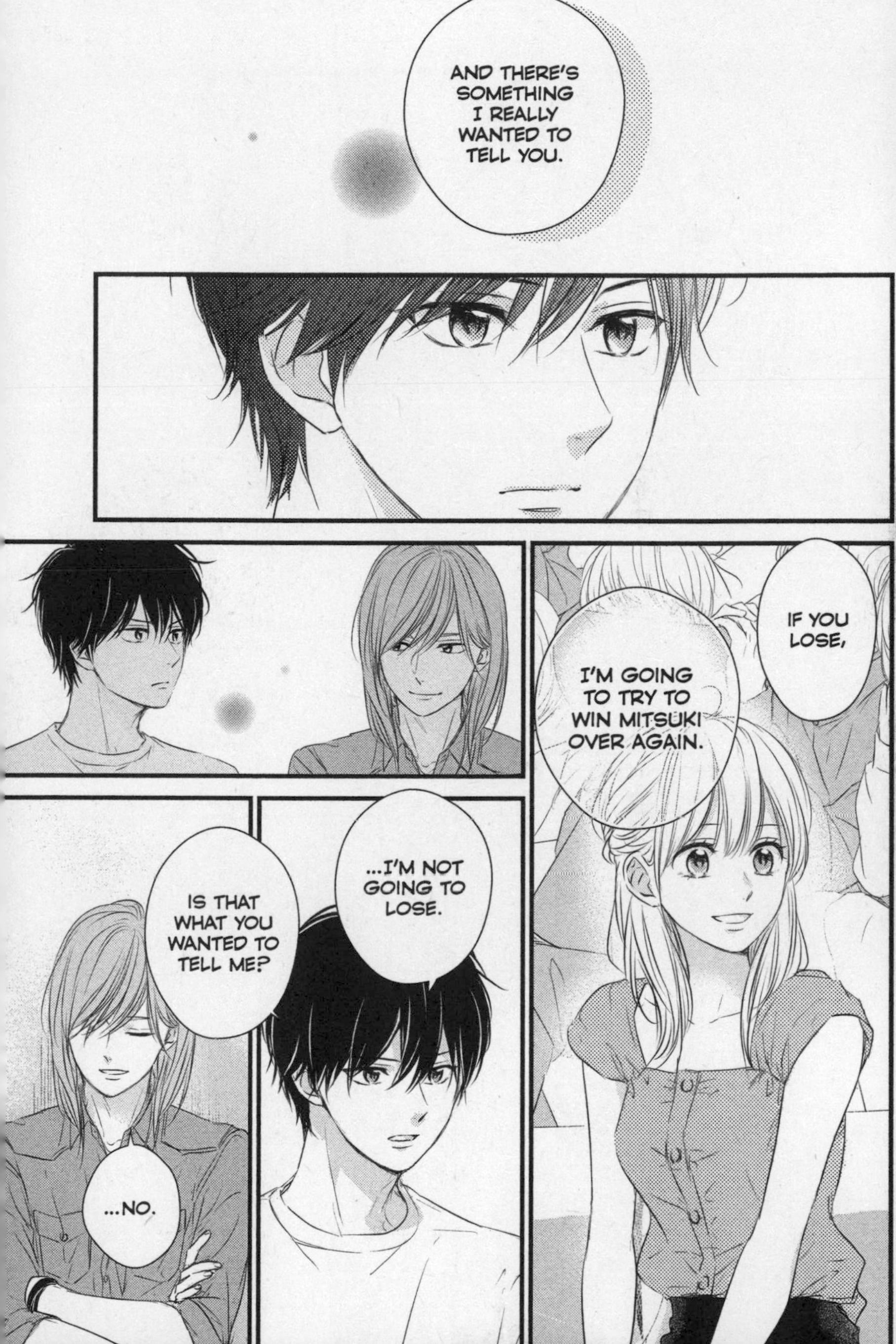
AND THERE'S SOMETHING I REALLY WANTED TO TELL YOU.
IF YOU LOSE,
I'M GOING TO TRY TO WIN MITSUKI OVER AGAIN.
...I'M NOT GOING TO LOSE.
IS THAT WHAT YOU WANTED TO TELL ME?
...NO.

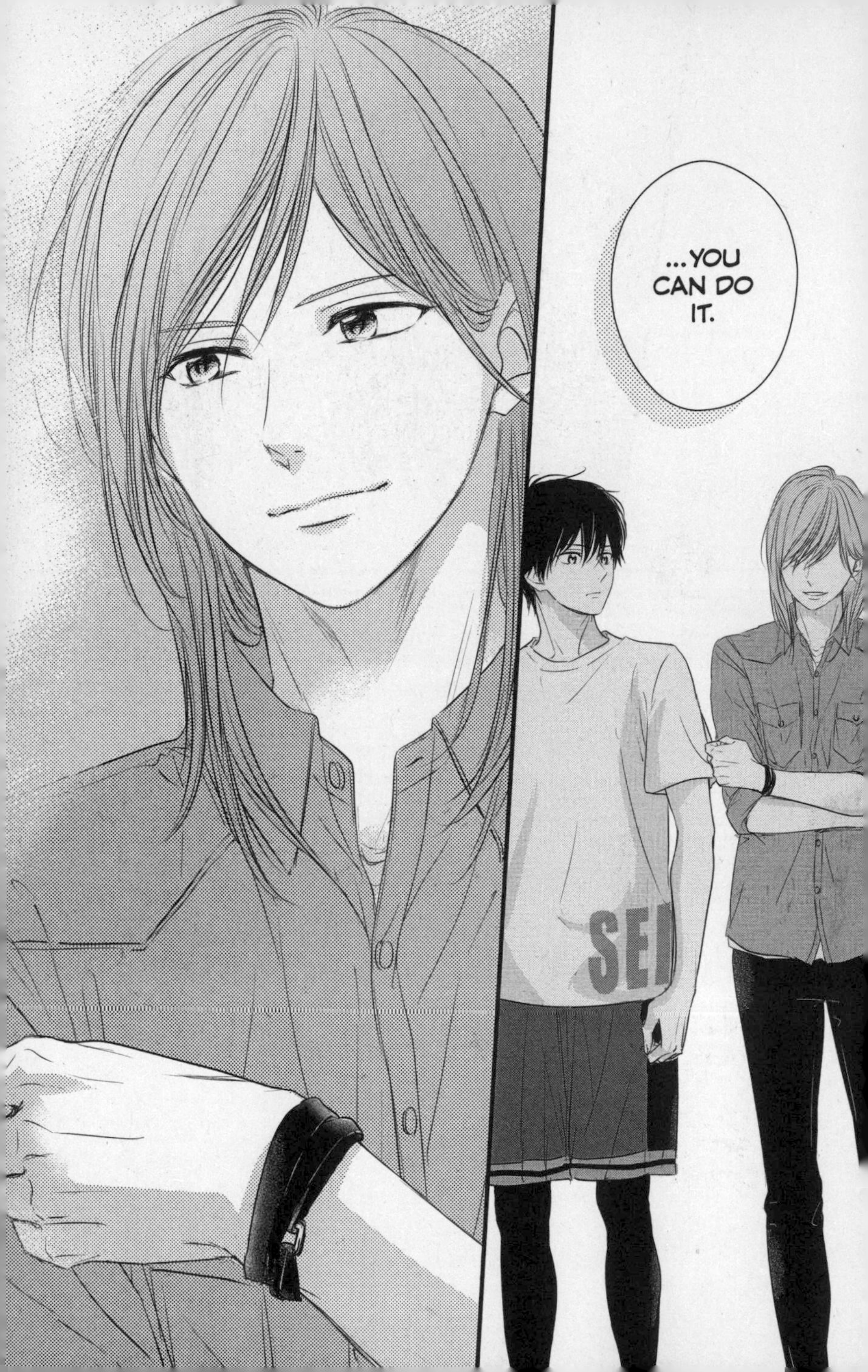
...YOU CAN DO IT.
SEI

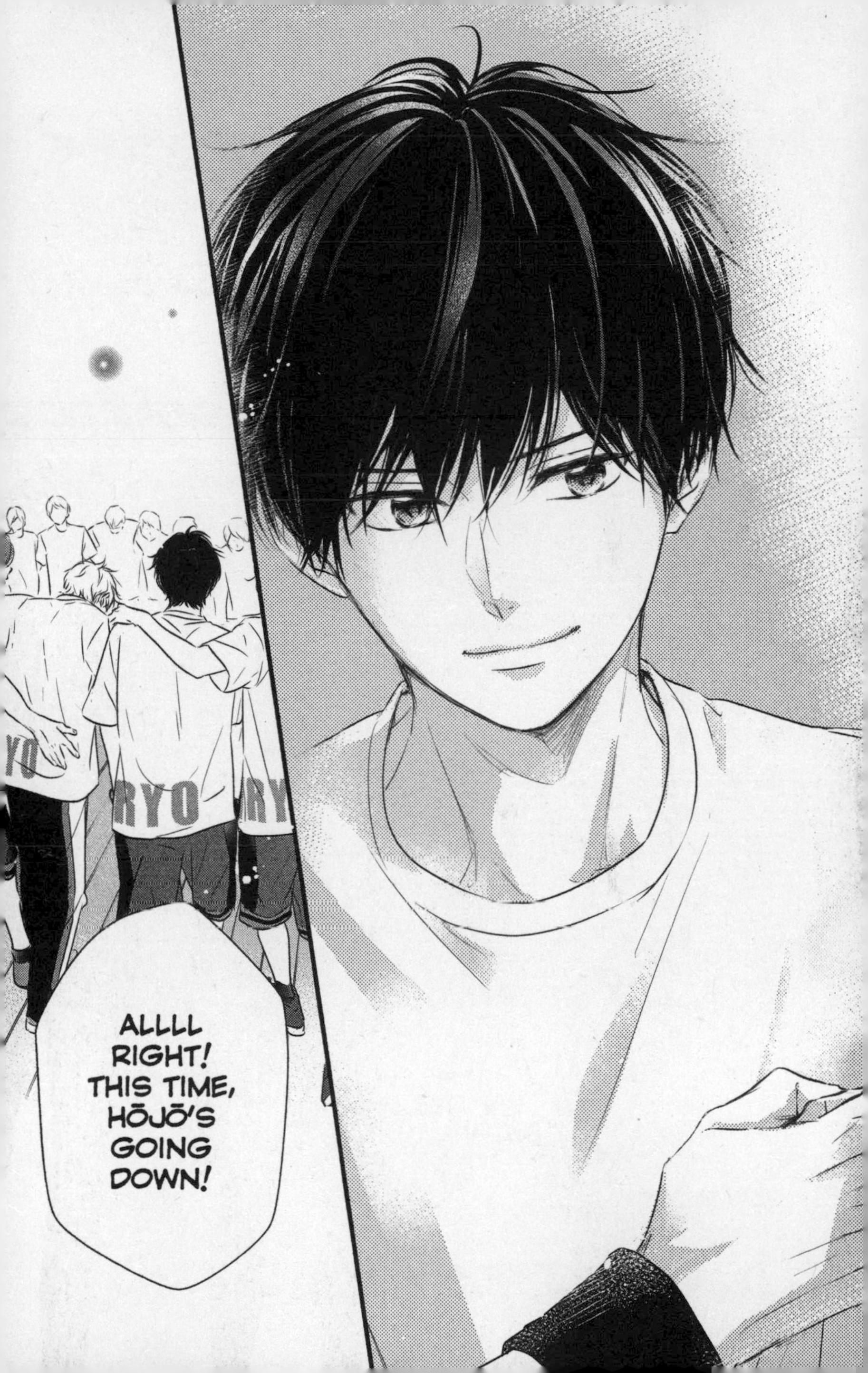
RYO
RYO
RY
ALLLL RIGHT! THIS TIME, HŌJŌ'S GOING DOWN!

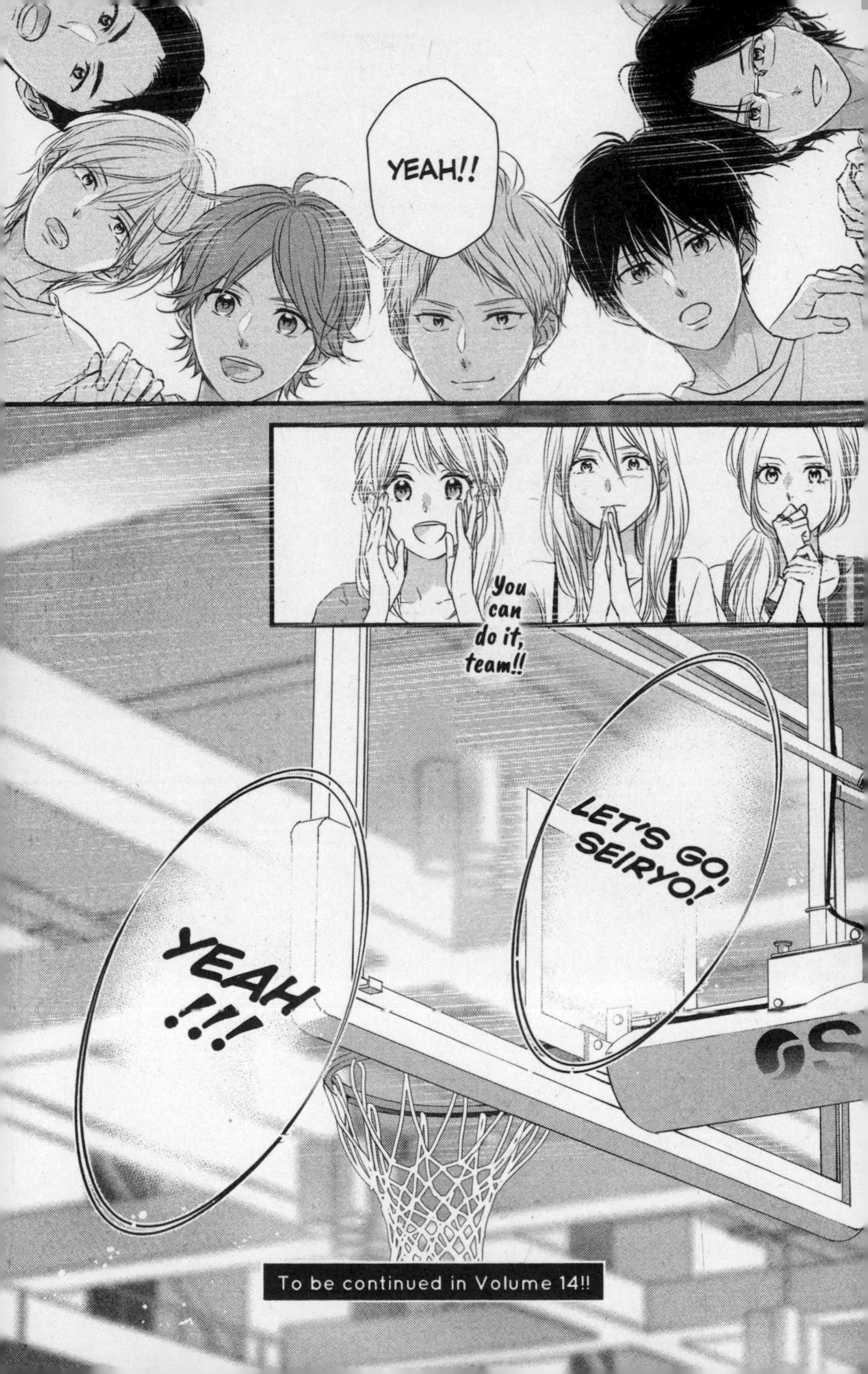
YEAH!!
You can do it, team!!
LET'S GO, SEIRYO!
YEAH!!!
To be continued in Volume 14!!

Bonus Manga

Mitsuki's Reddest Day

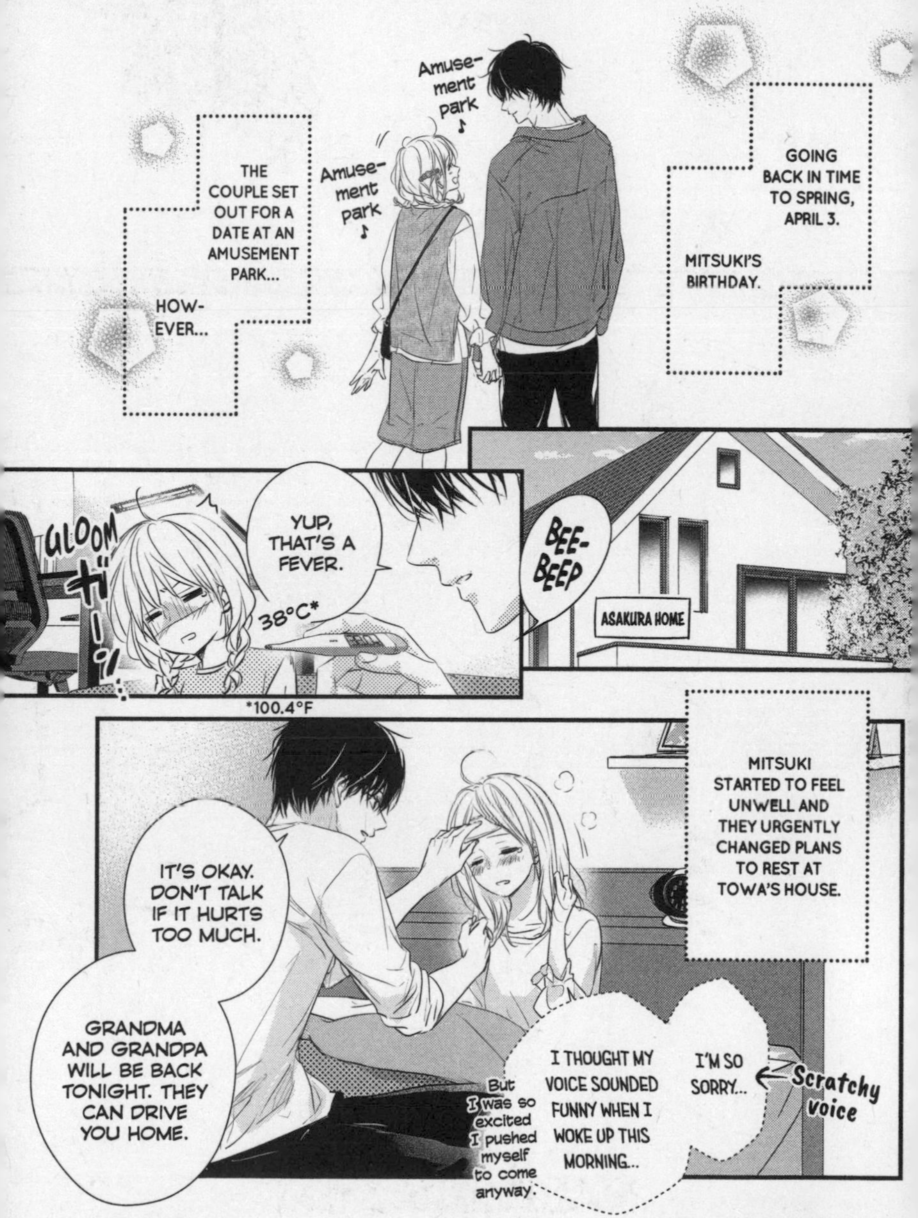
GOING BACK IN TIME TO SPRING, APRIL 3.
MITSUKI'S BIRTHDAY.
Amusement park ♪
Amusement park ♪
THE COUPLE SET OUT FOR A DATE AT AN AMUSEMENT PARK...
HOWEVER...
BEE-BEEP
ASAKURA HOME
YUP, THAT'S A FEVER.
38°C*
GLOOM
*100.4°F
MITSUKI STARTED TO FEEL UNWELL AND THEY URGENTLY CHANGED PLANS TO REST AT TOWA'S HOUSE.
Scratchy voice
I'M SO SORRY...
I THOUGHT MY VOICE SOUNDED FUNNY WHEN I WOKE UP THIS MORNING...
But I was so excited I pushed myself to come anyway.
IT'S OKAY. DON'T TALK IF IT HURTS TOO MUCH.
GRANDMA AND GRANDPA WILL BE BACK TONIGHT. THEY CAN DRIVE YOU HOME.

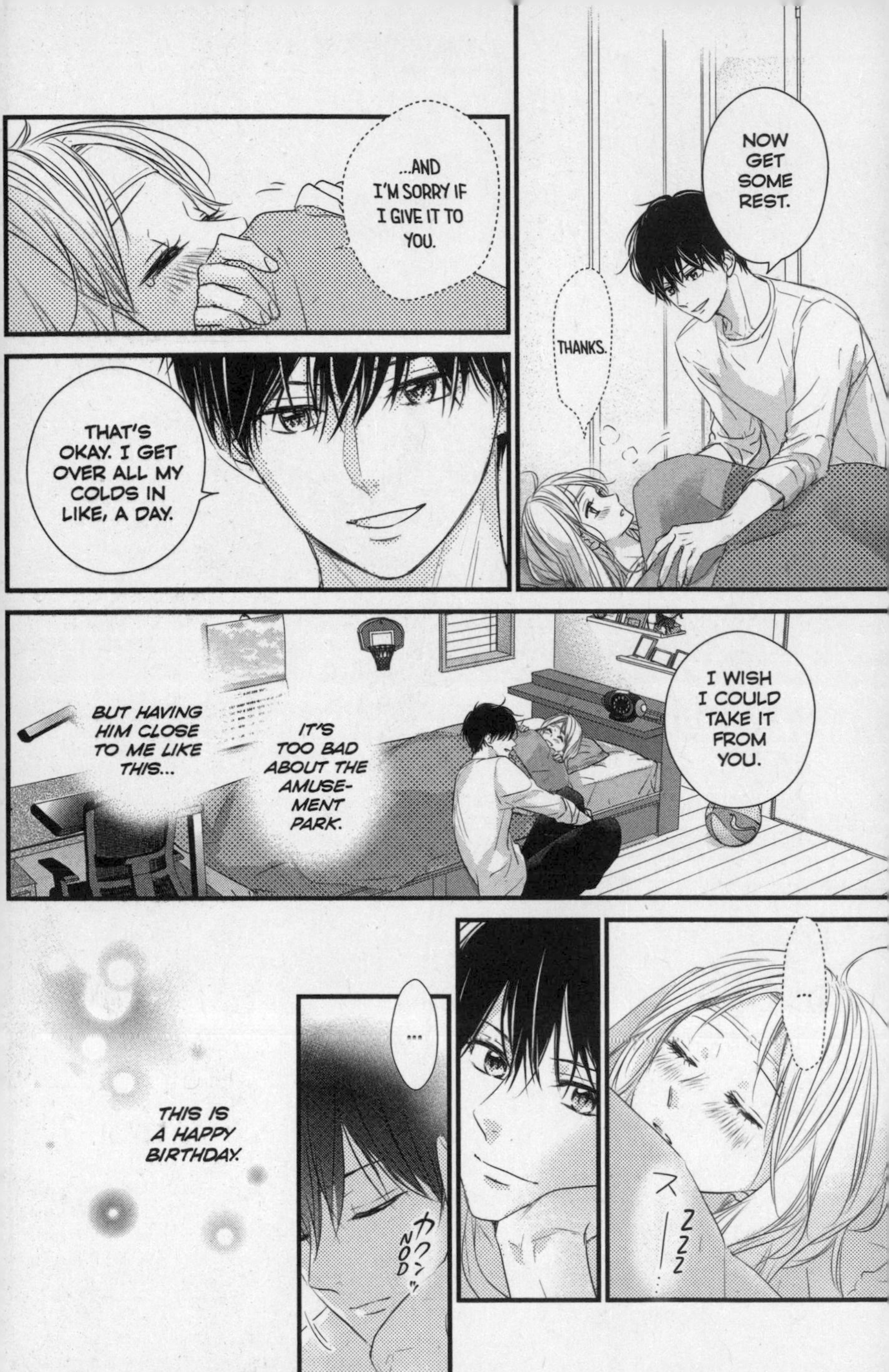
NOW GET SOME REST.
THANKS.
...AND I'M SORRY IF I GIVE IT TO YOU.
THAT'S OKAY. I GET OVER ALL MY COLDS IN LIKE, A DAY.
I WISH I COULD TAKE IT FROM YOU.
IT'S TOO BAD ABOUT THE AMUSEMENT PARK.
BUT HAVING HIM CLOSE TO ME LIKE THIS...
...
ZZZ
...
NOD
THIS IS A HAPPY BIRTHDAY.

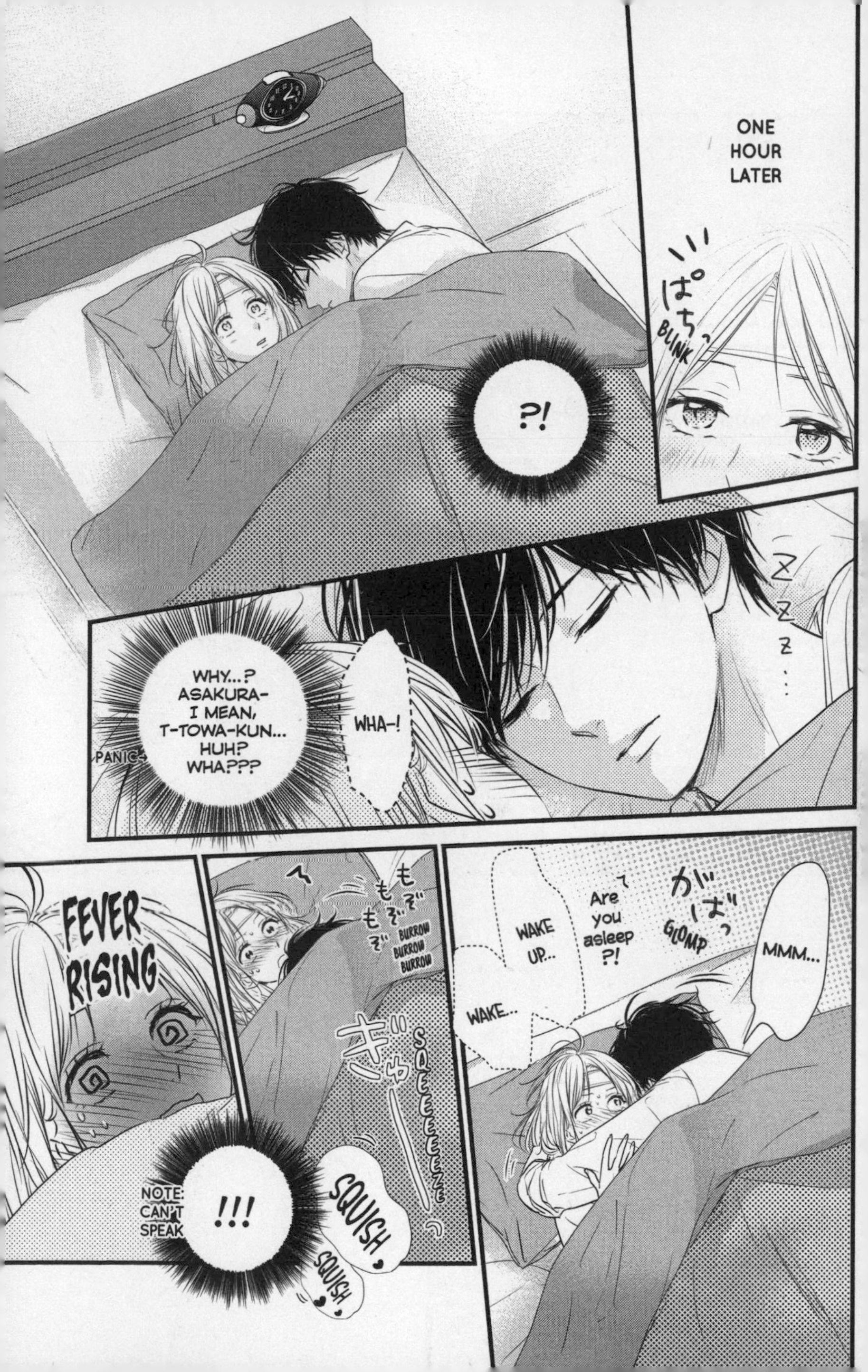
ONE HOUR LATER
ぱちっ
BLINK
?!
Z Z Z . . .
WHA-!
WHY...? ASAKURA- I MEAN, T-TOWA-KUN... HUH? WHA???
PANIC
MMM...
がばっ
GLOMP
Are you asleep?!
WAKE UP...
WAKE...
もぞもぞもぞ
BURROW BURROW BURROW
ぎゅー
SQEEEEEZE
SQUISH
SQUISH
!!!
NOTE: CAN'T SPEAK
FEVER RISING

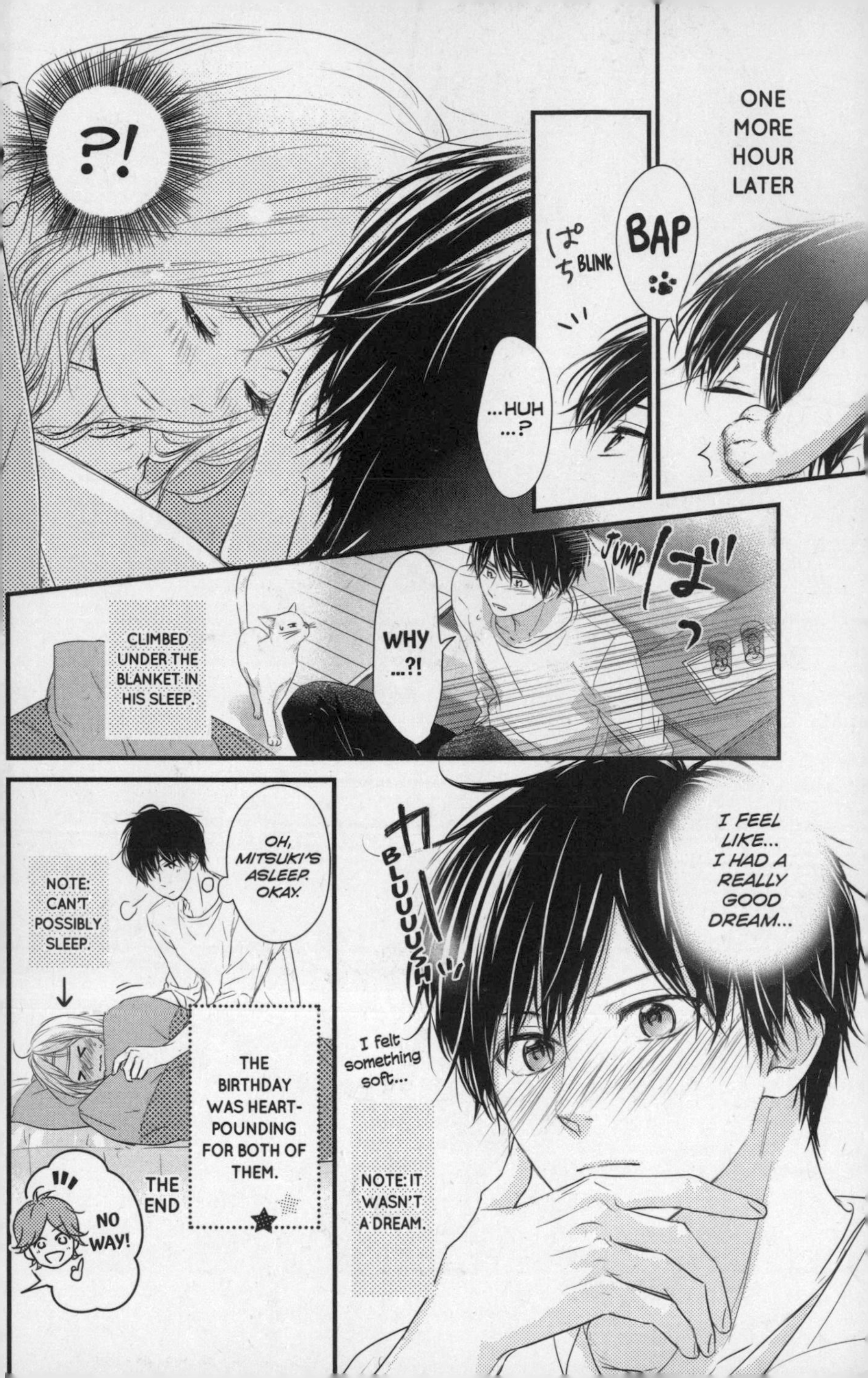
ONE MORE HOUR LATER
BAP
ぱち BLINK
...HUH ...?
?!
JUMP ばっ
WHY ...?!
CLIMBED UNDER THE BLANKET IN HIS SLEEP.
I FEEL LIKE... I HAD A REALLY GOOD DREAM...
カー BLUUUUSH
I felt something soft...
NOTE: IT WASN'T A DREAM.
OH, MITSUKI'S ASLEEP. OKAY.
NOTE: CAN'T POSSIBLY SLEEP.
THE BIRTHDAY WAS HEART-POUNDING FOR BOTH OF THEM.
THE END
NO WAY!

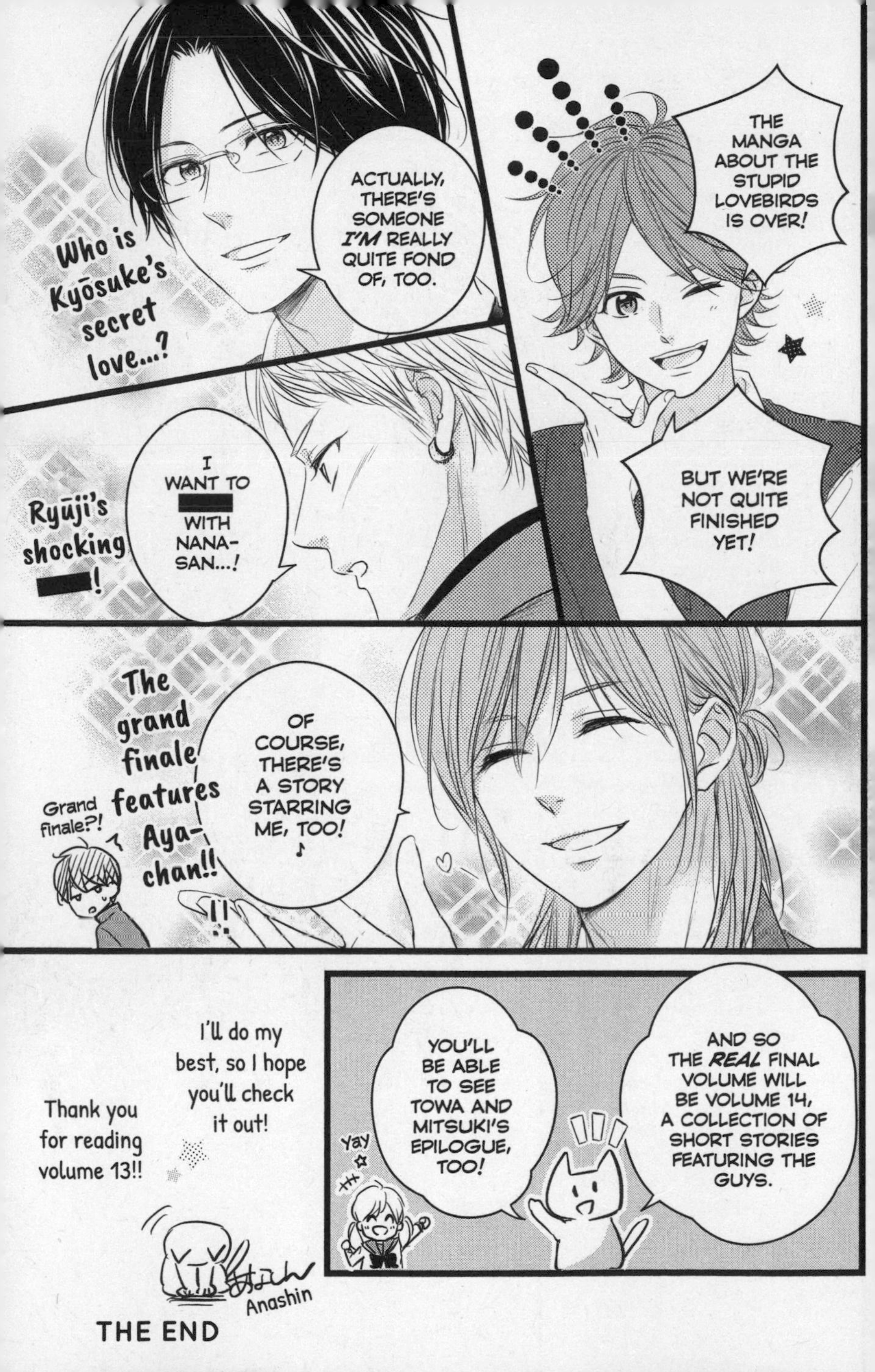
THE MANGA ABOUT THE STUPID LOVEBIRDS IS OVER!
BUT WE'RE NOT QUITE FINISHED YET!
ACTUALLY, THERE'S SOMEONE *I'M* REALLY QUITE FOND OF, TOO.
Who is Kyōsuke's secret love...?
I WANT TO [redacted] WITH NANA-SAN...!
Ryūji's shocking [redacted]!
OF COURSE, THERE'S A STORY STARRING ME, TOO! ♪
The grand finale features Aya-chan!!
Grand finale?!
!!
AND SO THE *REAL* FINAL VOLUME WILL BE VOLUME 14, A COLLECTION OF SHORT STORIES FEATURING THE GUYS.
YOU'LL BE ABLE TO SEE TOWA AND MITSUKI'S EPILOGUE, TOO!
Yay ☆
I'll do my best, so I hope you'll check it out!
Thank you for reading volume 13!!
Anashin
THE END

Translation Notes

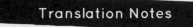

White Day, page 48
White Day is a follow-up holiday to Valentine's Day. It falls on March 14, and it is the day when anyone who received chocolate or other gifts on Valentine's Day will return the kindness with a gift of their own. Traditionally, the gift is something marshmallow related (hence the name White Day), but these days, the gifts are not restricted to those kinds of things.

WHITE DAY...

Horror test, page 95
Specifically, she asks if it's a "test of courage" known as a *kimo-dameshi* or "test of your guts." Young people will choose a frightening location, usually rumored to be haunted. They'll take turns walking a path through it alone or in pairs to see if they have the courage to make it all the way through. Sometimes other members of the group will dress up as ghosts and demons to improve the chances that something will go bump in the night.

Being so polite, page 157
More specifically, Nanase is complaining about Ryūji's use of *keigo*—polite speech, which is generally used for people the speaker is not on familiar terms with. Nanase is an older woman, so Ryūji started out using *keigo* to speak to her, because he didn't want to be rude. Now that they're in a relationship, she wants him to talk to her like they're equals.

UGH.
YOU'RE BEING SO POLITE AGAIN.
I told you to stop that.

waiting
for spring

Waiting for Spring 13 is a work of fiction. Names, characters, places, and incidents are the products of the author's imagination or are used fictitiously. Any resemblance to actual events, locales, or persons, living or dead, is entirely coincidental.

A Kodansha Comics Trade Paperback Original
Waiting for Spring 13 copyright © 2019 Anashin
English translation copyright © 2020 Anashin

All rights reserved.

Published in the United States by Kodansha Comics, an imprint of Kodansha USA Publishing, LLC, New York.

Publication rights for this English edition arranged through Kodansha Ltd, Tokyo.

First published in Japan in 2019 by Kodansha Ltd, Tokyo.

ISBN 978-1-63236-942-0

Printed in the United States of America.

www.kodanshacomics.com

9 8 7 6 5 4 3 2 1
Translation: Alethea Nibley and Athena Nibley
Lettering: Sara Linsley
Editing: Haruko Hashimoto
Kodansha Comics edition cover design by Phil Balsman

Publisher: Kiichiro Sugawara

Director of publishing services: Ben Applegate
Associate director of operations: Stephen Pakula
Publishing services managing editor: Noelle Webster
Assistant production manager: Emi Lotto, Angela Zurlo